CONSCIENCE

Conscience

Four Thomistic Treatments

Benoît-Henri Merkelbach, O.P.

Michel Labourdette, O.P.

Reginald Beaudouin, O.P.

Edited and translated by Matthew K. Minerd

CLUNY

Providence, Rhode Island

"Among all human pursuits, the pursuit of wisdom
is more perfect, more noble, more useful,
and more full of joy."

-Saint Thomas Aquinas,
Summa contra Gentiles

* * *

Thomist Tradition Series

While his birth and death and everything in between remain confined to the thirteenth century, the intellectual legacy of St. Thomas Aquinas perdures to the present day. The Catholic Church continues to recognize the sapiential fecundity of this Doctor whom she invokes as "Common" and "Universal." God gave to the world through the wisdom of his Thomas a gift that does not expire.

There was only one Thomas. However, there have been many Thomists—philosophers and theologians who have assimilated the principles of his instruction and found the freedom that only the truth can provide.

The Thomist Tradition book series from Cluny Media arises from a dual conviction: (1) the thought of St. Thomas Aquinas contains an incomparable fullness of wisdom, and (2) the writings of the Thomists who followed him play a necessary role in mediating his wisdom to subsequent generations. Admittedly, those figures who constitute the Thomist tradition were by no means equals in regard to talent, influence, and renown. Moreover, their individual and collective contributions to the Thomist tradition elude facile comprehension or easy summary. Nonetheless, this series attempts to make available the key texts of figures—both classic and contemporary, major and minor—who rightly claim membership in the living tradition which bears the intellectual imprint of their master, Thomas.

The THOMIST TRADITION series makes these books available not merely as static works of antiquated value or anachronistic interest. Rather, the series is the fruit of our conviction that each Thomist has participated in a legacy perennially alive and perpetually relevant. Under this inspiration, each carefully selected volume in the series includes a new introduction that explains the book's original historical and speculative context. These introductions also outline their volume's enduring relevance to contemporary questions and disputes. Finally, the texts themselves have undergone extensive editorial review and certain footnotes have been added in order to highlight, explain, and clarify themes and passages of particular significance.

It is our sincere hope that this endeavor from Cluny Media will contribute to the renewed interest in the Thomist tradition among contemporary philosophers and theologians. For 800 years, Thomas and the Thomists have demonstrated unparalleled service in the defense and exposition of the saving truth Christ confided to his bride, the Catholic Church. The THOMIST TRADITION book series is designed both to honor that service and to provide the Thomists of today and tomorrow with resources for their own service to the Truth who sets us free.

Cajetan Cuddy, O.P.
General Editor

THOMIST TRADITION SERIES

*** TITLES ***

Metaphysics and the Existence of God
by Thomas C. O'Brien, O.P.

What Is Sacred Theology?
by Joseph Clifford Fenton

The Natural Law According to Aquinas and Suárez
by Walter Farrell, O.P.

Mary, Full of Grace
by Édouard Hugon, O.P.

Philosophizing in Faith: Essays on the Beginning and End of Wisdom
by Réginald Garrigou-Lagrange, O.P.

Conscience: Four Thomistic Treatments
by Réginald Benoît-Henri Merkelbach, O.P.,
Michel Labourdette, O.P., *and* Reginald Beaudouin, O.P.

Cluny Media edition, 2022

ACKNOWLEDGMENTS:
For permission to translate the works contained in this volume, grateful acknowledgment is made to the publishers of the sources noted under "Texts Translated" at the conclusion of the Translator's Introduction.

For more information regarding this title
or any other Cluny Media publication,
please write to info@clunymedia.com, or to
Cluny Media, P.O. Box 1664, Providence, RI 02901

VISIT US ONLINE AT WWW.CLUNYMEDIA.COM

ISBN: 978-1685950231

Library of Congress Control Number: 2022930361

Cover design by Clarke & Clarke
Cover image: Ludger tom Ring the Younger,
detail from *Portrait of a Doctor*,
about 1572, oil on wood
Courtesy of Wikimedia Commons

Contents

* * *

TRANSLATOR'S INTRODUCTION

* * *

The texts gathered together in this volume are an example of accidental archeological findings discovered in the midst of my other work. If the reader is to understand the content and meaning of a project such as this, it is important to understand what inspired the undertaking. Although a bit pugilistic in tone, we can fairly describe the besetting intellectual sin of the period between the 1940s to today as "intellectual patricide." With a vivacity greater than previous generations, we have become a people "of the future," telling our own tale instead of taking guidance from previous generations. Indeed, a sort of reflexive distrust (or open hatred) for the past is perhaps the basic intellectual temptation of the whole of the modern period from its inception. This distrust has grown with the centuries and has been quite destructive culturally, including in the Catholic world, as should be clear to anyone who looks with open and honest eyes upon the state of catechesis, philosophy, and theology, all of which are only gradually recovering from the iconoclasm of recent decades.

Granted, the *answers* needed for today and for the future are not found, in pure form, in the past. Nonetheless, *intellectual counsel* regarding the course to be traveled will be found in the inheritance received from former days. A lesson I am learning as a father, watching my children pass from infancy to toddlerhood and onward, is the fact that very little is "purely natural" for humans. Even something as simple as learning how and when to sleep must be enculturated, and do we appreciate well enough at every meal just how much trial-and-error (at times fatal error) has gone into the human awareness of what can and cannot be eaten? How much more is this true for the food that is truth!

Now, I do not draw from this fact a wholly-historicist, anti-foundationalist conclusion. More than text and interpretation exist. There is, in the end, a bedrock of reality—the reality of revealed truths, natural reality, moral reality, cultural-artistic reality, and logico-rational reality—upon which we can land our concepts, even as we quickly add thereto our activity, using all the tools articulated by humanity through the centuries. I'm not sure that my outlook is exactly the same as that of Alasdair MacIntyre,[1] but my general intellectual bent does rest on this sane fact, which is important for MacIntyre's own overall "project": human reasoning *necessarily* unfolds its activity within traditions, which are the means *through which and in which we grasp truths that transcend those very traditions*. The task of passing from obscurity to clarity in concepts is very difficult, as also is the discovery of perfect middle terms for our laborious undertaking of discursive reasoning. Thus, we owe much to our forebears and should listen to them!

No writers have been more influential upon my philosophical and theological thought than Jacques Maritain, Yves Simon, and Fr. Reginald Garrigou-Lagrange, O.P. When I bumped into the last writer also agreeing with complaints voiced by another influence on my thought, Josef Pieper, I had to set up and think, "What is this about?" In his little book, *The Four Cardinal Virtues*, Pieper, citing Frs. Garrigou-Lagrange and Benoît-Henri Merkelbach, comments on the way that the treatise on prudence fell into desuetude in later scholasticism.[2] This piqued my interest, and I ended up translating the texts by Fr. Garrigou-Lagrange ("Remarks Concerning the Metaphysical Character of St. Thomas's Moral Theology, in Particular as It Is Related to Prudence and Conscience") and Fr. Merkelbach ("Where Should We Place the Treatise on Conscience in Moral Theology?") for the English edition of the journal *Nova et Vetera*.[3] Interestingly, Fr. Garri-

1. My thoughts here are in fact closer to those found in Anton Pegis, *At the Origins of the Thomistic Notion of Man* (New York: MacMillan, 1963); Armand Maurer, *St. Thomas and Historicity* (Milwaukee, Wisconsin: Marquette University Press, 1979).
2. Joseph Pieper, *The Four Cardinal Virtues*, trans. Richard Winston, et al. (Notre Dame, IN: University of Notre Dame Press, 1966), p. 208, nn. 5 and 6.
3. See Reginald Garrigou-Lagrange, "Remarks Concerning the Metaphysical Character of St. Thomas's Moral Theology, in Particular as It Is Related to Prudence and Conscience," *Nova et Vetera*, Vol. 17, No. 1 (2019): pp. 245–70; Benoît-Henri Merkelbach, "Where Should We Place the Treatise on Conscience in Moral Theology?" trans. Matthew K. Minerd, *Nova et Vetera*, English Edition, Vol. 18, No. 3 (Summer 2020): pp. 1017–1037.

gou-Lagrange's essay was included, in a slightly emended form, in his *Le réalisme du principe of finalité*, a text very recently published in translation by Emmaus Academic as *The Order of Things: The Realism of the Principle of Finality*.[4] In this article, he cites not only Fr. Merkelbach's study but also a little book, *Tractatus de conscientia*, by Fr. Reginald Beaudouin, O.P., the teacher of a number of great Thomist lights from the early twentieth century, including the Dominicans Ambroise Gardeil, Marie-Benoît Schwalm, Pierre Mandonnet, and Antonin Sertillanges.

All of this led me to come up with the idea of translating Fr. Beaudouin's quite obscure text. While reading his treatise, I found myself plunged into the world of the great debates over probabalism which structured so much (although, contrary to certain popular narratives, not all) of moral theology from the time of Bartolomé de Medina, O.P. (1527–1580) down to the final casuistic texts of the early twentieth century. Truth be told, it is still a very difficult and daunting world of moral analysis, and it will take many more studies and reflection before we are able today to integrate this old debate into the context of contemporary concerns and questions. Still, first steps must be taken.

Thus, I expanded my project somewhat. At first, I thought I would publish Fr. Beaudouin's treatise together with Fr. Merkelbach's own sub-treatises on conscience in his massive *Summa theologiae moralis*. The latter Dominican arguably provides the fullest accounting for how to handle the integration of the probabalist debates into a truly Thomistic treatise on prudence. (This does not go without its own dangers, as will be seen in the essays that follow.) His "addendum" to the treatise on prudence is, however, quite lengthy, pushing beyond sane bounds for this current volume. Thus, I have come to think that it would be better that such a text be published on its own, as a separate treatise on the virtue of prudence. Moreover, I became aware, in the course of my own research, that Fr. Merkelbach's general outlook, despite being shared with a number of important Thomists, was not universally accepted by other great lights of the *schola Thomae*. The great twentieth-century moral theologian, Fr. Michel Labourdette, O.P., whose course notes are finally being published

4. See Reginald Garrigou-Lagrange, *The Order of Things: The Realism of the Principle of Finality*, trans. Matthew K. Minerd (Steubenville, OH: Emmaus Academic, 2020), pt. 2, ch. 6, pp. 273–286.

in French, represents a proponent of a view that cautions against directly connecting the judgment of conscience with that of prudence.[5]

Finding myself at odds with so great a moral theologian (and, also, on this point, somewhat so with my friend and collaborator, Fr. Cajetan Cuddy, O.P.), I crafted a slightly different idea for the volume. Instead of fully presenting Fr. Beaudouin and Fr. Merkelbach as "the definitive Thomist approach to conscience," I decided to present them along with the more general, historical problem of the treatise on conscience. Thus, I have included Fr. Merkelbach's own scholarly overview of this history, along with a selection from Fr. Labourdette concerning the topic of conscience as discussed in the *Prima secundae*, wherein the problems arising from the "theologies of conscience" are laid out in critical fashion.

Frs. Merkelbach and Beaudouin are not completely guilty of the charges leveled by Fr. Labourdette. Therefore, I present all of these thinkers together here, including in this volume Fr. Merkelbach's treatise on conscience *in generali*, leaving his further lengthy developments *in speciali* (in the treatise on prudence) for a later day. My own dispositional conservatism is hesitant to say, with Fr. Labourdette (and someone like Fr. Servais Pinckaers), that the whole of the questions raised about probabilism and conscience were wrong-headed, as if three hundred years of moral theology deserves *no* integration into a beatitude-centric moral theology today. Rather, we need to encounter the best of the Thomist teachers from the previous era and ask how to organically develop our theology today. This will also require historical studies on the probabilist debates. Some such works have been written of late,[6] but the fact that the 1936 study

5. This view is articulated very well in an excellent pair of articles by P.-M. Noonan, "Auriga et Genetrix: Le rôle de la prudence dans le jugement de la conscience," *Revue thomiste*, Vol. 114 (2014): pp. 355–77 and 531–68. I will discuss this point at greater detail below in my introductory essay.

6. Of particular note is the important study by Rudolf Schuessler, *The Debate on Probable Opinions in the Scholastic Tradition* (Leiden: Brill, 2019). Likewise, Stefania Tutino, *Uncertainty in Post-Reformation Catholicism: A History of Probabilism* (Oxford: Oxford University Press, 2018); Julia Fleming, *Defending Probabilism: The Moral Theology of Juan Caramuel* (Washington, DC: Georgetown University Press, 2006); Barbara Fuchs and Mercedes García-Arenal, eds., *The Quest for Certainty in Early Modern Europe: From Inquisition to Inquiry, 1550–1700* (Toronto: University of Toronto Press, 2020).

Also see Ian Hacking's older but related study, with his own particular historical claims regarding the novelty of the notion of probability that emerged in the mid-seventeenth century, *The Emergence of Probability: A Philosophical Study of Early Ideas about Probability, Induction, and Statistical Inference*, 2nd ed. (Cambridge: University of Cambridge Press, 2007).

by Fr. Deman in the *Dictionnaire de théologie catholique*[7] remains a primary overview historical study cited by many itself bears witness to the fact that renewed interest is needed, now that the Catholic iconoclasm of the mid-twentieth century has somewhat passed. The current volume is envisioned solely as "triggering off" this much-longer project of recovery. Thus, in the spirit of such new research, I have included my own synthetic essay, integrating much of what I have gained in the course of working on this volume in discussions with others concerning these topics. In it, I try to lay out, in a truly Thomisitic manner, a general physiognomy of the different types of judgments used in "moral reasoning," broadly construed. The position articulated there is my own, presented as the fruit of years of reflection on the nature of the judgment of conscience, in dialogue with the great lights of the Thomist school.

Allow me to end with a direct statement regarding the ecclesiastical politics of the day. This volume *is not* written as part of the contemporary discussions and debates going on in the Roman Catholic Church regarding the reception and interpretation of the Second Vatican Council and the aftermath thereof. My liturgical-ecclesial home is the Ruthenian Catholic Church, a humble outpost of Eastern Catholicism, made up of a poor and generally forgotten people. Obviously, one cannot be unaware of these issues in the greater Catholic Church, but when one lives as a canonically Eastern Catholic (especially in so small a church), one cannot help but forget the heat and rage involved in some of these battles. Thus, I am firing no shots with this book, although it contains quite traditional Western authors. My intellectual training was in scholasticism, a training which I continue to employ in service of the Church, even while my teaching is sensitive to the unique intellectual and spiritual needs befalling those who are members of the Byzantine *sui iuris* Churches that send men to be formed at our seminary. Nonetheless, merely because I am translating old scholastic figures does not mean that I am taking up a party-position in the questions and debates shaking the Western Catholic world today. Thus, I am not writing in order to restart some supposedly glorious era but, rather, to reconnect us, today, to important thinkers and themes from the past.

7. Thomas Deman, "Probabilisme," *Dictionnaire de théologie catholique*, Vol. 13, No. 1, ed. E. Amann, et al. (Paris: Letouzey et Ané, 1936), col. 417–619.

Scripture citations in this volume are drawn from the Revised Standard Version and the Douay-Rheims translations of the Bible. They are marked as such, with the latter being used where the Vulgate is cited in Latin by the author being translated. All citations from Denzinger are drawn from Ignatius Press's forty-third edition of the text.

The task of compiling, translating, annotating, and editing such a volume is not a "one man show." Thus, I would like to recognize a number of people involved in the writing of this volume. For access to this difficult-to-obtain text by Fr. Beaudouin: the staff at the Woodstock Library at Georgetown University. For permission to use my already published translation of the article by Fr. Merkelbach: Dr. Matthew Levering and the staff of *Nova et Vetera* (English edition). For their insights and helpful corrections throughout the process of writing and translating the texts in this volume: Fr. Cajetan Cuddy, O.P., Dr. Thomas Howes, and James Bryan. Finally, but most importantly, for their willingness to take on this project, the good men at Cluny Media, whose untiring publishing work will guarantee that many texts which risked being lost will be saved for my children's generation: Scott W. Thompson and John Emmet Clarke (for whose editorial work on this volume I feel the greatest gratitude).

I dedicate this volume to the memory of my grandfathers, Joseph ("Sonny") Juriga and Byron ("Kenny") Minerd, men of simple, devoted character who taught me more about forming a right and certain conscience than any book of casuistry, probabilism, or moral theology (whether *in generali* or *in speciali*) ever could.

TEXTS TRANSLATED

Beaudouin, Reginald. *Tractatus de conscientia.* Edited by Ambroise Gardeil. Paris: Gabalda, 1911.

Labourdette, Michel. *Les actes humains. "Grand cours" de théologie morale,* vol. 2, pp. 204–245. Paris: Parole et Silence, 2016.

Merkelbach, Benoît-Henri. "Tractatus de conscientia in generali." In *Summa theologiae moralis*, 5th ed., vol. 1, 186–206. Paris: Desclée de Brouwer, 1946.

______. "Note: Quelle place assigner au traité de la conscience?" *Revue des sciences philosophiques et théologiques*, vol. 12, no. 2 (1923): pp. 170–183; "Where Should We Place the Treatise on Conscience in Moral Theology?" trans. Matthew K. Minerd, *Nova et Vetera*, English Edition, vol. 18, no. 3 (Summer 2020): pp. 1017–1037.

* * *

A SYNTHETIC OVERVIEW OF CONSCIENCE AND PRUDENCE IN MORAL REASONING

Matthew K. Minerd

INTRODUCTION

Words take on a life of their own. If ever there were need for proof of "semeiosis," the action of signs, we see it operative here in the developing and shifting meaning of our words. The weight of history, of unspoken hopes, of hidden evils, indeed the heavy load of culture itself all press upon the usage of words, often without us realizing that this influence is operative. A mere survey of the many metaphors that structure our discourse can help us sense how greatly our *thought* itself is nudged along by the kind of "unspoken cloud" that surrounds each and every word and phrase that we use.[1] It requires a great deal of asceticism to determine a single sense for our terms (or at least a proportionally single sense, in the case of analogical terms).

This scenario holds quite true for the word "conscience," a term touching upon realities central to human experience and action. Without even venturing outside of the restricted scope of the Catholic world, we can find ourselves faced with many different acceptations of the term "conscience": (1) self-awareness ("psychological conscience / consciousness of self"); (2) the sense for ultimate moral values ("*synderesis*" and "faith-infused *synderesis*" in the order of grace); (3) a particular power of mind related to judging moral matters ("moral sense" or perhaps, in more traditional philosophical terms, practical reason); (4) the voice of God deep within our souls intimating to us what is right or wrong; and (5) in strict Thomistic terms, "an application of knowledge to a particular act whether past, present, or future."[2] This last definition, however, has left many open questions for Thomists concerning whether conscience belongs to "moral science" (i.e., "reflective analysis on cases of conscience"),[3] to the domain of purely practical reason (i.e., when it is right and certain, to prudence, and otherwise, to imprudence),[4] or to something seemingly in between, utilizing moral science but not reducible thereto, without however being a judgment of prudence.[5]

In the contemporary edition of the *Catechism of the Catholic Church*, we find that even in the seemingly placid world of Roman declarations there is some need for exactness. Ample room is made for each of the

1. See George Lakoff, *Metaphors We Live By* (Chicago: University of Chicago Press, 2003). For a generally Thomistic reflection on the nature of language, see Étienne Gilson, *Linguistics and Philosophy: An Essay on the Philosophical Constants of Language*, trans. John Lyon (Notre Dame, IN: University of Notre Dame Press, 1988).
2. See *ST* I, q. 79, a. 13; I-II, q. 19, a. 5 and 6; *De veritate*, q. 17.
3. Such is the position, for example, by Cajetan Cuddy, "St. Thomas Aquinas on Conscience," in *Christianity and the Laws of Conscience: An Introduction*, ed. Helen M. Alvaré and Jeffrey B. Hammond (Cambridge: Cambridge University Press, 2021), pp. 112–31; Ralph McInerny, "Prudence and Conscience," *The Thomist*, Vol. 38, No. 2 (1974): pp. 291–305; Servais Pinckaers, "Conscience and the Christian Tradition" and "Conscience and the Virtue of Prudence," in John Berkman and Craig Steven Titus, eds., *The Pinckaers Reader: Renewing Moral Theology*, (Washington, DC: The Catholic University of America Press, 2005), pp. 321–358; P.-M. Noonan, "Auriga et Genetrix: Le rôle de la prudence dans le jugement de la conscience," *Revue thomiste*, Vol. 114 (2014): pp. 355–77 and 531–68; H.-D. Noble, *La conscience morale* (Paris: Lethiellieux, 1932), esp. pp. 52–56 ("Le jugement de conscience et le jugement d'action," a very distilled and well-argued section, although one whose conclusions seems to be somewhat at variance with other claims made in this very excellent study); somewhat by Reginald G. Doherty, *The Judgments of Conscience and Prudence* (River Forest, IL: Aquinas Library, 1961); in Jacques Maritain, at least in texts like "La rectitude du vouloir," in Maritain, *Loi naturelle ou loi non-écrite*, ed. Georges Brazzola (Fribourg: University Editions, 1986), pp. 63–78. For more details of the history of this position see both Noonan and Doherty.
4. Such is the position held by certain members of the Thomist School like John of St. Thomas, Fr. Beaudouin, and Fr. Merkelbach, as will be seen in the texts gathered in this volume. It was also the position of Fr. Garrigou-Lagrange, as can be seen in texts like Garrigou-Lagrange, "Remarks Concerning the Metaphysical Character of St. Thomas's Moral Theology," pp. 245–70 (substantially the same as *The Order of Things*, pt. 2, ch. 6); "Prudence's Place in the Organism of the Virtues," *Philosophizing in Faith: Essays on the Beginning and End of Wisdom*, ed. and trans. Matthew K. Minerd (Providence, RI: Cluny Media, 2019), pp. 153–170; *De beatitudine, de actibus humanis, et habitibus* (Turin: Berruti, 1951), 373–396. Also, see Benedict Merkelbach, "Note: Quelle place assigner au traité de la conscience," *Revue des sciences philosophiques et théologiques*, Vol. 12, No. 2 (1923): pp. 170–83; see *Summa theologiae moralis*, 5th ed., vol. 2, *De virtutibus* (Paris: Desclée de Brouwer, 1947), pp. 43–140; Reginald Beaudouin, *Tractatus de conscientia*, ed. Ambroise Gardeil (Paris: Gabalda, 1911).
5. Such seems to be the position held by Fr. Michel Labourdette in the essay included in this volume. See Michel Labourdette, *Les actes humains* (Paris: Parole et Silence, 2016), pp. 204–45; Labourdette, "Morales de la conscience et vertu de prudence," *Revue thomiste*, Vol. 50 (1950): pp. 209–27.

various senses above, in particular (2)–(5). Indeed, some version of the last seems to be the primary sense operative in the 1992 *Catechism of the Catholic Church*, especially in §1778: "Conscience is a judgment of reason whereby the human person recognizes the moral quality of a concrete act that he is going to perform, is in the process of performing, or has already completed." By citing, however, the less-than-technically-exact language of *Gaudium et spes*, §16, the *Catechism* ends up involving the other senses listed above—except for (1), given its unique, non-strictly-moral character:

> Deep within his conscience man discovers a law which he has not laid upon himself but which he must obey. (3) Its voice, ever calling him (2) to love and to do what is good and to avoid evil, sounds in his heart (5) at the right moment... For man has in his heart a law inscribed by God... His conscience is man's most secret core and his sanctuary. (4) There he is alone with God whose voice echoes in his depths.

Similar terms can be found, for example, in the pre-conciliar schema *De ordine morali christiano*.[6]

On the whole, *Veritatis splendor* clearly presents conscience in line with (5),[7] relegating the other senses to a secondary status (at least secondary in *signification*, although they involve fundamental principles making the judgment of conscience itself possible). To say that conscience is a particular kind of judgment-act, we have to ask, "Where does this act come from?" In finite being, actions are "accidents," requiring a subject in which to inhere, as well as various principles to give them being. This dependence leads some such principles to be themselves called "conscience," for as St. Thomas Aquinas says concerning this issue, thereby justifying the various usages of Sts. Jerome, Basil, and John of Damascus: "It is customary that causes and effects be named after one another."[8] Thus, for him, although conscience is a particular act of judgment (5), we can also say that it depends upon practical reason (3), coming to birth through our ability to elicit primordial moral insights (2), ultimately bearing witness to the Eternal Law like a voice of God within us (4) and revealing something

6. See *Schema de ordine morali christiano*, trans. Joseph A. Komonchak, available at https://jakomonchak.files.wordpress.com/2012/09/on-the-christian-moral-order.pdf, ch. 2.
7. See Pope John Paul II, *Veritatis splendor*, §§32 and 54–64.
8. *ST* I, q. 79, a. 13. Also see ad 1 and 3.

about ourselves as moral agents (1). All of these senses can have a home, but they do not designate the same thing, and they take their point of reference in consideration of (5), which provides the focal meaning for the other usages.

For those taking up the stricter Thomist language of (5), emphasizing the act-character of conscience, there still is more to be discussed. The present volume looks to provide a resource for discerning this question, while also hoping to enable future thinkers to carry forward the position of the Thomist school, all the while purifying and clarifying its vocabulary. As noted above, (5) has three sub-divisions:

(5a) Conscience is a judgment of "moral science." It is somewhat speculative in character. (Some will say it is *speculative*,[9] while others, in order to note its uniquely moral character, will say that it is *speculatively practical*.[10]) It is concerned with the morality of a given particular action as performed by any given person, although not necessarily *myself*. Thus, it is not part of prudential reasoning *at all*, for even when one takes counsel, one must already be considering *one's own potential action*, given that prudential counsel already presupposes an *efficacious* intention of the end to be achieved *by me*.

(5b) Conscience is a judgment of prudence or imprudence. It is practical in character, and even if one here speaks of things being "speculatively practical," that is only because one wishes to retain the designation "utterly practical" or "practically practical" for the command of prudence. On this view, any casuistry already seems to involve some degree of prudential reasoning, at least "participatively" by someone who is *giving* counsel to *someone else*, and not to any given, unspecified person.[11]

(5c) Conscience would be some sort of unique judgment, distinct both from prudence and from moral science, used when formulating a judgment about the rightness or wrongness of a potential act to be per-

9. See above, note 3.

10. See, for example, the text from Jacques Maritain in note 3 above; see also, *Existence and the Existent*, trans. Lewis Galantiere and Gerald B. Phelan (New York: Pantheon, 1948), p. 52, n. 3. On this terminology in general, see Matthew Minerd, "Appendix 2: On the Speculative, the Speculatively-Practical, and the Practically-Practical," in Garrigou-Lagrange, "Remarks Concerning the Metaphysical Character of St. Thomas's Moral Theology," pp. 266–270.

11. See Reginald Garrigou-Lagrange, *De beatitudine*, p. 4: "But casuistry does not seem to be something that is *per se* distinct from prudence, for perfect conscience, which is right and certain, is an act of prudence." Also, see the thinkers listed in note 4 above.

formed, without however, being concerned with its full fittingness for me, *here and now*.[12]

All of these distinctions likely seem overly scholastic, fussing over the smallest crannies of the meanings of terms. Yet this is far from true. At stake in the use of such terms is the very structure of practico-moral[13] reasoning, which such terms seek to describe. Now, from an "apologetic" perspective, it must be admitted that common parlance generally speaks about conscience as directing *my actions here and now*. That is, it somehow seems to imply the very *discursus* of moral reasoning undertaken by the moral virtue of prudence (and, for the Christian believer, supernatural infused prudence[14]), thus having a sense akin to (5b). Often, too, conscience is spoken of as being a particular power (3)—"My conscience tells me to do this"—often also implying that is a kind of ultimate "moral sense" (2). Even for the partisans of (5a)—conscience-as-moral-scientific-casuistry—it will be important to have the ability to distinguish their sense of the term "conscience" from that used in contemporary language since what is referred to by the latter is a real, experiential datum. While exactness of terms will require the drawing of appropriate distinctions for someone holding position (5a), nonetheless, it would be pastorally and interpersonally disastrous to respond by shutting down the conversation merely because of an honest disagreement over term. Rarely will this response engender an open mind in one's hearer. Without becoming soft of head,

12. See note 5 above.

13. In distinction from practical-artistic / practical-technical reasoning, like that applied in the useful and fine arts.

14. Throughout this essay, I will take for granted certain Thomist positions such as that concerning the infused moral virtues, held by way of theological deduction, though not held *de fide*. For a good introduction to this topic, see Romanus Cessario, "What Causes the Moral Virtues to Develop," in *The Moral Virtues and Theological Ethics* (Notre Dame, IN: University of Notre Dame Press, 1991), pp. 94–125; Ambroise Gardeil, *La vraie vie chrétienne*, ed. H.-D. Gardeil (Paris: Desclée de Brouwer, 1935), pp. 101–117; Reginald Garrigou-Lagrange, *The Three Ages of the Interior Life*, vol. 1, trans. M. Timothea Doyle (St. Louis, MO: B. Herder, 1947), pp. 59–66; *The Theological Virtues: Faith*, trans. Thomas à Kempis Reilly (St. Louis, MO: B. Herder, 1964), pp. 26–29. The latter volume is an incomplete, somewhat-altered translation of Fr. Garrigou-Lagrange's original text. I will not, however, here get involved in the debates on this topic as found in authors like Mattison, Knobel, Porter, Dahm, McWhorter, and others. My general position is that the infusion of the Christian moral virtues does not efface the acquired moral virtues, which remain as the proximate principles of a variety of human acts which, however, can be extrinsically ordered to charity and thereby integrated into the overall living of the Christian life.

however, we do need the magnanimity of someone like Aquinas, who is always ready to make a distinction instead of harping on "good Thomist terminology," as if Thomism were the arcana of a priesthood of specially educated elitists who can dole out wisdom to the masses, using a rigid and inflexible verbiage.[15]

In Catholic circles, there is a kind of common idea that the importance of conscience was only truly recognized by the post-conciliar Church, with the aforementioned passage from *Gaudium et spes*, as well as in the Declaration on Religious Liberty, *Dignitatis humanae*. An unreflective, popular narrative would have one believe that conscience was generally suppressed by pre-conciliar theologians and clerics exercising their rigid priest-craft within the confessionals: many black-and-white rules, but no freedom of conscience. From such a perspective, one ends up with a hermeneutic for the history of moral theology like that of Fr. James Keenan: *A History of Catholic Moral Theology in the Twentieth Century: From Confessing Sins to Liberating Consciences*.[16] Such a view of history is common. Yet, as Fr. Keenan is well aware (as evidenced by his own defenses of casuistry), the world owes a great debt to "pre-Conciliar" Catholic moral theology for the development of topics surrounding conscience. Indeed, the progressive moral theologian Fr. Charles Curran knew quite well that one must say that "the most extensive development in the understanding of conscience in the Catholic tradition came in the context of the manuals of moral theology that emerged at the end of the sixteenth century and continued until Vatican II."[17] Curran goes

15. As any reader will note, *of course*, I am a believer in the arcana of technical terminology. It is the mark of any mature discipline that it use a terminology that can help to stabilize the conceptual usages in that domain of discussion. However, not every discipline needs to be treated as though it has stipulated univocal terms, after the manner of mathematics. This is above all the case when we are dealing with notions that are vital and central to human experience, drawing on quite-varied bases for different people, thus having different connotations. Note well, I speak of *terms* not of *concepts* and, moreover, sometimes the terms used in a given context must be abandoned for the use of rigid technical terminology, lest misunderstanding arise. I only plea for a kind of magnanimous use of terminology by Thomists, lest we get caught speaking to ourselves, with our own terms, solely about ourselves and about what we have said.

    On this topic, see Jacques Maritain, "Sur le langage philosophique," in *Réflexions sur l'intelligence et sur sa vie propre*, 3rd ed. (Paris: Desclée de Brouwer, 1930), pp. 336–341.

16. See James F. Keenan, *A History of Catholic Moral Theology in the Twentieth Century: From Confessing Sins to Liberating Consciences* (London: Bloomsbury Academic, 2010).

17. Charles E. Curran, "Conscience in the Light of the Catholic Moral Tradition," in *Conscience: Readings in Moral Theology*, Vol. 14, ed. Charles E. Curran (New York: Paulist Press, 2004), p. 7.

on in this same passage to talk about the legal tone of much of this content,[18] and there is truth to this point, for as we will see in a chapter drawn from the work of Fr. Michel Labourdette, O.P., included in this volume, the treatment of conscience and freedom would come to be presented on the model of a courtroom proceeding between two litigants: Who has rights in this matter, the law or freedom?

As we shall see, especially in our general essays by Frs. Labourdette and Merkelbach, if anything, the theological treatise on conscience risked coloring the whole of moral theology. The great debates over probabilism—namely, the problem concerning "just how probable" our knowledge must be in relation to our moral acts[19]—raged just as harshly between the sixteenth and eighteenth centuries as did the famous controversy *De auxiliis* between the Jesuits and the Dominicans concerning questions related to predestination in the sixteenth and early seventeenth centuries. These theological debates also elicited Magisterial condemnations against both laxists and Jansenist rigorists,[20] and the entire structure of moral texts

18. Here we can have significant agreement with Curran's observation, despite the other problems involved in his thought. The dominance of law as the primary motif of moral theology was one of the ills which arose in part due to nominalistic currents of thought within theology in later scholasticism. The most generally accessible overview of this point of history can be found in Servais Pinckaers, *The Sources of Christian Ethics*, trans. Mary Thomas Noble (Washington, DC: The Catholic University of America Press, 1995), pp. 240–279; *Morality: The Catholic View*, trans. Michael Sherwin (South Bend, IN: St. Augustine's Press, 2003), pp. 7–64. Note, however, that many Thomists in Pinckaers' own day were well aware of this problem (as is obvious when paging through the works of Garrigou-Lagrange, Gardeil, Maritain, Merkelbach, Labourdette, and others). He most definitely was not the first person to decry this state of affaris.

19. See H.-D. Noble, *Le discernement de la conscience* (Paris: Lethielliux, 1934); P. Richard, *Le probabilisme moral et philosophie* (Paris: Nouvelle Librairie Nationale, 1922); P. Mandonnet, "Le décret d'Innocent XI contre le probabilisme," *Revue Thomiste*, Vol. 9 (1901): pp. 460–481, 520–539, and 652–673; Mandonnet, "La position du probabilisme dans l'Eglise catholique," *Revue Thomiste*, Vol. 10 (1902): pp. 5–20; Mandonnet, "De la valeur des theories sur la probabilité morale," *Revue Thomiste*, Vol. 10 (1902): pp. 315–335; and Fr. Thomas Deman's article "Probabilisme," *Dictionnaire de théologie catholique*, Vol. 13, No. 1, ed. E. Amann, et al. (Paris: Letouzey et Ané, 1936), col. 417–619. For important related studies, see Ambroise Gardeil, "La certitude probable," *Revue des sciences philosophiques et théologiques*, Vol. 5 (1911): pp. 237–266, 441–485; "La topicité," *Revue des sciences philosophiques et théologiques*, Vol. 5 (1911): pp. 750–757; and L.-M. Régis, *L'Opinion selon Aristote* (Paris: Vrin, 1935). Also see note 6 in the Translator's Introduction to this volume.

20. See Alexander VII, Decree of the Holy Office against the Laxists (Denzinger, nos. 2101–2167); Innocent XI, Decree of the Holy Office concerning Probabilism (Denzinger nos. 2175–2177); Alexander VIII, Decree of the Holy Office against the Jansenists (Denzinger, nos. 2301–2332).

would become bloated with discussions concerning the binding force of conscience, something quite distant from Aquinas's own explicit dicta. The title of a recent scholarly volume by Matthew Levering captures the centrality of "conscience" for understanding much of twentieth-century moral theology: *The Abuse of Conscience: A Century of Catholic Moral Theology*.[21] Indeed, a companion volume of history could be written with the sub-title: *Centuries of Catholic Moral Theology*.

I suggest that the two be read together. In this introduction, my goal will be to lay out the various stages of moral reasoning from a strictly Thomistic perspective, in the hopes of distinguishing positions (5a–c) above. Disagreement over words and basic structure features heavily in these matters; less prominent is an actual difference of opinion and conclusions concerning the nature of conscience. Very often, Thomists use the term "conscience" to refer to quite different things. Consequently, instead of getting into the weeds of texts and articles at the beginning, I wish to lay out a kind of schema of moral reasoning, in order to provide a vocabulary for carrying forward the conversation among Thomists, above all those who are desirous to connect up today's conversations with the heritage of earlier Thomist thinkers. There has been much vogue in the post-Conciliar methodological bias in favor of a historical "return to Thomas," and a kind of antipathy for the traditional schools, for fear of adulterating Aquinas's thought. The concern is understandable and often, if not always, laudable. I have learned far too much, however, from my Thomist forebears to ignore them as my primary interlocutors. Why opt solely for contemporary authors, who are not exempt from the nominalism of modernity, and thus choose to ignore voices whose spirit is more closely animated by the same intellectual climate as that of the Angelic Doctor? Merely because we have the *Index Thomisticus* today does not mean that we are better situated than they. A heap of citations without

21. I have had the benefit of reading a draft of Dr. Levering's book, which will provide an excellent (and very much-needed) resource for scholars looking to get their bearings concerning the very manifold history of philosophies and theologies of conscience. Without this sort of history, a full understanding of what is at stake is not possible, and the conclusions that Dr. Levering draws from this study are of great use and power in trying to formulate a path forward after decades of decadence in Catholic Moral Theology. (Of course, especially after the promulgation of *Veritatis splendor*, there has been much positive work done, but building always takes much more time than does destruction.) The current text, however, is looking to fill a different hole and to perform a different task than does Dr. Levering's volume.

a clear articulation of principles can be more befuddling than a slightly skewed, albeit generally correct, articulation of basic outlines of the main illuminative points laying out a given domain of knowledge. Of course, a self-critical outlook will be needed, but such self-criticism can be performed *in the light of the principles* thus provided by such a general "lay of the (conceptual) land."

Having meditated for some time on the implications of these various positions held among Thomists concerning conscience, it seems to me, at least at this moment, that the basic questions facing us are: *Just how practical is moral-scientific reasoning?* And: *To what extent are the domains of moral reasoning (whether scientific or personal) internally differentiated?* To answer these questions, however, an entire realist *Critique of Moral Reasoning* would be needed. (The best model for beginning such a project can be found in Yves Simon's *A Critique of Moral Knowledge*.) Such an investigation would primarily be concerned with the *reflexive critique* involved in moral philosophy and moral theology *precisely as forms of wisdom*. Wisdom is distinct from science in that the former defends and explains its principles *in themselves*. Thus, a critical reflection must be established in all forms of discursive wisdom if they are to manifest truly their complete character *ut sapientiae*. This critique is much needed—written primarily, not as a textual study of Aquinas (or even of his great Commentators), but as an inquiry *into the problem itself*.[22]

I shall try to provide the outlines of such an epistemological critique, although doing so in a pedagogical and broad-brush manner. My primary

22. On the importance of placing textual analysis in its proper, subordinate place in Thomist speculation, see the excellent reflections by John C. Cahalan in "On the Training of Thomists," in *The Future of Thomism*, ed. Deal W. Hudson and Dennis W. Moran (Notre Dame, IN: American Maritain Association, 1992), pp. 133–147. His words ring true to this very day, and for whatever their weakness, the spirit that inspires them would do much, were it followed, to prevent Thomism from being the self-referential historical cul-de-sac which it forever risks becoming, both out of quite justified devotion to the profound thought of St. Thomas but also out of the more lamentable current of contemporary scholarship which is infused with a kind of historical relativism. There is forever a risk of treating St. Thomas's thought as if it could only, at best, be laid out for its own sake, as one particular manifestation of human thought, although historically situated and placed in the museum of the past. An outlook similar to Cahalan's animated the response offered to the Fourvière Jesuits by Frs. Labourdette, M.-J. Nicolas, and Bruckberger in *Dialogue théologique* (St. Maximin: Les Arcades, 1947). Fr. Bruckberger, although a tragic figure in many ways, gives a rousing call to arms at the beginning of this volume, a bit of Thomist rhetoric which should inspire all followers of the Angelic Doctor. (A translation of these texts is anticipated for publication by The Catholic University of America Press in 2022 or 2023.)

concern is *to propose a way forward* for trying to interpret different kinds of moral judgments, hopefully providing a point of reference for people who discuss conscience in positions (5a–5c). At one time, I was a bold adherent of (5b), which we shall find reflected in the lengthy texts by Frs. Beaudouin and Merkelbach published in this volume. I have begun to question some of the over-simplification operative in this position, and I am not even sure that it is entirely fair to place these two Dominicans strictly in that category, although it ultimately does represent their fundamental bent. Given all of this uncertainty, as well as many fruitful conversations that I have had with Cajetan Cuddy, O.P., Thomas Howes, Matthew Levering, and James Bryan, I shall propose in what remains of this essay a kind of Thomist outline of moral reasoning.[23]

The overview discussion that follows will be made up of two main sections. The first, and shorter, section will lay out the distinction between moral philosophy and moral theology. These discussions will help to provide the scaffolding needed for the concepts to be deployed throughout the remainder of this study. Most importantly, it will situate moral reasoning within the broader environments within which it finds its true meaning. The second section will provide a lengthy analysis of the various stages of moral reasoning. Because these discussions descend from the most speculatively-practical of judgments down to the particularized judgment of prudence, I have felt the need to write this section as a single, extended whole. The overall "arc" of the discussion is lengthy and must be considered in all of its aspects. The ending, however, will provide a summary of all the various types of moral judgments considered in this section.

23. I must also recognize the immense influence that long ago was exercised upon my thought by Jacques Maritain, "Appendix VII: 'Speculative' and 'Practical,'" in *The Degrees of Knowledge*, trans. Gerald B. Phelan, et al. (Notre Dame, IN: University of Notre Dame Press, 2002), pp. 481–489; Yves R. Simon, *A Critique of Moral Knowledge*, trans. Ralph McInerny (New York: Fordham University Press, 2002). See also Michel Labourdette, "Connaissance pratique et savoir morale," *Revue thomiste*, Vol. 48 (1948): pp. 142–179. Cf. William A. Wallace, *The Role of Demonstration in Moral Theology* (Washington, DC: The Thomist Press, 1962), pp. 71–94. This whole study is utterly admirable and deserving of a broader reading.

In the process of composing this introduction I could not help but be staggeringly surprised at how illuminating the insights of these texts have remained. I believe that what I present here is an honest Thomistic account and not merely some covert justification of Maritain and Simon. Rather, the fact that they were so rooted in the long-lived Thomist tradition (and not solely in the discussion in contemporary journals) gives them incredible ballast against the waves of critique which can be raised against their accounts on this or that point. I wholeheartedly recommend these two texts to the reader.

"THE WHITHER AND WHENCE" OF CONSCIENCE IN MORAL PHILOSOPHY AND THEOLOGY

To the degree that Thomist theology, precisely as a *sapientia-scientia*, a discursive form of wisdom,[24] is Aristotelian in form, it has a purely speculative finality. Based on the very principles of faith, as well as those principles of natural reason that are elevated for use in theological speculation, it seeks to provide some degree of understanding of the matters of faith, some *intellectus fidei*. The mysteries of faith are the lights of theological speculation; indeed, they give theology its uniquely unified character: it is the discursive sapiential-science of the supernatural revealed life of the Godhead. All that theology considers refers back to God in His eminent, Trinitarian mystery. In each of its treatises, theology is merely inflecting its consideration toward some Divine Reality: God Himself as One and Three, creatures considered as dependent upon this God as upon their source, human action as traversed from top to bottom by the divinizing life we are given in grace and glory, the mysteries of the Redemptive

24. For important but highly technical reasons, acquired supernatural theology must be referred to as a form of discursive wisdom, *sapientia*, and not *merely* as a science. This is a point not always made with sufficient clarity by Thomists, a point I reflect on at length in Matthew K. Minerd, "Wisdom be Attentive: The Noetic Structure of Sapiential Knowledge," *Nova et Vetera*, Vol. 19, No. 3 (2020): pp. 1103–1146. The interested reader should consult that text, along with the numerous authors cited therein in defense of this point.

    In defense of the broadly "scientific" form of Thomist theology, although with more or less emphasis on its unique sapiential duties, see "La théologie, Intelligence de la foi," *Revue thomiste*, Vol. 46 (1946): pp. 5–44; Raymond Léopold Bruckberger, "Dialogue théologique," in *Dialogue théologique: Pièces du débat entre "La Revue Thomiste" d'une part et les R.R. P.P. de Lubac, Daniélou, Bouillard, Fessard, von Balthasar, S.J., d'autre part* (Saint-Maximin: Les Arcades, 1947), pp. 9–18. Marie-Rosaire Gagnebet, "La nature de la théologie speculative," *Revue thomiste*, Vol. 44 (1938): pp. 1–39, 213–255, 645–674; "Un essai sur le problème théologique," *Revue thomiste*, Vol. 45 (1939): pp. 108–45; "Le problème actuel de la théologie et la science aristotélicienne d'après un ouvrage récent," *Divus thomas*, Vol. 46 (1943): pp. 237–270.

    As has been noted by Donneaud, however, there is already some "give" in Gagnebet in the direction of recognizing the "supra-scientific" offices of wisdom. See Henry Donneaud, "Un retour aux sources caché sous son contraire: Rosaire Gagnebet contre Louis Charlier sur la nature de la théologie spéculative," *Revue thomiste*, Vol. 119 (2019): pp. 577–612. Gagnebet almost certainly gets such offices from Garrigou-Lagrange, who, although he tends to speak in terms of "theological science" and "theological conclusions," also emphasizes in various texts the importance of the supra-scientific duties of theology, for example, in Reginald Garrigou-Lagrange, "Theology and the Life of Faith," *Philosophizing in Faith*, pp. 421–43. See also the excellent Kieran Conley, *A Theology of Wisdom: A Study of St. Thomas* (Dubuque, IA: The Priory Press, 1963); Mark F. Johnson, "The Sapiential Character of *Sacra Doctrina* in the Thought of St. Thomas Aquinas: The Appropriation of Aristotle's Intellectual Virtue of Wisdom," Ph.D. diss. (Centre for Medieval Studies, 1990).

Incarnation by which this life is extended to all, the mystery of the Church as His mystical body, the sacraments as the "separated instruments" by which Christ acts even today through His Church, and so forth. No topic covered in theology remains untouched by this overall order and unity of theology. No treatise stands on its own, for each "part" of theology is in fact animated by a single soul: *God considered in the intimate and supernatural life of the Godhead, reflectively known through the faith-illuminated discourse of reason.*[25]

And yet, the only "science" that knows God in a single, eternal, ever-actual, undimmed flash of knowledge is God's own self-knowledge. In the spiritual life, this fact is reflected in the various purifications by which our faith (and our knowledge of all things in light of faith) is rendered increasingly akin to that knowledge—above all by the ways of supernatural unknowing through the mediacy of charity which here takes on the character of objective causality (*sic amor transit in conditionem objecti*), we silently "taste" the supernatural realities at work in the depths of our soul where God dwells.[26] In the hereafter, our knowledge of God will be direct. Nonetheless, the "light of glory," by which our minds will be made capable of that immediate, beatifying knowledge, will not render our mind's equal to God Himself. This "subjective capacitating" offered by the light of glory will leave a kind of gulf between our non-comprehensive proportioning to this vision and the comprehensive knowledge that God has of Himself.[27] In faith, mystical experience, and the vision of God,

25. That is, He is known in accord with what theologians after St. Thomas's day would come to call "virtual revelation" in distinction from the "formal revelation" grasped through supernatural faith. On this topic, see Matthew Minerd, "Translator's Appendix 1: Concerning the Formal Object of Acquired Theology," in Garrigou-Lagrange, "Remarks Concerning the Metaphysical Character of St. Thomas's Moral Theology," pp. 261–266. See my slight qualifications, however, in Minerd, "Wisdom be Attentive: The Noetic Structure of Sapiential Knowledge," p. 1108, n. 13.

26. For good overviews on the Thomist theology of the divine indwelling, see Reginald Garrigou-Lagrange, *Love of God and the Cross of Jesus*, trans. Jeanne Marie, vol. 1 (St. Louis, MO: B. Herder, 1948), pp. 136–173; an excellent study can be found in Francis Cunningham, *The Indwelling of the Trinity: A Historico-Doctrinal Study of the Theory of St. Thomas Aquinas* (Dubuque, IA: The Prior Press, 1955). A classic speculative study of this can be found in Ambroise Gardeil, *La Structure de l'âme et l'expérience mystique*, 3rd ed., vol. 2 (Paris: Gabalda, 1927). Also see J.-H. Nicolas, *Les Profondeurs de la Grâce* (Paris: Beauchesne, 1969), pp. 126–141.

27. In other words, God in His self-knowledge and the blessed in their knowledge of Him have the same *obiectum formale quod* (the Uncreated Deity), while differing as regards the *obiectum formale quo* (clearly and comprehensively seen versus clearly and non-comprehensively seen).

we are faced with truly divine acts, resting on divine motives: God who supernaturally reveals Himself, whether obscurely, in the unspoken "taste" of experience, or as clearly seen.

Yet, as discursive beings who must win our way to knowledge—through progressive judgments, premises, and conclusions—it befits us to have a form of divinized-yet-human knowledge of the mysteries: acquired supernatural theology. This knowledge will be marked by our condition as a kind of spirit who is "temporally dilated."[28] Our organism is made up of many ordered parts, in all of which the soul is present. So too, in our sciences (and our sapiential-sciences), we find that our discourse must be spread out over many chains of reasoning, definitions, and indeed even in the very observation of data (or, we might say, the establishment of the facts unique to this or that form of discourse).[29] For theology, all is *one* under the unity of its subject and principles: God in His inner mystery, lived by man, returning to Him through the Redemptive Incarnation in the Church, who applies that redemption and divinization through the ages. Yet, given the discursive character of our intellect, there are *many* theological treatises.

In moral theology, the great hinge is Aquinas's Treatise on Beatitude. It connects moral theology to the entire circuit of theology, passing from God and His Providence (*Prima Pars*) to man who is called to participate in His Beatitude (*Secunda Pars*) to Christ who brings beatitude by trampling death, being resurrected, applying the fruits of salvation through the Church and the Sacraments, and ultimately leading us to ultimate beatitude in the hereafter (*Tertia Pars*). One can rightly say that "the attraction of the Divine Beatitude does not only function as the teleological lodestar for the entire economy of our knowledge of God, of which theology is an integral part, but it also leaves its mark upon the formal structure

28. See the powerful study by Anton Pegis, *At the Origins of the Thomistic Notion of Man* (New York: MacMillan, 1963); also, see its conceptual continuation in Armand Maurer, *St. Thomas and Historicity* (Milwaukee, WI: Marquette University Press, 1979).

29. Fr. Labourdette devotes a profound section to this topic in "La théologie, Intelligence de la foi," pp. 26–34. See also Yves Simon, "Philosophers and Facts," in *The Great Dialogue of Nature and Space*, ed. Gerard J. Delacourt (New York: Magi Books, 1970), pp. 139–62; Maritain, *Degrees of Knowledge*, pp. 60–64; also see the insightful and lucid reflections in Michael D. Torre, "Yves R. Simon, Disciple of Maritain: The Idea of Fact and the Difference Between Science and Philosophy," in *Facts are Stubborn Things: Thomistic Perspectives in the Philosophies of Nature and Science*, ed. Matthew K. Minerd (Washington, DC: American Maritain Association / The Catholic University of America Press, 2020), pp. 19–39.

of a complete theological exposition."[30] Theology bounds from beatitude to beatitude: God's "immanent" Trinitarian beatitude; the participation in this beatitude which is our ultimate end; the giving of this beatitude which overflows in Christ from the greatest of all "graces," the "Grace of Union."[31]

Rightly did Fr. Jacobus Ramirez compose a massive five-volume treatise merely on this one treatise of theology.[32] Aquinas learned well from Aristotle's *Nicomachean Ethics* that we must place the ultimate end at the head of moral matters. In comparison, however, with the great light offered to moral philosophy by the primacy of the ultimate end in all its discussions, the light offered here is even greater. With an uncreated radiance, the supernatural life of divinization offered in grace will illuminate all that must be discussed: the virtues, which now are transformed by the addition of the theological virtues and the infused moral virtues; the passions, which must be understood so that they may be raised to divine heights (just as they were in Christ's own humanity); the treatment of law, which now makes room for the New Law of grace; the virtues themselves are transfigured and elevated, while still also leaving human values in place too. And likewise, *our account of practico-moral reasoning cannot fail to be altered by all of these supernatural data.* The theologian must explain *not merely the natural process* of human moral reasoning but must also take up that reasoning to explain how it is that the child of God manifests (or fails to manifest) his or her destiny through free action in the pursuit of beatitude.

And yet, this was not to be the order of things for many formed in moral theology. A confluence of nominalism and voluntarism in late scholasticism shifted the focus of moral speculation away from beatitude and objective moral norms toward the freely-willed imposition of law by a divine law-giver.[33] With increasing tendency, morality appeared to be determined by the *imposition* of the moral rule, not by its *intrinsic moral character.* The simple schematization, familiar to all at least since the time

30. Emmanuel Durand, "The Practice of Trinitarian Theology as Wayfaring Pilgrims," in *Divine Names in Human Words: Explorations in Theology*, trans. Matthew K. Minerd. (This text is to be published by The Catholic University of America Press in 2022.)

31. See *ST* III, q. 2, a. 10.

32. See Jacobus Ramirez, *De hominis beatitudine: In I-II Summae theologiae divi Thomae commentaria (qq. i-v)*, vol. 3 (in 5 parts) of *Opera omnia*, ed. Victorino Rodriguez (Madrid: Conseo Superior de Investigaciones Científicas, 1972).

33. See note 18 above.

of Plato, could be put as follows: Is something wrong because God so commands, or does He command it precisely because it is wrong? Understandably aware of the contingent nature of the created order and how the natural moral law depends upon God's good pleasure, Duns Scotus tilted the discussion of moral obligation in the direction of such voluntarism. And even if (according to the classic interpretation of Scotus[34]) he restricted God's voluntarism to the "second tablet" of the Ten Commandments (those not directly concerned with God), this kind of voluntarism would become far more marked with the passage of time. Thus, the "ethics of the befitting and beatifying good" would be replaced by an "ethics of law and obligation." Moral questions would be slanted in the direction of "What do moral norms hold?" and away from "How does this act concretely build virtue and deepen the life of beatifying grace?"

Neither outlook necessarily excludes the other, but they will transfigure each other when they bring them into their own domain. Thus, an obligation-centric moral theology will tend to transfigure the virtues into *precepts*. As a consequence, prudence will become a kind of legalistic conscience, weighing out the rights of this or that obligation. The "inventive" character the moral life of virtue will be replaced with a desire to figure out how to avoid crossing the line of sin. Moral theology, in short, will come to be above all a science of obligations to be weighed out and of sins to be avoided. No doubt, spiritual theology will compensate for these theological deformities, and such has been the case for so many great saints and preachers of the Church. The Western Church, to name but a few figures, has St. Francis de Sales, St. John Eudes, Jacques-Bénigne Bossuet, and St. Thérèse of Lisieux. In the East, the movement to compile and spread the *Philokalia*, undertaken by Sts. Nicodemus the Hagiorite and Macarius of Corinth, bore into Orthodox Christianity a great abundance of moral-ascetical wisdom from desert monasticism. The relations between moral theology and spiritual theology are close. Thus, where moral theology slackens, spiritual theology can, under the right conditions, bring its own compensations.[35]

34. Although this interpretation is being nuanced today. See Thomas M. Ward, "A Most Mitigated Friar: Scotus on Natural Law and Divine Freedom," *American Catholic Philosophical Quarterly*, Vol. 93, No. 3 (2019): pp. 385–409.

35. On the relationship between moral theology and spiritual theology, see Michel Labourdette, "Qu'est-ce que la théologie spirituelle?" *Revue thomiste*, Vol. 92 (1992): pp. 355–372.

On the other hand, a beatitude-centric moral theology will provide an outlook that is ultimately broad enough to incorporate an obligation-centric framework, albeit only at the cost of showing the latter its delimited domain. Obligation is derivative upon the notion of the good, in all of its many ramifications throughout the various virtues. Thus, a beatitude-centric moral theology will search out the place to consider the weighing out of cases of conscience, of the battle of "law and freedom," forever realizing that doing so is only part of the story. Such a theology will be well apprised of the fact that the true core of moral reasoning is to be found in the virtue of prudence, which requires the careful touch that comes from the virtuous life. It must weigh out these particulars, and this will mean that no guidance of conscience is fully written out on paper in advance. Universal maxims will exist—for the good is imperious in its demands—but they will not vie with each other as they did in the great debates over probabilism, i.e., seeking out just how much certainty is necessary in order to act. For centuries, this issue was, for many, *the* burning question. A beatitude-centric moral theology will say that it is *a* question, but not *the central one*.

In theology, the debates over probabilism occasioned the solidification of a particular treatise which became central for many thinkers, leading to a restructuring of the apparatus of moral theology: the treatise on conscience. This treatise did not exist separately for St. Thomas. He treats of conscience only in passing in *ST* I, q. 79 a. 13 and in *ST* I-II, q. 19, a. 5 and 6 in the sub-treatise on morality[36] within the treatise on human acts. The famous Bishop Francis Kenrick of Baltimore, however, begins his *Theologia moralis* with the treatise on human acts immediately followed by a treatise on conscience.[37] No doubt, he felt quite justified in doing so, for the treatise on conscience stands at the head of many great moral theologians' works, including the *Theologia Moralis* of St. Alphonsus of Liguouri.[38] And we may merely reference a work such as the *Ad Theologiam*

Also Reginald Garrigou-Lagrange, "Addenda: On the Nature of Spiritual Theology" in *The Three Ages of the Interior Life*, vol. 2, trans. M. Timothea Doyle (St. Louis, MO: B. Herder, 1948), pp. 652–654.

36. See note 55 below.

37. See Francis Patrick Kenrick, *Theologia Moralis*, vol. 1 (Mechelen: H. Dessain, 1860).

38. See St. Alphonsus Liguori, *Moral Theology*, vol. 1, trans. Ryan Grant (Post Falls, ID: Mediatrix Press, 2017), pp. 23–159.

Christianam Dogmatico-Moralem of Daniello Concina, O.P., to see an utterly learned (over seven hundred pages in length) discussion of the problems of conscience, which nonetheless places all of this heavy freight at the head of moral theology, within a matrix that is quite different from that of St. Thomas's own opening to the moral part of the *Summa theologiae*.

The consequences of this shift of perspective in moral theology, however, were disastrous, dis-equilibrating the very nature of the theological life. Indeed, as Matthew Levering argues very cogently in his recent work, *The Abuse of Conscience: A Century of Catholic Moral Theology*,[39] once the basic frameworks of faith were shaken during the 1950s onward, this conscience-based framework of morality had nothing left to stand upon. It can indeed be argued that progressive theologians and philosophers of this era were not reformers; rather, they were themselves the ill-begotten fruit of a theological synthesis that was intrinsically unstable and, for a time, had survived solely through external supports of sanctity or, in some cases, fear of authority.

Much of the vexation felt in Orthodox circles against "Roman legalism,"[40] and the loss of the centrality of divinization and theosis in moral theology is almost certainly due to this shift of focus. It is, however, in my estimation dangerous to act as if such "legalism" is a purely Roman issue. It is a bent of mind that is quite natural to the very warp and woof of vocabulary used in Sacred Scripture, given its derivation from the revelation of the Old Covenant.[41] Indeed, the language of law is found throughout the liturgical language of the East. In comparison with a sane Christian understanding of law and obligation, however, the language of conscience-centric and obligation-centric moral theology does have a dry and desiccated character.

Yet let us not cast aside previous generations. They had true concerns, even if their answers were uneven. Rather all limp along. Therefore, instead of polemics, we should try instead for *engagement*. For our part, let

39. Matthew Levering, *The Abuse of Conscience: A Century of Catholic Moral Theology* (Grand Rapids, MI: Eerdmans, 2021).

40. At least when it is not actually just an expression of the antinomianism of the recent era of thought.

41. And let us never forget the great love we should have for this law. Psalm 119 deserves a kind of meditative savor all the days of our life! For a beautiful reflection on this topic, see C.S. Lewis, "Sweeter Than Honey" in *Reflections on the Psalms* (New York: Harvest Books, 1958), pp. 54–65

us turn now to an engagement with the core of our problem: *the noetics of conscience*, reflected on and integrated into a beatitude-centric framework of moral theology (and a virtue-ethics, happiness-centric moral philosophy). This content should in turn frame, in particular, the *highly* technical sections of the works by Frs. Beaudouin and Merkelbach in this volume.

THE STAGES OF MORAL REASONING AND THE VARIOUS KINDS OF MORAL JUDGMENTS

The following is an attempt to categorize the various judgments that are possible within the moral domain. As such, it will likely fail to fulfill completely any one reader. This introduction, however, is written in the spirit of being an "essay," an attempt to outline these matters. My goal is to push onward within the Thomist school, although without being overly solicitous about the various categories of contemporary debates concerning moral reasoning within contemporary Aristotelian and Scholastic academic literature. These debates are important, and they touch upon vital points of interest. Contemporary academics, however, can tend to become lost in one particular problem to the detriment of trying to give a full overview of the problem at hand. My goal is to synthesize what I have gained from my own masters, whose names will be obvious in the notations accompanying my reflections.

The "Speculatively Practical" Starting-Points of Moral Reasoning

The entire "descent" of the most "directive" of moral truth, namely prudential truth, is itself marked at its start by a form of knowledge which has a speculative character—technically, a *speculatively practical* character.[42] At the birth of moral knowledge, we have a form of knowledge that is at once *ultimately directive* while, however, retaining the overall character of speculative truth. In the declarations of the natural *habitus* of *synderesis* (along with its supernatural correlate, to which I will refer as "faith-synderesis"), we find ourselves faced with truth declared after the model of speculative truth: *per conformitatem ad rem*. Here, truth is measured insofar as there is conformity between knowledge and reality. In speculative knowledge,

42. This section should be read in parallel with Matthew K. Minerd, "A Note on *Synderesis*, Moral Science, and Knowledge of the Natural Law," *Lex Naturalis*, Vol. 5 (2020): pp. 43–55.

truth arises when the subject and predicate, which are *objectively* distinct are, in fact, *really the same* in some way.[43] Thus, the predicate "to be pursued and done" is really the same (as a property) as "the (moral) good," such that we can say, "The good is to be pursued and done." *In the very reality that is moral being itself,*[44] this assertion is true in a direct and non-inferential way. It is *per se notum*, "self-evident," *intellectually seen* without any objectively illative discourse.[45] So too, when we say, "Where a debt is owed, it must be recognized and repaid appropriately," we are asserting something *per se notum*, self-evident, which will remain present in all of our various acts of justice, throughout all of the various species which make up that great and vast domain of our interpersonal life. Through *synderesis* and faith-*synderesis* we have the very foundations for the moral life. It is through this knowledge that we are in touch with the formal-intellectual "norm" which will be the measure of our action, the very nature of moral activity that prudence will need to trace out existentially for each of us in a unique way, although never departing from the "norm."[46] And

43. See John C. Cahalan, "The Problem of Thing and Object in Maritain," *The Thomist*, Vol. 59, No. 1: pp. 21–46; Jacques Maritain, *The Degrees of Knowledge*, pp. 96–107 and 127–136; Yves R. Simon, *An Introduction to the Metaphysics of Knowledge*, trans. Vukan Kuic and Richard J. Thompson (New York: Fordham University Press, 1990), pp. 136–149; Reginald Garrigou-Lagrange, *Thomistic Common Sense: The Philosophy of Being and the Development of Doctrine*, trans. Matthew K. Minerd (Steubenville, OH: Emmaus Academic: 2021), p. 54.

44. See Jacques Maritain, *An Introduction to the Basic Problems of Moral Philosophy*, trans. Cornelia N. Borgerhoff (New York: Magi Books, 1990), p. 36: "What makes a man good, not relatively but absolutely speaking? It is not external goods, not bodily or even intellectual goods... It is action as flowing from freedom, good action, which makes a man good absolutely speaking, action which is the supreme actualization of being. Here we have good as moral value; *we are in the order of formal causality* [emphasis mine]. The good as *moral value* [emphasis original]. Here we are faced with a new order, the moral order; a new universe emerges and is revealed to us. If human action were simply a natural event, resulting from the interaction of a constellation of causes at work in the world, we would only need to consider the universe of nature. But human action is introduced into the world as a result of free choice, as something that depends not only on that whole which is the world, but on the absolute initiative—irreducible to factors interacting in the world—taken by another whole which is myself, my own person, so that I am responsible for the act in question."

45. Although subjectively illative discourse may well be necessary. On this topic, see Garrigou-Lagrange, "Theology and the Life of Faith," pp. 430–431, 439–443.

46. The notion of norm must be understood very carefully, lest one fall into a form of legalism. Thomist morality is *first and foremost* grounded in the notion of the "fitting good" (*bonum honestum*), that which is morally good *for its own sake*. Thus, the ultimate resolution of moral obligation is found in the line of intrinsic formal causality: the formal befittingness of a given moral essence, grasped through *synderesis* or faith-*synderesis*. Importantly, then, this means that the notion of *end* is not the ultimate terminus of Thomist moral analysis. This observation is expressed with lucidity by Fr. Austin Woodbury: *God is not the Highest*

let us never forget that at its very beginning, such knowledge is not *our personal truth*. It is a truth measured *per conformitatem rem*. Even in the very personal and very "creative" activity of prudential reasoning, we have a pre-given contact with the nature of virtuous human activity, as well as with the virtuous activity to be performed by the child of God. This is the rock upon which we build, the immobile axis of our activity.

Still, "objective justice" is not a *thing*, at least in the sense in which the term "thing" is normally used. It is *a kind of act*, indeed an act of the will, meaning that it is spiritual in nature, even if, given our hylomorphic constitution, it is incarnated in particular physical actions. There is a sense in which "subjective justice"[47] is *the quality that subjectively inheres in our soul*. In order to perform acts of justice, we need the psychological quality, the *habitus*, or virtue, of justice. Just as the (subjective-formal) concept is a quality *inhering in* the soul that passes from potency to act in knowing,[48] enabling actual knowledge of reality (i.e., in the "objective concept"),[49]

Good (even for Himself) because He is the Ultimate End (even for Himself); rather, He is the Ultimate End precisely because He is the Highest Good. See Austin Woodbury, *Untitled Manuscript on Ethics*, The John N. Deely and Anthony F. Russell Collection in the Latimer Family Library, St. Vincent College, Latrobe, PA: "Note (many Thomists miss this) that the concept of the FITTING GOOD is the dominating concept of the Thomistic concept of moral philosophy, not the concept of THE ULTIMATE END. God is the ULTIMATE END because He is the SUPREME GOOD (Supreme FITTING good); [it is] not [the case that] He is the Supreme Good because He is the Ultimate End." An excellent analysis of related matters can be found in Jacques Maritain, *An Introduction to the Basic Problems of Moral Philosophy*, 141–160.

47. My use of "subjective" and "objective" are technical, and they do not trace the contemporary use of this terminology. To be "subjective" is to exist "in natural being in a given substance / subject"; to be "objective" is to exist *intentionally*, though in vital relationship with reality, which is presupposed for the very possibility of objective existence. On this topic, I owe an endless debt to John N. Deely. He discusses this distinction in many places throughout his works. For a powerful, late-career account, see John N. Deely, *Purely Objective Reality* (Berlin: Mouton de Gruyter, 2009).

48. Although, technically, the formal *ratio* for the uttering of a concept / internal word is not wholly due to the indigence of our intellect. There is a sense in which it is called for because of the superabundance of intellection, which aims at *expressing to oneself* that which one knows. (If this were not the case, the *ratio analogata* of the *verbum mentis* could never be applied to the generation of the Word *in divinis*.) See J.-H., Nicolas, *Synthèse dogmatique* (Fribourg: Éditions Universitaires, 1985), §62; also see the beautiful explanation of this in John of St. Thomas, *Cursus Philosophicus, Naturalis philosophiae*, vol. 3 (pt. 4, *De ente mobile animato*), ed. Beatus Reiser (Turin: Marietti, 1937), q. 11, a. 1 (349a11–23).

49. See John Frederick Peifer, *The Concept in Thomism* (New York: Bookman Associates, 1952), pp. 132–212; Maritain, "Appendix I: The Concept," in *The Degrees of Knowledge*, pp. 411–41; Simon, *Introduction to the Metaphysics of Knowledge*, pp. 127–136. The final volume, as beautiful as it is difficult, should be the *terminus a quo* of any contemporary Thomist discussion of knowledge.

so too the virtue of justice and the psychological acts of which it is the immediately elicitive principle enable something new to exist in the order of purely moral-intentional being: objective justice. The nature of such justice is the "*rem*," the *hard-and-fast reality*, to which our judgments of synderesis are conformed. Thus, in place of saying, "Conformity to the thing," I prefer to say, "Conformity to reality," enabling us to take "reality" in the broadest sense possible.[50] Therefore, we see that synderesis above all is concerned with *enunciating truths of potential human actions* (e.g., *objectively what justice is and requires*), not, primarily, the psychological states of soul involved in the various virtues (e.g., *subjectively what justice is as a virtue inhering in the will*).[51]

50. The most poignant example of the broad scope of the notion of "res / reality" can be found in cultural artifacts such as *money, vehicles, furniture*, and other such things. Although all of these realities are incarnated in particular physical realities, their essences are not reducible thereto. A qualitative abyss separates the physical and monetary properties of a dollar bill. Since, however, we can define the essence of these kinds of things, they are not mere *per accidens* heaps. They have their own existence in the moral and artificial domains. If we can define them, we can also form propositions concerning them, and if we can form propositions, then we have forms of speculative truth involving these realities—through conformity to their particular kinds of reality. Even for those who may be skeptical about these musings (which I sketched out at some length several years ago in the essay cited below), one can also consider the case of logic as a science. We can discuss the properties of syllogisms, statements, and definitions, but according to the *strictest* of Thomist positions, logic is concerned with *second intentional relationes rationis*, not with psychological qualities of the soul. See Matthew K. Minerd, "Thomism and the Formal Object of Logic," *American Catholic Philosophical Quarterly*, Vol. 93, No. 3 (2019): pp. 411–44.

I often wish that Fr. Garrigou-Lagrange could have just slightly altered his meaning of *rem* in response to Blondel's understandable concerns late in life. See Blondel, "Correspondence," *Angelicum*, Vol. 24 (1947), p. 211: "When the reproach is registered against me, claiming that I overlook the absolute sufficiency of the definition of truth, 'Adaequatio rei et intellectus,' I should be the one to protest against this reduction to the words *res* et *intellectus*, which do not suffice to exhaust everything involved in these matters: indeed, *res* does not suffice for designating the loftiest realities, and the intellect does not exhaust the science of things and of beings, nor the reality of the intimate activities [*opérations*] of our conscience or our duties, nor the profound truth of our supernatural destiny." Note, however, that Fr. Garrigou-Lagrange does respond to the latter concern, actually, by pointing out the way that affective knowledge supplements and completes notional cognition, without, however, substituting it.

51. This is, of course, a topic calling for great elaboration. Even if we consider, however, the most obvious case from Aquinas's own words, the first principle of practical reason enunciates a truth that is *not merely philosophical-psychological in character*: "The good must be done and evil avoided." There is a very important topic of philosophical psychology which underlies this insight, "The object of the will is the good, to be accomplished in human acts, however far that latitude may extend, if only obedientially." Another, related truth is, "All free human acts will be elicted insofar as they are seen as being good." The latter two statements are wholly speculative, "psychological" but not "moral," *never destined to be intrinsic formal measures of a human action, though they underlie them (for the speculative*

Now, obviously, there is no high wall between the speculative and the practical for a Thomist.[52] The famous dictum that, by way of extension, the speculative becomes practical,[53] remains unquestionably true. Action is not a free-floating reality—neither ontologically nor experientially. A moral (or immoral) action is necessarily a free action. Freedom, precisely as such, is not the formal constitutive of what *morality* is; however, freedom is a necessary condition for the very possibility of morality, of *esse morale*.[54] Without the very nature of the will (in *esse naturae*) as a

order is presupposed for the most basic speculatively-practical truth). When we act, however, we can say: "That is a good that was seen as something to be done." The most speculative declaration of *syndresis* is already practically oriented, though it declares *how things are and must be* in human action. Something similar could be considered, for example, in a contrast between *temperance* as known through *synderesis* vs. how it is known in philosophical psychology. In the former, we have: "Desires are to be pursued in a way that is moderated in line with the higher goods of human activity." In the latter, we have: "Virtues are possible in the concupiscible appetite insofar as the latter is open to being measured and ruled (in a 'political fashion') by practical reason." The latter truth is very important, and it puts us in touch with the *subjective-natural* reality of the virtue of temperance. The former, however, puts us in touch with the very *objective content* aimed at by the virtue of temperance. In a poor family, the father eats only the end bits of meat left over from his children, thus ensuring that everyone has adequate nourishment, despite the fact that he himself ends up eating somewhat less enjoyable meat. We will look at him and say: "That is action moderated in line with the higher goods of human activity." It is only by verbal artifice that we would strive to assert that the truths pertaining to the psychology of human acts *directly* inform his very activity.

52. For this reason, I generally subscribe to Ambroise Gardeil's way of discussing *synderesis*, an outlook that has greatly influenced my own exposition, although Fr. Gardeil at times seems to use *language* that would make *synderesis* seem "purely speculative," although it is, in fact, (as will be seen in Fr. Beaudouin's text, which Gardeil edited) *speculatively practical.* See Ambroise Gardeil, "Intelligence and Morality," trans. Matthew K. Minerd, *Nova et Vetera*, Vol. 16, No. 2 (2018): pp. 660–661.

53. See *ST* I, q. 79, a. 11, sed contra.

54. This topic deserves a word, even beyond what I have said elsewhere about it. Martin Rhonheimer states, in "The Perspective of the Acting Person and the Nature of Practical Reason," in *The Perspective of the Acting Person*, ed. William F. Murphy (Washington, DC: The Catholic University of America Press, 2008), p. 212: "Every deliberately chosen human act, on the other hand, already *necessarily* has an object at the moral level, because its object is this exterior act itself, as a 'good understood and ordered by reason.' To deny this is to fall into physicalism. Traditionally, to avoid this danger, it was customary at this point to resort to the *Deus ex machina* of the mysterious 'transcendental relation of the physical object to the moral norm.'" His language is quite wrong from the very start in describing the Thomist position in this manner, which, in fact, is language more akin to certain nominalist positions about the formal constitutive of morality. As is clear from a cursory reading of the relevant texts, Thomists would say "actus humanus" (or some variant thereof) where Fr. Rhonheimer says "physical object." The difference is not merely verbal. Fr. Rhonheimer's comment on this point is vexing because it cuts off his many *very good* insights from the chief metaphysical backing that would help to defend his thought against his critics.

spiritual appetite, there would be no discussion of its free action (*in esse morale*). In fact, the entire philosophical psychology of human acts functions as a kind of presupposed condition for the possibility of morality. For this reason, Thomists used to subdivide clearly the *Summa theologiae*'s treatise on human acts (*ST* I-II, q. 6–21) into two parts, the first (q. 6–17) being concerned with the philosophical psychology involved in human acts (*De actibus Humanis in suo esse psychoogico*), and the second (q. 18–21) devoted, from its very start,[55] to their moral being (*De actibus*

I have defended the Thomist notion of transcendental relation elsewhere in Reginald Garrigou-Lagrange, "There Cannot Be Genuine Sensation Without a Real Sensed Thing," *Philosophizing in Faith*, ed. Matthew K. Minerd, trans. Thomas DePauw and E. M. Macierowski (Providence, RI: Cluny Media, 2019), pp. 116–119; the notion was famously fought by Fr. Anton Krempel in *La doctrine de la relation chez saint Thomas: Exposé historique et systématique* (Paris: Vrin, 1952). For a defense, see John Poinsot, *Tractatus de Signis: e Semiotic of John Poinsot*, 2nd ed., ed. and trans. John Deely and Ralph Austin Powell (South Bend, IN: St. Augustine's Press, 2013), pp. 462, 473, n. 114, 477–78, n. 119, 499, and 500, n. 139.

See Merkelbach, *Summa theologiae moralis*, vol. 1, pp. 107–11 (*De essentia et speciebus moralitatis*); Garrigou-Lagrange, *De beatitudine*, pp. 307–318; Austin Woodbury, *Ethics*, John N. Deely and Anthony F. Russell Collection in the Latimer Family Library, at St. Vincent College, Latrobe, PA, sec. 3, ch. 7, a. 2 (Metaphysical Essence of Morality); Josephus Gredt, *Elementa philosophiae aristotelico-thomisticae*, vol. 2, ed. Eucharius Zenzen (Friburg: Herder, 1961), *Ethica generalis*, ch. 3, §1 (pp. 372–376); Charles René Billuart, *Summa sancti thomae*, vol. 2 (Paris: Palmé, 1872), *Tractatus de actibus humanis*, diss. 4 (*De actibus humanis in esse moris*), a. 1 (*In quo consistat moralitas in communi actuum humanorum?*), pp. 283–288; Antoine Goudin, *Philosophia iuxta inconcussa tutissimaque Divi Thomae dogmae* (Paris: Sarlit, 1857), q. 4 a. 1 (pp. 114–115); John of St. Thomas, disp. 8, a.1 (pp. 617–639); also see the subsection of a. 2, "Quid sit ponitas naturae et quomodo se habeat ad moralitatem?" pp. 640–644; Salmanticenses, *Cursus theologicus*, vol. 6 (Paris: Victor Palmé, 1878), *De bonitate actuum humanorum*, disp. 1, dub. 1–3 (pp. 3–29); Jean-Baptiste Gonet, *Clypeus theologiae thomisticae contra novos eius impugnatores*, vol. 4 (Paris: Vivès, 1876), disp. 1, a. 1 and 2 (pp. 3–12); Jacques-Casimir Guerinois, *Clypeus philosophiae thomisticae contra veteres et novos eius impugnatores*, vol. 7, *Ethica* (Venice, 1729), q. 5, a. 1 (pp. 312–323).

55. See Leonard Lehu, "À quel point précis de la Somme théologique commence le Traité de la Moralité," *Revue Thomiste*, Vol. 33 (1928): pp. 521–532. To this end, the reader should take care in consulting Fr. Ramirez's references, for he cites somewhat uncritically several works by Dom Odo Lottin, O.S.B., who should be consulted only for historical details and not for systematic positions in moral philosophy, at least for a Thomist interpretation of matters. Ramirez's deepest position seems to agree more closely with the position taken by Lehu, whom he does cite, although without dwelling much on his text. The great scholastic battle between Lehu and Lottin is actually of great interest in the question of *esse morale*, and his brief works deserve better note than they have heretofore received. He was influential not only on Fr. Martin Rhonheimer but also on the future Pope St. John Paul II. See Leonard Lehu, *La Raison: Règle de la Moralité d'après Saint Thomas* (Paris: Lecoffre, 1930); Karol Wojtyla, *Lecciones de Lublin (II)*, trans. Rafael Mora Martín (Madrid: Ediciones Palabra, 2013), pp. 66–71.

humanis in suo esse moris).[56] Fr. Austin Woodbury in his lectures stressed the importance of seeing this distinction between *ens naturae* and *ens morale*:

> The threshold concept in moral philosophy is that moral ought [i.e., in distinction from the ontological "ought"]. You can't take the first step in morals until you get that concept—the concept of a moral ought as distinct from a physical ought in human free acts—the free act as free has a diverse rule from the physical rule.[57]

I see no reason to abandon this categorization, nor these discussions, as though they were so many post-Aquinas subtleties.[58]

In matters surrounding the natural law, this represents the foundation for many misunderstandings and the incapacity for certain parties to talk to each other adequately. The great debates that somewhat rock the world of Catholic journals inevitably present this dyfunction. For example, the proponents of the so-called "New Natural Law" emphasize, even if they do not use the term, the unique character of *synderesis*, its primarily moral character and implications, being less worried directly with the questions of natural philosophy and metaphysics that undergird the apprehension of moral norms.[59] On the other hand, many Thomists are solicitous to maintain the bond between our moral reasoning and natural

56. See Jacobus M. Ramirez, *De actibus humanis* (Madrid: Vives, 1972), pp. 469–548; Benoît-Henri Merkelbach, "Le traité des actions humaines," *Revue des sciences philosophiques et théologiques*, Vol. 15 (1926): pp. 185–207.

57. Austin Woodbury, *Untitled Manuscript on Ethics*, The John N. Deely and Anthony F. Russell Collection in the Latimer Family Library, St. Vincent College, Latrobe, PA. Lest the reader misjudge Fr. Woodbury to hold that this "ought" is utterly primordial, see the text cited in note 46.

58. I would be remiss if I did not, however, cite the work of Duarte Sousa-Lara, "The *Ordo Rationis* and the Moral Species," *Josephinum Journal of Moral Theology*, Vol. 17, No. 1 (2010): pp. 80–125.

59. There is obviously a great variety among such writers and thinkers, some opting for a more "preceptive knowledge" concern as regards fundamental moral norms and others for integrating their insights into a virtue ethics framework. The famous beginning point for so many of these discussions was Germain G. Grisez, "The First Principle of Practical Reason: A Commentary on the *Summa Theologiae*, 1–2, Question 94, Article 2," *Natural Law Forum*, Vol. 10 (1965): pp. 168–201. A very good and appreciative overview of this vein of moral analysis can be found in Martin Rhonheimer, "Practical Reason, Human Nature, and the Epistemology of Ethics: John Finnis's Contribution to the Rediscovery of Aristotelian Ethical Methodology in Aquinas's Moral Philosophy: A Personal Account," *Villanova Law Review*, Vol. 57 (2012): pp. 873–887.

teleology.[60] As Fr. Martin Rhonheimer astutely noted, we find ourselves even today faced with the great debate between Dom Odo Lottin and Fr. Leonard Lehu concerning the philosophical meaning of reason as the rule of human action.[61] (I would say that this is "l'affaire *esse morale*"; however, that is my particular preoccupation.[62])

Schematically, we could arrange thinkers within the Catholic fold between two tendencies, one being Kantian (in the sense that such thinkers would risk separating practical reasoning from natural teleology rather starkly[63]), and the other being naturalistic (in that such an intellectual

60. Above all, see Steven J. Jensen, "The Role of Teleology in the Moral Species," *The Review of Metaphysics*, Vol. 63, No. 1 (September 2009): pp. 3–27; *Knowing the Natural Law* (Washington, DC: The Catholic University of America Press, 2015); and Steven A. Long, "*Veritatis Splendor* §78 and the Teleological Grammar of the Moral Act," *Nova et Vetera*, Vol. 6, No. 1 (2008): pp. 139–56; *The Teleological Grammar of the Moral Act* (Naples, FL: Sapientia Press, 2007).

61. See Martin Rhonheimer, *The Perspective of Morality: Philosophical Foundations of Thomistic Virtue Ethics*, trans. Gerald Malbary (Washington, DC: The Catholic University of America Press, 2011), p. 162, n. 108; *Ethics of Procreation and the Defense of Life: Contraception, Artificial Fertilization, and Abortion*, ed. William F. Murphy (Washington, DC: The Catholic University of America Press, 2010), pp. 11–12, n. 16: "When in preparing the study *Natur als Grundlag der Moral*, I came across Lehu's book; it was an important discovery for me, and one that had a decisive influence on my reading of St. Thomas. Lehu, in fact offers an interpretation of the doctrine of St. Thomas in which Thomas's statements on reason as the measure and rule of morality, on the moral object, prudence, and *recta ratio*, as well as the natural law, are seen in a systematic and coherent unity." For a very clear history and outline of this debate, see Ludovicus N. Hamel, "Controversia Lehu-Elter, Lottin circa regulam moralitatis secundum S. Thomam," *Antonianum*, Vol. 7 (1932): pp. 377–384.

62. See Matthew K. Minerd, "Beyond Non-Being: Thomistic Metaphysics on Second Intentions, *Ens morale*, and *Ens artificiale*," *American Catholic Philosophical Quarterly*, Vol. 91, No. 3 (Summer 2017): pp. 353–380.

63. Immanuel Kant, fearing that freedom would be impossible in a Newtonian world of mechanism, was led to erect a high wall between the physical-speculative world of appearances from the moral-intelligible world of freedom. In the Kantian world, the metaphysics of morals is ultimately a kind of dualism of viewpoints which man must have concerning himself: physically determined yet morally self-determining. The die had been cast long before Kant, for modern metaphysics and epistemology had imprisoned itself by so many ill-fated choices. Yet, I have forever looked upon Kant with awe. In comparison with the many "chatty" philosophical scribblers of modernity, he is a beautiful albeit poisonous flower of German scholasticism, turned now upon itself in a self-critique which proclaims the ultimate, tragic intellectual implications of choices made long before. Thus, in the question facing us, for Kant, natural being and moral being—and hence, by extension (and more directly related to the topic at hand), speculative reason and practical reason—are separated by a high wall, which bears witness to the great divide of the modern soul between physical exteriority and moral interiority, forever seeming to imply a pre-existing harmony between two wholly different orders. An excellent reflection on issues relevant to this topic can be found in Robert Sokolowski, *Moral Action: A Phenomenological Study* (Bloomington, IN: Indiana University Press, 1985), esp. pp. 1–77 and 143–90.

bent would risk deducing moral knowledge *directly* from the order of speculative truth about human nature). If we were to rank a scale between these two extremes, we might be able to class them as follows, from Kantian risks to naturalistic risks: Germain Grisez, "earlier" Alasdair MacIntyre, John Finnis, Robert George, Fr. Martin Rhonheimer, Fr. Leonard Lehu, the "later" MacIntyre, Fr. Stephen Brock, Steven Long, Steven Jensen, and Dom Odo Lotin / Fr. Edmund Elter.[64] After Frs. Rhonheimer and Lehu, a shift occurs, where concern with natural teleology and the primacy of speculative truth tends to assert itself rather strongly as one passes to the right beyond their names in this list. My own position is effectively right between them, appreciating Fr. Rhonheimer's defense of the unique position of the acting subject, while partial to Fr. Lehu's maintenance of the older Thomist school's language, above all on the language of *ens morale*. I do not believe that any of the parties above actually wish to be "Kantian" or "naturalist." Nor do I even propose the schema as being something definitive. It is merely intended to clarify my own situation in these debates.

At the interstices between the speculative and the practical a very important turn of perspective takes place. In the practical domain, all of our knowledge takes its origin in a first principle which not merely declares how things are but, moreover, how they ought to be: *The good is to be done and evil avoided.* The intellectual *habitus* by which this principle is grasped is *synderesis*, the parallel to *intellectus* in the practical order:

See Immanuel Kant, *Groundwork of the Metaphysics of Morals*, trans. Mary Gregor (Cambridge, UK: Cambridge University Press, 1997), pp. 61–62 (4:457–458): "The human being, who in this way regards himself as an intelligence, thereby puts himself *in a different order of things* and in a relation to determining grounds *of an altogether* different kind when he thinks of himself as an intelligence endowed with a will, and consequently with causality, than when he perceives himself as a phenomenon in the world of sense (as he also really is) and subjects his causality to external determination in accordance with laws of nature… [He goes on to say that this doesn't involve any contradiction.]"

"The concept of a world of understanding is thus only a *standpoint* that reason sees itself constrained to take outside appearances *in order to think of itself as practical*, as would not be possible if the influences of sensibility were determining for the human being but is nevertheless necessary insofar as he is not to be denied consciousness of himself as an intelligence and consequently as a rational cause active by means of reason, that is, operating freely" (italics added in the first paragraph).

64. For this list, I am particularly indebted to Dr. Thomas Howes for checking my classification regarding the proponents of the "New Natural Law" tradition, with which he is much more professionally familiar than I.

Where does this process begin? There can be no doubt concerning St. Thomas's thought on the matter. It begins with the *intellectus principiorum*. And it is at this first instant that these two movements of the intellect, practical knowledge and speculative knowledge, are differentiated from each other. Indeed, it is the only formal diversification that St. Thomas recognizes at this level of foundational intuitions. A single virtue suffices for all the speculative principles, whatever might be their degree of immateriality. For the first principles of practical knowledge, however, there must be another one: "*synderesis*." It is a derivative virtue, supposing the *habitus* of speculative principles without which it would itself lose its own light. It is, however, a distinct virtue, finding its originality in the practical character of the knowledge that it establishes and strengthens. What is the character of this knowledge?

It does not yet essentially affect the very type of truth attained in these primordial intuitions. It is by their conformity to reality that these immediate judgments are true. They are, however, at the root of what practical truth necessarily retains of an intellectual character. They translate on to the level of immediately evident intellectual knowledge the first postulates of the order of action and its very requirement for regulation, for rectitude, and for conformity to that which in each case is the very principle of action: the end. Knowledge already is, although from a distance, fundamentally oriented toward the action to be ruled. Hence, it takes charge of the direction of the dynamism that the first impulses of the will inaugurate. Never will there be a [moral-]practical process that does not imply at least this first perception of a kind of measure to be taken in the action so that it may be right and so that it may not lack its true finality. Henceforth, the intellect knows that it has another office aside from purely knowing. It knows itself to be the directive light of that which is a principle of affection and of realization in us...[65]

65. Michel Labourdette, "Connaissance pratique et savoir morale," *Revue thomiste*, Vol. 48 (1948): pp. 149–150. On the distinction between the two *habitus*, see John of St. Thomas, *Material Logic*, trans. Yves R. Simon, John J. Glanville, and G. Donald Hollenhorst (Chicago, IL: University of Chicago Press, 1965), q. 26, a. 1 (pp. 508–509); Michel Labourdette, "Connaissance pratique et savoir morale," pp. 149–151. Also see Reinhard Hütter, "Equipped for Beatitude—To Be Good Is to Do the Truth: Being, Truth, the Good, and the Primordial Conscience in a Thomist Perspective," in *Bound for Beatitude* (Washington, DC: Catholic University of America Press, 2019), pp. 151–174; and for a

This is why we have found ourselves faced with "l'affaire *esse morale*"—an affair that none seem to speak of directly, although in the end it calls for metaphysical adjudication—and it was adjudicated once upon a time! The traditional Thomist school emphasized the fact that the moral rule of acts is different from its merely physical rule.[66] This is evident if we consider the end aimed at by the virtue of temperance regarding our desires. Temperance with regard to food is concerned with more than health. Rather, it is ruled by the whole "order of reason," which takes into account, for example, our duties to others. This is why it is possible for someone to be intemperate by being far too concerned with finding "perfectly healthy" food.[67] Such concern can lead one to fail in duties to family, to others, etc. Moreover, there could be cases in which self-harming abnegation (*obviously* as ruled by prudence) could be temperate when the demands of the common good call for such abnegation (e.g., in the context of war, in times of famine when trying to provide for one's family, etc.) The moral rule of temperance is far suppler than a merely natural-organismic rule.[68] Failure to heed this distinction between the moral rule and the physical rule can give birth to tragic misunderstandings, like those which, during the recent coronavirus pandemic, we have sadly witnessed between politicians (justly looking to follow their political-moral rule: "what is best for achieving *the common good of society*?") and medical advisors (justly speaking only in line with the rule of medical practice: "what is best for maximal *health* outcomes?").[69]

---

relatively recent account drawing connections between *synderesis* and knowledge of the natural law, see Katarzyna Stępień, "Synderesis and the Natural Law," *Studia Gilsoniana*, Vol. 3 (2014): pp. 377–398.

66. See the host of texts cited in note 54 above.

67. A witty example of this kind of intemperance can be found in C.S. Lewis, *The Screwtape Letters* (New York: Touchstone, 1982), ch. 17.

68. See the reflection on the distinction between a *medium rationis* and a *medium rei* in Garrigou-Lagrange, "Remarks Concerning the Metaphysical Character of St. Thomas's Moral Theology," pp. 258–60.

69. On the distinction between the natural and moral rules of actions, see Leonard Lehu, *La raison règle de la moralité d'après saint Thomas d'Aquin*, pp. 143–59; also, see the texts cited in Matthew K. Minerd, "Beyond Non-Being: Thomistic Metaphysics on Second Intentions, *Ens morale*, and *Ens artificiale*," *American Catholic Philosophical Quarterly*, Vol. 91, No. 3 (2017): pp. 353–379. More precisely, however, there is also a "technical-artistic" rule of acts too. When wiring a new house, there is also a "measure" / "rule" that applies to the good work of the electrician.

The reason for this disjunction is precisely because *synderesis*, the starting point of all moral reasoning, has a unique formal perspective: the directing of human action, albeit at a great distance and, ultimately, requiring the virtue of prudence. Granting the pivotal importance of "the moral perspective," however, Steven Jensen and Steven Long are correct in their concern to connect moral reasoning to speculative reasoning, and natural teleology. Without these latter connections, *synderesis*, a kind of "derivative *habitus*" would lose its light.[70] Still, this point remains: *synderesis* has a unique formal character in comparison with purely speculative knowledge. Here, in the domain of universal truths, we do indeed grasp truths "through conformity to reality."[71] For this reason, the Thomist school came to say that such knowledge is *speculatively* practical.[72] These are truths that are *intrinsically normative* and already function as a general ("remote") measure of human action. For this reason, they are speculatively *practical*.[73]

Thus, the great problem in these matters is easily summarized as follows: How do we pass from speculative truth to speculatively-practical truth? This question represents the better formulation, to Thomists, of the famous "is-ought problem," or of the so-called naturalistic fallacy. The problem at hand becomes even more pressing when we must pass from *conclusions deduced* in speculative knowledge to *insights grasped through synderesis*. Although moral knowledge has its own unique noetic character, involving less certitude and less crystalline clarity than what pertains to more purely speculative domains,[74] we must be careful not to reduce its intellectual content to the First Principle of Practical Reasoning merely because it is difficult to explain how it is that other *synderesis*-grasped truths come to birth.

70. See Labourdette, "Connaissance pratique et savoir morale," p. 150.

71. Practical truth in the strict sense will fall to prudence, which will directively declare its truth *as conforming to virtuous ends*. See Reginald Garrigou-Lagrange, "Prudence's Place in the Moral Virtues," in *Philosphizing in Faith*, p. 166.

72. Concerning this point of terminology, see note 10 above.

73. Thus, although the moral goodness spoken of in the first principle of practical reason presupposes its ontological foundation in the foundational ordering of all things to their own particular goods, precisely *as moral* (that is, *as measuring freedom*), it is not equivalent to its ultimate metaphysical foundation. See Austin Woodbury, *Ethics*, John N. Deely and Anthony F. Russell Collection in the Latimer Family Library at St. Vincent College, Latrobe, PA, no. 326C and also no. 196. This is a point not always evident in the language of Thomists, who are justly desirous firmly to place moral reasoning upon its ontological foundations.

74. Such is, of course, the excellent insight born witness to in *Nicomachean Ethics*, bk. 1, ch. 3.

To this end, consider a quite basic insight undergirding the natural moral virtue of religion: God must be worshiped. Or, less distinctly: The source of our being must be recognized in some way.[75] Whatever the level of distinctness, this basic insight requires some conceptual elaboration (something often implied in the basic knowledge had in a given culture). As the basic content of the virtue of religion, however, it also is something known through *synderesis*[76]—that is, something known in an *immediate manner* (without syllogistic inference through a middle term). The predicate is included as a property within the subject. How is this possible? Speaking wholly within the framework of the acquired moral virtues: if we are to avoid self-deception or naïve morality, we must discursively conclude that God exists, prior to being able to say, "God must be worshipped." But how then can this latter statement be *per se notum*? I think that some insight can be provided by a perceptive observation made in passing by John of St. Thomas:

> In moral-practical knowledge (*in practicis*), the principle, "God must be worshipped" is self-evident (*per se notum*). It is not contradictory, however, to say that practical principles would presuppose something that is speculatively known through discursive reasoning, given that practical knowledge arises from speculative knowledge, for the speculative intellect becomes practical by extension. Thus, following speculation, even discursive speculation, practical principles can arise which are not as much concerned with the truth of the thing [after the manner of purely speculative knowledge] as they are with fittingness in relation to an end. Thus, it does not follow that if "God must be

75. For an excellent reflection on the moral character of this virtue, see Michael Krom, "Civic Virtue Aquinas on Piety, Observance, and Religion," *American Catholic Philosophical Quarterly*, Vol. 88 (2014): pp. 145–153; Ambroise Gardeil, "Our Personal and Supernatural Self-Education by the Virtue of Religion," in *The True Christian Life: Thomistic Reflections on Divinization, Prudence, Religion, and Prayer*, trans. Matthew K. Minerd (Washington, DC: The Catholic University of America Press, 2022), pp. 146–183.

76. The reliance of the virtues upon *synderesis* is a topic not always given as much attention as it should. However, for a state of the literature on this topic, see Ryan J. Brady, *Conforming to Right Reason: On the Ends of the Moral Virtues and the Roles of Prudence and Synderesis* (Steubenville, OH: Emmaus Academic, 2022); Dominic Farrell, *The Ends of the Moral Virtues and the First Principles of Practical Reason in Thomas Aquinas* (Rome: Analecta Gregoriana, 2012). One justly wishes that *synderesis* were spoken of just as much (indeed more) than the natural law (without, however, doing away with the latter). See also my, "A Note on *Synderesis*, Moral Science, and Knowledge of the Natural Law," cited in note 42.

worshipped" is a practical principle "God" would be presupposed as being known prior to all discourse, whether practical or speculative. Rather, it suffices that it be prior to all practical discourse although following upon some speculative discourse, especially if that precept is understood as being concerned with God known in a particular and distinct manner.[77]

Although this is only an aside (and not a full analysis of the issues involved here), the remark clarifies how it is that *synderesis* provides a new beginning in the order of knowledge without, however, losing its contact with speculative finalities and speculative knowledge. The order of moral reason remains "derivative" without being a *direct*, objectively illative de-

77. John of St. Thomas, *Cursus theologicus*, vol. 1 (Paris: Desclée, 1931), *In ST* I, q. 2, disp. 3, a. 1, no. 18 (418B); see Simon, *A Critique of Moral Knowledge*, p. 28, n. 2. John of St. Thomas goes on to discuss how this particular precept is not the first principle of practical reasoning, taking up *ST* I-II, q. 100, a. 1 and 3 concerning the way that the precepts of the Decalogue are the first conclusions of the natural law. On this point, he seems to speak of all secondary principles as being *deduced* from first principles.

Regarding primary and secondary precepts of the natural law, see R. A. Armstrong, *Primary and Secondary Precepts in Thomistic Natural Law Teaching* (The Hague: Martinus Niijhoff, 1966); Sr. Mary Georgetta St. Hilaire, "Precepts of Natural Law in St. Thomas," Ph.D. diss. (St. Louis University, 1963); Vernon Bourke, *Ethics in Crisis* (Milwaukee: Bruce, 1966), pp. 116–19. Maritain seems to propose a way forward, although full treatment of his recommendations would need to take up the problem of knowledge through inclination even in the speculatively-practical domain (which seems to be implied by his position). Nonetheless, trying to save face for the inconsistency of talking about *per se nota* principles which are also conclusions (as Aquinas does), in light of the unique character of moral knowledge, Maritain comments in *Loi naturelle ou loi non écrite*, pp. 137–38: "Inasmuch as [the precepts of the natural law] are known through a non-demonstrable form of knowledge, they all correspond to what is *per se nota* in speculative reason. Inasmuch as they are given fruits, necessary concretizations of more primitive principles, they correspond to that which, in the order of speculative knowledge, are demonstrated conclusions. This simple comparison does not intend to liken them [fully] to demonstrated conclusions. They are *per se nota* forms of knowledge that concretize, in a natural manner, the common principles [of the natural law]. Thus, in what is spoken of here in a. 4, we find that which, in the practical order, corresponds to principles which are *per se nota sapientibus tantum*." See ibid., pp. 133–200.

The central issues concerning dogmatic development addressed by Garrigou-Lagrange in *Sens commun / Thomistic Common Sense* needs to be brought together with this issue of the practical order (along with the various discussions related and found in authors like Gardeil, Marin-Sola, Schultes, and others). It will bear much fruit for explaining the increase of knowledge of the natural law, as well as the relationship of this knowledge to that had through philosophical "moral science." Also, at the time of final editing of this volume, there was published a very interesting article deserving of integration into this topic, Barrett H. Turner, "The Law of Nations as Developing Moral Law: Two Interpretations of *ius gentium* in the Thomistic Tradition," *The Thomist*, Vol. 84, No. 3 (July 2020; printed July 2021): pp. 339–393.

duction from speculative premises. It is one thing for the human person to realize, even vaguely, that there is some source of being or that the human person is an intellectual being. The first point can be discussed in metaphysics, and the latter opens up many possible discussions within the speculative domain of "philosophical psychology." To then say, however, "I must act in accord with the truths that we grasp through intellection," or, to return to the case from above, "God must be worshipped," involves a very new perspective indeed: that of *synderesis*. This will color everything that follows: the noetic character of the speculatively practical *is never reducible to that of the purely speculative*.

To make this last, capital point clear, let us return again to the example from above, drawn from the exercise of the virtue of temperance. When we consider the food we should consume, our health is one of the factors that must be taken into account, and this consideration is important for the morality of our acts. In normal circumstances, *temperate* activity cannot involve actions that would be volitionally incorporated into activity which is deleterious to our health. Granted, there is much latitude here, given the fact that the "mean" of a temperate act is a *medium rationis*, an act highly malleable under the governance of the virtue of prudence. Nonetheless, this truth remains: the temperate person cannot fail to consider such matters of health.

But is this the whole story? A difficult case will reveal an important insight here. Stranded on a desert island are a fifty-year-old father and his sixteen-year-old son. Having been marooned for some time now, they have learned how to survive as well as possible in these difficult conditions. Some set of circumstances, however, has now caused them to be short on food. Somewhat like the men who allow women and children to escape a sinking ship, the father gives preference to his robust teenage son's need for food, denying himself *to the point of the father putting his own health at risk*. Will we be so bold as to say that this is an intemperate act? Or, perhaps, would it be wise to listen to a nominalist muse who would whisper in our ear, "In this case, the general law is abrogated; health cannot be achieved"?

No. It is here that the Thomist can stand erect proudly and note the solidity of the moral object of temperance: desire must not stand in the way of the order of reason (whether natural or supernaturally elevated). Here, faced with a question of justice toward his son, the father has chosen the difficult and self-sacrificial path. Such circumstances are rare, but they bear witness to this utterly important point: health is something ultimately pertaining to "natural being," whereas temperance's meaning fits into the overall moral ordering of reality. A biologist can speak of the speculative truth concerning the systemic-organismic effects of dietary reductions. (This is purely speculative truth.) A doctor can counsel through the "medical art," which declares the actions that seem necessary for achieving such health. (This is already practical, but not moral.) Moral philosophy and moral theology will come to speak of the *order of reason* (whether natural or super-elevated) that must be put into our actions through a consideration of the moral befittingness of an act: in this case, a father acting on the desire to seek health would act immorally. Health is not the proximate measure of moral acts; moral reason is. "Just as the good of health consists in a kind of commensuration of the humors in a way that befits an animal's nature, *so too the good of virtue* [i.e., *the moral good*] *consists in a kind of commensuration of the act to the rule of reason.*"[78]

The Thomist will say that in the circumstances under consideration, the father must seriously consider whether or not he will be a glutton if he decides to split the meager food evenly. One might object: A glutton, really? Yes, for the measure of temperance is not food but, rather, *desire for food in accord with the order of reason* (whether natural or superelevated): "Gluttony does not essentially and primarily signify [*importat*] an immoderate eating of food but, rather, an immoderate desire for eating."[79] It falls to the art of medicine to decide the measure of food in accord with our particular bodily constitution; it falls to moral reasoning, to *prudence*, to determine what is a moderate or immoderate desire for food.[80]

Thus, to summarize: (1) the anatomy of human bodily health is known by a biologist (speculative judgment); (2) the good of healthy practices is known by doctor or nutritionist (practical-artistic judgment); (3)

78. *ST* I-II, q. 72, a. 4. Here the advanced reader should meditate at length on the discussion in Leonard Lehu, *Philosophia moralis et socialis*, vol. 1 (Paris: Gabalda, 1914), nos. 152–58 (pp. 108–120). The "conclusion" texts speak volumes. Their exegetical foundation is so strongly attested to in Fr. Lehu's French volume that they are beyond dispute for anyone with open eyes: "For St. Thomas, the moral good essentially involves a relationship with reason [*respectum ad rationem*] as to its proper rule... *Human nature is not the proximate rule of the moral good....* Human nature, considered in a kind of abstraction prior to consideration of the eternal law [*considerata in momento anteriori ad legem aeternam*] and independent of it, *in no way* can be called the foundation of morality" (emphasis added).

79. *De malo*, q. 14, a. 2, ad 2.

80. See Lehu, *La Raison, Règle de la moralité d'après Saint Thomas*, pp. 126–27.

the moral good of temperate desire is stated by *synderesis* or described by the moral philosopher or moral theologian (speculatively-practical-moral judgment); (4) the moral good of temperance *for me* is rendered in a judgment of prudence (practically-practical-moral judgment). Between (1) and (2) there is a difference of perspective, and between both of them and (3) and (4) there is another perspectival shift.[81] The latter two involve "the perspective of the acting person." *What synderesis declares to us concerning the good of temperance must be described morally and not reductively as either biologistic or medical.*

Now, before continuing, we must note two further distinctions within *synderesis*, both of which are not always observed. A Thomist obviously must hold that "personal" morality includes within itself an order to the common good. The greatest practical-moral activities undertaken by man are those of justice, involving the shared life of persons and, ultimately, the acts of religion which order the whole of the creature to the common good who is God, the First Cause. Beyond such acts, there is something more divine still, contemplation, and ultimately this is the teleological center of all human activity, whether in the natural order or the supernatural order.[82] Still, the common good suffuses all activity, even that of the lowliest virtue, temperance, which receives its full human meaning from

---

81. Moreover, (3) and (4) are also noetically distinct, for the moral philosopher / theologian *will never, precisely as a moral philosopher or theologian,* be able to enter into all the details of prudence. This will require a shift of outlook: participatively prudential counsel to another person. There are also internal differentiations within (3). See Minerd, "A Note on Synderesis," p. 50.

On this topic, one should heed well the words of Cajetan in *In ST* I-II, q. 58, a. 5, no. 8: "Now, prudence (since it is right reason, whose work involves discourse) makes use of two premises which are the principles of the conclusion that it draws. The first premise is a proposition concerned with something that is known through *synderesis*. For example: 'the good of reason must be followed in both passions and in activities' [*operationibus*]. The second premise [of prudence's discourse] is, however, utterly particular, namely: 'the good of reason, here and now, must be preserved in such a matter, to this degree, etc., as regards boldness or anger.' And then the preceptive conclusion follows—*not in actu signato* [i.e., as expressed reflectively through discourse] (that is, in the form, 'therefore, this must be commanded [*praecepti*], chosen, and pursued by me,') *but, rather, in actu exercito* [i.e., directly in the exercise of one's moral agency], that is, [so to speak,] in the form, 'I am actually in the act of judging, commanding, choosing, and pursuing [this course of action]'). *Indeed, here we have what deceives many in this matter: they dispute about these propositions (of both synderesis and prudence) in actu signato; however, their nature and force must be seen in actu exercito*" (my translation).

I thank Dr. Thomas Howes for this excellent citation, taken from Martin Rhonheimer, *Natural Law and Practical Reason: A Thomist View of Moral* Autonomy, trans. Gerald Malsbary (New York: Fordham University Press, 2000), p. 147, n. 3.

its overall context in the hierarchy of virtues. We see temperance shine forth most especially when someone foregoes pleasure for the sake of the common good shared by the community, like the father allowing his children to have the best cuts of meat at dinner, or someone turning down a much-desired promotion to a high-stress work position in order to ensure that he or she can be present to his or her aging parents or in contact with his or her family. In the latter case, the shared common good of family life shines forth quite radiantly *in the self-abnegation* of temperance.[83]

The common good can *itself*, however, become the formal perspective of *synderesis*. The most basic insight of *synderesis* remains the first principle of practical reason ("The good is to be done and evil avoided"). This very principle, however, can be subject to internal variations, in accord with the analogy of proper proportionality: Just as *moral good* is said of the private moral good, so too is it said of the common good executed in shared action. For this reason, there is an internal differentiation within how we apply the first principle of practical reason, leading (at the very least) to those two natural common goods which are inscribed in our human nature, independent of any further elicited choice on our part: the family and the political order. This "perspectival shift" gives rise to new forms of prudence: familial prudence and political prudence.[84] Here, the First Principle of Practical Reason becomes, respectively, "The good of the natural family is to be done, and its evil avoided," and, "The good of the political community is to be done, and its evil avoided." Of course, a careful union of the

---

82. Indeed, this is even more so the case in the supernatural order, for while in the natural order we must perform the practices of the social-practical life in order to assure some space for contemplation, in the supernatural order, even our actions, insofar as they are meritorious, in fact will be the (meritorious) cause of God's bestowal of an increase in charity, which ultimately will proportion us for a more profound contemplation of God in the beatific vision, and to the degree that such charity can become the formal means of mystical experience exercised through the gift of wisdom, it already gives us—even, indeed above all, the simplest among us—an unspeakable foretaste of the eternal experience.

83. For excellent reflections on this phenomenon in the domains of courage and temperance, see Josef Pieper, *The Four Cardinal Virtues*, trans. Richard and Clara Winston, et al. (Notre Dame, IN: University of Notre Dame, 1965). Also, see my reflections in Matthew K. Minerd, "On the Lowly, Yet Vital, Importance of Chastity: A Response to His Excellency, Bishop Robert McElroy," *Homiletic and Pastoral Review* (November 2017).

84. See *ST* II-II, q. 50. Also, see Fr. Garrigou-Lagrange's analysis of political rule by the use of the virtue of prudence in his introduction to a French translation of St. Thomas's *De regimine principum*, "On Royal Government," in *Philosophizing in Faith*, pp. 239–50. Also see the admirable essays in Stanley Vodraska, *Philosophical Essays Concerning Human Families* (Lanham, MD: University Press of America, 2014).

various orders will be necessary. The good of one order will never, in fact, be opposed to the other orders since the virtues exist within an overall framework, which determines each one's place and office. Nevertheless, although we need not fall into the errors of Machiavelli regarding the distinction of political "expediency" from morality, we must distinguish personal morality from social morality.[85] Many moral dramas arise as prudence strives to tie together the various threads of personal morality with threads belonging to the political order, calling for great grace and moral rectitude.[86]

Another point of no small importance involves the place of faith and supernatural truth in constituting the insights that will guide our life from these speculatively practical heights. By previously referring to "faith-*synderesis*," I have already hinted at this new, supernatural perspective for moral truths. Catholic moral theology is often presented as being a kind of mere gilding of the natural law, often implying a position attributed to Francisco de Vitoria: "The evangelical law contains no other precept outside the natural precepts, with the exception of the precepts concerning faith and the sacraments."[87] The attribution here to Vitoria has always seemed somewhat strange, likely meaning that there is some qualification made by him elsewhere. In any case, it stands quite at odds with the Thomist doctrine of the infused moral virtues, a vitally important aspect of our moral organism if we are to understand the texture of human moral reasoning at all of its stages.

Because of the new, supernatural end that the human person receives through the gift of grace, each of the redeemed finds himself or herself faced with the need to measure his or her actions in accord with this end, not only by ordering natural virtue to charity[88] but also by eliciting actions that truly are means befitting the moral destiny of the Christian precisely as such.[89] In short, he or she stands in need of moral virtues that are pro-

85. For related reflections, see Jacques Maritain, "The End of Machiavellianism," in *The Range of Reason* (New York: Charles Scribner's Sons, 1952), pp. 134–164.

86. In order to have a sense for the great difficulties faced, one need only imagine the careful threading of duties of family with duties of ruling in the case of a virtuous political leader.

87. See Reginald Garrigou-Lagrange, "On the Relationship Between Philosophy and Religion," in *Philosophizing in Faith*, p. 383 (cited by Fr. [Jacques] de Blic S.J.).

88. Something which would only imply a supernaturality *quoad modum*, through final causality, without formally altering the act *quoad substantiam*. See Reginald Garrigou-Lagrange, *The Sense of Mystery: Clarity and Obscurity in the Intelectual Life*, pp. 206–216.

89. See the texts cited in note 14 above.

portioned to the new divine end. The Sermon on the Mount presents us with an image of the eminent holiness to which the Christian is called; indeed, the whole of the New Testament loudly proclaims this fact. How could one read the exhortations contained in the letters of Sts. Paul, Peter, or John without thinking that Christians have a kind of new morality, one which far outstrips the natural law, not overturning it, but fulfilling by a supernatural abundance that of which its "obediential potency" could not have even dreamed?[90] According to the Thomist school, this new moral calling requires a new set of *habitus* with their own, supernatural characteristics.[91] We must be vitally recreated, rendered capable of the *selves* we are called to be as agents of acts of Christian morality. This is the role played by the infused moral virtues, a role of striking beauty.

This means that *our very acts* must be transfused with an intelligible content that measures our powers, giving them this supernaturalized formality. What we need is *formal causality* in the order of the infused moral virtues. To this end, I have chosen to follow Fr. Merkelbach, who has proposed that faith instrumentally uses *synderesis* in order to declare how it is that truths are to apply to our action. Textually, he bases himself on the fact that, as a rule, St. Thomas refers to *synderesis* when speaking of the major premise of the so-called practical syllogism. My understanding is that this problem was only inchoately addressed by St. Thomas, thus a textual study may do little to solve the issue. Whatever one may say for the textual issue, the problem remains, whether Fr. Merkelbach's position is found in the very letters of St. Thomas's own works. Even if St. Thomas did not happen to raise this question of noetics, we must raise it: How does the knowledge that we have through faith descend vitally, somehow in relation to *synderesis*, into the prudential *discursus*?[92]

90. For a discussion of obediential potency, see Reginald Garrigou-Lagrange, *On Divine Revelation: The Teaching of the Catholic Faith*, trans. Matthew K. Minerd (Steubenville, OH: Emmaus Academic, 2021), ch. 12 (pp. 529–73).

91. This point comes out, in particular, in the texts from Gardeil and Garrigou-Lagrange cross-referenced in the previous note.

92. See Merkelbach, *Summa theologiae moralis*, 5th ed., vol. 1 of 3, *De principiis* (Paris: Desclée de Brouwer, 1947), pt. 3 (*De actibus humanis*; sub-treatise *De conscientia in generali*), q. 3 (*De conscientia Christiana prout est regula actuum supernaturalium*), nos. 216–19 (1:203–6). Merkelbach cites the work of Fr. Noble, *La conscience morale* (Paris: Lethielleux, 1923); also see this same point cited by Reginald Garrigou-Lagrange in *De beatitudine* (Turin: Berruti, 1951), 347. As we will see in Beaudouin's text, Fr. Gardeil speaks of this being faith. In a text for which I am still searching (owing to pandemic-imposed limitations of

For its own part, although faith is primarily speculative in nature, it is in fact *formally and eminently* speculative and practical (just like God's own knowledge). This is above all clear if we consider how the theological virtues proportion us to the divine mystery precisely in its supernaturality. The divine mystery stands before us here in the order of knowledge (faith) and of appetition (hope and charity), although ultimately according to the same formality: The Deity as such, the mystery of the triune God.[93] Precisely in the Deity, knowledge and love merge together, precisely by the exigencies of what each of these realities are, although in a way that stands above them.[94] Faith puts us into touch with such supernatural realities, and by a kind of wholly connatural overflow, it wells forth into our action, functioning not only to give us speculative assent to the truths of faith but also revealing to us what we are called to be in our supernatural destiny. Dynamically, this whole host of truths—think but a moment upon the Scriptures, where a host of such "moral-practical truths" illuminate our lives with a splendor that is divine—is gathered around its central axis: charity, in whose service all of these many virtues are requisitioned and called to arms.[95]

For some,[96] faith itself would provide for this beginning to the practico-moral syllogism; for my part, I allow that this proposal is indeed a

---

research), Fr. Ramirez speaks of "supernatural synderesis" as "faith as practical" (*fides ut practica est*). See Wallace, *The Role of Demonstration in Moral Theology*, p. 194, n. 93.

For a recent critique of this recommendation, see Paul Rambert, "Conscience et loi naturelle dans les manuels d'avant Vatican II," *Revue thomiste*, Vol. 119 (July 2019): pp. 428–29. His article contains much of interest and use in the matters to be discussed in detail in note 7 of the preface to the article by Fr. Merkelbach, below. The reader should take care, however, regarding the use of Dom Odo Lottin, whose systematic work is questionable in comparison to his historical erudition. Whatever might be the case, a Thomist position concerning moral principles cannot limit itself merely to *synderesis* as a natural moral *habitus* of first moral principles, for not only will the entire domain of acts of faith, hope, and charity be left out of consideration but, moreover, the entire domain of the infused moral virtues will be unexplained (for natural *synderesis* will never declare a word concerning the ends of moral virtues proportioned to the supernatural ends given through grace).

93. Although, a distinction of formal object *quod* and *quo* remain necessary here. See my brief translator comments in Reginald Garrigou-Lagrange, "Remarks Concerning the Metaphysical Character of St. Thomas's Moral Theology," 264n37.

94. See Reginald Garrigou-Lagrange, "On the Eminence of the Deity: In What Sense the Divine Perfections Are 'Formally and Eminently' in God," *Philosophizing in Faith*, pp. 341–60; Garrigou-Lagrange, "The Eminence of the Deity, Its Attributes, and the Divine Persons," in *The Sense of Mystery*, pp. 171–91.

95. See Gardeil, *La vraie vie chrétienne*, pp. 118–25.

96. This seems to be the case for Gardeil in notes accompanying Beaudouin's text.

possible solution to this problem. Nonetheless, following Fr. Merkelbach, I find that *synderesis* can be elevated somewhat like *intellectus* is elevated when philosophy is *used* by theology, thereby being traversed by the supernatural energy of faith, such that the theologian will resolve his or her conclusions in the light of faith, although a faith that has discursively set itself to its task by thus using reason instrumentally.[97] In fact, in moral theology, *synderesis* must be instrumentally used when super-analogies are proposed for matters pertaining to the supernatural order.[98] Why would it not also be possible, in the actions of the infused moral virtues, for such an instrumental use of reason to be operative as faith passes downward into our acts so as to incarnate its exigencies there? In this way, we would have an operatively complex, faith-*synderesis,* whereby the requirements of the life of grace would pass into the execution of the moral life. Moreover, this will mean that there is such a thing as a "Christian conscience," formally distinct from acquired moral conscience.[99] For now, what is important is

97. See Maritain, *Degrees of Knowledge*, pp. 268–70.

98. Thus, illuminated by faith, we say, "Just as, in the natural order, desires are to be pursued in a way that is moderated in line with the higher goods of human activity, so too in the supernatural order, we are called to self-abnegation of a higher order." It is a question of the superanalogy of faith, explicated by theology. Based on the sources of revelation, we are sure of the fact that there is a superior form of temperance in the Christian life. To form the analogy, however, faith must instrumentally use the insight from *synderesis*, illuminating it "from behind" with a loftier light, although one that is not out of line with its obediential potency, expressed in the natural order by the words, "in line with the higher goods of human activity (whatever those may be, if humanity can be elevated to them)." On the super-analogy of faith, see, J.-H. Nicolas, *Dieu connu comme inconnu: essai d'une critique de la connaissance théologique* (Paris: Desclée de Brouwer, 1966), pp. 237–316; Maritain, *Degrees of Knowledge*, 256–59; also, see Charles Journet, *The Dark Knowledge of God*, trans. James F. Anderson (London: Sheed and Ward, 1948), pp. 61–64 and p. 69, n. 20; *The Wisdom of Faith*, trans. R. F. Smith (Westminster, MD: The Newman Press, 1952), pp. 14–32.

99. This opens up, of course, the entire problem concerning the state of acquired moral virtues in the soul that has sanctifying grace. For a recent summary of the rather large literature devoted to this topic, see W. Scott Cleveland and Brandon Dahm, "The Virtual Presence of Acquired Virtues in the Christian," *American Catholic Philosophical Quarterly*, Vol. 93, No. 1 (Winter 2019): pp. 75–100. I am not convinced that I can agree with Cleveland and Dahm's conclusions, trying to split the difference between the position that states the acquired and infused moral virtues coexist (which would be, in the end, my own position, alongside many Thomists of yore), and that holding that the acquired moral virtues are subsumed by the infused moral virtues. Perhaps Cleveland and Dahm's use of the notion of virtual presence to prove their synthesis does stand in line with my own position. If all that they mean is that the obediential potency of the natural moral virtues is, in the case of the soul in a state of grace, actually ordered to the supernatural end, becoming "participatively" involved in the supernaturalized activity of the Christian person, then all is fine. But in such a case, the formal character of such actions *must* not be rendered instrumental

to see how it is that faith, which is *instrinsically supernatural* (*secundum supernaturalitatem quoad substantiam*), stands at the core of these other truths enunciated in line with the lofty new ends given to our moral life through grace. Thus, we have a dual starting point for the speculatively practical order: *synderesis* and faith-*synderesis*.

Two Paths from Synderesis: Moral Science and Prudential Discourse

Bearing all of this in mind, we can sense that speculatively-practical truth has something unique about it, a characteristic not shared by *purely speculative truth*. And the unique character of speculatively-practical truth is why it is *quite* important to be exact in distinguishing the speculative from the speculatively practical. Even if St. Thomas does not use the expression "speculatively practical," and even if he would seem at times to indicate that synderesis declares *merely speculative* truths, no Thomist can say this unqualifiedly since speculative truth is destined *solely* for knowledge. Never will it measure a human action. By contrast, speculatively practical truth is susceptible to being *the very measure of the will itself*.[100] Two paths open up before *synderesis*: directly toward action or toward speculation. By contrast, in metaphysics, natural philosophy, the natural sciences, etc., the route to action is indirect. It must pass through *synderesis*.

(or, at least, not solely instrumental). There must be room for the activity of the Christian to remain *natural* in its formality, even if it is dynamically ordered to the supernatural last end. Such acts would not become intrinsically and formally supernatural but, rather, extrinsically supernatural (*surnaturale quoad modum*), in the order of final causality. The Christian who votes in a civic election elicits *an act of natural justice*, which, no matter how much it is influenced extrinsically by his or her faith, *remains formally an act of natural justice*.

To some eyes, the maintenance of these two orders of virtues would seem to cause a schizophrenia for the Christian, called to act sometimes through natural prudence, while at other times through infused moral prudence. This concern is not unimportant, and I wager that if one misjudges the affair, the theologian likely will be implicitly led either to a form of monophysitism / monothelitism or to a form of Nestorianism in Christology. In order for the theologian to understand all of these points aright, a full integration into the Christological study of Christ's acts is necessary. (Thus, we see the unity of theology in great clarity.)

For hints and indications of the direction to go in these matters, see Jacques Maritain, *Science and Wisdom*, trans. Bernard Wall (London: Geoffrey Bles, 1944), pp. 210–20 ("Acquired Prudence and Infused Prudence").

100. This is a point at the heart of the thought of Maritain, Simon, and Labourdette. Some implications of this fact are summarized well in Wallace, *The Role of Demonstration in Moral Theology*, pp. 190–94 ("The Practical Character of Moral Theology").

The first principles of speculative knowledge are destined for speculation alone. This marks out an important distinction between *synderesis* and *intellectus*.[101]

Although the later school would add distinctions, St. Thomas himself already saw what later Thomists would make clear concerning the distinctions to be drawn between purely speculative reasoning and that form of speculative reasoning which is remotely ordered to moral action. We can see him clearly delineating moral philosophy from purely speculative knowledge in a text from the prologue to his commentary on the *Nicomachean Ethics*, where he is surely speaking in his own voice and was so interpreted by later Thomists[102]:

> There is a certain order which reason does not bring about but, rather, solely considers, as is the case for the order of natural things. There is another order, however, which reason brings about through its own activity in considering things, namely, when it orders its concepts in relation to each other, as well as the signs of these concepts, that is, words having a signifying value. Moreover, there is a third order which reason brings about in volitional activity through reason's own act of consideration, and a fourth order is that which reason, through its own activity of considering things, brings about in external things, of which it is itself the cause (e.g., a chest or a house).[103]

As he says earlier in the same prologue: Just as the internal order of a whole is subordinated to that whole's relationship to its end, so too the internal ordering of a given body of knowledge is ordered to the particular end of reason in that given domain. This ultimate ordering will give rise, respectively, to the various "noetic textures" that fall to the four domains mentioned above: purely speculative knowledge, logic, moral knowledge, and technical knowledge.

---

101. See note 51 above.

102. For example, see Antoine Goudin, *Philosophia iuxta inconcussa tutissimaque divi Thomae dogmata*, vol. 4 *Moralis et Metaphysica* (Paris: V. Sarlit, 1857), pt. 3 (*Ethica seu moralis*), quaest. praem., art. unic. (p. 1–6). A full study of how this text was used historically would be interesting, for this text is often quoted when later Scholastics attempt to place logic among the sciences as well.

103. St. Thomas, *In Ethic.*, proem.

Moral knowledge is marked by the fact that *human actions presuppose the knowledge and free activity of the human person*. This perspective in turn colors the considerations of moral matters. As this is laconically expressed in *Veritatis splendor*: "In order to be able to grasp the object of an act which specifies that act morally, *it is therefore necessary to place oneself in the perspective of the acting person*. The object of the act of willing is in fact a freely chosen kind of behavior" (emphasis added).[104] This fact does not, however, mean that all moral knowledge is the same as prudence or that its ultimate judgment is really nothing other than the terminal judgment that will rule the will's choice.[105] We will see that moral philosophy always has in the background of its reflection this nagging recollection concerning its data. Nonetheless, despite this very "practical" awareness, the moral philosopher (and theologian) travels a different path branching out from *synderesis*: The path of "moral science," a knowledge of the universal conclusions that can be drawn on the basis of the knowledge known through *synderesis*. In this essay, we will use this term to refer to both moral philosophy and moral theology, setting aside further distinctions in the natural moral sciences, which likely include other subjects, such as sociology.[106] Moreover, in the natural order, we will limit ourselves to *personal* moral philosophy, although not forgetting the existence of political morality, as well as familial ethics. (In the supernatural order, there is no such distinction, given the unity of theology as a sapiential-science.)

Granted, the moral philosopher is concerned with a whole host of speculative considerations. This is so true that it is easy to forget the unique character of *esse morale*. A great number of the treatises on beat-

104. John Paul II, *Veritatis splendor*, §78. The theme is widespread in Rhonheimer. For a direct presentation, see Rhonheimer, "The Perspective of the Acting Person and the Nature of Practical Reason," pp. 195–249. For examples of dissent against Rhonheimer, see Steven A. Long, "*Veritatis Splendor* §78 and the Teleological Grammar of the Moral Act," *Nova et Vetera*, Vol. 6, No. 1 (2008): pp. 139–156; Stephen L. Brock, "*Veritatis Splendor* §78, St. Thomas, and (Not Merely) Physical Objects of Moral Acts," *Nova et Vetera*, Vol. 6, No. 1 (2008): pp. 1–62; Steven L. Jensen, "Thomistic Perspectives?: Martin Rhonheimer's Version of Virtue Ethics," *American Catholic Philosophical Quarterly*, Vol. 86, No. 1 (Winter 2012): pp. 135–159. I cite Rhonheimer's critics at length, although, for my part, I feel closer to his camp on these matters.

105. See Philip Neri Reese in "The End of Ethics: A Thomistic Investigation," *New Blackfriars*, Vol. 95 (May 2013): pp. 285–294.

106. See Yves R. Simon, "From the Science of Nature to the Science of Society," in *Practical Knowledge*, ed. Robert J. Mulvaney (New York: Fordham University Press, 1991), pp. 115–136.

itude, on human acts, on passions, on virtues, on law, and on grace are taken up with questions that are concerned with what would be called *esse naturae* (or even *esse supernaturale*, in the case of grace and so many other supernatural realities). We must know the presupposed "background" that makes free action possible.

This need for certain points of "background foundational knowledge" is not unique to moral philosophy. Logic too requires some basic discussion concerning the three broad kinds of acts performed by the intellect: (1) defining in order to know simple intelligibilities, (2) complex judgments, and (3) reasoning. It belongs to philosophical psychology to consider all of the "quasi-metaphysics of knowledge" involved in these acts. The logician, however, needs to know something about these matters so that he can intelligently lay out the domain of second intentions, the very subject of logic.[107] In the end, this means that logic is "magnetized" toward the study of second intentions: definitions, propositional opposition, *suppositio*, syllogistic forms, sophistical fallacies, etc.

A similar "teleological magnetization" is present in moral philosophy. It is not a metaphysics of moral psychology but, rather, a study *of moral acts*. For the Thomist, the whole of morality, above all supernatural morality, is attracted by the one great (participatively[108]) eternal act which spreads out through all of our acts here below: beatitude. This is why the treatise on beatitude is like the soul of the whole of moral theology. It is a kind of hinge that bears witness to the overall structure of the *Summa theologiae*.[109] But this *one great act*, our participation in the pure actuality that is God, is spread out through many acts, themselves ramifying from a great host of virtues. For this reason, the whole of the *Secunda secundae*, with its careful classification of virtues and vices, is the great fruit toward which Moral Theology grows (and the similar point can be said of the philosopher's discussion of the virtues). Even where the psychology of the virtues must be studied,[110] the central concern in the various treatises on

107. See Minerd, "Thomism and the Formal Object of Logic," p. 433.

108. See Carl J. Peter, *Participated Eternity in the Vision God: A Study of the Opinion of Thomas Aquinas and His Commentators on the Duration of the Acts of Glory* (Rome: Analecta Gregoriana, 1964).

109. See note 30 above.

110. For example, throughout a number of the articles in the treatise *on habitus* in the *Summa theologiae*.

the virtues is to analyze the character of various human acts: acts of hope, faith, piety, geniality, etc. In "moral science," we want to understand the nature, principles, effects, etc., of such acts, all *precisely as acts brought about by free agents.*

For this reason, "moral science" by its very nature gives rise to casuistry, the study of various examples of acts.[111] No form of human knowledge is merely a kind of abstract speculation, detached from experiential contact. Human knowledge is abstractive. We see essences in *things*, particular things, wherein we seek to find that which cannot not be the case. And this abstractive moment is not merely a kind of ladder that can be kicked away. For all our mortal days, our intellectual knowledge will be marked by a need to judge in relation to the pre-intellectual basis from whence it was drawn.[112] In a discipline like moral philosophy, which is concerned with human acts, with all their attendant circumstances and variation, can we limit ourselves to a kind of disembodied knowledge of moral essences? No. Were we to do so, moral science would turn into a kind of simplistic sketch of moral essences, a kind of facile Phariseeism which would fail to see the rich character of human acts, along with the variegated circumstances in which those acts are, in fact, possible in human agency. In moral science, we want to know, for example, *just what are acts of justice*? And, indeed, it is only by considering these acts that we are able to abstract the general notion of justice and understand *the one formal character* (i.e., justice, prudence, etc.) *that is the same in multiple different acts of the same virtue.* For this reason, one is foolish if he wishes to do away with casuistry in moral philosophy or moral theology.[113] It represents one of its legitimate extensions and, in a way, its final fruit,

111. Very carefully, I avoid saying "cases of conscience," for reasons that will become clear, out of a great caution taken in order to avoid the confusions regularly encountered in these matters.

112. Thus, in the state of union with the body, the phantasm remains necessary throughout intellection. For a technical discussion of this, see Austin Woodbury, *Natural Philosophy, Psychology*, The John N. Deely and Anthony F. Russell Collection, St. Vincent College, Latrobe, PA, ch. 70 ("Necessity of Conversion to Phantasms"), p. 895–901.

113. For a defense of casuistry from a bent of moral theology that is not my own, see *The Context of Casuistry*, edited by James F. Keenan and Thomas A. Shannon (Washington, DC: Georgetown University Press, 1995). This text was written in response to discussions like those found in Albert R. Jonsen and Stephen Toulmin, *The Abuse of Casuistry: A History of Moral Reasoning* (Berkeley, CA: University of California Press, 1990). For an approach that is much closer to my own, see Brian Besong, "Reappraising the Manual Tradition," *American Catholic Philosophical Quarterly*, Vol. 89, No. 4 (2012): pp. 557–584.

uniquely placed in each of the articles discussing each of the particular virtues and vices considered in what used to be called "special moral philosophy / theology." Moreover, such casuistry enables moral science to connect up with its infra-scientific "neighbors" in literature, history, etc.[114]

Here, we see the unique character of "moral science" quite clearly. The basic data of moral science is almost always interwoven with this thought: What would I do in this or that situation? We cannot help but think about human acts without seeing them as *potential acts for myself, at least were I in that scenario*. "Moral science," however, which is more concerned with understanding the *nature* of acts, not *their full, existential position*, requires a great deal of intellectual asceticism. In "moral science," I must purify my knowledge of actions so as to say: For any person X, this action bears witness to virtue (or, alas, vice) Y.[115] Thus, we must strip out a number circumstances from the action, rendering it somewhat unreal; for when we are practitioners of "moral science" our concern is turned toward *the hunt for moral essences*, not toward potential activity.

How difficult is this intellectual asceticism! Here we are treating *utterly concrete actions*. Human actions, which almost always require a careful awareness of *the agent's own situation*,[116] are treated by "moral science" as if they could be abstracted from their circumstances. At first, this seems no different from speculative knowledge. Even in more particularized scientific disciplines, such as botany, the scientist *of necessity* must set aside

114. I generally think that Maritain's position concerning the "practically practical" sciences (or, as Simon wished, "disciplines") has a good deal to add here, enabling us to give such "moralists" a discipline that is more than mere opinion without guiding principle (and hence giving them something akin to a scientific character in their reflection). See Jacques Maritain, "Appendix VII: 'Speculative' and 'Practical,'" in *The Degrees of Knowledge*, pp. 481–89; Simon, *Practical Knowledge*, pp. 79–87.

For the question of history and its place in Thomist thought, see above all Jacques Maritain, *The Philosophy of History*, ed. Joseph W. Evans (New York: Scribner, 1957). Also, see the text by Fr. Armand Maurer cited in note 28 above.

115. See the treatment of *individuum vagum* in Wallace, *The Role of Demonstration in Moral Theology*, pp. 199–202.

116. This is above all true for the case of those actions, such as those of the virtues of temperance and courage, which are measured by a *medium rationis*. This important point, drawn from Beaudouin, was noted with great clarity by Fr. Reginald Garrigou-Lagrange in "Remarks Concerning the Metaphysical Character of St. Thomas's Moral Theology, in Particular as It Is Related to Prudence and Conscience," pp. 259–61. Even in the case of acts of justice, however, which are ruled by a *medium rei*, many unique points drawn from the agent will remain determinative, coloring the execution of the action. (For example, the debt of piety is indeed "measured" by the debt we owe to our parents. We ourselves, however, still must determine many details of just how this debt will be paid on this or that occasion.)

mere accidents in order to discover what are the proper accidents of a given plant being studied. Yet, too often, a kind of popularized Thomism simplifies this process. Accidents are critical for the human attempt to define things. We slowly travel *through* the accidents,[117] seeking to espy the essence of things. Accidental definitions are ***not nothing***, and very often they are part of the first stage of the great hunt that our intellect undertakes in the search for the essential character of what we are considering. Definition is a true accomplishment, not a mere "X-ray" of essences performed by the intellect.[118] But the ultimate goal of the hunt for definitions is properties and, where possible, specific differences, in order to provide us with a grasp of the *quiddity*, the "what-this-is-ness," of what we are considering. This is so strict a feat that some would see Thomism as being a kind of merciless intellectualism concerned with lifeless, abstract essences.

In human acts, however, accidents have a very different bearing. Because of the way that they are dynamically related to moral-practical reasoning, they can introduce new moral essences into our actions. In fact, our acts can have multiple moral *species*, even at times bestowed upon them by what would be merely accidental, at least in relation to what the primary object of our choice is.[119] To repeat an example, consider the father who decides to indulge himself at dinner when this will be detrimental to his children's health—especially when he has the option of eating less pleasing meat, thus providing himself with enough so as to continue

117. See Maritain, *Degrees of Knowledge*, p. 217: "As far as substantial essences are concerned, J. de Tonquédec was certainly right in noting against Rousselot that 'when it is a question of thinking substance [*sic*], even in the most imperfect fashion, the mind never "stops short at the accidents." That would be contradictory. It always regards something beyond them. But, *on the other hand, a moment is never reached when the mind, having left the accidents behind, "passes beyond" and "discovers" the bare substance. It is by remaining attached to the accident that it finds the means of seeing beyond… The mind always goes beyond the accidents, but [does so] by continually relying on them*'" (emphasis added).

118. See Robert Sokolowski, "Making Distinctions," in *Pictures, Quotations, and Distinctions: Fourteen Essays in Phenomenology* (Notre Dame, IN: University of Notre Dame Press, 1992), pp. 55–91; Reginald Garrigou-Lagrange, "On the Search for Definitions According to Aristotle and St. Thomas," pp. 21–34; See John Deely, *Intentionality and Semiotics: A Story of Mutual Fecundation* (Scranton, PA: University of Scranton Press, 2007), pp. 45 and 86.

119. See *ST* I-II, q. 18, a. 10 and 11; William Matthew Diem, "*Prima Secundae*, Q. 18 and *De Malo*, Q. 2: A Critical Comparison of Their Teachings Concerning Circumstances and Their Role in Moral Specification," *American Catholic Philosophical Quarterly*, Vol. 91, No. 3 (Summer 2017): pp. 447–471. On the possibility of multiple moral *species* (and, hence, something quite unique about *esse morale*), see *ST* I-II, q. 1, a. 3, ad 3; q. 18, a. 7, ad 1.

fulfilling his own duties. His action is arguably at once *intemperate* (*gluttonous*, in fact) and *unjust* (against the rights of his children). It is likely more intemperate than it is unjust (for the injustice is chosen *in view of* the intemperate desire for this food). Nonetheless, we have here two *moral species* interwoven in this action—along with some species of imprudence also. And if the father did this out of inordinate and uncalled-for fear for his own health, the act could arguably also bespeak yet another moral *species*, cowardice. All the virtues are indeed connected together in prudence. This is so important that, depending upon the particular circumstances of this agent, this person's character and knowledge, this situation, etc., one single human action is a knot of many circumstances which bear witness to its quite complex structure, often giving rise to several semi-essential moral *species*.

Despite this complexity, there is *real objectivity involved here*. Granted, it is very difficult to extricate it, and ultimately, moral science on many occasions *cannot judge this or that person's particular acts* without going beyond moral science.[120] It can only say: If this moral *species* is present, the action is good or evil, virtuous or vicious. Abstraction is not an impoverishment, and moral *species* are not mere "abstract precepts / norms." They are the very soul of our actions, their essential organizing principle, that which gives them meaning. The affirmation of objective moral *species* prevents us from holding that our actions merely float about upon an endless sea of relativistic circumstances—just as the affirmation of natural essences prevents us from holding that natural reality is nothing other than an endless flux of ever-evolving accidents. But, to perform truly moral-scientific reflection, we must abstract from the *hic et nunc*, and if the practitioner of moral science is true to his or her method, he or she will feel a unique melancholy at this harsh asceticism, far more than even the botanist in the midst of the most beautiful greenhouse.

Such is the nature of abstractive knowledge. It will forever create a kind of potential misunderstanding between the practitioner of "moral

120. In such cases, the person evaluating this act takes part in something akin to consequent conscience. Here, the virtue of "memory" (*ST* II-II, q. 49, a. 1) is needed for a sane recollection of past actions, as well as "understanding" (*ST* II-II, q. 49, a. 2) in order to judge such particular memories correctly. It is interesting, moreover, to consider how a good moral counsel from another person presupposes some degree of participation in these virtues in the agent whose action is being considered. The person who gives good advice must have affective connaturality with the person to whom advice is being given.

science" and the person who is tasked with being a practical guide. To the eyes of the person who is tasked with offering moral counsel, the practitioner of moral science will seem like he or she is living in the clouds, concerned with ideas, not with realities. And the moral scientist will look at the moral counselor as being someone who is always concerned far too much with particularities, a kind of relativist who won't answer the *essential* questions. An anecdote from Yves Simon perfectly captures this dynamic:

> Thus, from the very point of departure, moral sense gives normative judgment of direction, even though the object of thought is still abstract in the extreme. Then, as it progresses, practical thought adds to itself determination upon determination until, face to face with the singular case, it is ready to be posited in existence. That is what must not be forgotten when we stress the "abstract" character of moral science as compared with the concrete character of prudence. Practical discourse can indeed be conducted at various levels of abstraction, but it always remains, through its synthetic method, essentially related to existence. If, therefore, it is legitimate to speak of practical science, we must not forget that its generalizations and abstractions, no matter how valid, represent but various stages in a movement of the mind directed from the beginning to a concrete ultimate end.
>
> I have no doubt that it is because this is often forgotten that many moralists suspect all abstract discussions. For instance, several years ago, I found myself one night with some companions at the home of a priest of quite exceptional gifts; I cannot remember ever having met a more perfect example of the prudent man. The subject of the morality of games of chance arose, and we asked our host if it was legitimate *in itself* to bet a sum of money on a game of cards. He replied by invoking for us the image of ruined families, of health dissipated because of the passion for gambling, and suicides at Monte Carlo. Didn't we know that it is not permitted that one ruin one's family and one's health, or that one expose oneself to the temptation of suicide? Then we asked if money won at gambling is money honestly won. Is the contract, I asked, stipulating that the one who draws the ace of spades takes all the money on the table a licit contract? But there was no way to get a reply. This ideally prudent man refused to consider the question

> in the abstract, which would require him to dissociate factors that should be considered *all together* by the immediate rule of action. One could say that he exaggerated, for pushed to its logical extreme, such an attitude would make moral science impossible. But if this attitude indicates that we are not dealing with a philosopher, it also and more importantly tells us we are dealing with a man possessed of the proper concern of the moralist.[121]

The point of all of this discussion has been to make clear that the term "casuistry" is used to cover reflective activities which are often quite noetically distinct and different in character. Traditionally, these different types of casuistry have been lumped together in a more-or-less inexact manner, leading moral-scientific casuistry to be treated as though it were homogeneous with other forms of reflection which are, ultimately, prudential (or, in the case of the counsel given by one person to another, "participatively prudential").[122] They are not the same, and moral-scientific casuistry will forever be inflected in a different direction from prudential casuistry. The former bends toward this speculatively-practical question: What is essentially the case here? The latter bends toward this practically-practical question: What is true and good for me to do here and now?

In short, no matter how practical the knowledge had in moral science might be, it is ultimately *speculative* in its character. It is concerned with conceptual analysis, with laying out the details that make up *moral essences*. It is not *directly* concerned with measuring human actions. Much like how theology is not the same as supernatural faith while, all the same being of great interest for faith, so too "moral science" derives from *synderesis* and faith-*synderesis* and remains deeply important for the perspective of the moral agent. There are cases in which the theologian can offer assistance in the declaration of *de fide* truths.[123] In a similar way, even the moral philosopher can help in the declaration of *per se nota* truths which, in fact, fall to the natural law, albeit to that special category of the natural law

121. Yves R. Simon, *A Critique of Moral Knowledge*, pp. 37–39 (slightly modified).

122. For this reason, Fr. Garrigou-Lagrange was led to hold that casuistry is really reducible to prudential reasoning, and truth be told, given the way that the "cases of conscience" were being treated in his day, they perhaps were, at times, a kind of quasi-prudential advice. See the text cited above in note 11 above.

123. See Reginald Garrigou-Lagrange, "Theology and the Life of Faith," in *Philosophizing in Faith*, pp. 421–43.

known as the *ius gentium*.[124] Moreover, even when someone does not have a highly developed *habitus* of "moral science," whatever degree of such "inchoate science" he has remains an abiding source of guidance of his or her prudential reflection. In short, in "moral science," we have a consideration, which remains speculative, and no matter how personal its "source material," it is forever marked by the *necessarily* abstractive character of its *speculatively* practical character. The aim of moral science is *knowledge*, not direction. Its truth remains *conformitatem ad rem*, conformity to reality.

Another kind of truth does exist, however—a truth which must *never* be univocally reduced to a shared genus with speculative truth: practico-moral truth. Between speculative truth and practico-moral truth, there is only an analogy of proper proportionality.[125] Speculative truth is concerned with the truth of reality, practical truth with *conforming our actions to the ends of the virtues which we intend to perform here and now in the concrete.* The ultimate judgment of prudence is utterly concrete; it is concerned with declaring what is to be done *by me, here and now, in these unique circumstances.* Moreover, *the ultimate act of prudence* is not the terminal judgment which brings our moral deliberation to a close but, rather, the command which will function as the very formal cause of the will in its execution of the act. The destiny of fully practical knowledge is not *to say something,* not *to express conceptually a truth.* Its goal is *to do the truth,* to shape the will through the very execution of the action. With fully practical truth, we are no longer seeking solely to know *how things are.* Instead, our primary concern is to direct our action: *to command how things must be.* So long as we maintain the clear and central role of *synderesis* and faith-*synderesis* (along with their discursive extension in moral-scientific knowledge) at the outset of this reasoning, there is no danger of pure subjectivism. Without this initial *conformity to reality,* everything would

124. See Maritain, *Man and the State* (Washington, DC: The Catholic University of America Press, 1998), pp. 98–101; *Loi naturelle*, pp. 51–56; James Schall, "Natural Law and the Law of Nations: Some Theoretical Considerations," *Fordham International Law Journal*, Vol. 15, No. 4 (1991): pp. 997–1030. The *ius gentium* may well be what we could call "enculturated moral science," intentionally present in the moral environs of a given society in a pre-scientific state. However, its most important core are those principles (themselves *per se nota*) which are merely explicated by moral philosophical reflection. See Minerd, "A Note on *Synderesis*," p. 50 (diagram sub-section 3b and associated notes 29–31). Also, see the work of Turner, "The Law of Nations as Developing Moral Law: Two Interpretations of *ius gentium* in the Thomistic Tradition," cited in note 77 above.

125. See Yves R. Simon, *Practical Knowledge*, p. 39.

float adrift on the sea of our caprice. With this first conformity, however, we are placed in touch with the natural law and the new law of grace.[126] Then we turn toward *action.*

Choosing the "Concrete Path" from Synderesis: *Turning Toward Prudential Reasoning*

Personal moral reasoning is not an affair of paging through an encyclopedia of virtues in order to say: This essence goes here; this casuistic case which would work for any person X would be great and fine, just as it is, with this vagueness, here and now for me. No, personal moral reasoning is concerned with synthetically gathering,[127] bit by bit, circumstance by circumstance, the very existential context of the action to be performed. We must bring into being—and this is why the will is so important here—an action which right now does not exist in the world. We must "posit," place, assert, and effect a new action, our action, a true actualization of ourselves, a participation in God's own providence, a true participation in the Eternal Law.[128]

Much foolishness has been utttered, however, concerning these matters, treating personal moral reasoning as though it were just a matter of situational suppleness, with "existential" considerations overriding the "essential" necessities of action. Purely situational or purely existentialist ethics must be deplored, for they will ultimately rob *synderesis* and faith-*synderesis* of any meaningful implication for our moral activity.[129] The true solution is to turn to the true and complete Thomist understanding of prudence, for it is here, in the exercise of prudence, that the "abstract" becomes real.

126. See Reginald Garrigou-Lagrange, "Prudence's Place in the Moral Virtues," p. 166. Moreover, see note 76 above.

127. For some direction on the use of "synthesis" in this language, taken up often from the later school, see S. E. Dolan, "Resolution and Composition in Speculative and Practical Discourse," *Laval théologique et philosophique*, Vol. 6 (1950): pp. 9–62; Wallace, *The Role of Demonstration in Moral Theology*, pp. 81–92.

128. The theme is repeated in Aquinas and will come up in our texts below as well. This is put very poignantly in John Paul II, *Veritatis Splendor*, §41: "Others speak, and rightly so, of *theonomy*, or *participated theonomy*, since man's free obedience to God's law effectively implies that human reason and human will participate in God's wisdom and providence."

129. For example, see Karl Rahner, S.J., "Principles and Prescriptions," in *The Dynamic Element in the Church*, trans. W. J. O'Hara (New York: Herder and Herder, 1964), pp. 13–41; "On the Question of a Formal Existential Ethics," in *Theological Investigations*, vol. 2: *Man in the Church*, trans. Karl-H. Kruger (Baltimore, MD: Helicon, 1963), pp. 217–34. For a Thomist response, see William A. Wallace, O.P., "Existential Ethics: A Thomistic Appraisal," *The Thomist*, Vol. 27 (1963): pp. 493–515. All of this is discussed at length in the book by Matthew Levering mentioned at the start of this introduction.

A discussion of the virtue of prudence is the real answer to the problem of "situational conscience," a point well summarized by Pope Pius XII in an allocution given on April 18, 1952:

> Let it suffice to cite St. Thomas's unsurpassed explanations concerning the cardinal virtue of prudence and the virtues connected to it (*ST* II-II, q. 47–57). His treatise shows his sense for personal activity and actuality, which contains whatever true and positive elements might be found in "situation ethics," while avoiding its confusion and deviations. Therefore, it will the modern moralist will find it sufficient that he continue along these same lines if he wishes to deepen his investigation into the new problems facing us today.[130]

Because of the importance of this matter, a brief *florilegium* of texts from Thomists on this matter will prove helpful. Fr. Gardeil notes that prudence is a matter of sifting out the grain and the chaff in our action, though it is also much more than this as well:

> No, nothing, not even the most trained spiritual flare, entirely replaces the insights analyzed in the rational light of this underappreciated supernatural prudence, for it has eyes to see and a ready instrument for rendering judgments. Thus, it would seem that prudence would only be a sieve, though one that is indispensable for preventing indigestible husks, the grinds that cannot be assimilated to the divine life, from passing through as though they were pure wheat flour.
>
> It is more, however. It is a faculty of organization. On account of the patient and directive work that it ceaselessly exercises over the practice of the virtues, not only are our hostile dispositions little by little eliminated, but beyond this, prudence also establishes a synergistic coordination of all our efforts on behalf of the good. is begets results having an assured technical value, a guarantee against the returns of disorder, and a solidity in our accomplishment, one that the inspirations of pure love do not provide by themselves. It is a good work that is meticulous and durable.[131]

130. Cited in Labourdette, *Les actes humains*, p. 245.

131. Gardeil, *The True Christian Life*, p. 84.

Fr. Garrigou-Lagrange describes this vital descent very well:

> *A Doubt.* How are these reflex principles [used in the probabilistic calculations of casuistry] related to St. Thomas's doctrine *concerning prudential judgment through conformity to right appetite*, exposited especially in *ST* I-II, q. 57, a. 5, ad 3?
>
> *Response.* The aforementioned reflex principles *are useful for establishing this conformity*. Indeed, St. Thomas says that the truth of the prudential judgment (especially for establishing the golden mean in the moral virtues in particular cases applying to me personally here and now) is through conformity to right appetite, or to right intention. Now, this intention applies the intellect to *having due diligence in knowledge of the laws and of the facts*. Now, when direct principles are lacking, one must have recourse to commonly received reflex principles. That is, one must consider *the side on which presumption stands*. And often from these principles one only has a greater probability, whereas practical moral certitude is had through conformity to right appetite, for "As a given man is, so does the end seem to him. [*Qualis unusquisque est, talis finis videtur ei*]." For example, if someone is chaste, those things that pertain to chastity seem to him to be good and suitable because they are conformed to his appetite, which has been rectified through chastity. Thus, the *rectitude* of the principles of moral science *descend, in a vital manner, through right reason* to one's judgment concerning singular actions.[132]

And likewise, he elsewhere points out just how personalized the judgment of prudence must be:

> How can we arrive at a certain judgment of conscience despite the fact that we experience invincible ignorance concerning many of the circumstances of human acts, for example, when it is a question of future contingents of which we must have foreknowledge in order to take all the necessary precautions? Likewise, how can I determine with certitude, here and now, in matters that directly concern me (and not you) the golden mean to preserve in matters of temperance, meekness,

132. Reginald Garrigou-Lagrange, *De Beatitudine* (Turin: Berutti, 1951), p. 389.

humility, courage, patience—all while this golden mean depends on many particular circumstances that are still known only in a vague manner (or, even at times are unknown), such circumstances including my temperament (be it high-strung, sanguine, or phlegmatic), my age, the season (be it summer or winter), my social status, etc., etc.? To what must we have recourse in order to have this practical certitude of conscience in the presence of such a diversity of conditions that we can only vaguely grasp? Ought I to weigh probabilities for and against this or that action? They must be considered, but does this suffice, even when one adds to them certain reflex principles that are more or less certain: a law that is in doubt does not oblige; the one in possession is in a better position? This investigation into probabilities [through casuistry] sometimes may be lengthy. It even surpasses the capacity of many and often leads to nothing that is actually certain.

St. Thomas provides a more profound solution to this question. He does not disdain the consideration of probabilities for and against a course of action. Nor does he disdain commonly received reflexive principles. He insists, however, before all else on a *formal principle* spoken of by few modern theologians even though it can be found even in Aristotle. This principle can be expressed: "*The truth of the practical intellect* (or, prudence) *is found in conformity with right appetite*," for, "*According to the way that a man is well or poorly disposed* (in his will and his sensibility), *so does the end appear suitable or not suitable to him*." The truth of the practical intellect (i.e., of prudence) consists in *conformity to rectified appetite*, that is, to the *sense appetite* rectified by the virtues of temperance and courage and above all to the *rational appetite* rectified by the virtue of justice and the other virtues of the will. In other words, pratico-practical truth consists in conformity with the habitually and actually *right intention* of the will, for as Aristotle says, "According to the way that a man is well or poorly disposed, so does the end appear suitable or not suitable to him." For example, he who is chaste, even if he does not know moral science, judges with rectitude (by way of the inclination of this virtue) concerning things relative to chastity. They appear to him as being good and obligatory.[133]

133. Garrigou-Lagrange, *The Order of Things*, pp. 274–75.

Fr. Ambroise Gardeil notes well the importance of casuistry (truly, whether it be in moral science or, as we will see soon, the domain of prudential counsel)—although it can only go so far:

> Behold what we must transpose into the domain of our supernatural conduct. It is not a recipe given once and for all so that we may govern some purely malleable substance. Nonetheless, it is a containment and domination of contingencies, less through a speculative and meticulous science of their details than through living experience and the vigorous cultivation of our power to decide, ceaselessly renewing and feeding it at the sources of a living love of God.
>
> The secret of this outlook will not be found in the manuals of asceticism or of casuistry that strive to predict every possible case and to provide lines of appropriate conduct corresponding to them. Such a book has its use, for it renders its services by furnishing authoritative models for resolving problems. Given that, concretely speaking, no equivalent case exists, however, onsite adaptation remains the proper task of our good personal government. Suggestions, orientations—yes, as many as you can desire! In the end, however, such casuistry cannot furnish wholly polished-off solutions that are practical on all points and imperative, applicable straightaway to every single concrete case. There is no prudence that is written on paper. In order to govern oneself well, a tactical maneuver is needed, one that is utterly versatile because it unfolds on the essentially moving terrain of human contingencies.[134]

And Maritain echoes this point in a passage which would seem extreme, were it not for his own acknowledgment of the role of moral intelligibility on a number of occasions (in the same work, as well as in others), as well as the close connection that his language has with that of Fr. Garrigou-Lagrange on these matters[135]:

> The same moral case never appears twice in the world. To speak absolutely strictly, precedent does not exist. Each time, I find myself in a situation requiring me to do a new thing, to bring into existence an act

134. Gardeil, *The True Christian Life*, p. 89.

135. See all of the texts by Fr. Garrigou-Lagrange cited in note 142 below.

> that is unique in the world, an act which must be in conformity with the moral law in a manner and under conditions belonging strictly to me alone, conditions which have never arisen before. It would be useless to thumb through the dictionary of cases of conscience! Moral treatises will of course tell me the universal rule or rules I am bound to apply; they will not tell me how I, in my uniqueness, am to apply them in my own unique context. No knowledge of moral essences, no matter how perfect, meticulous, or detailed it may be, no matter how particularized those essences may be (though they will always remain general),[136] no amount of casuistry, nor any chain of pure deduction, nor science can exempt me from my judgment of conscience, and if I have some virtue, from the exercise of prudence, in which exercise the rectitude of my willing must effect the accuracy of my vision.[137]

This point is made so often by Yves Simon that the best thing that one can do is read all of his texts on moral thought, texts which should be a *sine qua non* for all Thomist students of moral science.[138]

It should by now be evident what is at stake in personalized moral reasoning. We now, however, must attempt to understand the stages involved in this moral reasoning, for it involves many kinds of judgments, and an understanding of these various stages will help us determine the unique character of each of these judgments. To this end, I will lay out the classic table—developing slightly the presentations of Fr. Garrigou-Lagrange and Fr. Gardeil—of the acts of reason involved in moral-practical reasoning. No doubt this chart suffers from the limitations befalling a kind of "psychology of acts."[139] Nonetheless, it remains the best way to lay out the gradual process by which *synderesis*, faith-*synderesis*, and even moral science all descend down, *vitally and virtuously* into our acts.

---

136. See the text from Maritain, *Loi naturelle* cited in note 3 above. Also see the discussion of *individuum vagum* in the work by Wallace cited in note 115 above

137. Maritain, *Existence and the Existent*, p. 51 (slightly altered).

138. My own position is not isomorphic with Simon's but grappling with his thought on these questions will do the reader much good.

139. See Servais Pinckaers, "La structure de l'acte humain suivant saint Thomas," *Revue thomiste*, Vol. 55 (1955): pp. 393–412. The careful reader will sense the places in which I agree and disagree with Fr. Pinckaers' insightful (if, at times, overstated) critiques voiced in this article.

Acts of Intellect	*Acts of Will*
ORDER OF INTENTION (ENDS)	
1a. Judgment: "This end is good"; "Fear must not get in the way of doing truly virtuous activity"; "Where a debt is owed, it must be recognized and repaid appropriately."	1b. Inefficacious* *desire* for this end. * *Inefficacious* = Not applied to my action here and now, though it is a real and true affective appreciation of this good.
2a. Judgment: "This end can and *ought* somehow* to be attained here and now." * *Somehow* = through some means still to be determined, thus setting off the order of election / choice.	2b. *Efficacious intention*
ORDER OF ELECTION / CHOICE (MEANS)	
3a. *Counsel* concerning the means: "Perhaps these or those general circumstances will help you perform this action."	3b. *Consent* to diverse means, envisioned *in globo*
4a. *Practical judgment*: "These are the best means."	4b. *Election* (or, choice) of the means that seem to be the best
ORDER OF EXECUTION	
5a. *Imperium* or command that directs the execution of chosen means.	5b. *Usus activus*: The will applies the other faculties to the execution of the means.
	5c. *Usus passivus*: Passive application of other faculties, e.g., attention.
	1c[140] / 6. *Fruitio*, joy in the possession of the achieved end.

140. See note 149 below.

This chart must be read carefully. We must distinguish intellection and willing from each other. In each act elicited in this process, however, they are closely bound to each other in very important ways, indeed with increasing importance. They mutually interpenetrate each other, and in the final practical judgment (4a), the will's choice (4b) is the efficient cause of this final practical judgment, while the final practical judgment is the extrinsic formal cause of this choice. In this ultimate judgment, the interpenetration is profound, for the will must determine itself to *this or that particular good*, something which will never settle the will, which remains a power which desires the good in its full latitude. Thus, these two causes are prior to each other, although in different lines of causality. There is no contradiction involved here, but it is an example of a profound natural (or supernatural, as the case might be) mystery.[141] Every act contains a poignant example of the maxim "causes are mutually causes of each other." This is a deep and difficult matter, for which I recommend the works in which it is treated by Fr. Garrigou-Lagrange[142] and Jacques Maritain.[143]

At the start, let us note the three great divisions of this chart. Prudence presupposes a pivotal task of preliminary moral reasoning, *the order of intention*. It is in the order of intention that the moral virtues begin their first extension toward action. Indeed, without a firm intention emanating from the moral virtues, there will never be a prudential task, for the latter is concerned with *means*, which are always *that which is ordered to an end*. In moral actions, that which is intended will forever be the *most internal action, the target which prudence will hit or imprudence miss.*[144]

141. F.-X. Maquart, *Elementa philosophiae*, vol. 2: *Philosophia naturalis* (Paris: Andreas Blot, 1937), pp. 476–486.

142. A study of this maxim can be found in the final chapter of Reginald Garrigou-Lagrange, *The Order of Things*. Also see Garrigou-Lagrange, *God: His Existence and His Nature: A Thomistic Solution of Certain Agnostic Antinomies*, vol. 2, trans. Bede Rose (St. Louis, MO: B. Herder, 1949), pp. 306–338 and 370–72.

143. A digest of Maritain's position (heavily reliant on Fr. Garrigou-Lagrange) can be found in Jacques Maritain, "Freedom," in *Bergsonian Philosophy and Thomism*, trans. Mabelle L. Andison and J. Gordon Andison (New York: Philosophical Library, 1955), pp. 266–77. The theme can also be found in works by Simon.

144. Too often, the "external act" is held to be the act which is "outside" the agent's will (or the "physically external act"). While there is a sense in which this is the case, the first case of an internal-external action coupling is actually between the acts of intention and choice. For a recent treatment of this, see Duarte Sousa-Lara, "Aquinas on Interior and Exterior Acts: Clarifying a Key Aspect of His Action Theory," *Josephinum Journal of Theology*, Vol. 15, No. 2 (2008): pp. 277–316. Much of this rediscovery could have been sped along if one

Prudence will rely on the intention of the end throughout the whole of its own labor in seeking out the means. There can be no virtuous act without prudence, but it is also true that there can be no prudent decision without the moral virtues providing the "intentional strength" for the prudential *discursus*. In order to exist, this *order of intention* will give rise to the *order of election / choice*, wherein we will prudentially search out the means for our action, doing so again with a whole host of virtues to aid us in this task.[145] Even beyond choosing, the most important thing is *to do the good that is chosen*, and this will be yet another intellectual task: that of *ordering and commanding* the action to be done, something which is not merely a question of "following the recipe" from (4b) in the action in (5), for there are many traps along the path, and great virtue is sometimes needed in order to *execute* on what has been chosen. This execution, the *order of command*, will be the full perfection of the prudential activity. The choice serves the execution, not vice-versa.

The Important Presupposition: the Order of Intention

The root of this intention is something quite hidden and mysterious in our moral reasoning[146]: the simple willing of the end. Here is the profound source of the moral life. Here are *synderesis*, faith-*synderesis*, and even moral science now applied *to my potential moral action*. Here we can judge: "Being a dutiful parent is a good to be done"; "Fetuses must not be killed through abortive actions"; "Alcoholic beverages must be used in such a way that they maintain the order of good reason, proper desire, justice, and interpersonal decorum in our actions"; "Fear must not get in the way of doing truly virtuous activity"; etc. To the degree that these judgments enter into our chart, they are no longer being considered *merely* from the perspective of "why is this so?" In other words, we are no longer reflecting in a "moral scientific manner." Instead, we are considering them *as the initial springs for personal action*. They are part of this great dynamism of moral essences which pushes onward toward *my personal life, how I should live and act.*

had consulted Fr. Garrigou-Lagrange who made the same terminological point decades earlier in *De beatitudine*, pp. 345–71.

145. See the chart at the end of this introduction for a digest of all of these virtues involved with prudence.

In the first "simple volition" (or, *voluntas*, understood not as "the will" but rather as "primordial willing"), we have an example a point of great importance for moral reasoning, as well as concerning the very nature of "moral science" as well. It is very difficult—perhaps almost practically impossible—to set aside our own affective response to these judgments. How many moral philosophies are, at bottom, nothing more than a consecration of our own prejudices, passions, vices, unexamined opinions, or fears? Our own character and personal biases can exercise great influence on how we react to this first judgment. This essay cannot consider all of the difficult problems involved with the various sources of erroneous moral judgments, even in such universal matters. The strength of our assent to moral truths is not, however, a purely speculative affair, and our character matters a great deal. The maxim, "Qualis unusquisque est, talis finis videtur ei," most certainly applies here. The end will seem different to each individual, depending on his character. As evidenced earlier, the shift from *personal moral action* to *moral science* involves a new formal perspective, the latter being purely speculative and not directive. The two perspectives are, however, deeply interrelated. Most of our moral-scientific data must come from personal experience, and even when we gain understanding from others, literature, history, etc., we still filter so much of this through our own experience of the ends of moral actions. Let us be aware of the nature of the shift between personal-action judgment (1a) and a judgment belonging to moral science.[147]

This first judgment, along with the simple willing of the end will be the wellspring from which all future moral action will bud forth.[148] Without a genial and full love of the good, why would we ever truly *intend* (2a

146. See John of St. Thomas, *Introduction to the Summa Theologiae of Thomas Aquinas*, trans. Ralph McInerny (South Bend, IN: St. Augustine's Press, 2004), p. 60: "Before treating the second such will-act, namely, enjoyment, St. Thomas devotes two questions to asking what moves the will. The Holy Doctor does this because simple volition is the first act of the will, and here [the] will cannot be moved by anything willed before; therefore, the origination and cause of this first act is obscure and hidden…"

147. In most ways, I agree with the early-career observations made by Yves R. Simon in "Moral Philosophy," in *A Critique of Moral Knowledge*, pp. 41–49. Later in life, Simon seems to have erected a slightly higher (only *slightly*) wall between moral experience and moral science, especially when discussing the opening of the *Nicomachean Ethics*. See Simon, *Practical Knowledge*, pp. 41–47.

148. This is where I agree with the concerns voiced in the article by Fr. Pinckaers cited in note 139 above.

and 2b) to bring about this good for ourselves, or actually attempt to do these virtuous actions? At this very first point of "existentialization," the will already begins to rest in a good, rendered intentionally present by this first judgment, which presents this moral object to it as a good that could be pursued, if the circumstances allow for it.[149] Fr. Ambroise Gardeil describes this process precisely in a striking passage (written primarily from the natural perspective of *synderesis*):

> Therefore, the fundamental moral education will consist in forming THE HEART—that is, the will, envisioned in its initial act of taking pleasure in the good and the true end of the being who possesses it. It will not be a question of instruction, properly speaking. The intellectual formation of the heart depends upon a simple maieutic [i.e., clarifying one's ideas]. It consists in drawing the attention of the human being to the character of reason, which, in him, takes precedence over all the others and differentiates him from all that is inferior in him and around him to make him see that, things being so, the ends of his actions ought to be in harmony with this noble

149. Thus, we see that it is deceptive to think of *fruitio* as being solely the last step in this process, a kind of "resting on your laurels" at the end of our moral action. See John of St. Thomas, *Introduction to the Summa Theologiae of Thomas Aquinas*, pp. 60–61: "Having discussed the first act of will bearing on the end, [St. Thomas] goes on to another act which bears on the end absolutely, namely, enjoyment. This is not the perfect enjoyment that comes from the real attainment and possession of the end but an imperfect one which follows on the initial love which finds the end pleasant when it is had only intentionally. The end begins to move as what is first in intention. That is why St. Thomas treats enjoyment immediately after the will's simple act of volition. Although perfect and consummate enjoyment is the last of the acts of the will (all motion ceases once the end is attained), still the inchoate rest in the thing loved, when it is first had intentionally through love, follows immediately on the first simple act of will."

In fact, to the degree that an action is not merely a motion (*kinesis*) but an act (*energeia*), it is already always the case that you are doing it. The musician does not enjoy *fruitio* solely at the end of the organ piece, as the final chord fades away in the air, but, rather, experiences fruitive-joy throughout the whole activity. The duration of such cases of "energeia" does unfold throughout time, but it has the feeling of something like angelic duration, a kind of single pulsation of act dilated here-below, the spirituality of *art* shining on the moving substrate of material existence. The same is true of the person who is achieving a moral act, especially throughout the process of command (which has its own activity and adjoined virtues specifically deputed to it in particular, namely, foresight, circumspection, and caution). On the unique role played by these three virtues in the execution of an action, see *ST* II-II, q. 48, a. 1. Most especially, however, see Gardeil, *The True Christian Life*, pp. 131–33. Here, we have the ultimate conquest in the moral domain, analogically akin to the organist playing a highly technical fugue.

> part of himself, which completes him and totalizes him as a man and penetrates his spirit with the exigencies of these ends. As regards the formation, properly speaking, of the "heart," it consists in bringing about the natural reactions of the will in face of this evident goodness, to invite the will to consent to it. Such a consent has nothing of the character of being forced, nothing of the character of a violent action, for it is inscribed in the natural laws of a human will's unfolding. Still, it is necessary to aid him, who for the first time has arrived at this (or who returns to it), to make this personal effort. In this sense, and within their limits, our secular educators have been right to say, "Before all else, be personal." Yes, be personal—but not by making arise from you any innate thing whatsoever by a personalism of an arbitrary will; instead, be personal by letting loose your personal effort in the direction of the natural bent of your human will, which is, before all else, rational.
>
> This double formation of the general conscience and of the heart does not require speculation. It demands simply that one looks truly upon oneself and that one loves what one has thus seen. In this way, St. Thomas's conclusion is imposed: moral virtue cannot exist without understanding [*l'intelligence*].[150]

At this stage of things, *the very judgment* (1a) that provides the formal content for this affective attachment (1b) *is colored by the fact that it pertains to this person.* Here, the judgment, "Where a debt is owed, it must be recognized and repaid," is not being considered *solely* in its truth value (although this is implied, for *synderesis* is presupposed for all of this) but, in addition, it is being considered insofar as *justice is a potential good to be appreciated by me*, as *something in which I take a kind of (intentional-objective) rest and enjoyment.*[151] *This judgment measures this first "simple willing."* Its destiny is already "personalized." It is important to note this unique "coloration," and a full phenomenology of this act would explain just how this differs from the others that we have discussed, as well as those which we will discuss in what follows.

150. Ambroise Gardeil, "Intelligence and Morality," trans. Matthew K. Minerd, *Nova et Vetera*, Vol. 16, No. 2 (Spring 2018): p. 662.

151. Hence, *fruitio* is inchoately present from the start. See note 149 above.

The second type of judgment (2a) in the order of intention reaches far deeper into our subjective life. While the very first, simple willing is the root and source of all personal appreciation for the moral good, it remains somewhat "disconnected" from our current circumstances. No doubt, this is why the first kind of judgment (1a) is sometimes presented by scholastics as if it were a "velleity" or a mere wish: "This would be nice to do, if it were possible, but it is not." This likely overstates the case for how "disconnected" our "simple willing" is from our action. Nonetheless, a person who is reading a piece of great literature or watching a well-done documentary can be profoundly moved by the good presented therein (or, alas, for the vicious person, moved by the evils presented there), without, however, having any real concern with his or her personal action here and now. At most, such a person can think, "This is truly good. Were I presented with such a possible virtuous action, I too would approve doing it."

But, then, the day comes when this action is a real possibility. Faced with our particular circumstances and possibilities, we realize: *I must do this here and now*. In other words, we find that we must *intend* to do an action. In the judgment (2a) and willing (2b) involved in our moral reasoning, we take what had been somewhat "existentially disembodied" in simple willing and make it quite real for ourselves. Our judgment is no longer merely, "Where a debt is owed, it must be recognized and repaid," coupled with an abstract willing that affirms this as being good *for me*. In the judgment that rules our intention, we say, "A debt is here owed, so it must be recognized and repaid. *This is to be my end here and now.*" And if we have the virtue of justice, at least to some degree (even if it is only found in an inchoate and implicit form in the basic goodness of the will, which can never be lost),[152] we will stretch out toward this good, no longer as something *merely good in itself as a possible action*—as in (1b)—but *as something I will to be good, in my very action, although this will require certain means in order for it to be accomplished*.[153]

In a truly virtuous person, the volitional act of intention will spring from the depths of his or her virtue, which will provide, *in the order of*

152. See *ST* I-II, q. 94, a. 6.

153. Doubtlessly, insights drawn from Anscombe's work on intention must be incorporated into the moral psychology of the order of intention, though this is not our task here. See Elizabeth Anscombe, *Intention*, 2nd ed. (Cambridge, MA: Harvard University Press, 2000).

execution, the causality which is guided *in the order of specification* by the judgment of intention ("a debt is here owed, so it must be recognized and repaid. *This is to be my end here and now*"). Both causalities are needed, for this is not a mere question of knowledge but, rather, of knowledge that is *moving toward action*, meaning that this is not a merely intellectual affair but, rather, a kind of vital interaction of "head" and "heart" or, to put it better, of speculatively-practical intellection and virtuous (or at least incipiently virtuous) willing.[154] The whole work of prudence will be in the service of these virtues, which give all of the moral weight to the action to be performed, and if a given moral object is indeed sinful, this will be because it is not, ultimately, in line with virtuous ends.[155] There will be no prudential command without this intention, however inchoate it might be. From top to bottom, it provides the utterly essential *desire for the end* to be achieved, and if prudence succeeds, we can truly say that it is the intention that succeeds *in* the prudential action which brings it into existence.[156]

Prudentially Pushing on from Intention to Choice

Intentions alone do not bring about our action. Action brings about action. We must put together the means for accomplishing this intention. Here, we have an entire labor ahead of us, the labor of prudence.[157] As we will see, we must not think of prudence's activity as being a kind of "map

154. But notice how the "speculatively practical" is here descending toward the fully practical.

155. Thus, the person who chooses a sin for a "good intention" in fact vitiates that intention *and* builds up a vicious character in the opposed direction. In fact, even something like "to exercise responsible parenthood" or "to protect one's life in a virtuous manner" is vitiated by acts of contracepted sexual intercourse (a sin against the very nature of chastity) or by abortive actions (a sin against justice), for "to exercise responsible parenthood" or "to protect one's life in a virtuous manner" *imply the order of virtue* and are only in fact performed by the person who chooses objects that belong to that order. The sin found in the *object* also is a sin against the end which was not reached. Moreover, note that in the case of mortal sins, a sinful object not only inculcates opposed tendencies undermining the virtues and tending toward vice but also leads to the loss of grace and, at least, the loss of the theological virtue of charity, along with all of the infused moral virtues and the gifts of the Holy Spirit.

156. This point is repeated in all of the texts by Fr. Garrigou-Lagrange relevant to this matter. Of course, numerous other Thomists could be cited.

157. Again, recall what I said above about the various types of prudence. Here, we are simplifying things only to address *personal prudence, whether natural or supernatural.* St. Thomas, however, holds that there are formally different kinds of prudence. Generally, his vocabulary remains in the natural order here, though it would be interesting to discuss how this applies also to infused prudence for the Christian.

reading." We are not merely sitting in Pittsburgh, Pennsylvania, looking for one of the pre-arranged paths to Passaic, New Jersey. Sometimes, in simpler cases, this can indeed be akin to what we must do, following generally prescribed paths, adding our own little flair to them, speeding up here, slowing down there. Moreover, even in difficult cases, these paths, these general recommendations, will forever be of use. We need examples, and even "simple" examples are rich with lessons, often so rich that every future complexification will be nothing more than a further determination of a kind of primordial nucleus of moral insights, a kind of extension of "moral common sense." Such is the reason for the continued fecundity of myths and fables, understood in the most profound sense of these terms. In traveling from Pittsburgh to Passaic, one will either drive over the mountains or travel by circuitous paths. Maritain, a great proponent of the "inventive" character of prudence but one unafraid to speak up against mid-century French existentialism's desire to turn moral reasoning into a wholly unique and unrepeatable affair, is profound on this point:

> As for us [in comparison with the existentialists], we do not fear advice for human liberty. Fill it with as much advice as you like—we know that it is strong enough to digest them all, and that it lives on rational motivations which it manipulates for its purposes and of which it alone knows the efficacy. In sum, by suppressing generality and universal law, one suppresses liberty, leaving only chaos thrusting out of the night it resembles. For, in suppressing generality and universal law, one suppresses reason, in which freedom has its root, and from which so vast a desire flows into man that no explanation on earth and no objective solicitation, except Beatitude seen face to face, suffices to determine it.[158]

Indeed, such advice is so necessary that prudence requires a great host of auxiliary virtues that enable us to make the next stage of judgment, *counsel / deliberative judgments* (3a). In the stage of "deliberation," we must consider the various paths that might be taken in our activity. We must be ready to see moral truths in the particular cases we are consider-

158. Maritain, "Action," in *Existence and the Existent*, pp. 60–61 (slightly modified). Also, see the excellent quote from Gardeil, referenced in note 134 above.

ing ("understanding"), never tempted to distort our recollection of past actions but, instead, to draw upon them honestly without undue delay or precipitancy ("memory"). We must be ready to attend to those who have an "eye to see" because they have experience and moral wisdom, not tarrying too long there either ("docility"),[159] but ready and able to grasp the course of action that we must personally take ("shrewdness"). And when we try to put together the "moral syllogisms" that may or may not apply to us, we must reason well, connecting the universal needs of morality to the particular requirements of here and now ("reason").[160] And all of this must be ordered by a kind of "perfected overall coordination," a moral perfection that enables us to come to a final set of possible judgments of counsel / deliberation ("euboulia"). How great the virtue needed in order to fulfill, justly and rightly in this or that set of circumstances, the great Aristotelian maxim: *oportet consiliare tarde* ("one must be slow in taking counsel").[161]

These judgments are said to be *in globo*, general and still somewhat incomplete in character: "Perhaps these or those general circumstances will help you perform this action. I remember when doing this, this seemed to be the best path. Given your mood today, given the present circumstances, you should probably do X, Y, or Z." A whole host of these sorts of judgments can be marshalled for every moral decision.

In fact, although this kind of deliberation is most obvious when it comes to difficult choices, there are many day-to-day decisions which at least implicitly involve a kind of silent deliberation over the most anodyne

159. See Aristotle, *Nicomachean Ethics* (trans. Ross), VI, 11: "Therefore we ought to attend to the undemonstrated sayings and opinions of experienced and older people or of people of practical wisdom not less than to demonstrations; for because experience has given them an eye they see aright."

160. In fact, because of the way that the *vis cogitativa* is involved in all of this, as well as in the virtue of "understanding" discussed here, the reader should bear in mind everything relevant that is said in Daniel D. De Haan, "Perception and the *Vis cogitativa*: A Thomistic Analysis of Aspectual, Actional, and Affectional Percepts," *American Catholic Philosophical Society*, Vol. 88, No. 3 (2014): pp. 397–437; "Moral Perception and the Function of the Vis Cogitativa in Thomas Aquinas's Doctrine of Antecedent and Consequent Passions," *Documenti e studi sulla traditione* filosofica *medievale*, Vol. 25 (2014): pp. 289–330; Julien Peghaire, "A Forgotten Sense, The Cogitative According to St. Thomas Aquinas," *The Modern Schoolman*, Vol. 20 (1943): pp. 123–140, 210–229; George Klubertanz, *The Discursive Power: Sources and Doctrine of the Vis cogitativa According to St. Thomas Aquinas* (St. Louis: The Modern Schoolman, 1952).

161. See *ST* II-II, q. 53, a. 3, ad 3.

things. For example, the planning of a meal should always involve the exercise of temperance. There is a great deal of latitude here, however, given the way that in matters of temperance the "mean" of virtue is the sort of thing which is clearly determined by prudence itself. (In scholastic terminology, this is called a *medium rationis*.[162]) There are many potential options open to us *for dinner tonight*, all in view of *what I intend also to choose to make tomorrow, what the people involved like, etc.* Sometimes, temperance is explained with a simple example about, for instance, choosing whether to eat another piece of cake. Such simple examples hide, however, the truly symphonic nature even of this very simple virtue. Temperance provides the rectification of our concupiscible[163] appetite *in relation to higher goods*.[164] There are many paths open to us, ones that may in fact include wonderful delicacies today—but only if we choose to have them in a way that is not selfish, self-indulgent, etc. Deliberation requires a fullness of labor, for prudence is ever-active, constructing the circumstances of virtue in all of our free actions, even the most anodyne. Here too, the Gospel maxim is of no small importance: "He who is faithful in a very little is faithful also in much" (Lk. 16:10; RSV).

These judgments are marked by a truly affective character. Our moral judgments increasingly become right or wrong to the degree that they apply to *me* in *these circumstances*. Merely to draw one example, let us consider a friend whom we know to be wise in the matters we are deliberating about. Rather quickly, however, we realize that he or she here is giving us advice that is deeply affected by his or her temperamental needs, which differ greatly from our own. Thus, a very phlegmatic friend might tell us that vespers at a given monastery is edifying, a good way to fulfill our religious duties toward God on occasion, although we are members of the laity. Despite the fact that this friend has a good ear for music, however, he is not bothered that vespers at this monastery is often a bit cacophonous, for as a Benedictine monk once told me: the one quarter of the community who cares about music is made up almost solely of the musicians. Alas, however, our friend is potentially susceptible to overlook-

162. See *ST* I-II, q. 64, a. 2; q. 66, a. 3, ad 3; II-II, q. 47, a. 7. See the text cited in note 67 above.

163. I would say "desire-oriented affect," but it seems that the opacity of the old, technical terminology remains necessary.

164. See note 83 above.

ing real faults and deficiencies, and we are vulnerable to harsh judgmentalism which will isolate us from common prayer when it really would be a duty, even for a layman. *Given my temperament*, and *in these particular circumstances*, however, it would be a failure in "docility" for me to continually ask him advice about this, forever listening to his overly optimistic reasoning when *I know, in my current state of soul, how I will be enraged at the distracting cacophony of this particular monastic choir*. My judgments of counsel will not contain much from him, only enough to serve as a possible counterbalance to my own insalubrious hard-headedness.

Even when I do listen to him, however, these judgments will now be much more individualized than any judgment that I would have elicited in the casuistry falling to moral science. Here, we have a true kind of *prudential casuistry*, marked by my own situation: "Given my current mood, my recent experiences with the pitiable world of ecclesiastical music, my real need for shared prayer, my duties as a parent to expose my children to the common prayer of the Church in her various rites, the time since I last did it, my sense that I can curb my irascibility right now, etc., etc., it is at least arguable that I should consider going to vespers at the local monastery sometime soon, perhaps on a feast day on their calendar, so that I can hedge against lackluster musical performance and also can be buoyed by my sense of religious devotion to the given feast." That is a lengthy declamation, however, such is the nature of the judgment given in counsel. It will be subject to various nuances and various levels of complexity, and it will always have this sort of relationship to my current state of soul, virtue, etc. And even when the path is easy, this will be because, *given the demands of a given virtue or virtues, this path must be heeded*. Thus, we see, too, how the appetitive dimension ("consent," 3b) in this process is so very important.[165]

165. In what I have said here, I have needed to set aside the Holy Spirit's gift of counsel. My concern, although inspired by many of the theological problems involved here, is primarily limited to the issues of "moral psychology" involved in the debates over conscience. Nonetheless, this important topic should be considered in order to understand true Christian prudence. See *ST* II-II, q. 52; "'Let It Be So Now': The Gift of Counsel," in Walter Farrell and Dominic Hughes, *Swift Victory: Essays on the Gifts of the Holy Spirit* (New York: Sheed and Ward, 1955), pp. 105–129; Ambroise Gardeil, *The Holy Spirit in the Christian Life*, trans. anon. (London: Blackfriars Publications, 1953), 69–78; *The Gifts of the Holy Spirit in the Dominican Saints*, trans. Anselm M. Townsend (Providence, RI: Cluny Media, 2016), pp. 59–70; Garrigou-Lagrange, *The Three Ages of the Interior Life*, vol. 1, pp. 67–88; vol. 2, pp. 86–89, 218–21, 225–23, 475–77.

Yet a path must be chosen. At times, we have a number of paths open before us, a number of possible choices. This must all be condensed down into a final dictum: "This is what must be done." All of the various options gathered in counsel / deliberation must now be made *my own here and now*. No longer is it a question of "possible paths" but, instead, of *which path to take*. This is the stage of the final practical judgment and the choice that follows upon it. A common perception of Thomism is that it requires us to make the final practical judgment a quasi-speculative judgment, as if prudence were wholly intellectual (a claim that would be Scotist, not Thomist).[166] But this is not so. Prudence is at once intellectual and moral—requiring both intellectual and volitional perfection so that we may readily judge and act as is morally necessary. The ultimate practical judgment will never be ultimate without the causality of the will. Our will's choice depends on the practical intellect's final judgment in the order of formal causality, whereas the intellect's final judgment depends on the virtuous will in order to be ultimate: "The free will, by choosing, makes it be the case that the ultimate practical judgment is the ultimate one and actually directs the will, which accepts this direction."[167] Or, as Maritain summarizes so well:

> The second point of doctrine, which particularly controls the whole theory of the virtue of prudence, concerns the judgment of moral conscience[168] and the manner by which, at the center of concrete existence, desires intervene in the regulation of the moral act by reason. Here, St. Thomas makes the rectitude of the intellect depend on that of the will, and this by virtue of the existentiality—no longer speculative but practical—of moral judgment. The truth of the practical intellect is understood not as conformity to an extramental being but as conformity to a right desire; the end is no longer to know what is, but to bring into existence that which is not yet; further, the act of moral choice is so individualized, both by the singularity of the person from which it proceeds and the context of the contingent circumstances in which it takes place, that the practical judgment in which it is expressed and by

166. See Garrigou-Lagrange, "Remarks Concerning the Metaphysical Character of St. Thomas's Moral Theology," pp. 257–258.

167. Reginald Garrigou-Lagrange, *The Order of Things*, p. 336.

168. Although, as should be noted from comments above, Maritain at times seems to also place conscience in the domain of moral science.

> which I declare to myself, "This is what I must do," can be right only if, *hic et nunc*, the dynamism of my will is right, and tends toward the true goods of human life.[169]

Fr. Sebastian Samay, O.S.B., would be quite candid with visitors of his monastery who were considering a Benedictine vocation: "Do you know what you get from sitting on the fence? A sore ass." The slight vulgarity was meant to shock the hesitating vocation guest. With St. Thomas, however, we could merely say, after carefully deliberating, "*oportet operari velociter consiliata* ("we must be quick in carrying the counsel that we have taken").[170]

There is something very definitive about the judgment that needs to be rendered at the end of deliberation. The judgment (4a) which will provide the very formal content of the will's choice (4b) is utterly personal and determinative. This is not a question of considering, at some distance, the act to be taken. No longer are we doing the casuistry of moral science, nor even the "prudential casuistry" of counsel / deliberation. We are declaring the path forward, the judgment which will rule our choice: "This is what must be done." In the final practical judgment, we determine the indetermination of the will. In fact, the will *determines itself* while also determining (in the order of efficient causality) our final practico-moral judgment, which itself determines the will (in the order of specificative-objective-formal causality). This final judgment represents our most profound declaration *within ourselves* concerning what it is that we must do, here and now. A great mystery is involved here, where both intellection and virtuous volition meet. The Thomist interpretation of this moral psychology must maintain the golden mean between mere intellectualism and mere voluntarism, giving due praise to both the intellect and the will for their roles in this process.[171]

The Perfection of Prudence: Command

To illustrate the final practical judgment, spilling over into command, consider the following image—one which, hopefully, captures the ferocious energy of moral reasoning.

169. Maritain, "Action," in *Existence and the Existent*, pp. 50–51 (slightly modified).

170. *ST* II-II, q. 47, a. 9.

171. See notes 140–42 above.

We have considered a whole host of possible courses of action; this collection resembles a solar system filled with planets, debris, and so forth. At the center of the system, practical reasoning draws, like a star, all things to itself. Exercising a powerful gravitational attraction, this star begins to draw down to its most essential core, compressing the whole solar system, growing to an immense level of heat, incorporating all of this matter into its white-hot nuclear fusion. Then, at a certain moment, it reaches its point of determination, the smallest point where the stability of the fusion gives way to a super-nova.

Here, we have something metaphorically akin to the moment of choice. Deep within ourselves, *in our will*, we determine ourselves. We are won over by the good. Then, we must explode outward—we fashion the very act to be done, *commanding* our action. No longer are we declaring to the will, "This is what must be done." Rather, we are saying: "Do this." The mood is now imperative, and this is the tensest moment, when "head and heart meet." Our action spills outward—throughout our whole being and into the world, which we now *order*, which we now *command*:

> Have we now made clear the difference between choosing and commanding ourselves? Our choice, in sum, terminates and comes to its consummation within us. It is the act of a will that has been completely won over in advance by the sweetness of the love of God, an act of will that, moreover, in its spiritual grandeur is made to taste and embrace divine things. When we begin to command ourselves, however, we turn ourselves outward, toward an external world that is still ourselves, though no longer the superior *self* of reason and of the will but, rather, the *self* that is inferior and tainted by the passions, a *self* which does not know the divine beauty, our inferior *self* which includes our relationships with others—this terrible self, terrible, I say, precisely because it is other and, as such, is unmoved by the events that stir within us. We move ourselves from within when we choose, but we ultimately will be dealing with a world that is not instructed by the decisions that aspire to rule it. It is a world that is prepared to resist them as soon as they claim to penetrate into it and that indeed resists them as soon as their governance is impressed upon them.
>
> This difference of orientation between the choice that is brought to its consummation in "the interior man" and the command that

> looks upon "the exterior man" explains the difficulty that we experience in fully realizing our self-government, as well as the hiatus existing between our resolution (however energetic it might be) and our effective command. To choose and to command oneself belong to two different worlds.
>
> The tactic of our faculty of [self-]government thus finds itself faced with a new problem to be resolved: how to impress upon the will, which henceforth will be executive and directive [*réalisateur*], a sufficiently powerful impulse for overcoming all these difficulties.[172]

Here, too, there will be need of auxiliaries: caution, foresight, and circumspection, virtues necessary in order to carry out the task at hand.[173] The "doing of the deed" does not just unroll like a carpet before our feet. Often, the very thing that we have commanded requires continued insight, readiness, and careful attention. For example, I am hosting a friend for dinner, and decide to offer two cocktails, knowing my guest's ability to drink alcohol. Just after giving him the second drink, however, I realize that he must have had a drink before his arrival. Without insulting him, I must plot a course which can maintain both temperance and celebration. Such an instance as this would require great tact, but the judgments involved are not the same as any of the others. They are all adjuncts and auxiliaries to our command. They are the servants of the imperious dictates of the *imperium*, the command of prudence.

And in the midst of this activity, especially at those moments when its accomplishment is most keenly felt, we are filled with joy. Certainly, all human joys are fleeting here-below. Nonetheless, the will can take its rest in the accomplished good, echoing in a lesser but real manner: "Lord, it is good that we are here" (Mt. 17:4).

Summarizing the Judgments of Moral-Practical Reason

Now that we are in a position to gather together all of the possible candidates for the judgment of conscience, a summary of the judgments discussed thus far will prove helpful. The numbers in parentheses are related to the earlier chart:

172. Gardeil, *The True Christian Life*, pp. 129–30.

173. See ibid., pp. 171–73; *ST* II-II, q. 49, a. 6–8.

1. Moral-scientific judgments.[174]
   a. *Synderesis* and faith-*synderesis* in pure form: "Desires are to be pursued in a way that is moderated in line with the higher goods of human activity" (temperance).[175]
   b. Universal *conclusions* in moral science: "There is a way to moderate our reading of various publications" (conclusion drawn on the basis of the sub-virtue of temperance, studiousness).
   c. Casuistic judgments in moral science: "There are many cases in which online forums and comment sections tend to draw people into the sin of curiosity."
2. Personal-moral judgments.
   a. Pre-prudential judgments.
      i. The judgment of simple willing (1a): "It is good, *for me*, to appreciate the human goodness of moderating desires in line with the higher goods of human activity."
      ii. The judgment of intention (2a): "Today, while working, I must moderate my desires to look into news, etc."
   b. Prudential judgments.
      i. Deliberative judgments (3a).
         1. Memory: "When I kept my phone close by in the past, I was more likely to look at online articles, etc. Therefore, in the circumstances of my actions it would be better if I were to set my phone aside, etc."
         2. Understanding / Shrewdness: "This or that course of action is a real temptation to curiosity. This or that course of action will help me to avoid distraction."
         3. Docility.
            a. Judgment from the one giving advice: "When I work, this is how I keep myself from getting burned out without, however, dallying over various things online. Given your temperament and character, you should try X, Y, or Z."
            b. Judgment in the agent receiving the advice: "X, Y, Z are possible options, though given to me by someone

174. For further amplification on this domain of judgments, see the chart in Minerd, "A Note on *Synderesis*, Moral Science, and Knowledge of the Natural Law," p. 50.

175. Note, also, that these judgments can belong to the *ius gentium*, as things which are self-evident "to the wise" (*per se nota sapientibus*).

else, so they need to be interpreted in light of my own self-knowledge."

ii. Ultimate practical judgment (4a): drawn in light of *synesis* and/or *gnome*[176]: "Today, I must in fact choose to keep my phone away from me in order to help me measure my actions in line with the virtue of temperance."

iii. Command-related declarations (cf. 5).

1. Command: In the imperative mood: "Do this act of temperance."

2. Various judgments drawn through foresight, circumspection, and caution, all in the midst of the circumstances *of my performance of the action.*

Some Thomists have chosen to emphasize quite strongly the aspects of Aquinas's texts which would place the judgment of conscience in the domain of "moral science." Thus, in particular, its dictates would be found in categories (1c) in the listing directly above.[177] Others have sought to place the judgment of conscience primarily in the domain of prudential reasoning, stressing above all that when it is true and certain it is the final judgment which rules the choice (2b[ii]) directly above.[178] Maritain, in at least one text, seems to broaden this to include judgments involved in deliberation, (2b[i]) directly above; in other works, however, he does maintain clearly the speculatively-practical character of conscience in a way concordant with the "moral science" adherents.[179] Fr. Michel Labourdette, in contrast, seems to place conscience somewhere between prudence and moral science, but without clearly explaining how conscience can be formed by a particular virtue. (That is, he does not answer the questions: What virtue leads to the good use of conscience as a unique kind of judg-

176. These adjuncts will have their own unique roles, depending on the complexity of the case. Based on several texts in St. Thomas, Fr. Merkelbach believes that the character of *synesis* and *gnome* will be inflected toward giving *certitude* in their judgments, whereas *euboulia* will be focused more so on the truth and rectitude of the judgment in question. Obviously, these elements must be involved in all judgments of prudence. A full phenomenology of these forms of knowledge may help, however, to bear witness to the particular nuances and inflections found in their particular formal objects. See *ST* II-II, q. 51.

177. See note 3 above.

178. See note 4 above.

179. See note 3 above.

ment concerning particular acts? Is it moral science? Is it prudence? Is it something else?)[180]

Each of these positions has arguments in its favor, based on St. Thomas's texts as well as on the very nature of the issues at hand. As moral-scientific judgments, judgments of conscience would be concerned with an *individuum vagum*, some person X, but mostly concerned with knowing the "truth" of this judgment, not whether it applies directly to us. No matter what we say about "conscience," this judgment is quite necessary, and even those who are not moral philosophers or moral theologians will deploy such discernment in order to rectify their personal moral judgments. In fact, let us take great joy in the fact that *the moral-scientific truth of action* remains forever present as a possibility, able to support our prudential reasoning and to rescue us when we fall short in virtue!

On the other hand, if, as others hold, the judgment of conscience pertains to our prudential reasoning, then it involves a whole nexus of quite-personal possibilities, as is obvious if we consider the various kinds of judgments involved in counsel / deliberation. Thomists perhaps underappreciate the varying qualities of these judgments—elicited through unique *habitus* which function as quasi-integral parts of prudence.[181] Nonetheless, these qualities play an important role in forming prudential decisions, and to the degree that one draws conscience and prudence closer together, they should be recognized for their important role. Moreover, to the degree that we think of conscience in a personal (not purely "moral scientific") manner, we must not forget the profound sources of conscience, not only in *synderesis* but also in the first judgments in the order of intention, whereby our whole personal-moral organism is formed.[182]

CONCLUSION

An appreciation of the Thomist discussions of moral epistemology bears witness to a very multi-layered, complex analysis of human action, one

180. See note 5 above.

181. Here, a kind of phenomenology of practical reason would render great services.

182. In this regard, we would take a cue from St. Thomas himself, who, while noting well that conscience is concerned with the application of knowledge to a particular action, says in *ST* I, q. 79, a. 13: "Since *habitus*, however, are the principles of acts, sometimes the term 'conscience' is used for the first natural *habitus*, namely, 'synderesis.'" On this topic, see the text by Reinhard Hütter cited in note 65 above.

that is much suppler than anything offered in contemporary philosophical discussions, while simultaneously being open to the most profound, subjective aspects of moral life and freedom.

The texts contained in this volume present some of the most technical discussions of conscience in the Thomist school. Frs. Beaudouin and Merkelbach tend to combine conscience and prudence. For this reason, I have also included an essay by Fr. Labourdette, laying out the worrisome aspects of this *rapprochement* of conscience and prudence. In particular, his essay provides an introduction to the highly technical (and, to Fr. Labourdette's eyes, problematic) discussions that took place in the controversies over Probabilism.[183] These debates inspired the texts by Merkelbach and Beaudouin, and a mature Thomist cannot cast them aside as a "dead end" as does Fr. Labourdette.[184] These thinkers must be heard in order to ascertain in full what and how Thomists should think concerning conscience. Thus, I also present Fr. Merkelbach's own overview of how, from the fourteenth century onward, the treatise on conscience floated around the various theological treatises, accompanied by his outline of his own treatment of the topic of conscience.[185] I provide Fr. Beaudouin's text as a monument to the Thomist school which inspired my own masters, Frs. Gardeil and Garrigou-Lagrange. Painstaking and technical as it is, this text is filled with insights now missing from contemporary Thomist discussions. The selection, lastly, from Fr. Merkelbach's *Summa Theologiae Moralis* is a more systematic and synthetic presentation of an argument which shares much with Beaudouin, although the latter Dominican tends to be more occupied (not without some self-awareness) with some of the issues caused by limiting his discussions of conscience to the treatise on human acts.[186]

183. See note 19 above. Also see note 6 in the Translator's Introduction to this volume.

184. He is not alone, of course. Fr. Garrigou-Lagrange somewhat does, although even he incorporates these discussions into his *De Beatitudine*, pp. 373–96. As is well known, Fr. Servais Pinckaers is much more scathing about probabilism.

185. I thank *Nova et Vetera* for permitting me to republish this text in this volume.

186. I do draw the reader's attention, however, to the fact that Fr. Beaudouin on occasion speaks about how casuistry must be left to the particular treatises on the virtues, and quite often at pivotal moments refers to the way that the prudent person determines the rightness or wrongness of actions. On a number of occasions, these sorts of comments save his *Tractatus de conscientia* from falling into some of the legalistic problems that one finds in so much of this genre.

Regarding the way that probabilism affected the structure of moral theology, we must admit that the *Theologia moralis* of St. Alphonsus is not Thomism. (And this could be said more strongly about other authors in this vein of speculation.) The layout of St.

These texts are deeply insightful for Thomists attempting to present a philosophy and theology of conscience. Too many ecclesiastics and lay Catholics bandy about this word, "conscience," often doing great damage. Thomists must take up this discussion in earnest in order to show that Thomistic thought can address all of the profound issues of moral subjectivity while retaining the stern stuff of moral objectivity. We must have confidence that the principles of Thomism remain far more illuminative than the small flashes of insight that some gain through a kind of passing dilettantism with this or that theory or theme that is in the vogue. To have such confidence, we must turn to our masters. As Aristotle said in his *On Sophistical Refutations,* cited on occasion by Aquinas: *oportet addiscentem credere*, or, as the old Blackfriars translation expressed it so charmingly: "It behooves the learner to believe" (*ST* II-II, q. 2, a. 3). It is in this spirit that I have presented these texts and this introduction.

It is curious that St. Thomas found so small a place for conscience, discussing it briefly in the *Prima pars*[187] and in the *Prima secundae*,[188] and not mentioning it at all in the discussion of prudence. Fr. Labourdette (and others, doubtless) have seen in this an indication that St. Thomas wished to distinguish very clearly prudence and conscience. Such is not an entirely convincing assertion. One merely needs to think of the Augustinian theme of "superior" and "inferior" reason[189] in order to realize that

Alphonsus's text bears witness to the fact that his system of thought organizes itself in a way that is different from a truly Thomist moral theology. To this degree, one is understandably cautious in saying that the two systems cannot be wed in a profound way *at the level of their speculatively-practical* moral-scientific inspiration, whether this be in the domain of moral philosophy or that of moral theology. Yet, it seems that when Maritain spoke of the practically-practical moral disciplines that could be formed based upon St. Alphonsus's vocabulary, he had in mind above all texts like the *Praxis confessarii ad bene excipiendas confessiones*, that is, a text devoted to the study of how interpersonal casuistry can guide action close at hand (although still lacking the final determinations that belong to prudence in the agent himself or herself). In practical matters, the data of human experience are very important. St. Alphonsus's keen eye for *interpersonal / prudential casuistry* would certainly bring to light data that could be incorporated throughout the various treatises of moral theology. Think of how many cases of conscience could illuminate the descriptions of the various virtues treated in *ST* II-II, as well as their correlative sins! *Scientific casuistry*, focusing on the essences of moral matters, not upon counsel in the direction of acts, would be all the better founded upon this experiential basis.

Concerning St. Alphonsus and Thomism, see Maritain, *Science and Wisdom*, pp. 144–45; *Degrees of Knowledge*, p. 487.

187. See *ST* I, q. 79, a. 13.

188. See *ST* I-II, q. 19, a. 5 and 6.

189. See *ST* I, q. 79, a. 9; *ST* I-II, q. 74, a. 2; *De veritate*, q. 15, a. 2; *In II Sent.*, d. 24, q. 2, a. 2.

St. Thomas at times made sure to address the language of his day without fully incorporating all of these elements into the increasingly Aristotelian framework of his presentation of the powers and acts of the human soul. This is not to say that his remarks on these Augustinian topics of philosophical and theological psychology are unimportant; rather, we need not seek after greater systematic coherence where it is not, in fact, to be found. Historical studies are needed, but we must never neglect the need to think philosophically and theologically, to think *within Thomism*, not merely *about Thomism*.[190]

Perhaps such coherence can be found in St. Thomas's own writings. At a certain point, however, we must simply lay out the formal structure of the problem, along with all of its various elements. Then, in light of that overall presentation—and always within the space of the Thomist school, broadly understood and vitally in dialogue with our previous masters, not limiting ourselves to narrow textual purism—we should seek an answer to such pressing questions. Whether this introduction has been *Thomasienne*,[191] I can say that its intention has been to provide an account that is *Thomiste*, echoing with the voices of the *schola Thomae*.

May this enlighten what is at stake in our selections, provide the tools for guidance in these important matters, and perhaps, in some small way, give glory to God, the true "Immobile Axis" of our divinized-moral life.

190. To this end, I recommend the exhortation found in the excellent essay by Jack Cahalan cited in note 22 above. He is perhaps more temperate in his use of language than I can be at times, but the reader should recall that my generation of Thomists were reared by masters who themselves had suffered the shipwreck of the traditional *scholae*, when the great riches of the past schools were cast aside and ignored. Our zeal is well-intentioned, and we ask only to be allowed a little bit of space as we appreciate these great riches which we have found.

191. A French term for "Thomas's own thought," although one which I fear masks the fact that what one is doing is, in fact, fashioning a new form of being a "Thomist," but one with the 1960s (or Fr. Chenu in the 1930s) as a kind "year zero." (Not all explicitly think this, of course. Yet, the language leans in this direction by its own weight.) Pure history is rarely done in such studies, which do desire to hand on St. Thomas *as a teacher today, answering problems which are felt today*. Why not merely embrace the many Thomists who have been devoted to Aquinas? This is not slavishness, nor is it a question of being uncritical. It is an act of *intellectual piety*. Without their defense of Thomas, his work almost certainly would not be extant today.

BENOÎT-HENRI MERKELBACH, O.P.

* * *

Where Should We Place the Treatise on Conscience in Moral Theology?

ORIGINAL TEXT

Benedict Merkelbach, "Note: Quelle place assigner au traité de la conscience," *Revue des sciences philosophiques et théologiques*, Vol. 12, No. 2 (1923): pp. 170–183.

Originally published in translation in *Nova et Vetera*, English Edition, Vol. 18, No. 3 (2020): pp. 1017–1037.

* * *

TRANSLATOR'S INTRODUCTION

The topic of conscience has been at the center of many ecclesial discussions of late.[1] Much is to be said positively about the desire to emphasize the importance of the inner sanctuary in which moral judgment springs forth in our lives. To refer to the heavily-cited passage from *Gaudium et Spes* §16,[2] conscience does indeed represent a profound sanctuary in the heart of the human person. From its deepest roots in faith and synderesis,[3] as well as in the gains added by moral culture, philosophy, and theology, all the way to the terminal judgment of prudence, our moral reasoning (when it is indeed right and certain) sets the human person upon the path of the personal moral and divine self-governance[4] that "existentializes" the human conquest of freedom for the good.

Very often the term "conscience" is used somewhat loosely to refer to all of these aspects of moral reasoning. For St. Thomas, it had a more specific sense, properly referring to the act of moral judgment applying moral knowledge to a particular case (see *Summa theologiae* [*ST*] I, q. 79, a. 13). In the synthetic outlook presented in the *Summa theologiae*, conscience is not treated by itself as a subject set apart. Soon after the thirteenth century, however, it became normal to discuss the nature of conscience somewhere in the neighborhood of the treatise on human acts (i.e., *ST* I-II, qq. 6–21), often swelling the discussion with later controversies and subtleties, especially those that arose in the context of the great debates over probabilism. The history became incredibly complex, and we find ourselves faced with a question: "Is this the best solution for synthetically treating the nature of conscience?"

This article is presented as providing one possible approach to answering this question, one that seems seemed quite respectable to the famed

---

1. At the original time of the drafting of this translation and introduction, many of the debates surrounding *Amoris Laetitia* were much more heated. It seems that the world of ecclesiastical discussions moves at a speed nearly as quick as does the popular media, replacing one topic with another quite rapidly. Although I share in worries that have been expressed concerning the creeping inexactness of ecclesiastical language in these matters, I am in agreement with the reading of the exhortation in question provided in Matthew Levering, *The Indissolubility of Marriage: Amoris Laetitia in Context* (San Francisco: Ignatius Press, 2019).

   That said, this article has been translated as part a broader research project, undertaken in the hope of doing some small part to articulate a Thomist account of conscience drawing upon the wisdom of the Thomist school historically as providing guiding light for a more robust articulation of conscience than what is readily fashioned if one draws solely upon the several questions devoted to conscience *ex professo* in Aquinas (e.g., *ST* I, q. 79, a. 13; I-II, q. 19, aa. 5 and 6; *De veritate*, q. 17; *In II Sent.*, d. 24, q. 2, a. 4; d. 39, q. 3, a. 1, ad 1; d. 39, q. 3, a. 2; *Quodlibet* III, q. 12). For recent discussions drawn from a different, although faithfully Catholic, hermeneutic, see David L. Schindler, "Conscience and the Relation between Truth and Pastoral Practice: Moral Theology and the Problem of Modernity," *Communio*, Vol. 46, No. 2 (2019): pp. 333–385.

2. The text is cited in *Amoris Laetitia*, §222. A stand-alone history could be written concerning the uses *and misuses* of these words during the past fifty-five years of Catholic history. An interesting study would compare this to the preconciliar schema *De ordine morali christiano*, §§7–11 ("Draft of a Dogmatic Constitution on the Christian Moral Order," trans. Fr. Joseph Komonchak, available at jakomonchak.files.wordpress.com/2012/09/on-the-christian-moral-order.pdf). There is much to be said for reading the final wording incorporated into *Gaudium et Spes* as being interpretable in line with the more conservative wording of the schema, despite the way that this text was taken up by those who wished to find discontinuity in the Council's expressions.

3. Fr. Benedict Merkelbach has made interesting recommendations regarding the way that synderesis is illuminated in the supernatural order in order to declare the universal truths that motivate Christian conscience *qua Christian and* supernatural, both in the order of the theological virtues as well as the infused moral virtues; see Merkelbach, *Summa theologiae moralis*, 5th ed., vol. 1 of 3, *De principiis* (Paris: Desclée de Brouwer, 1947), pt. 3 (*De actibus humanis*—sub-treatise *De conscientia in generali*), q. 3 (*De conscientia Christiana prout est regula actuum supernaturalium*), nos. 216–19 (1:203–6). Merkelbach cites the work of Fr. Noble, *La conscience morale* (Paris: Lethielleux, 1923); also see this same point cited by Reginald Garrigou-Lagrange in *De beatitudine* (Turin: Berruti, 1951), p. 347.

   For a recent critique of this recommendation, see Paul Rambert, "Conscience et loi naturelle dans les manuels d'avant Vatican II," *Revue thomiste*, Vol. 119 (July–September 2019), pp. 428–29. Rambert's article contains much of interest and use in the matters discussed in detail below in note 7. The reader should take care, however, regarding the use of Dom Odo Lottin, whose systematic work is questionable in comparison to his historical erudition. Whatever might be the case, a *Thomist* position concerning moral principles *cannot* limit itself merely to synderesis as a natural moral norm, for not only will the entire domain of acts of faith, hope, and charity be left out of consideration but, moreover, the entire domain of the infused moral virtues will be unexplained (for natural synderesis will *never* declare a word concerning the ends of moral virtues proportioned to the supernatural ends given through grace).

4. This is an expression containing great power, used by Fr. Ambroise Gardeil in "La faculté de Gouvernement," in *La vraie vie chrétienne* (Paris: Desclée de Brouwer, 1935), pp. 101–89. This volume is scheduled for publication in translation by Catholic University of America Press in early 2022.

Thomist Fr. Garrigou-Lagrange.[5] In the text presented here by *Nova et Vetera*, Fr. Benedict Merkelbach (the author of the erudite and lengthy *Summa theologiae moralis*[6]) presents the results of his own research concerning these matters, providing a historical outline of the problem of conscience in the tradition of Catholic moral theology, as well as his opinion that a significant portion of this discussion should be conducted explicitly within the context of the treatise on prudence. Merkelbach and Garrigou-Lagrange[7] argued that if right and certain conscience is the judgment declared as prudence's *dictamen*-judgment (in distinction from the

5. See Reginald Garrigou-Lagrange, "Remarks Concerning the Metaphysical Character of St. Thomas's Moral Theology," pp. 245–270.

6. See Merkelbach, *Summa theologiae moralis*.

7. It is important to note, however, that a significant vein of critique exists among Thomists on this very point. Some are concerned about this annexation of conscience to the virtue of prudence, and this concern is understandable. Thomas's texts do at times emphasize the "speculative" character of conscience, to the point that some authors have seemed to hold that it is a purely speculative judgment and not a speculatively-practical judgment. On the meaning of this latter expression, coming from the later Thomist school, see my remarks in "Appendix 2: On the Speculatively-Practical, and the Practically-Practical," in Garrigou-Lagrange, "Remarks Concerning the Metaphysical Character of St. Thomas's Moral Theology," pp. 266–70.

In any case, I find that the main dividing line seems to be drawn between those who would have conscience be *only* a kind of judgment of "moral science"—that is, reflective moral thought, a kind of casuistic judgment (in moral philosophy and moral theology), not ordered *at all* to the direction of *one's own acts* but merely to the analysis of cases—and those who would say that conscience extends, also, beyond such scientific casuistry, to the domain of prudential (or imprudential) reasoning. Here, in the latter domain, the judgment of conscience no longer applies to any X whatsoever but, rather, to the acting subject himself or herself. It is important to remember that prudential reasoning does not *merely* pick up a judgment emanating from "moral science" in order to readily apply its not-fully-concretized judgment to the acting subject. Rather, this judgment would serve merely as a preliminary in the practical *discursus* involved in the prudential activity of deliberation. Much work remains to be done in order to arrive, then, at the terminal judgment of prudence, for a moral-scientific casuistical judgment still remains at a great remove from the full particularization of the act in question *for me, here and now, given my own character, weaknesses, strengths, circumstances, etc.*

When I first translated this article two years ago, I was an unqualified adherent to Merkelbach's and Garrigou-Lagrange's language on this topic. It was, however, the reading of an essay by Fr. Pius-Mary Noonan, O.S.B., that changed the strength of my claim here, finally realizing, for instance, what separated myself from the explanations given by thinkers like Fr. Cajetan Cuddy and Ralph McInerny, who distinguish conscience and prudence more cleanly than I generally do. I was (and still remain) wary of the fact that too often this latter position renders moral science too completely *speculative* and not *speculatively practical*. And on this head, I remain deeply indebted to what is found in Jacques Maritain, "Appendix VII: 'Speculative' and 'Practical,'" in *The Degrees of Knowledge*, trans. Gerald B. Phelan, et al. (Notre Dame, IN: University of Notre Dame Press, 2002), pp. 481–89. Although Maritain himself seems to carefully distinguish conscience and prudence, he refers to concretized moral reasoning as "conscience" as well, even as

imperium directing execution of the act), the only way to have a complete account of conscience is to discuss it in the company of the great host of

---

included in prudential reasoning (in the order of deliberation, if not the terminal practico-practical judgment guiding the will's choice). See the insightful chapter "La rectitude du vouloir," in Jacques Maritain, *Loi naturelle ou Loi non-écrite*, ed. Georges Brazzola (Fribourg: University Editions, 1986), pp. 63–78; cf. Maritain, *Existence and the Existent*, trans. Lewis Galantiere and Gerald B. Phelan (New York: Pantheon, 1948), p. 52, n. 3.

For two excellent histories and overviews on these two main veins of thought, see the following, superb studies: Reginald G. Doherty, *The Judgments of Conscience and Prudence* (River Forest, IL: Aquinas Libray, 1961); P.-M. Noonan, "Auriga et Genetrix: Le rôle de la prudence dans le jugement de la conscience," *Revue thomiste*, Vol. 114 (2014): pp. 355–377 and 531–568. For several others who voice similar concerns as those raised by Noonan, see: Michel Labourdette, *Les actes humains* (Paris: Parole et Silence, 2016), pp. 204–245; Labourdette, "Morales de la conscience et vertu de prudence," *Revue thomiste*, Vol. 50 (1950): pp. 209–227; Cajetan Cuddy, "St. Thomas Aquinas on Conscience," in *Christianity and the Laws of Conscience: An Introduction*, ed. Helen M. Alvaré and Jeffrey B. Hammond (Cambridge: Cambridge University Press, 2021); Ralph McInerny, "Prudence and Conscience" *The Thomist*, Vol. 38, No. 2 (1974): pp. 291–305.

Nonetheless, I cannot help but feel that *contemporary language* discusses conscience in a way that applies not merely to *moral science* but also to *personal-existentialized* moral reasoning. We cannot bend terms to fit a vocabulary that is no longer in use among our contemporaries (or, truth be told, by ourselves). I think Thomists lose the intellectual fight by a too-strict employment of a vocabulary which even Aquinas himself did not develop in detail. Here, as a matter of methodology, I am of like mind with the sage words expressed in John C. Cahalan, "On the Training of Thomists," in *The Future of Thomism*, ed. Deal W. Hudson and Dennis W. Moran (Notre Dame, IN: American Maritain Association, 1992), pp. 133–47.

Hence, voices like Fr. Garrigou-Lagrange's and Fr. Merkelbach's remain important in trying to craft a way forward in these matters. Moreover, St. Thomas himself seems to talk about conscience *both* in relation to personal-prudential reasoning and in relation to "moral-scientific-casuistic" reasoning. The texts cited by Fr. Cajetan Cuddy show the latter clearly enough. To name merely one text testifying to the former bent, consider this portion of the body of St. Thomas, *De veritate*, q. 17, a. 1: "Now, we use the word, 'conscience,' for both of these modes of application. Indeed, *inasmuch as knowledge* [*scientia*] *is applied to an act as directive of that act*, conscience is said to prod, urge, or bind. Inasmuch, however, as knowledge [*scientia*] is applied to an act by examining those things *which have already been done* conscience is thus said to accuse or cause remorse, when what has been done is found to be out of harmony with the knowledge [*scientia*] in light of which it is examined, or to defend or excuse when what has been done is found to have proceeded in accord with due reasoning [*secundum formam scientiae*]."

Perhaps such directing belongs solely to the order of moral-scientific reasoning. The use of *scientia* here in this early-career text of Aquinas could mean "moral science" or could merely mean "discursive reasoning" broadly speaking, whether practical or speculative in its mode of resolution. Later in his career, he would attribute to Augustine this kind of broad use of "science" (see *ST* II-II, q. 47, a. 4, ad 1). I admit, however, that later in his career, he does not use *conscientia* in the treatise on prudence. We are not here adjudicating whether this is of significance as regards his terminology and the development of his thought. I merely note this ambiguity, which is present throughout, for instance, the work of Beaudouin and Gardeil, bearing witness to an imprecision in the Angelic Doctor's own vocabulary. (Lest I raise too much ire for making such a claim, however, I happily will accept the well-grounded findings of others if brought forth.)

virtues that are annexed to prudence, aiding in the lofty and difficult task of rectifying our natural and supernatural self-government in the moral and divine life. We thus come to see conscience as being centrally involved in the "conquest of the good" that is the task of prudence. Prudence provides the context within which further discussions can then take place: the necessity of the virtues for rectitude of will in relation to the *ends* of the acquired and infused moral virtues, the relationship of prudence to faith, synderesis, and "moral science" (as well as moral culture), the perfection of prudence by the Spirit's gift of counsel, the nature of practical truth as helping us understand the certitude involved in conscience, and so forth. Yet, before the specific details are considered, it is best to know the general terrain. Why not turn to a great master of a former age to consider this matter—especially when that master provides us with an erudite article like the one being presented here?

Therefore, the intention of this translation is not to provide a mere "throwback" to past thought on the matter of conscience. Rather, it is to provide the reader with arguably one of the sagest Thomistic accounts concerning conscience presented by one of the great pedagogues of preconciliar moral theology. We will not find in the past all of the answers to the questions pressing upon the Church today concerning this much-vexed topic. Nonetheless, in all such matters, I think that most of us find ourselves to be beginners and learners, and whatever may be the case for the reader, I know well the fruit I have personally drawn from listening to those sage words of Aristotle's *De sophisticis elenchis*, cited on occasion by Aquinas: *oportet addiscentem credere*, as the old Blackfriars translation expressed it so charmingly: "It behooves the learner to believe" (*ST* II-II, q. 2, a. 3). In order to make new progress on these topics, let us first turn to a master, ourselves forearmed with docility, that great tool in the exercise of all forms of prudence—even academic prudence! Well-armed

If, however, the aforementioned application is performed in relation to *my* act (hence prodding, urging, or binding *me*), then we find ourselves in the domain of prudential reasoning, for moral science is one thing and prudential reasoning another, even if they are closely interrelated. Here, for whatever differences I have voiced in the past (and feel in the present, especially concerning a slight overemphasis on the *speculative* in the speculatively-practical domain), I find myself in agreement with the main thrust of the argument made in Reese, "The End of Ethics: A Thomistic Investigation."

In the end, at least to my eyes, "conscience" in Aquinas himself seems to straddle both moral science and prudence, and therefore, the way forward is for Thomists to lay out a teaching that is concerned with the problem and not with solely textual studies.

in this manner, we can indeed be that wise scribe of whom our Lord said, "Therefore every scribe who has been trained for the kingdom of heaven is like a householder who brings out of his treasure what is new and what is old" (Mt. 13:52; RSV).

* * *

WHERE SHOULD WE PLACE THE TREATISE ON CONSCIENCE IN MORAL THEOLOGY?

Benoît-Henri Merkelbach, O.P.

Through the course of the centuries, the theology of conscience has undergone notable development, above all from the time when Bartholomé de Medina, O.P., systematized moderate probabilism (1577). Moreover, discussion surrounding this topic continued its development in the wake of the controversies between the tutiorists and probabiliorists on the one hand and between the probabilists and laxists on the other (ca. 1650).

Before this (above all, from the thirteenth century onward), conscience was principally discussed in the treatise on human acts. In that treatise, however, such discussions were limited solely to the establishment of the general principles involved: "What is conscience? Why is it the rule of our acts? How does it bind, accuse, or excuse? What are the qualities required of it, especially as regards truth and certitude?" In speculative moral theology, true conscience and erroneous conscience (considered both as invincibly and vincibly erroneous) were discussed.[1] Sometimes (above all in specific questions addressed in the "moral summas" and "penitential cases"[2]) doubtful conscience was discussed.

Once this teaching began to undergo development, it quite naturally continued to be exposited in the context of human acts, adding to this discussion all the various questions which arise concerning conscience. Medina inaugurated this methodology, and it was taken up by all the principal commentators on St. Thomas, as well as by all the great theologians of the age. In this vein, the theory of conscience continued to be part of the treatise on human acts. Besides Medina, we can find[3] among the Dominicans [the following writers following this methodology]: Diego Alvarez (†1635); John of St. Thomas (†1644); Labat (†1670), Contenson (†1674); Gonet (†1681); Grossi (†1704); Gotti (†1742); Billuart (†1757); and Gazzaniga (†1799). Among the Jesuits: Azor (†1603); Vasquez (†1604); Suarez (†1617); Becan (†1624); Pallavicini (†1667); Platel (†1678); the professors of Würtzburg (1766–1771); and more recently Fr. Pesch. Among the Franciscans: Herincx (†1678); Reiffenstuel (†1704); and Henno (†1713). Finally, among the Belgian clergy: Wiggers (†1639) and Daelman (†1731), professors at Louvain; Sylvius (†1649), a theologian from Douai; and Perin (†1724), a professor at the Seminary of Namur. This is even the case for J.-B. Du Hael (†1706), for Tournely (†1729) at the Sorbonne, and for Laloux (†1853).[4]

The importance of this subject soon led many authors to compose a special treatise, separated from the treatise on human acts.[5] Neesen (†1679) and the Dominicans John Syrus de Uvadano (†1727) and Preingné (†1752) placed it between the treatise on human acts and the treatise on sin, setting all of these treatises before the treatise on law: Human Acts—Conscience—Sins—Laws. By contrast, Henry of St. Ignatius (†1720), Schmier (†1728) and Dens (†1775) followed the order: Human Acts—Sins—Conscience—Laws. In Boudart (†1707), we already

---

1. See St. Albert the Great, *Summa de creaturis*, pt. 2 (*de homine*), qq. 71–72; St. Thomas, *ST* I-II, q. 19, aa. 3, 5, and 6; *De veritate*, q. 17, a. 4; *In II Sent.*, d. 39, q. 3, a. 3; St. Bonaventure, *In II Sent.*, q. 39; Giles of Rome, *In II Sent.*, d. 39; and Scotus's discussion of this distinction in the *Reportatio parisiensis*.

   [Translator's Note: No indication is given as to which *reportatio* of Scotus's Parisian lectures is in reference here.]

2. See St. Thomas, *Quodlibet* VIII, q. 6, aa. 3 and 5, and IX, q. 7, a. 2. See also, St. Albert the Great, *Summa de creaturis*, pt. 2 (*de homine*), q. 72; Scotus, *In I Sent.*, prol., a. 2, no. 15; William of Paris [*Gul. Paris*], *De coll. Benef.*, a. 8; Jean Gerson, *De Praep. Ad mis.*, cons. 3.

3. We do not intend to furnish a complete classification. Even less is it our intention to undertake a full and continuous history of the treatise on conscience. Here, we will limit ourselves to citing the principal authors, above all those whom we have at hand.

4. Fr. de la Barre (in *La Morale d'après saint Thomas et les anciens scolastiques*) cites also Valentia, S.J. (†1603), Tanner, S.J. (†1632), Arriaga, S.J. (†1622), Ysambert (†1642), Arauxo, O.P. (†1664), and Salas, S.J. (†1612). We have not, however, been able to verify his accuracy on this matter.

5. Preparation for this change can be found in many theologians listed in the preceding category (such as Suarez and John of St. Thomas), who, while continuing to study conscience in the treatise on human acts, made it into a distinct chapter, which they relegated to the end of the treatise.

find the layout that will be dear to many modern theologians: Human Acts—Conscience—Laws—Sins.[6]

Already before this, the subject had taken on such importance in other authors that it overtook the importance of the treatise on human acts and was placed at the head of these treatises. Inspiration in this direction was able to be drawn from St. Antoninus, O.P. (†1459), who in his *Summa theologica moralis* follows a wholly idiosyncratic plan, beginning with the soul and its faculties, studying conscience (an act of the mind) before speaking about the will and voluntary acts. In any case, Laymann, S.J. (†1635), adopted the order: Conscience—Human Acts—Sins—Laws. Sporer, O.F.M. (†1714), followed him, while suppressing the treatise on laws, whereas Roncaglia (†1733) ordered them: Conscience—Human Acts—Laws—Sins. Illsung, S.J. (†1695): Conscience—Laws—Human Acts—Sins. And in contrast, Cuniliati, O.P. (†1759): Conscience—Laws—Sins—Human Acts.

In his *Medulla*, Busenbaum, S.J. (†1668), completely suppressed the utterly essential and fundamental moral treatise,[7] namely the treatise on human acts, probably on the pretext that students had acquired knowledge about it in their study of moral philosophy. He places the treatise on conscience at the head of his discussions, followed by the treatise on laws, relegating the treatise on sins to the more specific treatises on moral theology,[8] after the study of the commandments of the Decalogue! This plan was followed by Mazzotta (†1746) and by those who commented on Busenbaum, like Lacroix (†1714) and St. Alphonsus (†1787), who nonetheless interposed a small treatise on human acts before the treatise on sins.

Antoine, S.J. (†1743), no longer had a treatise on human acts. He presupposed and followed the order Conscience—Laws—Sins, though

6. He probably is not the first to do so. We have not discovered the origin of this ordering.

7. Translator's Note: The assertion is surprising, given that *the fundamental* treatise of moral theology is the treatise on beatitude. Hence, we have, for example, the lengthy five-volume commentary *De beatitudine* by Fr. Ramirez. And Fr. Merkelbach himself does not neglect this fact in his own *Summa theologiae moralis*. However, it seems that here he has perhaps slightly fallen prey to the spirit of the moral theology of his age.

8. Translator's Note: The traditional expressions "special moral theology" and "general moral theology" are a bit opaque in contemporary English. Roughly speaking, the division for Thomists was between the various treatises on the virtues found in the *Secunda secundae* and the more general principles discussed in the *Prima secundae*. It is rendered freely in this translation.

without separating them by any interval. This plan prevailed in modern theologians who preceded it with the treatise on human acts, which they reintroduced (Human Acts—Conscience—Laws—Sins). This order can be found in Collet (†1770), Voit (†1780), Gousset, Gury, Scavini, Van der Velden, Haine, Raphaël of St. Joseph, Pruner, Génicot, and others. Even among the Redemptorists, we find Konings and Aertnijs [following this order].[9] Likewise, this order is found in Lehmkuhl, who, however, detaches the question on probabilism from the treatise on conscience in order to place it in the treatise on laws. Again, it is found in Ballerini, who comments on Busenbaum and who, in order to remedy his deficiencies, composed an outline *de actibus humanis*, which he placed, by way of commentary, at the head of his entire work.

In addition to these general methodologies, some authors followed their own, idiosyncratic approaches. Noël Alexander, O.P. (†1724), follows the plan of the Catechism of the Council of Trent and inserts the treatise on conscience into the treatise on sins. Bonacina (†1631) had already done the same before this. And the Salamanca Carmelite moralists (1665–1724) combined the sequence Human Acts—Conscience—Sins into a single treatise, *de principiis moralitatis*, though they completely separated it from the treatise on laws.

Patuzzi, O.P. (†1769), first discusses the rules of morality: laws and conscience. Then he discusses the principles of morality: acts, virtues, and sins. Others still, like Müller and Bouquillon among contemporary authors, place the treatise on laws in the first place, then conscience, thus finishing with the treatise on human acts. This represents a confusion between the order of juridical science and the order of ethics. The former begins by studying the laws and envisions everything from their perspective. The latter has our actions as its proper and immediate object, given that it is the directive science of these acts. It studies other topics (i.e., laws, habits, virtues, faculties, motions, influences) only inasmuch as they are related to our acts. The theological works of Malines, Noldin, Tanquerey, and most recently Fr. Vermeersch mix together the two methodologies and adopt the plan: Human Acts—Laws—Conscience—Sins.

9. Marc, on the contrary, retains St. Alphonsus's order, although he does so while bringing the treatises on human acts and sins back into the general treatises on moral theology, immediately after the treatise on conscience and the treatise on law.

Others study conscience in a discussion set apart, which they do not integrate into the overall framework of ethics but, instead, place at its head.[10] Among these latter, we can cite Mercorus, O.P. (†1669), Thyrsus Gonzales, S.J. (†1705), and Concina, O.P. (†1756), for the probabiliorists and Terillus, S.J., for the probabilists. The outlook is the same in De Brocard ([†]1726) who, in this introduction, combines the teaching concerning acts with that concerning conscience.[11]

Finally, quite recently, Fr. Sertillanges, in his *Philosophie morale de saint Thomas d'Aquin*, places conscience in the specific ethical treatises, after the study of all the particular virtues.

* * *

How are we to orient ourselves in the midst of such chaos? Are we not forced to conclude that, in the end, it does not ultimately matter where one chooses to house the doctrine on conscience? Or, on the contrary, should we say that it ought to be assigned a determinate place? Should it be studied with human acts or, rather, should it depend on the study of laws? Does it belong to the general ethical treatises? Or, instead, should it be cut up into several sections and connected to different parts of ethical science?

In recent days, this question has been raised in explicit terms. Already in 1884, the Carmelite, Raphaël of St. Joseph, wrote:

> According to right order, the treatise on conscience follows the treatise on human acts, both because it is the *proximate and formal* rule [of human acts] and also because in the treatise on human acts we discuss the human (or, moral) act *abstractly*, whereas in the treatise on conscience, we discuss the same act *concretely*. Indeed, as we said

10. **Translator's Note:** Arguably, in context "morale" should be translated "moral theology." Yet for faithfulness and (in some cases readability) I will use the indifferent term "ethics." Nonetheless, one should recall that moral theology is not a separate discipline from theology as such but, instead, is an integral part of acquired theological wisdom. Fr. Merkelbach himself notes this point in his *Summa theologiae moralis*, vol. 1, nos. 1–6 (esp. 3). Also, Fr. Merkelbach himself is a little ambiguous at times, using expressions that are more appropriate for moral philosophy than moral theology. The reader should note this ambiguity, although his overall framework is arguably that of moral theology.

11. This work figures in the *Cursus theologiae* of Migne.

elsewhere, in *Quodlibet* III, q. 12, a. 2, St. Thomas writes, "A human act is judged to be virtuous or vicious in accord with an apprehended good, toward which the will is moved, and not in accord with the act's material object.[12]

Fr. Reginald Beaudouin, O.P., is of the same opinion:

> St. Thomas discusses this argument briefly in *Summa theologiae* I-II,[13] q. 19, aa. 5 and 6, and in passing in other places. He holds that its proper location is found in the place where he treats of the human act inasmuch as it is moral [i.e., the treatise on human acts in I-II, qq. 18–21[14]], for properly speaking, the goodness of the will depends on its object. The will's object is proposed to it by reason, however, for the understood good is the object proportioned to the will.... And therefore, the goodness of the will depends on reason in the same way that it depends upon its object (*ST* I-II, q. 19, a. 3).[15]

This opinion did not find favor before the eyes of Fr. Leonard Lehu, O.P. (to whose side Fr. Dominic Prümmer, O.P., rallies),[16] who treats of conscience after sins, *habitus*, and laws:

> Fr. Beaudouin thinks that the proper place [for discussions concerning conscience] is found in the treatise on morality, following the example of St. Thomas, who treats of conscience in *ST* I-II, q. 19, aa. 5 and 6. In response to this opinion, one can say that this was indeed the case in St. Thomas's day, when the entire question on conscience was reduced to these two questions: "Does erroneous conscience bind? Does erroneous conscience excuse?" Since the treatise on conscience nowadays

12. Raphäel of St. Joseph, *Institutiones fundamentalis theologiae moralis* (Alosti: Vernimmen, 1884), tr. 2 (*De conscientia*), in proem.
13. **Translator's Note:** Reading "II-II" as "I-II".
14. **Translator's Note:** See Leonard Lehu, "À quel point précis de la Somme théologique commence le Traité de la Moralité," *Revue Thomiste*, Vol. 33 (1928): pp. 521–532; B.-H. Merkelbach, "Le traité des actions humaines dans la morale thomiste," *Revue des sciences philosophiques et théologiques*, Vol. 15 (1926): pp. 185–207.
15. Reginald Beaudouin, *Tractatus de conscientia*, ed. Ambroise Gardeil (Paris: Gabalda, 1911), p. 4.
16. See Dominic Prümmer, *Manuale theologiae moralis*, vol. 1 (Friburg: Herder, 1914), no. 141, note 1.

> finds itself to have been greatly amplified, however, it is fair to ask ourselves: "According to the logical order, which should come first, the treatise on laws or the treatise on conscience?"
>
> *Conclusion: According to the logical order, the treatise on laws must be placed first, with the treatise on conscience coming afterwards.*
>
> *This can be proven in two ways.* (1) It is the office of conscience to apply universal laws to particular cases. Now, "Nobody can suitably apply one thing to another unless he knows both, namely both that which is to be applied and that to which it is applied" (*ST* II-II, q. 47, a. 3). Therefore, knowledge of the laws is a prerequisite for the treatise on conscience.
>
> (2) Modern treatises on conscience chiefly focus on the problem of probabilism, which is entirely concerned with the conflict between the rights of the law and rights of freedom. Thus, in such discussions, we often read, "The law is in possession [of its rights].... Freedom is in possession [of its rights]." Now, in order to justly resolve a given quarrel, the prudent judge must know the rights of both contending parties. Therefore, the controversy concerning probabilism would be settled according to the wrong order of procedure were it exposited before the rights of the law.[17]

Before this, Fr. Lehmkuhl, S.J., had certainly posed the question to himself and practically resolved it (in 1883) by dividing up the doctrine on conscience (as we saw in passing above). Considering this solution in its general outlines (and without approving all the details of applied morality that are encountered in Fr. Lehmkuhl), we believe that it could indeed be the most logical and best resolution of this matter because the doctrine of conscience, in its full breadth, contains a general part and a specific part.

The general part serves as a continuation of the theory of human acts. Indeed, it is even an integral part of this topic. Conscience is the proximate, formal, and intrinsic rule of our actions, and it is impossible to understand the general principles of conscience without knowing why, how, and in what conditions it is the sure rule. Thus, with St. Thomas, we must continue to exposit this portion in the treatise on human acts

17. Leonard Lehu, *Philosophia moralis et socialis*, vol. 1 (Paris: Gabalda, 1914), no. 341.

or must form it into a small treatise set apart, one which would follow the first part of the treatise on human acts. Indeed, logically, this part precedes the treatise on laws. In ethics, everything is studied on account of our acts, and in the study of the latter, the proximate and intrinsic rule (i.e., conscience) must logically precede the remote and extrinsic rule (i.e., law). It also precedes the study of *habitus* (i.e., virtues and vices). These latter can be the principles of human acts, but they are not a constitutive element of them.

This general part contains only the three following points: (1) conscience is the rule of our actions; (2) this rule must be practically true or right; (3) it must be certain.[18]

This subject, however, also includes a specific part. In the latter, we come to envision questions that are more practical in nature, being more determinate and more concrete, concerning the practical details involved in forming a true and certain conscience for oneself:

1. How does one acquire a right conscience?
2. How does one set aside an erroneous conscience?
3. When and how must a superior or confessor reform the erroneous conscience of his inferior or his penitent?
4. How does one educate one's conscience?
5. What kind of certitude does conscience require?
6. How does one form one's conscience in cases of negative or positive doubt?
7. When one can form only probable opinions aiming solely at

18. If we were to divide the treatise on human acts and the treatise on *habitus* into three parts, respectively envisioning according to their psychological, moral, or supernatural being, we could adopt the same division for the treatise on conscience in general:

I. On conscience according to *esse physicum* (or, psychological existence)—What is conscience? (See *ST* I, q. 79, a. 11.)

II. On conscience according to its *esse morale*:

1. It is the rule of human acts;
2. It must be right; is it a right rule when it is…
   - … true conscience?
   - … invincibly erroneous conscience?
   - … vincibly erroneous conscience?
3. It must be certain.

III. On conscience according to its *esse supernaturale*.

For this last part, inspiration could be drawn from the articles published by Fr. Noble in *Vie spirituelle*.

the permissibility or soundness of our acts, what legitimate use may one make of probable opinions?
8. What is the species or gravity of the sin of the person who acts against his conscience or with an insufficiently formed conscience?
9. And so forth...

The eighth question obviously presupposes the treatise on sins. Most of the others presuppose the treatise on laws and the general principles concerning right which are explained there, such as: *the condition of the possessor is better; a law that is in doubt does not obligate; the fact is not presumed but must be proven; [in a doubt] one must stand for the value of the act; positive biases are to be broadened, offensive ones restricted* ["Favores sunt ampliandi, odiosa restrigenda"]; a *commanding law does not obligate with a great inconvenience*; *in obscure matters, what is least* [*minimum*] *is to be held, etc.*

Therefore, the specific part [of the treatment of conscience] presupposes and applies the entire general theory of laws. Likewise, it presupposes the treatise on sins. Now, we are no longer in agreement with Fr. Lehmkuhl when he places it at the beginning of the treatise on laws. We are even less in agreement when he places the study of lax conscience and of scrupulous conscience in the general part. We believe that these issues presuppose the general ethical treatises and belong to the specific ethical treatises.

Merely scanning the statement of some of the questions that we just noted and even more so, when we read them in [treatises on conscience in works of] theology, we get the impression that we are reading treatises belonging to "special ethics" [i.e., those which treat of the various virtues], given the diversity of immediately practical applications set forth in such treatises on conscience. Indeed, this impression can only increase when the study of lax or scrupulous conscience is added to it, topics that are usually addressed in the same treatise.

Therefore, we think that the treatise on conscience must be divided up. The first part must remain among the general ethical treatises. It envisions conscience in its most *general* aspects and establishes that it is the rule of all our actions, though on the condition of possessing the two qualities of truth and certitude. The second part, which is much more considerable in size, will emerge in the specific (or, applied) ethical treatises. It will examine each of the *particular states* or *species* of conscience (true, erroneous, doubting, probable, lax, scrupulous, and perplexed) in order to see whether each is a legitimate rule of action, then the practical ways to acquire, on these various hypotheses, a sufficiently true and certain conscience, and finally the different ways that one can sin in relation to conscience.

It will be objected that this breaks up the unity of moral teaching. We respond by saying that nothing prevents one from sacrificing a little bit of unity on a particular point, like that of conscience, in view of the unity of the entirety of moral science. The synthetic order of the whole obviously must hold primacy. He who would consider the subject of conscience all by itself could not divide it up. If, however, he studies conscience from the perspective of human acts and that of the various circumstances of these acts, the general order can require him to separately consider certain parts that touch on each other so as to better connect them, respectively, to the great divisions of the whole.

Again, one may well object that it is useless for the same subject to be treated two times, for it will be necessary to repeat the general part when one addresses the specific part, on pain of not understanding the latter. In response, let us first of all note that this second objection completely destroys the first, since, by recalling and applying the principles explained in the general part, the unity of the whole doctrine will be placed in full light. The reproach of duplication, however, is unmerited. One could register the same complaint against every other general ethical treatise. If the objection had some merit, one would need to refuse to divide the sciences into a general part and a specific part. The general principles that are concerned with laws are applied to all the commandments of God and the Church. Nonetheless, one does not claim that the principles and commandments must be gathered together into a single whole. The principles of human acts have their own application and must be recalled throughout the whole of ethics. Must we conclude from this that we no longer need to study them separately, apart? The notion of sin is found in all the species of sins, and nonetheless the study of different sins does not enter into the treatise on sins in general. Thus, the study of *various states* of conscience must not enter into the treatise that considers conscience *in general*, although it presupposes the principles that are established in that treatise.

Therefore, just as we separately study, on the one hand, human acts, law, virtue, sin in general, and on the other hand, the different species of acts, of laws, of virtues, and of sins in particular, so too we must study conscience and its qualities in general in the general ethical treatises, coming to discuss, only later on, in applied ethics, the various species of conscience and the means for acquiring a conscience having all the qualities required.

The fact that this latter part itself has a universal scope does not demonstrate that it must be incorporated into general morality. Legal justice, obedience, and charity (above all the order of charity) all likewise have their own general scopes. Nonetheless, the study of these particular virtues belongs to the specific ethical treatises. Likewise, the particular virtue of prudence and the way it must proceed in order to rightly form its act well (i.e., right conscience) do not cease to belong to the specific ethical treatises merely because those virtues govern all our actions and, for this reason, exercise a universal form of influence. The only things that belong to the general ethical treatises are the principles that are completely universal, governing human acts, conscience, law, virtue, or sin, all envisioned in general.

* * *

If the doctrine on conscience predominantly belongs to the specific ethical treatises, the next question is: "Where should it be placed in that section?" Without a shade of doubt, it should be connected to the treatise on prudence. The judgment of conscience is an act commanded by prudence, though prepared and posited by the virtues that are connected to it: *euboulia* (good counsel), as well as *synesis* (good sense) and *gnome* (the sense for exceptions).[19] Therefore, the study of prudence and conscience must unhesitatingly be pursued together. As a result, the treatise on prudence will receive the unique recognition it deserves.

It is dumbfounding that the most perfect, most essential, and most fundamental of the moral virtues occupies such a diminished position in

19. *ST* II-II, q. 51, a. 2, ad 1: "It pertains to prudence to counsel (and judge) well *by commanding it*, to *euboulia* (and *synesis*) *by eliciting it*." *ST* I-II, q. 57, a. 6, ad 1: "Prudence makes use of good counsel (and judgment) not as though its *immediate* act would be to counsel well (and to judge well), for it perfects this act *by the mediation of* the virtue of *euboulia* (and *synesis*), which is subject to it.

moral science today—a quite bizarre state of affairs indeed, given that no good act can fail to be simultaneously prudent. Students and even professors are so blind to its importance that many manuals pass over it in silence, or if they do speak about it, the entire treatise is reduced to four or five pages. As soon as it is connected to conscience, its exceptional importance will stand forth in its peerless character. To bring this point to the fore, we merely need to entitle this treatise: "On prudence and the virtues connected to it, considered in the formation of conscience."

Hence, we must face the question set before us: "How should the treatise on prudence be ordered?" We will furnish two responses to this question.

The first option is to unite the theories of prudence and conscience, simultaneously envisioning the cardinal virtue and the annexed virtues, introducing the doctrine of conscience into the overall plan of prudence, such as it was constructed by St. Thomas.[20] This is what is suggested in the following table.

GENERAL CONSPECTUS

THE TREATISE ON PRUDENCE AND THE VIRTUES CONNECTED TO IT, CONSIDERED IN THE FORMATION OF CONSCIENCE

Introduction

1. On the various states of mind: doubt, opinion, and certitude with its various species.
2. What are *synderesis*, moral science, conscience and law, and prudence?
3. Definition of prudence.
4. Necessity of prudence.[21]
5. Division of the treatise.

Part 1: On Prudence in Itself

Q. 1: On the subject in which prudence inheres [i.e., the intellect-as-practical].

Q. 2: On the object of prudence.

20. See *ST* II-II, qq. 47–56.
21. See *ST* I-II, q. 57, a. 5.

- Q. 3: On the acts of prudence:
  - (a) On its acts in general.
  - (b) On conscience taken specifically.[22]
    - (i) Its definition.
    - (ii) Its various species.
    - (iii) It is the conclusion of reasoning.
    - (iv) It is the rule of human acts.
- Q. 4: On the *habitus* of prudence.
  - (a) From the perspective of being a virtue.
  - (b) From the perspective of truth: practical truth suffices (wherein true and erroneous conscience are discussed).
  - (c) From the perspective of certitude: it suffices to have practical (or, moral) certitude broadly speaking.
- Q. 5: On the cause[s] of prudence.
  - (a) On those having prudence.
  - (b) On the generation, increase, and corruption of prudence.

Part 2. On the Parts of Prudence

- Q. 1: On its integral parts.
- Q. 2: On its subjective parts.
- Q. 3: On its potential parts.
  - (a) On those parts in general.[23]
  - (b) On *euboulia*, which is a prequisite in deliberation for the formation of right conscience:
    - (i) On the obligation of employing solicitude in the formation of one's conscience.
    - (ii) The means to be employed in its formation.
    - (iii) The forming of right conscience in oneself and in others.
  - (c) On *synesis* and *gnome* in the formation of certain conscience:
    - (i) In a negative doubt.
    - (ii) In a positive doubt.
    - (iii) In a state of opinion.

22. This consists in a summary of what had been explained in the treatise on conscience in general.
23. The special gift of the Holy Spirit called "counsel" could be introduced here.

(iv) In a state of perplexity.
(v) In a state of scrupulosity or of laxity.

Conclusion: On the practical formation of certain conscience in oneself and in others.

Part 3. On the Sins Opposed to Prudence

Q. 1: On sins opposed by defect.

(a) On imprudence in general and on the sin of acting against conscience.
(b) On precipitancy and on the sin of acting without right conscience (i.e., with a vincibly erroneous conscience).
(c) On thoughtlessness and on the sin of acting without a certain conscience.
(d) On inconstancy and on the sin of acting with a scrupulous conscience.
(e) On negligence and on the sin of acting with a lax conscience.[24]

Q. 2: On sins opposed by excess...

(a) On false prudence.
(b) On craftiness.
(c) On guile and fraud.
(d) On excessive solicitude.

Prudence could, however, just as well be studied separately by following the order established by St. Thomas and then adding the treatise on the annexed virtues envisioned from the perspective of the formation of conscience, thus adopting, for example, the following plan.

GENERAL CONSPECTUS

THE TREATISE ON PRUDENCE AND THE VIRTUES CONNECTED TO IT, CONSIDERED IN THE FORMATION OF CONSCIENCE

(*To be placed immediately after the treatise on prudence ordered in accord with St. Thomas's treatise*)

24. Scrupulous conscience and lax conscience could be connected to precipitancy and thoughtlessness.

Introduction

1. The virtues connected to prudence exist so that the judgment of conscience may be rightly formed. Indeed, good counsel is ordered to the right practical judgment through which counsel/deliberation is brought to its terminus, just as the right practical judgment is ordered to the command that commands the judgment of execution. Therefore, just as commanding is the proper and most important act of prudence itself, so too the judgment of conscience (which is formed from prerequisite counsel and in accord with which prudence's command must itself be rendered) is the proper or most important act of the annexed virtues which prudence utilizes for its own end. Thus, after we have spoken about prudence itself, we now come to those things that must be said concerning the virtues connected to it, viewed from the perspective of the practical formation of conscience.

2. From general moral theology, we know:

(a) What conscience is and how it is distinguished from synderesis, moral science, law, and prudence;
(b) That it is the conclusion of [practico-moral] reasoning;
(c) That it is the proximate and subjective rule of human acts;
(d) And that, however, in order for it to be such a rule it must be right (from the perspective of its object) and certain (from the perspective of the subject).

3. Having posited these points, since we do not always have right and certain conscience immediately and easily, we must now investigate how one is to proceed prudently in practice in order to form a conscience that is right and certain in the various states or circumstances that are involved in conscience's activity.

All the defective states of conscience, just as well are reduced to three categories: a defect in truth, a defect in certitude, and a defect in truth together with a defect in certitude. Therefore, we must discuss:

(1) The discovery and formation of right conscience for the sake of removing errors (this belongs, in particular, to *euboulia* because rectitude in judgment especially depends upon preceding deliberation).
(2) The formation of certain conscience for the sake of doing away with uncertainty (this is particularly concerned with *synesis* or *gnome* because certitude is a quality of judgment).

(3) The way to form right and certain conscience in a case of uncertainty that is coupled with error (where aspects of both *euboulia* and *synesis* are observed together).

Part 1: On the Formation of Right Conscience for the Sake of Removing Errors

Q. 1: On the obligation to undertake the inquiry [of counsel] with care and to form a right and true conscience, as well as concerning the means for achieving this.

Q. 2: On the species of conscience considered from the perspective of the object (i.e., from the perspective of rectitude).

Having established the inquiry needed for the discovery of [the judgment of] conscience, when we consider matters from the perspective of conscience's object, we know that this can be either true or erroneous (whether vincibly or invincibly). Hence, we must ask whether there are several rules for acting prudently (i.e., in a practically certain manner):

(a) On true conscience.

(b) On invincibly erroneous conscience.

(c) On vincibly erroneous conscience.

Q. 3. On the practical formation of right conscience in oneself and in others (on how to discern erroneous conscience—on how to set it aside—on the obligation to teach those who labor under erroneous conscience—on the education of conscience)

Part 2: On the Formation of Certain Conscience for the Sake of Eliminating Uncertainty

1. On various states of mind: doubt, opinion, certitude, and their various species.

2. After bringing a diligent inquiry and deliberation to its close, man either arrives at direct certitude of conscience or remains in a state of doubt or opinion. Hence, we ask:

(a) What kind of certitude suffices so that conscience may be the rule of acting prudently and in a practically certain manner?

(b) In the case of doubt or of opinion, how can someone (in accord with prudence) form an indirectly certain conscience which is the rule of acting prudently, doing so in a practically certain manner?

3. Various systems have been devised in order to resolve these questions.

Q. 1: On the quality of the certitude required for conscience

Q. 2: On the species of conscience, considered from the perspective of the subject and of certitude:

(a) On negatively doubtful conscience.
(b) On positively doubtful conscience.
(c) On opining or probable conscience.
(d) On the right and prudent use of probable opinions.

Q. 3: On the practical formation of certain conscience in oneself and in others.

Q. 4: On the sin of the person acting against conscience.

Part 3: On the Formation of Right and Certain Conscience in the Case of Uncertainty Together with Error

A single question on the species of conscience considered from the perspective of the object and the subject at once:

(a) On perplexed conscience.
(b) On lax conscience (definition and division—signs—causes and effects—remedies—imputability).
(c) On scrupulous conscience[25] (definition—signs—causes and effects—remedies—imputability—methods for directing scrupulous people)

We did not wish to consider, in a disconnected manner, each of the virtues that are connected to prudence. Indeed, for now, the best position seems to be that *synesis* and *gnome* undergo the same process in forming the judgment of certain conscience. The only difference that exists between them arises from the principles that they invoke.[26] With regard to

25. We take the words "lax conscience" and "scrupulous conscience" in the proper sense of an actual judgment, and not, like many theologians, in the sense of a habitual disposition to scruples or laxity.

26. If one were of another opinion on this matter, one could add a part: "On *gnome* in the

the counsel of *euboulia* and the judgment of *synesis* or of *gnome*, these two acts naturally call for each other: judgment presupposes certain deliberation, and deliberation is brought to its close by a judgment.

Therefore, good conscience simultaneously flows from two virtues.

As we indicated on the plans erected above, however, *euboulia* plays a preponderant role in the formation of right and true conscience, whereas *synesis* and *gnome* play a preponderant role in the formation of certain conscience. The rectitude (or truth) of a [practico-moral] judgment principally depends on one's prior deliberation, whereas certitude depends above all on the judgment itself. This seems to be in conformity with St. Thomas's doctrine:

> To one ultimate end, which is to live well in a complete manner, there are ordered various acts according to a kind of gradation, for counsel precedes, judgment follows, and finally there is the command which is related to the ultimate end. The other two acts are, however, remotely related to each other. Nonetheless, they themselves have certain proximate ends: counsel has the end of *discovering those things that* (truly) *must be done* and judgment has *certitude* as its end.[27]

This is why erroneous conscience declaring an evil course of action to be taken is a defect of *euboulia*, and the craftiness that seeks false ways is an abuse of counsel:

> There is no good counsel involved either in taking counsel (or, deliberating) for an evil end, or in discovering evil means for arriving at a good end—akin to how, in speculative matters, one fails in one's reasoning either by coming to a false conclusion or by arriving at a true conclusion on the basis of false premises because one has not made use of a suitable middle term [in one's reasoning]. And therefore, each of the aforementioned cases are contrary to the notion of *euboulia*.[28]

formation of certain conscience." St. Antoninus (*Summa*, pt. 1, tit. 3, ch. 10) seems to connect the reformation of scrupulous conscience to equity (ἐπιείκεια [*epieikeia*]) and consequently to *gnome*. Cajetan, however, limits the role of equity to the cases in which the law becomes harmful.

27. See *ST* II-II, q. 51, a. 2, ad 2.

28. *ST* II-II, q. 52, a. 1, ad 1; see also q. 55, a. 3, ad 2.

By emphasizing these different roles, one could entitle the first part of the second plan laid out above, "On *euboulia* in the formation of right conscience," and the second part, "On *synesis* and *gnome* in the formation of certain conscience." In the third part, counsel and judgment will be of nearly equal importance: "On *euboulia* and *synesis* in the formation of conscience that is simultaneously right and certain."

* * *

Of the two methods syncretized in the two tables that we laid out above, our preferences, quite frankly, stand with the second. First of all, it respects the excellent ordering of the treatise on prudence as it was conceived of by St. Thomas. It would be a shame to break up this marvelous unity or even to cast the slightest shadow over it. Moreover, it helps to emphasize the perfect unity of the teaching concerning the formation of conscience by synthesizing it into a single whole.

Moreover, St. Thomas always treats the annexed virtues, their acts, and the sins opposed to them after having treated the cardinal virtue in question. It is quite astonishing that he made an exception for prudence and did not raise specific questions for the virtues that are connected to it. The second method attempts to fill in this lacuna, all the while remaining within the general framework of the *Summa theologiae*. This is also the method that we have adopted for our students.[29]

29. Translator's Note: As always, I owe a debt of gratitude to the editors at *Nova et Vetera*, whose careful eyes are always such a great help in the process of reworking and editing translations. Likewise, I am grateful to Mr. David Capan, who kindly helped in the editing of this article with a spirit of true generosity.

MICHEL LABOURDETTE, O.P.

* * *

Comments on Conscience

ORIGINAL TEXT

Michel Labourdette, *Les actes humains*, "Grand cours" de théologie morale, vol. 2 (Paris: Parole et Silence, 2016), pp. 204–245.

* * *

TRANSLATOR'S INTRODUCTION

This text is drawn from the course notes of Fr. Michel Labourdette, O.P., published recently by the *Revue Thomiste*. Together with Fr. Marie-Joseph Nicolas and Raymond-Léopold Bruckberger, he was engaged in the polemics surrounding the *Nouvelle théologie* crisis in the 1940s, articulating a position that was harmonious with that presented by their older confrère, Fr. Reginald Garrigou-Lagrange. Likewise, he spent many years as the editor of the *Revue thomiste* and was a *peritus* at the Second Vatican Council.

As one of the great pedagogues of moral theology of the twentieth century, Fr. Labourdette deserves a hearing as someone testifying to these matters from within the Thomist school. He is less well-known than his fellow Dominican moral theologian, Fr. Servais Pinckaers—an unfortunate fact, for Fr. Labourdette's presentation of moral theology is much in harmony with Fr. Pinckaers's, while maintaining closer contacts with the earlier Dominican-Thomist school of theology.

In this text, Fr. Labourdette discusses, in outline, a number of the problems involved in the topic of conscience. He is less sanguine than Fr. Beaudouin concerning some of the developments that occurred during later scholasticism and in the modern era. His position deserves a hearing in order to provide a sober critique of casuistry and the overburdening of moral theology with questions of conscience. As is reflected in the text below, I have chosen to avoid rhetorically altering the rather dry style of his course notes.

* * *

COMMENTS ON CONSCIENCE

Michel Labourdette, O.P.

ARTICLES 5 AND 6: THE PROBLEM OF CONSCIENCE

In articles 5 and 6, St. Thomas asks himself about what happens to the morality of one's act when reason errs by following or thwarting a "*ratio errans*," an erring reason. Indeed, at the beginning of each of these articles, he will be content with tersely noting that this problem is exactly the same as that which is posed, in other terms, when one asks whether "erroneous conscience" compels one to act or, instead, excuses. Here, in our treatise on morality, this will be the only express inquiry into moral conscience and, in fact, throughout the whole of the *Secunda pars*, St. Thomas will not return to it. Yes, here and there he will use the term "conscience," as does everyone, but nowhere will we find him fashioning even the smallest "treatise" devoted to it.

Now, you merely need to open up a modern manual of moral theology in order to be quite well apprised that the idea of conscience has there, by contrast, become the central notion guiding practically the entire systematization of moral science. Not only has the very treatise on conscience (along with the treatise on laws, which is closely connected with the treatise on conscience) become the great treatise of general moral theology [*morale générale*], taking on greater importance than the treatise on the last end, but, moreover, we find that the other treatises come to be elaborated in function of the treatise on conscience and in accord with the categories specified therein.

Clearly, for some cause or other, wrongly or rightly, the perspective has here profoundly shifted. We will need to ask about this alteration, which was immensely important, not only for the scientific elaboration of morality but even for the commonly-held outlook held by most people, as well as for a particular, rather-common conception of the Christian life.

Let us begin, however, by speaking about St. Thomas's text. Thereafter, I will discuss modern moralities of conscience.

I. MORAL CONSCIENCE ACCORDING TO ST. THOMAS

The best means for understanding the brief texts in the *Summa theologiae* is to illuminate them by [St. Thomas's] earlier texts. We find that he dedicated one of the disputed questions *De veritate* (namely q. 17) to the topic of conscience. We will read the whole of it, for it only is made up of five articles. Then, we will reflect on the text of the *Summa theologiae.* [The basic texts of St. Thomas to be considered are:]

1. The Disputed Question *De conscientia* (*De veritate*, q. 17).
2. Articles 5 and 6 of our text in *ST* I-II, q. 19.

[We will first begin with] the Disputed Question *De conscientia*:

- *On the nature and character of Conscience*
  - What is it? (a. 1)
  - Is it fallible? (a. 2)
- *On the obligation imposed by Conscience*
  - Does it obligate? (a. 3)
  - Does it obligate even if it is erroneous? (a. 4)
  - In indifferent matters does it obligate more than a religious superior's command? (a. 5)

1. *On the Nature of Conscience*

What is the referent for the term "conscience"? Is it a faculty, a *habitus*, or an act? And if, as will be shown in article 1, it is an act, what are its characteristics? In other words: is it subject to error?

De veritate, q. 17, a. 1: *Is conscience a power, a* habitus, *or an act?*

ANNOTATION

Let us set aside St. Thomas's particular remarks dedicated, in passing, to conscience considered as a judgment of existence ("psychological conscience"). We certainly could say much more about this particular topic, for example, by drawing on what St. Thomas says concerning self-knowledge. This is not the place, however, to discuss this topic. It is mentioned here only to situate the issue of moral conscience, which is the essential concern in this question. How does St. Thomas conceive of it?

1. To our eyes, moral conscience seems to be an act of practical reason, although one which ultimately is not, properly speaking, elicited by a particular *habitus* but, rather, depends on many different kinds of *habitus*, as well as on a whole host of various kinds of knowledge, both currently experienced and also retained in our memory. It is essentially an application of what one knows (in the broad sense of the word "to know") to the evaluation of a particular act, either to be performed or already performed.

Undoubtedly, the fundamental element of such applied knowledge is whatever one derives from the *habitus* which is called *synderesis*, a *habitus* having a constitution in line with the *habitus* known as *intellectus*, insight into first principles. Through *synderesis*, reason grasps and formulates for itself, in normative judgments, the first moral principles, the main, self-evident elements of the natural law. When faced with something presented as being good, we grasp that we must do it and that we must avoid that which is presented as being evil. We grasp this as immediately as we do the principle of identity or the principle of *raison d'être*,[1] at least *in actu exercito* and without immediately reflecting upon them.

For an intellect such as ours, however, which is essentially a "*ratio*," a discursively reasoning intellect, no intuitive grasp [of principles] suffices or leads knowledge to its terminus. An entire investigation takes shape here, a *dicursus*, all in accord with the data of experience and the first forms of evidential knowledge. This *discursus* strives (where it can) to attain scientific certitude [that is, discursive, certain conclusions based upon the first principles guiding the *discursus*]. Most often and in most cases, it remains infra-scientific, either because of our failure to reach the necessary universality (something that does not prevent it from being certain in

1. Translator's Note: Many would call this the principle of sufficient reason. By this term, he means "the principle concerning the way that things variously have reasons for their being." He likely draws this terminology from his teacher, Fr. Reginald Garrigou-Lagrange, who generally was quite careful not to call the "principle of *raison d'être*" the "principle of sufficient reason." See Reginald Garrigou-Lagrange, "On the Search for Definitions According to Aristotle and St. Thomas," *Philosophizing in Faith*, pp. 25–26, n. 6.

particular cases) or because it does not reach certitude and leads the mind solely to an opinion, or perhaps even does not suffice to help it emerge from doubt. All of this constitutes an ensemble of insights which are of use for each person in thinking about his life and acts.

Moral conscience will simply be the act by which the mind gathers together and applies to a particular case all the various kinds of knowledge that can be of use in illuminating it, all depending on the need at hand: *synderesis*, moral science, infra-scientific convictions and opinions, experience, memory, and so forth. In this act, various *habitus* are exercised and refined. Conscience is not, however, the act of any of them in particular. And, of course, for the Christian, next to *synderesis*, faith, along with everything connected to it, develops therefrom.

2. Therefore, conscience is an act, a judgment. This judgment is undoubtedly of the practical order, a judgment that rules action. Is it the final judgment that reason would bring to bear upon one's concrete action or, rather, does our *intellect* still have something further to do? This is far more serious a question than it seems to be at first sight. Depending on how we answer it, we will find that we have before us one of two opposed moralities, and when we come to discuss this point later on, you will see the full scope of what is at stake in this matter. For now, however, let us content ourselves with gathering together the crucial teaching found in ad 4 (in the first series of objections involved in this article).

In this text, St. Thomas draws a clear distinction between the judgment of conscience and the judgment of choice [*election*]. Without a doubt, the judgment of conscience is practical and normative, just like the various types of knowledge that it uses (*synderesis*, moral science, etc.), but it must have a truth that is speculative in nature, that is, through conformity to the reality of things [*aux choses*]. This is what St. Thomas means in saying, "It consists purely in knowledge (*in pura cognitione consistit*)." A judgment of conscience is objectively true or false inasmuch as it is or is not conformed to objective requirements. Yes, quite certainly, the instinct of affection and of moral sentiment serve in posing it and in rectifying it. In the end, however, it sets forth what is true or false concerning an action's objective morality.

Now, after this, there still is more to be done, even on the part of the intellect and practical reason. It still must bring about the truth of action by reaching a judgment that is characterized by a truth that is no longer speculative in nature but, instead, practical, that is, a judgment whose truth consists in being conformed to action, to being its interior rule and immanent directive idea. This implies, "an application of knowledge to desire [*affection*]," since action must be rightly ordered to its end, which is pre-contained in desire [*affection*]. This will involve an intellectual task which will need to be fulfilled, and St. Thomas delegates to it a virtue which holds a central place in his morality: *prudence*. What prudence must rectify is not, directly, the judgment of conscience which, in reality, precedes it, but, instead, the judgment of choice [*election*] and the command.

With this in mind, we can understand why St. Thomas never mentions prudence among the *habitus* applied to a particular case by the judgment of conscience. For him, conscience is prior to prudence. And he emphasizes that, even with a true judgment of conscience, one can still "err" ("*errare*") in the judgment of choice, namely, that which stands in need of the intellectual virtue of prudence.

3. Now, anticipating a topic that we will develop at greater length later on in our discussion, after St. Thomas's time, it happened that, to the degree that the idea of conscience came to be placed in the foreground, so too was the notion of prudence placed in the background. Historically, all of this took place as though they were two notions at odds with each other. Nearly everything that St. Thomas said about prudence and its properly practical truth was transferred to the judgment of conscience, giving rise to the rather odd systems that we will come to speak about later on, leading to the demand that objective truth (required by St. Thomas for the judgment of conscience) be replaced by the need for good faith, which one believed to be equivalent to that of the practical truth which is characteristic of prudence. And many Thomists, beginning with Billuart,[2] perplexed by the problems involved in organizing these various data, believed that they could arrange everything by saying that true conscience is the very act of the virtue of prudence, namely, its judgment, a claim which contradicts, at once, the distinction proposed by the ad 4 we are here considering, as well as St. Thomas's own forever-repeated assertion that conscience is an *act* which is not reducible to particular *habitus*—prudence

2. Translator's Note: This is historically inexact. This trend is attested to at least in John of St. Thomas, as can be seen in the works by Doherty and Noonan cited in the Translator's Introduction to this volume.

no less than others, since he never names it among the *habitus* applied by conscience to a particular act.

De veritate, q. 17, a. 2: *Can conscience be mistaken?*

Annotation

1. Conscience is not something passively impressed within us, a kind of innate knowledge that is purely received. It implies activity on the part of our reason and is the fruit thereof. The first data upon which it is based and from which it sets forth are indeed the object of a spontaneous form of knowledge, that of *synderesis*, and when it comes to assessing an act which is nothing other than a particular realization of an [self-]evident principle, the judgment of conscience is itself stated with full certitude. More often, however, we will find that we need to undertake an investigation, attentively reflecting on things and comparing them to each other, reasoning by taking into account all of the various data. In this way, error can slip into our moral reasoning and lead to a judgment of erroneous conscience.

2. St. Thomas, who defined conscience as an act of practical reason, is here concerned with identifying the sources of properly intellectual errors in conscience. These are the proper, formal, and immediate causes of error in the judgment of conscience: the use of false ideas or the incorrect application of true principles, whether through precipitancy or through negligence in one's inquiries, etc. Among errors of this kind, we must class all sorts of prejudices, unquestioned received ideas, and pressures coming from our social environment. There are ways of seeing things and lines of conduct that one never seriously bothers to examine or critique because everyone in one's surrounding environment thinks or acts in this way, etc.

This teaching, however, must be supplemented by what St. Thomas says elsewhere in *ST* I-II, q. 17, concerning the influence of the will upon the intellect. There he tells us that, beyond those forms of [self-]evidential knowledge which impose themselves as necessary, the will can inflect our judgment in the direction of its own affective dispositions. In such a case, when one would have a clear view of things, so long as he were to considerate the matter seriously and with some desire for objectivity, the will can nonetheless interrupt our examination, turn away its attention, etc. All of this will be a common cause of errors of conscience. Granted, it may be, at times, a more remote cause which will be, in fact, intellectually translated into the use of false ideas or malformed reasoning. We can say quite certainly, however, that it is the cause of those errors which we most frequently commit, errors which, in any case, are most grave precisely because they will not be completely involuntary.

3. All of this means that conscience is something that is cultivated. True, it is not a *habitus*. It implies, however, many *habitus* that are all used together. These *habitus* develop through exercise and come to be refined. Discernment comes to be more rapid and surer. Many intellectual dispositions which will also be integral parts of prudence are necessary here and will develop and grow through the exercise of conscience. This activity of cultivating conscience is not, however, purely intellectual in character. As soon as we are concerned with objects that are of interest to human life, even if studied in a purely speculative manner, our volitional dispositions will matter a great deal. *A foritiori*, this is true when we must draw from such knowledge an immediate rule for our action. Conscience stands in need of a general climate of rectitude, of fidelity to the light, a kind of desire for objectivity which enables us to step back from our personal affective reactions. Modern moralists insist on the duty to be genuine and to faithfully listen to and follow one's conscience; and nothing could be more accurate. St. Thomas did not demand anything less than this. He will forever add, however—a point which is a somewhat more forgotten—that what is primordially necessary is a great love for the truth *in itself*. For conscience, the problem of truth is not first and foremost that we be in agreement with ourselves, that we be sincere and simple. Rather, first of all and essentially, we must be in accord with the objective order of things, the natural law, and ultimately, the eternal law.

In our discussion below, St. Thomas's formulas will seem severe to our eyes. We will need to understand them aright. These appearances will all come from the fact that St. Thomas does not readily and easily admit that an error concerning the natural law or even, going further still, concerning a sufficiently promulgated law, could be completely involuntary and entirely innocent. And in that very case when it would be (something which he does not entirely rule out), we will see that his conclusion will be utterly different from what contemporary moralists say.

We must first, however, continue our investigation into what he says in *De veritate*.

2. *On the Obligation of Conscience*

To say that conscience can be mistaken is quite a grave conclusion to draw. How will we still be able to say that it sets an obligation for us? And, if it is true that it obligates, will we need to say that this holds true even in those cases when it is mistaken? Moreover, if it obligates even when it is deceived, does this mean that the command of a legitimate superior will not take precedence over it?

Here, we have the problems that are considered in the next three articles. In the *Summa theologiae*, we will find formulations that are more precise and more nuanced. The explanations offered in *De veritate*, however, will prepare us to understand the later ones.

De veritate, q. 17, a. 3: *Does conscience obligate?*

Annotation

1. Obligation is an essentially moral notion. The fact that the word involves an image drawn from the bodily world is a common linguistic fact. Properly speaking, it means: the imposition of some kind of necessity upon a free will. What kind of necessity? Not coercion [*coaction*], which cannot be exercised upon a will. Nor interior necessity through determination to a single act (*ad unum*), something which is incompatible with freedom. Rather, it imposes "conditional necessity," which is addressed expressly to an intellect: "If you wish to attain this end, take up this means, without which you will fail to reach it." This is a necessity which the will must make its own through free acceptance of it, *presuming* that it wills the proposed end. If I will to go to England, I must either sail or fly there; however, I will not be able to walk there.

In the moral order, based on the first determination to the Good and to the End precisely as the final end (a determination which is not an obligation but, rather, a natural ordination), everything will be obligatory for me which appears as being necessary for reaching my end, for realizing this Good. Now, this is intimated to me by Him who presides over the order of the universe, namely God, whose Eternal Law is found within me in a participated form in my natural inclinations such as they are submitted to reason, in His express revelation, in the orders of legitimate superiors, and so forth.

As regards the idea of a counsel, in the sense in which it is contrasted with a precept, it means the following: something is solely the object of counsel when it represents a better course of action for me, one which would enable me to tend more readily toward my end; however, without performing it, I can remain good and turned toward this end. Thus, St. Thomas will say in *ST* I-II, q. 108, a. 4: "A command is imposed with necessity, whereas counsels are left to the free choice of the person to whom they are given. (*Praeceptum necessitate imponit*—in the precise sense of obligation discussed a moment ago—*consilium autem in optione ponitur eius cui datur.*)"

2. Given that this is the nature of obligation, we immediately can see that conscience is neither the source of obligation, nor its foundation. It presupposes and transmits it. It is the indispensable intermediary by which an obligation reaches us. Just as coaction requires physical contact where the efficient causality may be able to be exercised, so too obligation requires knowledge as a kind of spiritual contact. Nothing can ever be imposed upon me except through a judgment of conscience. The only way that anyone is bound is through his conscience.

If he is indeed bound, however, this is because the obligation that conscience makes known does not come from conscience itself. Its definitive and constant foundation is founded on the Eternal Law. Thus, you can see the profound truth contained within the traditional metaphor stating that conscience is God's voice within us. Through it, we come into contact with a precept which ultimately receives its authority from the Eternal Law. In a. 4, ad 2, St. Thomas will say: "That which conscience declares is nothing other than the divine command coming to him who has a conscience. (*Conscientiae dictamen nihil aliud est quam perventio divini praecepti ad eum qui conscientiam habet.*)"

Nonetheless, we must not draw from this metaphor the simplistic idea of a kind of immediate inspiration. Conscience is not a kind of Mount Sinai. As we said in relation to the previous article, we arrive at the judgment of conscience through our rational activity, and this is why it can be false. The obligation that it involves, however, one which exists intimately within us, is forever reducible to the Eternal Law.

This really only serves to pose, all the more acutely, the problem taken up in the next article: how does this rule retain its authority given how it depends so readily and easily on the errors to which we are susceptible? Does it do so in an unconditional manner? What are our duties toward it? Thus, anew, we pose the problem of erroneous conscience, no longer for knowing whether it can exist (a. 2) but, rather, in order to know how it continues to obligate and to what degree it does. This is already at stake in ad 4.

De veritate, q. 17, a. 4: *Does erroneous conscience obligate?*

Annotation

I will not linger over this article in particular, for it represents the problem that we will find in the *Summa theologiae*, where it will be treated more broadly and with greater nuance. Let us limit our observations here to the essential points.

We defined obligation as being the imposition of a necessity. Obligation properly so called exists only for free acts that presuppose a first act of will concerned with a given end. To say that we are obligated to do something in order to attain this or that given end does not directly mean that we will perform a good deed by doing it. This directly means, however, that we will perform an evil deed if we choose not to do it. This is how we transgress the conditional "necessity" which is the very nature of obligation [*en quoi consiste l'obligation*]. The fact that we do not sufficiently define obligation by merely stating the fact that one does well by fulfilling it is made clear by considering how counsels hold. In their case, one acts well by following them, at least if the counsel is good. Counsels, however, are not obligatory, for one does not do evil by not following them.

Consequently, the problem concerning the obligation belonging to erroneous conscience is not precisely concerned with knowing whether one will act well by acting in conformity with it. That is a later problem, one which certainly does arise, although it requires other principles for its resolution. The true problem is concerned with knowing whether one does evil by transgressing an erroneous conscience. And thus, it does not matter whether it is a question of objectively indifferent, good, or evil things.

The essential response is that we cannot transgress what conscience presents as being an obligation without thereby agreeing to transgress the divine law, something which is obviously a sin.

If then, however, that which conscience falsely presents as an obligation is already a sin, we find ourselves in an impossible situation, what theologians call "a case of perplexity (*casus perplexus*)": sin is inevitable. We will sin by performing the act (since it is a sin), yet we will sin by not performing it (since we would thereby transgress our conscience). Ad 8 examines this case. It will be posed, however, with even greater clarity by the next article.

De veritate, q. 17, a. 5: *In indifferent matters, does conscience obligate more or less than a superior's command?*

ANNOTATION

The case is specified in the title and depends on the medieval controversies concerning erroneous conscience. Here, we have a case which everyone recognized as presenting a situation in which erroneous conscience obligates: the object in question is intrinsically indifferent, but through an error we believe that it is evil and forbidden by God. Then, we receive a command from a superior to whom we have vowed obedience. Let us suppose that he has in no way abused his power. Like a purely positive law, this makes a line of conduct which was intrinsically indifferent now obligatory for us. In conscience, however, I believe that it is evil. What should I do?

To fulfill this precept for my superior, in opposition to my awareness in conscience that I am doing something evil, is assuredly a sin. Whatever the activity might materially be, we formally consent to transgressing something that we believe to be a divine precept.

To refuse to fulfill the superior's command in order to remain faithful to erroneous conscience would also be a sin, not through conformity to my conscience but, rather, because I would thereby disobey a legitimate command. My subjective error in no way invalidates the legitimate precept. This second sin, however, is less grave than that which would be committed by acting against my conscience.

But then, do I find myself faced with an inevitable sin? Is this indeed one of those cases which are called "a case of perplexity (*casus perplexus*)," which was spoken of in ad 8 in the previous article? No, for this "perplexity" arises from a prior defect which is itself avoidable. And it is natural that, if it remains, problems follow upon it on all sides. For example, as St. Thomas says (and he will repeat the point often): if I am vain, I wish to be known of by others; but, here, see that I must give alms which, in this precise case, I am truly obligated to give. Thus, presupposing my intention to act out of vainglory, whatever I do, I will sin: either through vanity if I give these alms, or by transgressing the precept to give alms if I abstain from doing so. There is, however, another possible course of action: I can change my intention and renounce my vanity. The same is true for the case of erroneous conscience. It is not astonishing that, for as long as this error remains, it will involve problems no matter what I do; however, there is another possible path forward. In short, I could correct this judgment.

I told you that we will find severe formulas in St. Thomas. It is clear that the last one causes problems. What he says in *De veritate*, in fact, suffices for resolving it; however, the *Summa theologiae* will take up the terms with much greater clarity.

Here, let us at least note the lofty idea of conscience that St. Thomas fashions for himself. It has a side that is open solely to God, receiving its command only from Him, and everything else is subordinated to this. We do not need to judge the commands given by a superior, but we must always render judgment for our own actions and, therefore, for the fulfillment of commands that are received.

In the *Summa theologiae*

In the *Prima pars* (*ST* I, q. 79, a. 13), while speaking about the powers of the soul, St. Thomas asks whether we must hold that conscience is numbered among these powers. He responds, as he does in *De veritate* (q. 17, a. 1), that conscience is neither a power nor a *habitus* but, rather, an act: the application of the knowledge [*science*] that one has concerning a given action to a given case. A number of *habitus* concur in this act, though in dependence upon a first *habitus*, namely, *synderesis*, which for this reason is sometimes called conscience. This adds nothing to what we read in *De veritate*, but it does show us that St. Thomas has indeed retained the idea that he had formed, at the start of his teaching career, concerning the nature of conscience. We will find it again in *ST* I-II, q. 19, a. 5 and 6.

In those texts, however, St. Thomas poses the problem in more general terms. In the preceding articles, he showed that reason, as a participation in the Eternal Law, is the proper rule of moral acts. Obviously, he is speaking of reason as eliciting the act by which it pronounces the morality of an action. This act is nothing other than conscience, and if the judgment thus pronounced is false, we find ourselves faced with the problem of erroneous conscience. We thus come to envision its consequences:

* When the will transgresses it: is it evil?
* In the case when the will obeys it: is it good?

ST I-II, q. 19, a. 5: *Is the will which departs from erroneous reason evil?*

Annotation

1. As in *De veritate*, St. Thomas begins by setting forth an opinion which he will combat, one which was held by the early Franciscan masters. It wished to limit the obligation of erroneous conscience solely to those cases involving effectively indifferent objects. As soon as intrinsic good or evil is involved, the Eternal Law, so to speak, takes up all of its rights, and erroneous conscience no longer has any regulatory effect. What is essential is that the act be conformed to the Eternal Law.

(a) This opinion is quite representative of medieval morality and, even while refuting it, St. Thomas will not deny its spirit, as will be shown quite clearly in the next article. Moral goodness is conceived as being conformity with an objective order founded upon God. This is what has primary importance. There is a truth which man does not make, a truth which is independent from him. It determines an order into which man must place himself, an order where he is neither the center, nor the measure, of things.

What the opinion held by these Franciscan Doctors misunderstands is the *intermediary* role played by conscience. They were right to think that conscience cannot substitute itself for the divine law. The precept, however, reaches us through conscience, and conscience merely needs to present an act to us as being obligatory and, then, the omission of this act would be a sin: whatever the matter may be, one agrees to transgress the divine law.

(b) In *De veritate* (q. 17, a. 4), St. Thomas, examining the same opinion held by the Franciscan Doctors, was not content to oppose his own conclusion to theirs along with his proof thereof. Moreover, he pointed out a confusion that they committed: they feared that, in universally admitting that erroneous reason obligates, we would need to say that one would perform a good deed when acting in conformity with it. Thus, we would need to place right and erroneous conscience on the same footing and conclude: to transgress one's conscience, whether it be right or erroneous, is always evil; to follow one's conscience, whether right or erroneous, is always good. Thus, all things would be turned upside down: morality would be judged not primordially by the divine law and the truth of things, but rather, by conscience; the definitive criterion for judging our action would not be the divine law which conscience make known to us but, rather, conscience itself. St. Thomas was not opposed to them on this point. He merely responded, however, with some vivacity, that there was another question involved in that issue. To say that erroneous conscience obligates means, directly, that it is evil to transgress it. This does not imply, however, that it would be good to follow it. And to make this distinction clear, he called upon the notion of a counsel: it is good to follow a good counsel; however, this does not mean that counsels obligate.

2. This second issue was not studied *ex professo* in *De veritate*, although it was clear enough that St. Thomas would not settle it by affirmatively stating: "To follow an erroneous conscience is good." By referring to the case of perplexity (*casus perplexus*) and to his conclusion concerning the religious who sins either by violating his conscience when he obeys his superior [*prélat*] or by following it (because then he disobeys his superior), he committed himself to a completely different path of reasoning than the one that had raised concerns for the Franciscan Doctors.

In the *Summa theologiae*, he dedicates a. 6 to this problem. Its terms are well known. On the one hand, *to act against one's conscience* is always a sin, for even if such conscience is erroneous, this means that one agrees to transgress the divine law. On the other hand, *to act in accord with one's conscience* is to will to fulfill the divine precept. Even if conscience is erroneous, will this always be a good act?

ST I-II, q. 19, a. 6: *Is the will that acts in accord with erroneous reason good?*

1. Note well how the conclusions are formulated, in particular the second. Even in the case of a totally involuntary and innocent error, St. Thomas does not say (as the title of the article invited him to do) that the will conformed to erroneous conscience is good but, rather, only that it is not evil. Such an error, which he obviously judges to be rare, except in the domain of particular circumstances and of contingent facts, *excuses*; it does not, for all that, have the power to produce moral goodness. What it produces is an involuntary act and, in the beginning of the conclusion, St. Thomas recalls that involuntariness suppresses the entire notion of morality, be it good or wicked.

And this is why, in response to the first objection, which asks how it is that parity does not exist between the two cases (on the one hand, to violate an erroneous conscience is a sin because this involves willingness to violate what one believes to be the divine law; on the other, a good act would be performed in conforming oneself to an erroneous conscience because one believes that it is the divine law), he responds that the good is more demanding than is evil. It does not suffice that something appear as good to conscience. It must be good.

Along the same lines, ad 2 summarizes this: the Eternal Law is the unfailing principle of moral goodness and rectitude, not human reason, for the latter can be mistaken. Thus, in order to be right, it does not suffice that the will be in agreement with reason.

2. As regards the question of ignorance and error in relation to the voluntary character of actions, simply see q. 6 and the explanations I provided there. In particular, recall the distinction between ignorance of law [*ignorance du droit*] and factual ignorance [*ignorance du fait*]. St. Thomas was not unaware that both of them can be truly involuntary and innocent, but he thought that ignorance of law is exceptional, not normal. Why? Because we always are obligated to know the law, and in order for ignorance to excuse our action, we would need to have truly done everything possible in order to know it. This would be all the less likely to the degree that a given law [*droit*] is closer to the first principles of the natural law.

Conclusion

1. *The Place and Role of Conscience*

1. What is at the heart of St. Thomas's account of morality is the notion of the Good, the good as a transcendental property of being, therefore presupposing being and, for a spiritual appetite, presupposing true being, already grasped by the intellect and presented by it [to the will]. The good thus proposed constitutes for the will, at once and indissolubly, its object and its end. The ultimate explanatory notion around which the theology of human mores will thus be organized is that of God, who is the Ultimate End because He is the Sovereign Good, calling us to share in His own beatitude. Appreciated in its objective value as that which is supremely deserving of love while simultaneously being experienced in its attractive power, the Sovereign Good demands that it be loved for its own sake above all things and that it be the end of all of our acts of willing.

The notion of our ordering to the End immediately corresponds to this notion. This ordering is not purely formal and void, arbitrary, and as it were, externally imposed but, rather, is the ordination of a (super-elevated) nature which tends toward this Good as to its own fulfillment and perfection. Now, nature has an objective structure, and all natures have an objective structure; grace itself has its essential necessities. In this way, an order of things comes to be determined, with each thing therein being inserted into its own particular place, an order wherein it tends, in its own particular manner, toward the Supreme Good. Where is the principle and guarantee for this order of things which is fundamentally inscribed within their natures and, in that which falls to their historical achievements, is dependent upon God's design, His good pleasure, and the economy of providence? In the Divine Wisdom as ordering and governing the universe, in what we have called the *Eternal Law*. For every being, the good will correspond to this ordering, in conformity to it. Evil will be found in deviating from it.

For a rational and free creature, this conformity or opposition will take on a new dimension which is proper to it. Such a creature is not ordered passively in accord with the Eternal Law. He orders himself. He formulates the natural law for himself, ruling himself through reason. He connects back to the Eternal Law through a form of cognitional activity that expresses this law to him and rules his actions. Thus, good and evil take on a moral sense for him, characterizing an activity over which he has mastery and responsibility. The Eternal Law is applied to each of his acts by his own reason through a regulative-measuring [*régulateur*] judgment which is called *conscience.*

2. What role does conscience play? Its role is to make known the requirements of the Eternal Law in particular actions, to make good and evil known, to intimate obligation. Pay heed to the word "obligation." It characterizes something that is known as being required in order to attain a good end. So long as this end is that of nature (elevated by grace), obligation is connected precisely to that which leads nature [or, elevated nature] to its perfection, its good. To follow an obligation will not be to go against the grain of nature but, to the contrary, to go forward in line with its deepest desire, toward its full flowering. Deviating from one's obligation is what is contrary to one's nature.

Without a doubt, obligation is imposed by another; however, in the end, this *other* is the very one who is our End, our Good. When conceived in this way, obligation illuminates our free will, rationally and objectively sustaining it. No duty will be more profound than that of interiorizing obligation through love, making what one must do precisely that which one wills, with all the impulse implied by the word "to will." The fact that obligation comes from another solely results from the fact that we are not the measure of good and evil but, instead, are placed within an order which is the divine order, and our conscience's sole role is to enable us to perceive its requirements.

Now, the fact that this conscience is fallible represents an important observation. Error can slip into it. This gives birth to many problems, the most fundamental being: how are we to assure rectitude in the ruling of its moral life, to remain in the good and to avoid evil, with a conscience which can be mistaken? It is precisely here that medieval morality takes on its full meaning.

2. Problems of Conscience

Instead of tarrying about in the accidental, even if it happens to be frequent, St. Thomas and the theologians of the Middle Ages insisted on what is normally [and essentially] the case. They were primarily concerned with affirming the *per se*, not the *per accidens*.

Conscience has a role which is *subordinate* in relation to the Eternal Law and to the truth of things. It is not what makes goodness exist, no more than it would make obligation exist. Its primordial duty is *to be true*, to conform us to the divine order. When it falls into error, this will at least be a defect and, often, already a fault, for each person must do everything he can in order to avoid this kind of error.

Thus, we have a fundamental duty, one that is prior even to that of following our conscience, namely, the duty to do everything possible in order for our conscience to be true, objectively true. In this sense, prior to being responsible before one's conscience, one is *responsible for one's conscience*.

Thus, St. Thomas will serenely write these words, which have sent shivers down the spines of generations of moralists: "Every action performed against the law is always evil and is not excused by the fact that one followed one's conscience. (*Illud quod agitur contra legem semper est malum, nec excusatur per hoc quod est secundum conscientiam.*)" (*Quod.* VIII, q. 6, a. 3). In the normal order of things, to say that a human act would be opposed to the divine law is the very definition of sin. An error of conscience does not change its nature. It is, perhaps, the sign that one did not do everything necessary for remaining in the truth (see *Quod.* I, q. 9, a. 3 and III, q. 12, a. 2, ad 2).

Clearly, if the theory of conscience limited itself to this observation, it would represent a rather-frightening form of rigorism. Nonetheless, this is what must be said first, and everything else that is said concerning conscience must not lead one to forget this point.

1. From this perspective, it is not astonishing that we do not grant "erroneous conscience" the same rights to be the regulative principle of our acts as we do to right conscience.

Admittedly, all moralists will agree in saying that these two forms of conscience differ inasmuch as right conscience obligates by itself and always, whereas erroneous conscience only obligates for as long as it endures and because it is believed to be right, although the duty to change it remains. In fact, however, for as long as it endures, modern moralists practically came to treat these two forms of conscience as though they were the same, admitting that one could do good by following an invincibly erroneous conscience.

St. Thomas never says this. No, he makes quite the opposite point. To contradict one's conscience, whether true or false, is indeed always evil. Everyone agrees on this point. To conform oneself to a true conscience is always good. To conform oneself, however, to an erroneous conscience is, generally speaking, a sin because, above all in cases of errors concerning right [or, law], *the error itself is culpable.* If the error, however, happens to be innocent and invincible, erroneous conscience completely excuses from the sin, though the act that is performed is not, for all that, rendered good. Rather, it is rendered *involuntary,* which means it is neither good nor evil.

2. There are, however, more complex cases. Up to this point, we have been presupposing that such conscience is "certain." This is why it obligates us not to act against it and, if erroneous, it can happen that it excuses the person who follows it. But what if one *is in doubt*? I might have some sense that what I have thought of doing could indeed be a sin. If, upon reflection, I rule out this fear and remain persuaded that I am doing something good, there really is no special case involved here. Rather, we just return to what we have spoken of up to this point: my conscience is

perhaps erroneous; however, I believe that it is true and certainly cannot act in opposition to it.

If, by contrast, some doubt seems to be well-founded and I am unable to free myself from this hesitation, then I suspend my judgment (and this is the very definition of doubt as lived and exercised). The need to act, however, presses upon me: what must I do? St. Thomas generally [*universellement*], along with all medieval theologians, had a ready answer: I must take *the safer path* [*au plus sûr*]. To accept the risk of sinning is to accept sin itself. Far from granting a right to accept an action ("since it is in doubt, I can do it"), doubt indicates that a risk is at hand, one that we do not have the right to take, for it is the risk of sin.

This is the common [medieval] teaching, which contemporary historians call "medieval tutiorism." But pay heed to an important point! The word "tutiorism" also has another, different sense, more normally designating a different historical reality, namely, one of the systems that proliferated among the moralities of conscience, set in opposition to probabilism. I will discuss it below, and you will see that it is something completely different. Although the term is the same, there are two different senses involved. This second kind "tutiorism" will represent a form of absolute rigorism, quite distant from St. Thomas's own moral theology [*morale*].

3. Indeed, in all cases when the evidence at hand is not dazzlingly clear, will we need to take the safer path, that is, the most severe one? Certainly not. St. Thomas knew very well, as did Aristotle before him, not only that there are different kinds of certitude depending on the various orders of objects and necessities, but also that the order of contingencies does not lend itself to ready and easy certitude. Conscience is based on evident principles, but their application to a given, particular case can be rendered difficult by the tangled mess of circumstances, effects and causes, possible failures, and so forth. Between, on the one hand, certitude characterized by full and tranquil adherence to one side of an alternative and, on the other, doubt which, properly speaking, indicates the absence of full adherence, the suspension of judgment, there are intermediary attitudes, the most characteristic of which is *opinion*. In the proper sense of the term, opinion is the state of mind leading someone to adhere to one side of an alternative, while retaining a kind of concern that the other side might be true. Why does the mind so adhere? Because the assertion bringing it to a halt seems well-founded to it; it seems "probable." This means that it

seems *probably true* to this person. The only normal and definitive object of assent, that which the mind forever seeks to attain, is the truth. That which is true, known with evidence, provides the foundation and justification for certitude. That which is likely, that which is probably true, provides the foundation and justification for opinion. It is quite clear, however, that the "probable," so conceived, has a right to justify an assent only as an approximation of the truth, from which it draws all of its value. It cannot be isolated from this ordination to the truth, outside of which it does not justify adherence.

When faced with two contrary assertions, neither of them being evident to me or indubitably guaranteed ([as holds for the case of knowledge through] faith), one of two things is possible: *either*, I do not shake this doubt, thus not truly adhering to one of the two, and in that case, I must choose the more certain one; *or*, I do truly adhere to one of the two, giving it my assent because it is supported by reasons that render it probably true. The latter is not certitude, but it is an opinion undergirded by a solid motivation; it is indeed what I think about this particular problem [facing me]. Note that for this very reason, in such a case I will hold that the contrary position is probably false.

Well, St. Thomas fully recognizes that a "probable" conscience—that is, an opinion in the proper sense—is, although lacking certitude, a just and sufficient rule of action. With it, we are no longer in doubt and are in no way required to "take the safer path." The truth, sufficiently attained under the guise of probability, prevails over the fear of sinning.

Note these various words, along with what St. Thomas means by them: doubt, opinion, and probability. We will soon witness how their meanings will shift, leading the same terms to be used in support of diametrically opposed positions.

4. Above all, however, in St. Thomas's moral theology [*morale*], conscience is not everything! In order to assure rectitude in action, other resources are indeed at hand, primarily the virtue of prudence. This is not the place to analyze it. Moreover, even before the treatise dedicated to it in *ST* II-II, we will need consider it in *ST* I-II, already here forming a rather precise idea of it when we come to study the intellectual virtues.

For now, let us at least specify that, for St. Thomas, the judgment of conscience does not represent the intellect's absolutely final word in relation to action. It is not the last practical judgment. Much more still needs to be done after the judgment of conscience is rendered, indeed not mere execution, but rather, the work of practical reason *fashioning the truth of action*. It must fashion this truth from within, as its immanent directive idea, because it finds its truth no longer in being conformed to its object (after the manner of speculative truth) but, rather, by being conformed to action. And this cannot exist without this directive idea itself, right reason in our acts (*recta ratio agibilium*), being conformed to the supreme principle of action: its end, such as it must be pre-contained in the appetite which tends toward it [through intention]. In short, through the interaction of knowledge and affection, prudence's task is to impress its rational golden mean on an act which it makes to be in conformity with rectified appetite (i.e., rectified in relation to the virtuous ends of the person).

This represents a completely different kind of judgment than that of conscience, and this is why St. Thomas never names prudence among the *habitus* which must concur in the act of conscience. Nonetheless, most authors persist in identifying these two judgments. What they thereby distort, however, is the very idea of prudence, and it is not astonishing that, while the treatise on conscience would come to undergo great development, the place of prudence came to seem quite inexplicable for such authors....

II. MORALITIES OF CONSCIENCE

What I am here calling "moralities of conscience"—which in my opinion, as a conception of the theology of human mores, must *en bloc* be set in opposition to St. Thomas's moral thought—took on a particularly important and characteristic historical realization: *probabilism*. Later on, others defined themselves in relation to it and developed their own systems in the midst of controversies with it, either by exaggerating its principles and tendencies, as was the case for "laxism," or by reacting against it, as in the cases of "probabiliorism," equiprobabilism, and tutiorism. While these systems are mutual enemies, they nonetheless are siblings. By the very way that they pose the problem of morality, they are all of the "probabilist mold."

Probabilism had an extremely turbulent history, although its vicissitudes are quite instructive. Naturally, many tendencies and various currents favored it coming to birth, but the principle which supposedly gave rise to it was explicitly formulated in the sixteenth century by the Dominican, Bartolomé de Medina. Adopted from the start by the great theologians of the Society of Jesus, it increasingly became, as it were, a kind of theological good belonging to the Society, which defended probabilism against the winds and tides that buffeted against it. In general, the Dominicans thought themselves to be faithful to St. Thomas by opposing to probabilism the system called "probabiliorism," which in fact, does respect certain requirements of moral thought in these matters, though while remaining, in the end, a morality of conscience, precisely because probabiliorism accepted probabilism's way of posing the very question and problems at hand. Obviously, I cannot here present this history in detail. You will find it thoroughly documented in the monumental article, "Probabilisme," by Fr. Deman in the *Dictionnaire de théologie catholique.*

For my part, I will merely present the fundamental positions of the moralities of conscience, then showing you how various "moral systems" developed on the basis of these data. Finally, I will attempt to assess them from several angles.

1. *Fundamental Positions*

To extract the fundamental positions from a doctrinal whole is not to retrace and follow along its historical genesis but, rather, requires us to take this whole at its terminal point of development or, at least, at the point when it has reached maturity, having taken on its full proportions. Thus, my precise concern here is not to seek out what the "founders" of probabilism intended or thought they were doing. Rather, I would like to describe, in its essential lineaments, the system that emerged from their principles, progressively changing the entire appearance of moral theology [*morale*].

(a) The statement of the moral problem.

(b) The great notions employed.

(a) *The statement of the moral problem.* As a result of the tendencies which animate nominalist and voluntarist thought, the fundamental notion of the Good, the object and end of the will, gradually was replaced with a derivative notion which came to take the central place in moral matters, causing an overall perspectival shift: the notion of *obligation.* Is not morality the science of "what one *must* do"?

Having thus become a "first-order notion," the idea of obligation found itself cut off from its most profound justifications. Why must we do this and avoid that? Because it is commanded. Is something commanded because it is good? Or is it good because it is commanded? Such metaphysical speculation will hardly ever be bothered with anymore. Obligation: it is the law, the command, increasingly conceived of in the voluntarist sense as a precept that is imposed as a positive datum, no longer understood, above all, as expressing and formulating a requirement of a nature tending toward its own good but, rather, as something intimated by another concerning the conduct that one must follow.

What is obligation addressed to? To a free will. Increasingly, the response will be: "to freedom," *tout court.* Granted, this is an understandable assertion, but it means, in fact, that the word "freedom" has come to lose its metaphysical sense as a property of the will, a property founded on a given nature and explainable only on the basis of a first determination to the Good as such. In the "practical" morality that will be formulated within this perspective, freedom will come to be essentially defined as: "the inborn right to do whatever is not forbidden." (Hear this as meaning: everything that is not clearly and undoubtedly forbidden.)

Obligation and *freedom*: here we have the two essential and antithetical notions which will lay the foundation for the very way that all moral problems will come to be posed. They are clearly correlative and defined in relation to one another. And obligation is necessarily conceived as being something troublesome, impinging upon freedom, which previously had the "right to do otherwise."

Thus, the great and decisive question in morality will obviously be that involving the *discernment of obligation*, the identification of its certitude. Now, we have a means specially charged with this task: *conscience.* Conscience, St. Alphonsus de Ligouri tells us, is a tribunal which must decide between two litigants: freedom and the law. Each litigant has its rights. After examining them, conscience will pronounce its sentence. The *raison d'être* and sole ambition of all "systems of morality" is to bring aid to this examination.

(b) *The central notions employed.* Before the tribunal of conscience, freedom and law plead their rights: how will a decision be reached? According to their temperaments and principles, moralists will be led to favorably prejudice one or the other. For the great majority—in any case, for probabilism, properly so called—freedom is the first, inborn property. Obligation is what must prove itself, and so long as it does not succeed at doing so, freedom "has possession." That is, obligation will be recognized only if it is beyond doubt and resists all quibbling brought against it.

Faced with this alternative and the need to make a pronouncement, conscience will find itself in different conditions. Two principles of distinction intertwine in order to change the situations:

(1) Conscience renders a judgment which will be effectively true or false. Therefore, from the perspective of its *conformity to the object, right* conscience will be distinguished from *erroneous* conscience.

(2) Conscience can, however, adhere with greater or lesser firmness to this same judgment, be it true or false. Thus, from the perspective of *subjective adherence*, various states will come to be distinguished: *certitude, probability*, and *doubt.*

These various notions are not new. A number of them, however, indeed those which are most frequently utilized, will undergo a semantic shift which will involve great perspectival changes.

(1) *Certain conscience.* Certitude is characterized by a firm assent. Through evidence or faith (even, in certain cases, human faith, of course), it involves the reasonable exclusion of all hesitation and of all fear that the contrary might be true.

Certain conscience always obligates:

* If it is true, it obligates by itself and always. It cannot be changed without one falling into sin.
* If it is erroneous, it obligates in an accidental manner, inasmuch as it is thought to be true, and for as long as it endures. One has not only the right to change it, but indeed, the duty to do so.

Everyone agrees upon these principles. As we have seen, the difference is concerned with erroneous conscience: it is understood that it is always a sin to transgress it; however, what about when we conform our action to it and follow it?

For St. Thomas, this will also generally be a sin, above all in errors concerning right [or, law]: "That which is done against the law is always a sin and cannot find an excuse in the fact that it is done in accord with one's conscience. (*Quod agitur contra legem semper est peccatum, nec excu-*

satur per hoc quod est secundum conscientiam)" (*Quod.* VIII, a. 13 / q. 6, a. 3). The error can, however, be truly involuntary and, therefore, innocent. This will generally be the case for a factual error [*erreur de fait*], though it can also be true for an error concerning a law / right [*erreur de droit*]. The former kind of error, without any doubt, truly excuses. To follow it is not a sin, for it is *involuntary*, thus excluding both good and evil at the same time.

Modern moralists also admit, of course, that a vincible error cannot entirely excuse. On the one hand—and not without reason—they give a much larger place to involuntary error, while, on the other hand and above all (and here is the point of opposition), they think that such an error not only excuses but, moreover, that the act that depends upon it is effectively good. On this precise point, invincibly erroneous conscience is treated as being equivalent to true conscience.

(2) "*Probable*" *conscience.* With St. Thomas, we said that, for want of certitude (which it is often difficult to attain in the order of concrete and contingent actions as soon as the action's circumstances are complex), conscience can reach a conclusion that is solely an opinion. In its first and proper sense, *opinion* is a state of mind that truly adheres to an assertion, although with a kind of hesitation, still fearing that the contrary assertion may be true. It attains the truth only under the guise of "the probable." In certitude, the mind attains its proper object, *the true*, and nourishes itself upon it; in opinion, it tends toward it, by adhering to what seems *probably true* to it. If it adheres, however, this is only on account of this light of the truth. The probable is only a pathway toward the truth; it nourishes the mind and has a right to direct action only through this approximation of the truth. If an assertion wins our assent because it seems probable, by that same token it is clear that the contrary assertion becomes improbable. From this perspective, at one and the same time, nobody can have two opinions which are contrary to each other calling for a possible choice; and if no opining assent is yet possible, this is because for such a person, each of the terms involved is not yet truly probable.

In the new moral theories [*nouvelles morales*], the words "probable" and "opinion" will be commonly used in a derivative and noticeably different manner.

Progressively, and with increasing force, such theories would detach probable judgments from the mind [that elicits them]. Likewise, the term "probable" would no longer imply that one fashions a true assent, thus leading the notion of probable judgments to be disconnected from the truth (in place of which, on its own level, probability is substituted as if it were something having its own, self-contained consistency], without reference to the truth toward which a "probable opinion," in the traditional sense, tends, although with fear of error]). Thus the "probable" ends up becoming a kind of practical intermediary between the true and the false. One no longer thinks, "probably true," or, "probably false," but rather, "probable," *tout court*. Thus, it comes to be defined: an assertion that rests on one or several reasons capable of motivating a good man, without fully convincing him. Now, these reasons gradually came to be reduced to the form of probability which is most easily known in an objective and impersonal manner, so-called extrinsic probability: authority, in other words, the name and number of the authorities who defend this assertion.

At the same time, "opinion" gradually ceased to designate a firm, interior adherence to a way of looking at things. Thus, it too took on an objective and impersonal sense, practically becoming synonymous with "probable assertion" [in the modern sense of "probable"]. Thus, an opinion would simply be an assertion that has, on its side, objective probabilities in the sense explained above. This is an acceptable derivation, in accord with the laws of the analogy of attribution; but we must not forget the primary analogate: opinion is, first of all, a given state of mind.

In this objective sense, it is no longer absurd to say that two contrary "opinions" were present to the mind. This does not mean that one adheres to two of them at once. No, they are objectively presented as "opinions." Suppose that I adhere to one of the two. I will then continue to say that the other remains a probable opinion. Thus, for each case of conscience, I will begin by enumerating the opinions at hand, those that support the law and the others in support of freedom, ranking their various degrees of probability. Indeed, they will be more or less probable depending on whether they are based on reasons that are more or less serious and, above all, depending on whether they have better or less good guarantors among "authorities." This enumeration and classing of opinions became the great tasks to be performed in moral analysis.

Therefore, we here have conscience, faced with a given number of opinions which are more or less probable, more or less in support of either the law or of freedom. It must decide between the law and freedom. What will it do? This is the precise point that would divide the various moral systems formed in these debates. Before setting them forth for you, however, another capital notion still must be explained.

(3) *Doubting conscience.* Our moralists were very much occupied with the problem of "*conscientia dubia,*" doubting conscience. In the preceding case, conscience assesses the probabilities and gives itself positive reasons for justifying the choice that it makes concerning a solution for concrete action. Doubt is, however, a more embarrassing state: there is no sufficient probability at hand on any side. In such a state of mind, we fear that what we would like to do might be a sin. And yet, there is no objective element at hand for enabling a resolution to this matter. What are we to do in such a case?

We have seen that St. Thomas and all the medieval moralists responded: we must take the safer path and avoid what we think is a sin; for as long as the doubt is not resolved, to do the latter would be to accept the possibility of sinning and, consequently, to accept the very sin in question. This solution is so obvious that nobody will reject it. Everyone continued (and still continues) to affirm that to act with an unresolved doubt concerning the sinful character of what one does is to perform a sin. Given, however, that this line of conduct can prove to be too demanding, above all for delicate consciences, the new morality took up the task of elaborating a method that would enable one to resolve doubts of conscience right away. Must you emerge from your doubt? Yes, we will indeed emerge, attaining not only probability but, indeed, "certitude," and this suffices for "forming one's conscience."

Suarez has the honor of making a distinction which struck it rich, thus becoming the foundation for the entire morality of doubts of conscience and the methodology to be employed in delivering oneself from it. Behold: we can never act with *a practical doubt* concerning the value of our action; however, by reflexively forming our conscience, we can place its doubt upon the *speculative* level (where it will be inoffensive) and thus act with a *practical* certitude that we are acting "well." Now, whence will we draw this certitude? *Ex hypothesi,* in such a case, we have no proper principle which is able to settle the case in question, no objective element which suffices even for forming a true probability. Be that as it may, we can have recourse to principles that are utterly common, ones that are extrinsic to the case at hand, principles which will come to be called "reflex principles," which will be of use precisely in these sorts of embarrassing cases. These reflex principles will be the point that divides the various systems, and I will explain this briefly in a moment. But here is an example. Do I have the right to perform this action? I do not see more reason for one side or the other, as much for freedom as for obligation. If this is how things remain, I must take the safer path. I invoke a reflex principle, however—namely, the famous line: "A law which is in doubt does not obligate. (*Lex dubia non obligat.*)" At once, I leave the appropriate solution for my case to later "speculative" investigations and can be practically certain that since this obligation is doubtful for me, it does not exist for me at this moment. With a peaceful mind, I can choose the freedom of acting as I please. Even if this is an error, on the condition that I am acting in good faith, this "practical certitude" guarantees for me not only that I will be excused of committing a fault but also that I will do something good.

2. *The Various Systems of Morality*

As I said above, the first-born of the great moral systems of conscience was probabilism. All the others are defined in relation to it, taking up its particular way of positing the moral problem, along with its various notions, though drawing different conclusions and, naturally enough, correspondingly increasing the confusion experienced both for confessors and by believers' own consciences.

Therefore, let us begin with probabilism. We will then find it easy to quickly describe the other systems. They will differ from each other essentially on two points:

* The use of probability.
* The choice of reflex principles, as well as their extension.

(a) *Probabilism.* The two eternal litigants, forever antagonistic toward each other, law and freedom, assert their respective rights before the tribunal of conscience.

1. Let us suppose that each of them can invoke probable opinions: Suarez on one side and Sanchez and Caramuel on the other. What is the task falling to conscience? It weighs out the various probabilities, placing them at their particular degrees and comes to conclude that one set is greater than the others. For example, the opinion favoring the law is clearly more probable than the opinion favoring freedom.

The essential principle of probabilism—which, as I said, we owe to the Dominican Bartolomé de Medina—is that merely because we find an opinion which is more probable than its opposite does not require us to follow it, provided that this opposed opinion still has some kind of objective probability. (Most will add: "still serious [probability].") Therefore, in good conscience, we will be able to set aside the side the we think to be more probable and follow the one that we think to be less probable, nonetheless on the condition that we still judge it to be probable.

With that, endless debates were aroused, being maintained by the confusion that was fostered by a given use of the words "opinion" and "probability." We could not separate them any further from the living activity of the mind, nor more fully set out of consideration the relationship that the probable should have with the truth. The probable is isolated and considered separately apart. What makes it the rule of action is no longer the fact that it draws closer to the truth, for one can do what one judges to be less probable, in other words, in good English, what is "less probably true," and therefore, probable false. What makes it the rule of action is solely the fact that it might be "probable," indeed independent of every interior adherence by the mind, for, quite obviously, such adherence can be given neither to two contraries at the same time, nor to that which seems to me to be explicitly less probable. This represents a canonization of "that which is intrinsically probable" [in abstraction from the adherence of the mind, for which the "probable" must, in fact, be understood as "probably true"]. Thus, we will be able, at least at different times, to successively utilize contrary opinions for one and the same case.

2. Let us suppose, however, that, while examining the case being presented by these litigants, conscience does not succeed at finding true probability (in the objective sense explained earlier) on behalf of either side. Authorities have not discussed the problem at hand, or at least, perhaps, we are not familiar with what they may have said. And even while studying the concrete case, the questions posed by conscience remain unresolved. We know that conscience has a resource: reflex principles. All that remains for us to do is to "form our judgment of conscience."

Strict probabilism will be characterized among the other systems by the fact that, among these principles, it gives the first place and universal value to that which states, "A law which is in doubt does not obligate. (*Lex dubia non obligat.*)" Inasmuch as the obligation is not proven, freedom holds possession. Perhaps the law does indeed exist and of itself has a weighty obligation. For me, however, this will be the object of later investigations. My doubt has become "speculative." Right now, thanks to this universal principle, I have *practical certitude* that I am not obligated. Let the law prove itself. I need not search after it, for I am born free. It is up to the law to establish its rights!

(b) *Exaggerations of probabilism: laxism.* Obviously, no author openly professes a system which would be called laxism. This name was given to the tendency and doctrines of certain authors who pushed probabilism to its extremes. They were condemned by the Church, not collectively as professing laxism, but in the form of propositions that they held to be "probable." The Magisterium judged these propositions to be scandalous and "lax." You will find an instructive list of them in Denzinger, nos. 1151–1215 (DS, nos. 2101–2165). Among others, there you will find that it is "probable":

* That the precept of charity does not obligate one to perform more than one act of love of God in one's life;
* According to more moderate thinkers, that one is not required to perform more than one once every five years;
* That the precept to love our neighbors is imposed only upon our external actions but not upon the internal acts of affection;
* That one can desire that one's father die, not as an evil for himself, but inasmuch as this would be something good for us, for example, if he would leave us a nice inheritance, etc.

You can understand how the entire effort expended by orthodox probabilism will be undertaken in order to distinguish itself from laxism, whereas that of its adversaries will be to corner it and show that this is impossible. What are the doctrinal differences?

1. For the use of probabilities, where probabilism says, "One can follow the less probable opinion, provided that it still be truly probable," laxism, without perhaps saying something else, will act as if the most tenuous probability always suffices, for example, but a single authority, whoever it may be. Thus, as soon as the falsity of an opinion is not blindingly evident, one can always hold that "some probability" remains and profess that one can follow it.

2. For the solution of doubts concerning conscience, the difference lies in the interpretation and, subsequently, the extension, of the principle: *Lex dubia non obligat.*

An orthodox probabilist will strive to maintain: a law which is neither certain nor solely probable (excluding all "serious" probability for freedom) does not obligate.

For a laxist, this will simply mean: a law that is not certain does not obligate. And this goes very far indeed, for even if it is extremely probable, and even if freedom has but a very weak probability in its favor, one can say that a law is "doubtful." Doubt is no longer characterized, as it is in St. Thomas, by the absence of interior assent. It is no longer characterized any longer, as it is for the probabilists, by the absence of probability on both sides. Rather, it is characterized by the fact that the law, even one that is very probable, from the very moment when it is not certain, has a small margin that can cast doubt on the matter.

Clearly, few laws will resist being subject to such treatment. When is it truly impossible for us to be able to formulate the smallest of difficulty concerning some matter, either concerning its intrinsic character or concerning how it should be interpreted?

3. Nonetheless, we must recognize that this danger is something which the principle, *Lex dubia non obligat,* carries within itself, for there will always be a tendency to translate *lex dubia* as "a non-certain law (*Lex non certa*)," while forgetting that such a law can be probable and [*indeed*] solely probable. That is why it became necessary to find other limitations. Today, all probabilists teach that there are three great orders belonging to this case, wherein we do not have the right to use this principle, requiring us to take *the safer path*:

* *When the validity of a sacrament is in question.* Pope Innocent XI condemned a proposition saying, "In conferring the sacraments, it is not illicit to follow the probable opinion with respect to the validity of the sacrament, disregarding what is safer. (*Non illicitum in sacramentis conferendis sequi opinionem probabilem de valore sacramenti, relicta tutiore,* etc.)" (Denzinger, no. 1151; DS, no. 2101 [slightly altered]). Here, we must take the path which is more probable and safer.
* *When the strict rights of another person are in question.* The condemned proposition: "I think that probably a judge can

pass judgment according to opinion, even one that is less probable. (*Probabiliter existimo iudicem posse iudicare iuxta opinionem etiam minus probabilem*)" (Denzinger, no. 1152; DS, no. 2102 [alt.]).

* *When some grave spiritual or temporal injury is in question.* We do not have the right to eat food when we are in doubt as to whether it might be highly [*gravement*] poisonous, nor *a fortiori*, do we have the right to give it to another person.

At least in these various cases, doubt never frees us from the obligation to follow the safer path.

(c) *Reactions to probabilism.* As you might imagine, probabilism, above all when it was still poorly distinguished from laxism, was truly scandalizing, at least outside of the schools. It seemed to open the door to all kinds of relaxations. For example, in Pascal's *Lettres provinciales*, we do certainly see partisan passion and polemical skill, but likewise and obviously, quite-sincere and legitimate indignation [at this state of affairs].

Among theologians, after the craze of their first successes, the reaction was profound and tenacious. Unfortunately, however, it let itself be closed up in the very terms of the probabilist way of posing the problem, and we must recognize that, on this terrain, probabilism turned out to be stronger. It had to overcome very grave crises and to restrict the scope of some of its principles, including the sacrosanct words, "A law which is in doubt (as regards its validity [*validité*]) does not obligate. (*Lex dubia non obligat.*)" There can be no question, however, that after coming very close to condemnation (and perhaps even having incurred it, for the whole affair is obscure), it finally conquered and earned full rights of citizenship within the Church, where it flourished no less than did Molinism.

(c. 1) *Tutiorism.* The easiest reaction is always to allow oneself to be carried to the opposite extreme. Tutiorism represents the exact opposite of laxism. In other words, posing the moral problem in the same terms, it resolves it in the opposite manner. It thus led to an outrageous rigorism which the Church equally censured.

1. Tutiorism owes its name to the fact that its supreme reflex principle is that one must always take the "safer path," that is, *in the direction of obligation*, unless freedom is completely certain. Laxism led to the practical expulsion of probability on behalf of the law: doubt frees one even

from a very probable law. For its part, tutiorism will lead to the practical expulsion of probability in favor of freedom. We could say that, in place of the principle, "A law that is in doubt does not obligate (*Lex dubia non obligat*)"—understood in its laxist sense as stating, "A law which is not absolutely certain... (*Lex non absolute certa*)"—tutiorism simply substitutes the principle, "A doubtful case of freedom does not exist (*Libertas dubia non existit*)," understanding it also as, "a freedom which is not absolutely certain (*Libertas non absolute*)." In order for obligation to exist, the slightest probability suffices. Certitude is required for freedom. This is, in any case, "the safer path." For laxism, the supreme category is freedom; for tutiorism, security is supreme.

2. While expositing St. Thomas's thought above, I told you that it has also been called a form of tutiorism and is connected to "medieval tutiorism." Doubtlessly, it would be better just to avoid this kind of terminology, which could lead to equivocation. Such medieval tutiorism has nothing in common with the tutiorism that we are now discussing. The term *tutiorism* is used with different meanings. These two outlooks do not apply this principle of safety in the same way, and their doctrinal inspirations are completely different.

(*i*) The words do not have the same sense. As soon as we find ourselves within a morality of conscience, the words "doubt" and "opinion" are no longer opposed to each other precisely as two states of mind, with one being firm adherence and the other suspension of all judgment. Rather, they take on an impersonal meaning. Opinion comes to be an objectively probable assertion, meaning that we can have many of them concerning the same subject (obviously because one has set out of consideration the adherence of the mind), and doubt is thus an assertion for which no supporting probability has been found, meaning that this assertion is "doubtful."

(*ii*) Thus, the principle, "In a case of doubt, the safer path must be taken," does not at all have the same point of application. In St. Thomas, it holds when the mind cannot manage to make a pronouncement, thus remaining in suspense. It is in no way applied in the case when the mind assents to an opinion and judges, for example, that freedom is probable, for in that case, obligation becomes, by that very fact, improbable, probably false for it. In this case, one can very well choose the side of freedom. For tutiorism in the modern sense, this remains a case of laxism, and one must go in the direction of obligation, that is, toward the safer path, since freedom is only "probable," in other words, not absolutely certain.

(*iii*) And this opposition is explained by the wholly-different inspirations animating these two doctrines. For modern tutiorism, the supreme category is security, just as laxism holds that it is freedom. For St. Thomas and "medieval tutiorism," the supreme category is *the truth*. If it is attained even under the guise of the probably true (opinion in the strong sense of the term), it prevails over security, for it implies something much better. We speak of complete security only when the truth totally eludes the mind in every fashion, even in an approximation of true probability to which one could adhere.

(c. 2) *Probabiliorism.* Probabiliorism can be considered the general reaction of the Dominican School, above all during the era of the great controversies with the Jesuits.

Its name comes from the fact that it categorically rejects the fundamental principle of probabilism: the right to follow a probability which one judges to hold even in the least way. To the eyes of the probabiliorists, this seems contrary to the requirements of the mind, which obviously can truly adhere to only one opinion at a time and, while adhering to it, detaches itself from others. Likewise, it seems contrary to the nature of the probable, which justifies only on account of the truth which it draws toward, thus meaning that *to be less probable* means that something becomes *improbable*.

I believe that this reaction is sound and can, in fact, avail itself of St. Thomas's teaching. Probabiliorism as a whole and as a system, however, is assuredly not Thomist morality. It remains a morality of conscience, the prisoner of its terms and its overall posing of the problem. Despite its aforementioned rectification of the notion of probability, probabiliorism retains the methodology of enumerating opinions and weighing out probabilities. Above all, however, it retains the idea (one that is so foreign to St. Thomas's own thought) of forming a doubtful conscience by using reflex principles, with the admirable result of transforming the state of this conscience at once into a speculative doubt and practical certitude.

On this point, probabiliorism is content with limiting the scope of the principle, *Lex dubia non obligat.* It does not admit the idea of a supreme principle and thinks that, depending on the domain involved, we must sometimes have recourse to this principle and at other times to another. For example, in matters of justice, we need to have recourse to, "The possessor has a better position. (*Melior est conditio possidentis.*)" At bottom, here, it does not manage to avoid a kind of eclecticism, which enables it to avoid the excesses in both directions (rigorism or laxism), though without giving the impression of a unique vigor.

Moreover, it does not avoid fencing in the virtue of prudence, which, yes, is spoken of by probabiliorism. (Indeed, all thinkers continue to speak about it to a greater or lesser extent). But by being interpreted and understood in the vocabulary of conscience and on the level of problems of conscience, it loses its true meaning and everything that makes it unique.

(d) *Equiprobabilism: St. Alphonsus.* As happens for all authors who have managed to acquire exceptional authority, St. Alphonsus is—and was—claimed by all camps. Fiercely fought against during his own lifetime, both by the probabiliorists and the probabilists, his memory has become the subject of battles which still endure, some wishing to say that he was a probabilist (and it seems that he was one during one period of his life), with others saying that he fought against probabilism with weapons drawn from probabiliorism (and it is certain that he did fight it). In reality, St. Alphonsus desired to be a man holding to the golden mean, and to this end, he elaborated his own personal system: equiprobabilism. In reality, its principle was already posed by a certain Eusebius Amort, to whom St. Alphonsus himself refers.

1. Prior to being ordained, St. Alphonsus was a man of the law, and he forever retained its spirit and reflexes. He was the one who most clearly formulated the fundamental position concerning the moral problem involved in moralities of conscience: the confrontation of freedom and law, demanding an equitable ruling. Now, what was striking to him was the fact that one group (the probabilists and, *a fortiori*, the laxists) were, from the outset, favorably prejudiced toward freedom, while the others (above all the tutiorists, although, to a large extent, the probabiliorists as well, who in general were rather severe) were favorably prejudiced toward the law. Prejudice does not, however, make for a good judge, who by his very essence must be equitable. His dominant desire will be to hold an exact balance: the use of probabilities without prejudice for either of the litigants. This will be equiprobabilism.

2. Therefore, one will not say, "The law is what must bring forth proofs on its behalf," no more than one will say, "Freedom must bring

them forth." This will depend on their condition in the case at hand. The supreme principle will be neither, *Lex dubia non obligat* (a favorable prejudice toward freedom), nor *Libertas dubia non existit* (a favorable prejudice toward the law), but, rather, it will be, "The possessor has a better position (*Melior est conditio possidentis*)." The first thing to be determined is knowing which of the two holds possession [of its rights in this case]. It will be up to the other to prove this and to bring forth, if not certitude, at least a truly serious probability.

For example, consider a case where there is doubt concerning the existence of a law. In such a case, freedom holds possession. The law will begin to obligate only if it manifests is valid rights. Suppose, however, that, on the contrary, there is doubt concerning the cessation or application of the law to us. This law certainly exists, and one is not sure whether it has ceased; or it is certainly in force, but we are not sure whether it applies to us. In such cases the law holds possession and freedom must bring forth proofs on its own behalf. For as long as it does not do so, we must hold that we are obligated to follow the law.

"The possessor has a better position (*Melior est conditio possidentis*)." Behold the golden rule. By means of it, we will interpret and limit the *Lex dubia non obligat*, which thus loses its character as being biased against the law, consequently doing away with its dangers of slipping into laxism.

3. He who was not in possession must prove that he is the possessor. If he brings forth certitude, the question is settled. If he brings only a probability, this must be clearly dominant, and St. Alphonsus professes that one *must* follow the dominant probability.

In this way, he will find himself in the crosshairs of [his] two adversaries:

(*i*) When the existence of a law is in question, freedom holds possession. The law must bring forth at least a dominating probability. Before reaching this degree of probable certitude, however, its probability can be noticeably stronger than that of freedom, which has only a favorable prejudice on behalf of its prior possession. Nonetheless, one can still follow freedom, for the proof of the law has not been truly made. The probabilists cheer and the probabiliorists protest.

(*ii*) When the cessation of a law is in question, the law holds possession. Freedom must prove itself and bring forward at least a dominating probability. Before arriving at this point, such probability can be notable.

One cannot yet follow it, however, since the law holds possession. The probabiliorists approve and the probabilists protest.

3. Assessment of the Moralities of Conscience

(a) *The Church and probabilism—St. Alphonsus.* The history of the relations between the Ecclesiastical Magisterium and probabilism is quite instructive. It gave rise to great concern for the Church, resulting in successive condemnations of propositions drawn from the casuists, up to the day when St. Alphonus de Ligouri, on the very terrain of probabilist morals, with their intellectual instruments and their ambitions, composed the monumental work which he called his *Moral Theology.* Through an immense labor, he addressed and characterized the various opinions that had emerged up to his day. They were examined by a holy conscience, with an exceptionally sure judgment. I believe that we can say that the providential role that St. Alphonsus was called to play was, in the very midst of the probabilist moralities, to give birth to *collection of sure moral opinions.* In so doing, he rendered the Church a dazzling service. She declared him a Doctor of the Church on account of the balance expressed in his solutions, which were distant at once from rigorism and from laxism, thereby giving mighty strength to the liquidation of Jansenism.

Much more, a Decree by the Sacred Penitentiary (July 5, 1831), in a carefully measured-out response, declares that a professor of moral theology can teach *without risk* (*tuto*) the solutions offered by St. Alphonsus, without, for all that, raising concern regarding those who prefer to follow other recognized authors who have proven themselves (*probatis*), and that moreover, one should not raise concerns for a confessor who would follow St. Alphonsus's opinions in a quasi-blind manner without disputing them, suggesting them solely on account of his authority, because the Holy See has found nothing in them which would deserve censure. By this declaration, the Holy See clearly wished for St. Alphonsus's solutions—very consciously are solutions spoken of, not justifications, nor systems—to serve as the norm in the midst of the proliferating host of opinions being presented as probable, more probable, equiprobable, less probable, etc.

Thus, it is forever invaluable to know, in a given particular question of morality, what St. Alphonsus thought about the matter, for he exhibited exceptionally sure judgment in his practical solutions. It seems clear to me, however, that between his theoretical conception of morality and the doctrinal edifice of St. Thomas's thought, a choice must be made for one side or the other. There is something more involved here than differences of perspective. They cannot be amalgamated into a hybrid which would at once denature them both. Between the two, there is nothing less than a veritable revolution.[3]

(b) *The opposition of two moralities.* We must indeed recognize the fact that, with the advent and development of the moralities of conscience, moral theology took on a completely new appearance. That which was not yet fully clear at the beginning has now become fully manifest. Let us draw to a close by making this point clear.

1. For St. Thomas, what we call moral theology is in no way a separate and independent discipline, not to the slightest degree. It is one part of the unified discipline of theology, without involving even the slightest truly formal distinction of its subject or its light. It is forever, and above all else, the science of God. Thus, it is organized around God the Ultimate End, for He is the Sovereign Good, calling His rational creature to partake in His own divine beatitude. In theology, we study this return to God in its various requirements, those that hold for man's nature and those that hold for the gratuitous gift of grace, along with those that hold for the historical conditions of a humanity which has fallen through original sin but has been redeemed by Christ and gathered into His Mystical Body. In this order concerning our return to God, it does not limit its outlook to any particular domain, neither to sin, nor to precepts, nor to counsels, nor to asceticism, nor to mysticism. It embraces everything, so long as it is related to God the Ultimate End, leading man to his full and complete flowering in the beatific vision by studying all of the possibilities involved in his intermediary progress in virtue and holiness.

In this whole that is theology, the human person holds a place of first importance, for he returns to God through his free acts. The route that he must follow, however, has been traced out for him. He is not the one who makes the truth; he conforms himself to it and allows himself to be penetrated by it. By conforming himself to the truth of things, determined by the Eternal Law, he realizes ever more fully his own truth and goodness, that of his nature and of his supernatural vocation.

3. TRANSLATOR'S NOTE: Here, we have a point of quite clear difference between Fr. Labourdette and Frs. Beaudouin and Merkelbach, the latter who strive to integrate elements from St. Alphonsus.

Conscience plays a capital, albeit subordinate, role in this. A spiritual being can be bound only through the intermediary of conscience. Precisely speaking, conscience is nothing other than the application of this knowledge to particular acts. By it, the requirements of the divine order reach us. In this sense, it is the voice of God within us—at least if it exactly translates the Eternal Law. Its fundamental duty is to be true and conformed to the objective requirements of this Law, which are at once the laws of our perfection and our beatitude. Thus, it has so sacred a character that one cannot transgress it without thereby agreeing to transgress the Divine law. It can, however, be mistaken, and it is clearly important that we must do everything we can in order to avoid and correct such errors, which often will be faults in themselves (voluntary *in causa*); and even when they excuse because they are completely involuntary, they cannot be the principle of moral goodness. Erroneous conscience does not supplant the Divine Law, and our consciences' most urgent duty will be to once again place itself in the truth.

Yet when we know the moral truth, even in a particular case, it still must be done. We still must conform our acts to it and introduce this truth into our acts as their rule, their immanent rectification. Such acts are not unimportant, facile consequences of such knowledge. There are acts which are moral, good or bad, less good or better. This is the entire role to be played by prudence. In its fidelity to objective truth, it gives them their *practical truth* through the agreement between knowledge and love [*affection*], the rectitude of everything that enters into them from our spiritual and sense life, and through our personal decision, the free consolidation, by means of our own choice, of the means that lead to God. In this judgment of choice, taken as the typical [act] of the prudential labor,[4] the quasi-creative quality of freedom manifests itself, making man not only aware of his moral duty but, moreover, truly moral, morally good, consolidating himself in moral perfection and holiness through the virtues. Here, the whole of one's subjectivity, with all of its human depths, pushes itself forward in conformity with the divine order, making this order its own, interiorizing, making it into its very own life. In its concrete agreement with virtuous ends, present as the very weight impelling and inclining the will, error can no longer be present, except in a wholly involuntary form

4. Translator's Note: Although the command remains its principal act.

which, on this level, cannot taint the practical truth of conduct, actively conformed to its rule.

2. Let us not pass over to the *moralities of conscience.* Everything changes here. One simultaneously forgets both the meaning of the fundamental subordination [of morality] to the objective order, to the divine order of things, and the meaning of the truly personal activity found in the mystery of subjectivity and its life of knowledge and love [*affection*]. Through a veritable overturning of things, one that is astonishingly paradoxical (although this fact is not always appreciated), moral theology simultaneously falls into *subjectivism concerning the moral rule* and *a depersonalization of concrete action.*

(*i*) *Subjectivism concerning the moral rules.* Henceforth, conscience is what becomes the sovereign mediator. Certainly, theologians continue to say that conscience must be true, and care is taken to assure this. As soon, however, as one affirms that even when false (through an involuntary error) conscience remains the principle of moral goodness, meaning that its verdict effectively prevails over objective conformity to the Divine Law, the ultimate arbiter must be acknowledged: conscience itself. Then, whether or not one so wishes, the principle of assessment slides from objective truth to good faith. The only thing that comes to be important is that you be true to your conscience. It is above all necessary that the error be involuntary, which means that one acts "in good faith." Thus, even error no longer causes any evil. It becomes practically negligible. "Be of good faith, and not only are your acts excused, they are all just as good as though you were living in the truth."

Everything else is connected back to this primordial inspiration. *The notion of the probable*: what is essential is no longer that it be probably *true*; this is not what is first and foremost in importance. Rather, what is important is that it be sufficiently authorized so as to guarantee good faith. Whereas St. Thomas understood probability only as being subjectively lived in a personally held opinion which is true as an approximation of the truth, henceforth from this perspective, it becomes a kind of quasi-objective, impersonal datum, whose meaning is, at bottom, the fact that is *a guarantee of good faith.* One has the intention to obey, but the law has not proven itself.

And this same inspiration is the source for the curious technique used in forming one's conscience by excluding practical doubt. Refer the doubt to the level where objective truth is no longer in question, and it will no longer be important. Let a reflex principle come to assure your good faith, however, and you can thereupon "rectify your intention" and act with peace of mind. You are "practically" certain that you are doing good, despite the doubt that remains concerning the objective truth.

(*ii*) And you can see how it was only a matter of time before this transition to subjectivism through the substitution of good faith for objective truth would become, on the level of concrete action, an impersonal and mechanical form of reasoning, now wholly objective, but precisely where it should no longer be so. [Here, within the pseudo-prudential labor of the "moralist of conscience,"] it is no longer a question of weighing out of opinions that are one's own, that animate one's own life. These are replaced with other peoples' opinions, often three, four, or five of them. Whatever you yourself think, this is what will rule your action, not to make it true, to *guarantee it*, for at this moment, one's entire practical intellectual activity has been brought to a close. There is nothing to be done except an action that is thus ruled extrinsically, being judged from on high. Yes, prudence will still be spoken of, but it will be placed upon the same level as conscience. It was of use in "prudently" assessing opinions. Completely lost here is the sense for the creative character of free activity, as subjectivity pushing forth, in its vitality as knowledge and love.

Now, I am well aware that even in the midst of moralities of conscience, there were reactions against this sort of use of probability. Probabiliorism tends to replace it in line with true opinion and the approximation of the truth; equiprobabilism is employed in order to preserve it against the excesses that isolate [*séparent*] it through too much desire for the truth as such. There should, however, be no illusions. Probabilism is what triumphed. In relation to the terms in which the problem has been posed, it remains the most logical position. By that very fact, it is the most typical form of the moralities of conscience. In probabilism, we have the clearest manifestation of this system's most genuine inspiration.

3. It will no longer be astonishing that this morality, inspired by voluntarism, which places the idea of "commandment" in the foreground (and, correlatively, the intention to obey in good faith), would become "intellectual" in the worst sense of the term. Nothing more purely cerebral than probabilistic casuistry could be conceived of, nothing more cut off from subjective life and from love [*affection*]. It is a mechanical

calculation, a pseudo-universal schematization of individual cases, with a technical accounting tally in hand for each opinion.

And, by contrast, St. Thomas, who is all-too-readily called "intellectualistic," is the one who, in his conception of prudence, places in relief—to the point of making this into an absolutely decisive element—all the values of love [*affection*], knowledge by connaturality, and personal activity and responsibility. Although prudence has quite logically become a synonym for remaining out of harm's way, safe and secure, according to St. Thomas, by contrast, it is the virtue of personal decision, of engagement in responsibility and in the affirmation of freedom.

And here we see why morality has become, for many, at least in its lowliest region [*dans une zone inférieure*], an investigation into what, according to St. Thomas, is most opposed a truly moral life and to prudence: *recipes*, that is, the use of ready-made decisions, the mechanization of moral judgment through the impersonal resolution of cases of conscience which are supposedly typical and settled once and for all. For St. Thomas, it is utterly essential that the prudential command be singular, that it be usable only once. The prudential decision is always new, always to be discovered. The life of prudence is a daily creation of moral and spiritual values.

(4) According to St. Thomas, it is unthinkable to say that we must separate moral theology, ascetical theology, and mystical theology into different disciplines with different objects. The theology of our return to God does not stop within a certain region, in a certain domain of human acts, those which would be "commanded" or "forbidden." It embraces everything, and even if we would like to form a science of commandments, he would respond, as he does in the treatise on the various states of life, that the first commandment, that of charity, is given without measure, so that we can say, in line with his customary manner of explaining these matters: the perfection of charity falls under a precept. Of course, the moralities of conscience conceive of this differently, and Suarez will advance an opposition between precepts and counsels in a way that will utterly change the meaning of this contrast, becoming the commonly received interpretation.

In short, moral theology in the Thomist sense leaves nothing out of consideration in everything concerning our return to God, from the flight from sin up to the loftiest mystical states. We are never finished responding to its requirements.

Probabilism very consciously limits itself to the discernment of sin, doing so in kind of juridical and essentially impersonal way. It would not dare to present itself as a "rule of life." And, I am not alone in saying this. One of the purest contemporary probabilists, Fr. Noldin, S.J., wisely remarked: "If a Christian were to do in the service of God nothing more than what the law strictly demands in accord with the principles of Probabilism, he would assuredly lead a life hardly deserving to be called 'Christian.' (*Si homo christianus in servitio Dei nil aliud ageret, nisi quod stricte lex ex principiis Probabilismi postulat, profecto vitam ageret parum homine chrisitano dignam*)" (in Prümmer, p. 225, n. 155). There could be no better recognition (nor one presented with such modesty) of the true ambition of moral theology understood in the probabilist sense: learning how to glide up to the edge of sin without falling into it... In order to accomplish something more than this, one must turn to another science.

* * *

In our own days, it is not difficult to see that there is a reaction afoot, one that is fundamentally anti-intellectualist, anti-objective, etc. It readily looks at things from the perspective of "the dialectic of history." I told you that probabilist moralities led to a complete overturning of things by introducing subjectivism into the level of the moral rule and by leading, by contrast, to a wholly impersonal objectivism precisely where it is harmful, misunderstanding the entire living dynamism of prudence. Today's reaction rises up against this objectivism (which in fact is illusory), although without, for all that, giving up the claims of subjectivism regarding the moral rule.

Thus, the contemporary reaction leads to pure subjectivism. There no longer are any objects, nor any universal rules. The creative activity of conscience is placed at the first rank of things, alone competent in particular cases, which no universal law can embrace. The sovereign arbiter is said to be situational conscience. For every choice, it creates its own value, which is never an objectively assessable value, etc.

These ideas have taken on such importance that, as is well known, the Magisterium has felt the need to intervene. His Holiness Pope Pius XII has spoken of it many times, in particular in his radio message on March 23, 1952, and in his allocution on April 18, 1952. It is interesting to note that what he recommends is that we return to St. Thomas's treatise on *Prudence*:

> Let it suffice to cite St. Thomas's unsurpassed explanations concerning the cardinal virtue of prudence and the virtues connected to it (*ST* II-II, q. 47–57). His treatise bears witness to his sense for personal activity and actuality. It contains whatever true and positive elements might be found in "situation ethics," while avoiding its confusion and deviations. Therefore, the modern moralist will find it sufficient that he continue along these same lines if he wishes to deepen his investigation into the new problems facing us today.

Prudence plays its precise and complete role in our subjective activity, in all that it is, in its vitality as knowledge and love [*affection*]. It is in no way opposed, however, to the objectivity of conscience. Much to the contrary, it calls for it and requires it. There, it finds the source of its truth, from which it fashions the living truth of moral action. This is the meaning of "making the truth," certainly not speculative truth, which is not something to be made and is only a regulative element[5] for action, but rather, the truth of life and of action, in all its human density, with all the various elements included in it, above all on the side of the utterly-important source of action which is not intelligence but, rather, affectivity.

5. **Translator's Note:** He means that although speculative truth is presupposed for practical agency, it is not of the same order as even speculatively-practical truth. On this, see the text from Fr. Labourdette cited in notes 64 and 69 of the Translator's Introduction to this volume.

REGINALD BEAUDOUIN, O.P.

* * *

De Conscientia

ORIGINAL TEXT

Reginald Beaudouin, O.P., *Tractatus de conscientia*, ed. Ambroise Gardeil, O.P. (Tournai: Desclée, 1911).

* * *

TRANSLATOR'S INTRODUCTION

I am here reproducing the main speculative content of Fr. Beaudouin's *Tractatus de conscientia*, edited posthumously by Fr. Ambroise Gardeil, O.P. For the sake of space and focus, I have omitted some basic front matter concerning Fr. Beaudouin and the text more generally. His work is thoroughly marked by the theological controversies over probabilism and the resolutions offered by St. Alphonsus. Fr. Beaudouin attempts to wed the Thomist philosophy and theology of conscience with St. Alphonsus's equiprobabilism. On occasion throughout the text, I provide brief notes in order to indicate how Fr. Beaudouin's work may be synthesized in a fuller, more balanced account of moral theology and of moral reasoning. If this text is read as primarily fitting into the theological treatise on human acts (cf. *ST* I-II, q. 6-21), any of its apparent shortcomings fall away, for Fr. Beaudouin himself makes clear that further development is needed: *in the appropriate other theological treatises*, not this moral-theological treatise, which belongs quite early in the overall objective structure of moral-theological reflection.

* * *

DE CONSCIENTIA

Reginald Beaudouin, O.P.

INTRODUCTORY QUESTION: ON CONSCIENCE IN GENERAL AND ITS DIVISION

1. *The Order to Be Followed in the Theological Treatise on Conscience and Its Connection to the Overall Structure of St. Thomas's Summa*

St. Thomas briefly discusses this subject in *ST* I-II, q. 19, aa. 5 and 6, likewise taking it up, in passing, in other texts. He establishes the proper location for it where he treats of the human act inasmuch as it is moral: "(For) the goodness of the will properly depends on its object. Now, the object of the will is proposed to it by reason, for the object that is proportioned to the will is the understood good... And therefore, the goodness of the will depends on reason in the same way that it depends on its object."[1]

Now, the object of the will is found not only in the end, but also in those things that are directed to the end [i.e., the means]. Therefore, the goodness of the will depends on reason in two ways: first, in *intention*, that is, in the very desire for the end (which itself presupposes right apprehension of the end through *synderesis*); second, in *choice*, which presupposes right deliberative and discursive [*consiliativum atque ratiocinativum*] reason concerning those things that are directed to the end. Now, the discourse of practical reasoning is brought to its terminus at the practical judgment, that is, at *conscience*, which bears witness concerning the goodness or wickedness of the act in question, and, applying itself to the will, subjects the latter to itself, directing and ruling it.[2] Therefore, for good reason, St. Thomas connects this consideration to question 19, which is concerned with the question of the goodness or wickedness of the interior act of the will.[3]

2. *Some Questions*

Sub-question 1: *What does the term "conscience" signify?*

The *term* "conscience" signifies "the application of knowledge [*scientiae*]

---

1. *ST* I-II, q. 19, a. 3.
2. **Translator's Note:** Note here a potential underrating of the role of command in the prudential discursus.
3. In order for this exposition, which is perhaps briefer than what would be of use to those who are not experts in St. Thomas's ways, to be a little clearer, we will set out a synopsis of it. This synopsis, according to the order devised by St. Thomas himself, sets forth the movements of both the intellect and of the will that concur in bringing about the integrity and consummation of a given morally perfect act. [**Translator's Note:** See the end of this question for the chart that is placed in this footnote.]

   See Billuart, *Summa Sancti Thomae hodiernis academiarum moribus accommodata Tractatus de actibus humanis*, diss. 3, *Proemium, horum autem*; Antoine Goudin, *Philosophia iuxta inconcussa tutissimaque D. Tomae dogmata, Ethica*, q. 2, a. 3; Frins, *De actibus humanis psychologice spectates* (Fribourg en Brisgau, 1897). Also, see the entries "Acte humain," "Consentement," Counseil," and "Election" in the *Dictionnaire de théologie catholique*; Gardeil, *La crédibilité et l'apologétique* (Paris: 1908), p. 8.

   Cajetan, in *In ST* I-II, q. 17, a. 4, no. 2, seems to move away from the common ordering of these twelve movements, on account of his admission of certain reflex acts into his synopsis (cf. nos. 3 and 4 in the same commentary), as well as on account of a tacit understanding of one or the other [movements] examined by us. The aforementioned order, however, which I myself have taken from the most excellent writing of Master Fr. Beaudouin, seems to be more conformed to St. Thomas's own texts once they have been fully accounted for and carefully compared to each other.

   Note that the *judgment* placed under no. 3 [on the chart below] pertains to the intellectual virtue that is called *synderesis* and, moreover, to theological faith, which in practical matters is equivalent to a kind of supernatural synderesis, and, finally to the demonstratively proven conclusions of Moral Science (whether one refers to Theology or to Natural Ethics). However, the act of *intention* described under no. 4 is reduced in natural matters to morally fitting intention (or, *right appetite*), and in supernatural maters to the theological virtues of hope and charity. [**Translator's Note:** And in line with what Gardeil says elsewhere, in *La vraie vie chrétienne*, also to the infused moral virtues other than infused prudence. Also, supernatural faith can arguably be operative in the order of intention. On this, see my comments in the Translator's Introduction.]

   Finally, the acts of *counsel, the practico-practical judgment,* and *command* are themselves acts that are ascribed to prudence (whether acquired or infused). See *ST* II-II, q. 47, a. 8 (in the treatise on prudence) and q. 51. However, on the manner in which choice and intention themselves participate in the moral virtues that follow prudence, namely justice, courage, and temperance, see q. 58, a. 1 and 5 with nos. 6 and 7 in Cajetan's commentary on *ST* II-II, q. 47. (Editor's Note)

   Translator's Note: No article given for Cajetan's commentary.

to something." Thus, *conscire* designates, as it were, "to know simultaneously." Any given knowledge, however, can be applied to something. Thus, conscience cannot name some specific *habitus*, or some power. Instead, it names the act itself, namely the application of some knowledge-related [*cognosciviti*] *habitus* or of some knowledge to a given object—in this case, as all admit, to particular acts exercised by man.[4]

Now, knowledge [*aliqua notitia*] is applied to a given act *in two ways: in one way*, inasmuch as we consider whether an act exists or existed; *in another way*, inasmuch as we consider whether an act is "*right or not right*," *good or evil*.[5]

First: Indeed, according to the *first manner of speaking*, conscience is the application, to a particular act, either (*a*) of sense knowledge such as memory, by means of which we recall something that was done in the past, or (*b*) of the senses by means of which we perceive this or that particular act which we are now doing. And because the intellect perceives that it understands and comes to know its own nature by knowing its act,[6] the term "conscience" is transferred by some philosophers to signify this kind of cognition (whether habitual or presently taking place), which they call "psychological conscience."[7] According to them, this is nothing other than, "The faculty or act by which our soul perceives or can perceive itself and its own affects or activities."

Second: *According to the second manner* of speaking, however—namely that pertaining to knowledge of the rightness or wrongness of an act—a given act of knowledge [*aliqua notitia*] is applied to a particular act so that one may thereby know whether the act is right or not, good or evil.[8] Now, properly speaking, this is "moral conscience," for it is applied to a particular act by a *habitus* of practical reason, namely the *habitus* of synderesis and the *habitus* of wisdom, by which the superior reason is perfected, and

4. See St. Thomas, *De veritate*, q. 17, a. 1.
5. See ibid.
6. See *ST* I, q. 87, a. 3.
7. Translator's Note: The ambiguity is not as easily expressed in English, for we would be more likely to say, "psychological consciousness." I have retained "conscience" because Frs. Beaudouin and Gardeil are in fact expressing a potential equivocation on *conscientia*.
8. See *De veritate*, q. 17, a. 1.
9. Translator's Note: On the topic of superior and inferior reason, a terminological theme taken over from Augustine, although not deployed systematically by Thomists on the whole, see *ST* I, q. 79, a. 9; *De veritate*, q. 15, a. 4; *In II Sent.*, d. 24, q. 2, a. 2.

the *habitus* of science by which inferior reason is perfected,[9] whether all of them together are put into practice, or only one of them; and through this application [of such universal knowledge to particular acts,] one judges whether a particular act is good or evil.

There are two ways, however, that knowledge is applied to an act in order that we might know whether or not an act is right: first, after we have performed an act, it can be examined by [*ad*] the *habitus* of science in order to determine whether or not it is right; second, we are directed through the *habitus* of science to something to be done (as good) or not to be done (as evil).

Hence, along these two lines, there can be two types of such conscience. On the one hand, there is *consequent* conscience, through which we consider past things by applying to them our knowledge for making judgments concerning an act's goodness and wickedness. On the other hand, there is *antecedent* conscience, through which we consider future things.[10] Now, each of these two kinds of conscience seems to have unique properties. Indeed, inasmuch as knowledge [*scientia*] is applied to an act in order to direct it (i.e., in the form of antecedent conscience), conscience is thus said to *instigate*, *influence* [*inducere*], or *bind*. Inasmuch as knowledge is applied, however, to an act in order to examine things that we did in the past (i.e., in the form of consequent conscience), conscience is thus said to *accuse* or *gnaw*, when what we have done is found to be at variance with the knowledge at hand as we examine that act, or to *defend* or *excuse*, when what we have done is found to be in harmony with the knowledge at hand in the examination of the act [*secundam formam scientiae*]).[11]

Now, in either form, conscience involves the same sort of consideration, for through one and the same *habitus* of science, we examine what we have done and likewise also direct and deliberate concerning things to be done. Such examination is not only concerned with things done in the past but also with things to be done in the future, whereas deliberation is only concerned with things to be done in the future. Therefore, in moral science, it suffices that we consider conscience concerning things to be

10. See Scavini, *Theologia moralis universa, ad mentem S. Alphonsi* (Paris: Lecoffre, 1863), vol. 1, p. 61, n. 1.

11. See *De veritate*, q. 17, a. 1.

done, for by thus studying the nature of antecedent conscience, we may easily render a judgment concerning an act after it has been performed, asking whether it is right, good or evil.[12]

With Scavini,[13] we categorically reject the opinion held by some, namely, that there is no such thing as antecedent conscience. This error arises from a confusion of *psychological* and *moral* conscience.[14] Yes, our inner sense (or, psychological conscience) perceives an act only as present. By contrast, however, moral conscience judges concerning the goodness or wickedness of an act that has been performed or is to be performed. If this fact were denied, the whole of moral science would thus be overturned.

Sub-question 2: *How is conscience defined, inasmuch as it is applied to the act as directing it?*

Response. Conscience is commonly defined: *The practical judgment (or, dictamen) of reason by which we judge what is to be done here and now (as good) or to be avoided (as evil)*. Let us consider the parts of this definition.

First: It is a "judgment (or, *dictamen*) of reason," namely an act of the intellect, thereby excluding the opinion of those who say that conscience is a power or a *habitus*. Indeed, a power cannot be set aside, nor can a *habitus*, except with great difficulty. We can, however, freely set aside and change [our judgments of] conscience. Hence, as was said, conscience signifies an act, namely the actual application of knowledge or science to a particular act.[15]

Second: We say that it is a judgment "of practical reason." Thus, it is not an act of the will, but, instead, of the intellect. It is not, however, an act *of the speculative intellect*, because it does not stop in contemplation but, instead, is an act of *the practical intellect*, for it directs the execution of a work to be done and is a *science of the heart*.

Third: Likewise, we say, "By which we judge here and now." And, thus, conscience differs:

12. **Translator's Note:** Note, however, the role of consequent conscience, understood along Fr. Beaudouin's lines, is quite important for having an analysis of the way that moral memory is involved in prudential reasoning.

13. Scavini, no. 62.

14. **Translator's Note:** As noted above, the distinction is not as necessary in English, as the ambiguity is less likely to occur. We would likely more readily use the term "psychological *consciousness*."

15. See *ST* I, q. 79, a. 12 and 13.

(a) *From synderesis*, whose judgement focuses on the universal practical principles, that are, as it were, grafted on to our nature, for example: *The good is to be done and evil avoided.* The judgment of conscience, however, is concerned with particular actions and declares—not universally, but rather, particularly—that an act, clothed in all of its circumstances,[16] is good or evil.

(b) *And from prudence*, which is right reason concerning things to be done, from which conscience is distinguished as an act is from the *habitus* by which that act is elicited. Thus, since prudence is a virtue, it always is concerned with practical things that are true and good. Since conscience is an act, however, it can err, as will be discussed below, and can be concerned with practical things that are false.[17] Right conscience, however, coincides with the act of prudence that is called judgment, for there are three acts of prudence, namely, to deliberate, to judge, and to command.[18]

Fourth: And it is said that it is concerned with things that are here and now "to be done." This portion of the definition distinguishes it from *consequent conscience*, by which we examine those things that we have done, as well as from *the command* [issuing from prudence or imprudence], by which we order to execution those things that we have judged to be good or evil. Indeed, as St. Thomas says,[19] reason can declare or warn about something in two ways:

> In one way, reason can make an absolute declaration, which is expressed by means of a verb in the indicative mood, as when someone says to another person, "This is what you should do." Reason, however, sometimes declares something to someone by moving that person to do that thing. In this case, its declaration is expressed by means of a verb in the imperative mood: "Do this."

16. **Translator's Note:** This is exactly where the distinction between a "vague individual" and a prudential judgment comes into play. See the Translator's Introduction for more information.
17. See St. Thomas, *De veritate*, q. 17, a. 2, ad 7.
18. See *ST* II-II, q. 47, a. 8 and q. 51; Billuart, *Summa Sancti Thomae, Tractatus de prudentia*, a. 2 (*De actibus prudentiae*).
19. *ST* I-II, q. 17, a. 1.

The first way pertains to conscience, whereas the second pertains to the command or [*vel*] to the judgment of choice, as St. Thomas says.[20] And for this reason it sometimes happens that the judgment of choice is perverted, while the judgment of conscience remains right, as when someone examines something to be done and judges that it is evil (for example, *stealing*), but when he begins to apply himself to the act, on account of concupiscence or some other circumstances, his reason is bound, rejecting the *dictamen* of conscience, and he commits an act of theft. Thus, he errs in choosing, not in the judgment of conscience but, instead, acts against conscience. Indeed, he is said to act in bad conscience inasmuch as what is done does not agree with the judgment of knowledge [*scientiae*].

Fifth: It is to be done as good or avoided as evil: that is, not as a transcendental or [meta]physical good or evil, but as moral good or evil; *truly* good or evil, not only as an apparent good or evil, as has often been said.

Corollary

The judgment of conscience is a conclusion of the particular practical syllogism. Its *universal major premise* is proclaimed by synderesis, for example: *The good is to be done, but evil avoided. The particular minor premise* is, however, sometimes furnished by superior reason and sometimes by inferior reason, for example: *Theft is prohibited by the divine law* or *by the human law.* And from these two propositions conscience infers: *Therefore, theft is to be avoided as evil.* Theologians generally call this final judgment "practically-practical" because it immediately precedes the execution of the action.[21]

How is conscience divided? Conscience is commonly divided in two ways: first, from the perspective of the object; second, from the perspective of the assent or that of the subject assenting.

From the perspective of the object, it is distinguished into *right* and *erroneous conscience.* From the perspective of its assent, however, it is distinguished into *certain*, *doubtful*, and *probable conscience.*

The first thing we must consider is conscience from the perspective of its object.

20. See *De veritate*, q. 17, a. 1, ad 4.

21. Translator's Note: One point to note, throughout this text, is Fr. Beaudouin's underemphasis on the mutual causality exercised between the intellect and will. He is not unaware of it, but the rhetoric can lead one to miss this point.

EDITORIAL APPENDIX: LISTING OF THE STAGES OF THE HUMAN ACT

The following chart[22] expresses the twelve movements (or, partial acts) of both the will and the intellect concurring to the integrity of a morally perfect act, according to the teaching of St. Thomas in *ST* I-II, q. 8-21.

Act of the Intellect	*Act of the Will*
I. WITH RESPECT TO THE END (ORDER OF INTENTION, Q. 8)	
1. Simple *apprehension* of our perfect good / end (q. 9, a. 1).	2. *Simple willing*, an inefficacious desire for the good simply apprehended (q. 8).
3. *The judgment* of synderesis proposing the end already apprehended as befitting to reason (or, as a good that is fitting and able to be pursued) q. 19, a. 4ff.	4. Efficacious *intention*, the act by which the will tends in an absolute manner to the end proposed by synderesis as befitting and able to be pursued (q. 8, a. 1 and 4; q. 19, a. 7ff.). *This is also called:* RIGHT APPETITE.
II. WITH RESPECT TO THE MEANS ORDERED TO THE END A. *Order of Choice*	
5. *Deliberation* concerning apt means for obtaining the befitting end already efficaciously intended (q. 14).	6. *Consent*, whereby one approves all the means that are apt for bringing about a given befitting end, without giving preference to one over another, having discovered these apt means through deliberation (q. 15).
7. *Practical judgment*, conformed to right appetite, by which certain means are preferred and proposed	

22. TRANSLATOR'S NOTE: This chart was included in Fr. Gardeil's lengthy footnote above. It has been placed here.

Act of the Intellect	*Act of the Will*
to the will as being more apt for the attainment of the intended fitting good (q. 15, a. 6; q. 13, a. 3). *This is properly called* MORAL CONSCIENCE, which declares: "This is to be done by you here and now."[23]	8. *Choice*, the act by which the will efficaciously chooses the more apt means in preference to the others (q. 13).

B. *Order of Execution*

9. *Command* of the intellect ordering the will, in a fully efficacious manner, so that the chosen means may be placed into execution.	10. *Active use*, the act by which the will utilizes man's other powers so that they may efficaciously lead the chosen and commanded means for the end intended to their ultimate outcome.
	11. *Passive use*, the act of the powers of man executing the command. *This is called*: THE COMMANDED ACT (q. 16, a. 1).
	12. *The enjoyment* in the will following upon the consummated moral act (q. 11).[24]

N. B. *Since the will is not moved unless it is moved by the intellect, and in turn, the intellect is applied to the exercise of its power* [facultatis] *by the will, it follows that he who reads the synopsis above may continuously pass from the movement of the intellect to the movement of the will, and from the movement of the will to the movement of the intellect, namely, by following the order of*

23. TRANSLATOR'S NOTE: Reading "hic et nunc" for "nunc nunc".

24. TRANSLATOR'S NOTE: Recall, from the introduction, however, the way that enjoyment is intentionally present from the start of the action.

the numbers which are knowingly placed next to each other for this reason. (Editor's Note, Ambroise Gardeil)

QUESTION I: ON CONSCIENCE, CONSIDERED FROM THE PERSPECTIVE OF ITS OBJECT

Article 1: *On Right Conscience and the Obligation to Follow It*

§1. ON RIGHT CONSCIENCE

Sub-question 1: *What is right conscience?*

Conscience[25] is called "right" in contrast to "erroneous." Now, because this contrast is drawn from the perspective of the object, we must explain them both together. Therefore, *right* conscience is that which declares *the truth*, whereas *erroneous* conscience is that which declares *falsity as though it were true.*[26] Or, in accord with St. Thomas's way of thinking about this matter, *right* conscience is that which declares *something as really and truly conforming to right appetite*, whereas *erroneous* or *erring* conscience is that which declares *something as conforming to right appetite, although it is not really and truly conformed to it.*

Now, the reason for this is that truth and falsity in conscience's practical judgment is different in character from truth and falsity as they are found in speculative judgment.[27] On the one hand, the truth of the speculative intellect holds through the intellect's conformity to reality.[28]

---

25. In order to avoid confusion through the multiplication of distinctions, we here are abstaining from using the title "PRIOR PART," which nonetheless seems more fitting for this question, as is clear from §2, *Preliminary Notes* in Question II. Otherwise, we have left intact the other divisions deliberately employed by the author, along with their titles, on account of their clarity. Nay, we have taken care to preserve the orthography of certain words, regardless of their datedness [*antiquitatem*]. (Editor's Note, Ambroise Gardeil)

    Translator's Note: This footnote is associated in the original with the question heading.

26. See St. Alphonsus, *op. cit.*, no. 3, (H. p. 2; G. p. 3).

27. See St. Thomas, *In VI Ethic.*, lect. 2.

28. **Translator's Note:** As has become my normal manner of translating this expression, I opt for "to reality" than "to the thing," for in the case of judgments like those enunciated through *synderesis*, conformity is made in relation to the reality of a given moral essence, which while being ultimately based upon the nature of things is, nonetheless, measured *secundum esse morale*. Here, "thing" takes on its analogical breadth, a point I discuss in Matthew Minerd, "Beyond Non-Being: Thomistic Metaphysics on Second Intentions, *Ens*

Depending upon whether the reality [in question] is or is not [what it is enunciated to be or not be], the intellect affirming or denying is said to be true or false.[29] On the other hand, the truth of the practical intellect holds through conformity to right appetite / right desire [*appetitum*] for a due end. This desire for the due end, however, also presupposes right apprehension of the end, which takes place through reason,[30] and once such rectified appetite concerning the intention of the end exists, the intellect then undertakes deliberation and discursive reasoning concerning those things that are directed to the end [i.e., the means]. Indeed, as we have said, the will's object is something proposed to it by reason.[31] Therefore, if reason proposes something so that it is really and truly conformed to right appetite, conscience is called right and declares the truth. If reason, however, proposes something as being conformed to right appetite when, it is not really and truly conformed to it, conscience is then called erroneous and declares falsehood as though it were something true. For example, someone sees another person in danger and, hence, intends to save the latter precisely because this would be a good action. In this case, his desire [*appetitus*] is right on account of his right apprehension concerning the end. If this person believes, however, as did Cassian,[32] that we are permitted to lie in order to do something good or to avoid some evil, judging in conscience that lying is necessary in order to arrive at this most excellent end, this conscience is said to be erroneous, for it declares a falsehood as though it were the truth, judging that something is conformed to right appetite when, in reality, it is not—for a lie is never good but, rather, must always be avoided as an evil.[33]

---

morale, and *Ens artificiale*," *American Catholic Philosophical Quarterly*, Vol. 91, No. 3 (July 2017): pp. 353-379; "The Analogy of Res-ality," *Reality*, Vol. 1 (2020): pp. 124-145.

29. See St. Thomas, *In I Perihermen.*, lect. 9.

30. See *ST* I-II, q. 19, a. 3, ad 2.

31. See *ST* I-II, q. 8, a. 1.

32. Translator's Note: See the seventeenth of John Cassian's *Conferences*.

33. Right conscience is *per se* true and good, and erroneous conscience is *per se* false and evil. *Per accidens, from the perspective of the subject*, however, it can happen that right conscience may be false and evil, and erroneous conscience may be true and good, for it is surely the case that that which is good can take on the character of evil, or that which is evil can take on the character of good, on account of the apprehension of reason. For example, he who condemns a plaintiff whom he believes to be innocent is guilty because even if the judgment [*sententia*] is, of itself, true, nonetheless *per accidens* it is false because it is not in conformity with the rules of prudence. [continued next page]

Sub-question 2: *How many forms of right conscience are there?*

Response. Right conscience is understood in a three different ways, namely: as *permitting, counseling,* and *commanding or prohibiting.*

Permitting conscience is that which proposes acts which are indifferent, objectively speaking, consequently *per se* not imposing the binding force [*ligamen*] of a command or a prohibition. I said, "*per se*," because if the object, which of itself is indifferent, is clothed with its circumstances, this can introduce necessity for the individual case, depending on the given person's station in life.

Counseling conscience is that which proposes counsels, insofar as the latter are distinguished from precepts, by way of persuasion and exhortation. A counsel, however, is concerned with those things that pertain to perfection, but by no means with those things that impose a necessity [for someone to need to act, as is the case for precepts].[34] It can obligate only after the manner of the [given] counsel itself, by which one is obligated *inasmuch as one may not scorn* [it], though without thereby requiring the fulfillment thereof. Thus, we have the Scholastic axiom: "He who neglects a counsel does not sin, so long as he does not hold it in scorn."

Commanding or prohibiting conscience is that which *binds* and *obligates,* imposing the necessity that one do or not do an act, through the necessary force of the law. St. Thomas uses "to bind" and "to obligate" interchangeably.[35] Conscience binds lest we act against and obligates so that we may act according to it.[36]

On the other hand, erroneous conscience can be true and good. For example, when someone, led by an invincible error, lies in order to save an innocent person, that person does not sin. Indeed, although of itself this judgment [*sententia*] may be erroneous, *per accidens,* however, it is conformed to the rules of prudence, and is true and good.

The reason for this is that both forms of conscience (i.e., right and erroneous) have something in common, namely, that they declare that which is conformed to right appetite. From the perspective of the assenting or declaring subject, however, that which is truly conformed is not seen as being so conformed, and vice-versa, as is clear from the examples given above. (See *ST* I-II, q. 19, aa. 5 and 6, where examples of fornication and faith in Christ are given.)

34. **Translator's Note:** Here, we have an example of the weakness of these sorts of questions of conscience. The primary concern is with discovering the border between what is required and what is free to choice. The latter domain, however, has many shades of obligation as well, all depending upon the agent in question. (This will be admitted, however, by Fr. Beaudouin, when he discusses the *medium rationis,* the mean of reason, later on below.)

35. **Translator's Note:** This point is likely taken from the beginning of the text of Billuart (cited in the next note) where he addresses the position of Durandus of St. Pourçain concerning the senses of "to bind" and "to obligate."

36. See Billuart, *Summa Sancti Thomae, De actibus humanis,* diss. 5, a. 2.

On the other hand, conscience is said to *release someone* [*solvere*], allowing him or her to retain freedom of action, when such conscience judges that the will is neither bound by a necessary prohibition, nor obligated through the necessity of a precept. Thus, properly speaking, the question concerning the binding or obligation of right conscience is concerned with *commanding* or *prohibiting* conscience.

§2. ON THE OBLIGATION OF RIGHT CONSCIENCE

Conclusion. Right conscience binds and obligates. That is, it binds by prohibiting, such that we may not act against it [without sinning], and it obligates, such that we must act in accord with it.

First Proof. From the authority of the Apostle Paul to the Romans (14:23; DR): "All that is not of faith is sin." Now, as St. Thomas explains,[37] faith can here be understood in two different ways. On the one hand, it can be understood as pertaining to faith which is a particular virtue. On the other hand, it can be understood as referring to conscience. These two senses, however, differ only as particular and universal. Indeed, what we hold in a universal manner by faith, conscience applies to the work that was done or to be done. Therefore, it is said that he who eats [food sacrificed to an idol] and discerns [that it would be right not to have eaten it] is thus condemned, for this is not from faith. Nay, it is contrary to the truth of faith and contrary to the conscience of the person who eats such food.

This is how the Holy Fathers and [most] Theologians understand this passage from St. Paul.

Second Proof. From reason. When the Eternal Law prohibits, it binds so that we may not act against it, and when it commands, it obligates such that we must act in accord with it. Now, right conscience commands or prohibits on the strength of the Eternal Law. Therefore, it binds and obligates.

Proof of the minor premise. Indeed, right conscience is nothing other than the application and promulgation of the Eternal Law, brought about by us, through natural reason or through revelation added above and beyond that. Consequently, it participates in the two properties of the Eternal Law from which it is derived: first, *it judges concerning things to be done*, as the proximate rule subordinate to the Supreme Rule, and second, *has a*

37. St. Thomas, *In XIV Rom.*, lect. 3.

coercive or obligating power. Thus, St. Bonaventure said: "Conscience is, as it were, God's herald and envoy. What it declares it does not command on its own but, instead, does so, as it were, from God, like a herald disseminating the king's edict."[38]

38. *In II Sent*, bk. 2, dist. 39, a. 1, q. 3. Cf. St. Thomas, *De veritate*, 17, a. 3.

It is of assistance here to refer to this whole article, which is truly worth its weight in gold. Indeed, the doctrine it hands on is the foundation of things that will be discussed in this treatise. Moreover, there he proposes the arguments that St. Alphonsus of Liguori used to support himself in establishing his theory of equiprobabilism.

"I respond that it must be said that conscience certainly binds.

To see how it binds, however, we must bear in mind that binding (a term that is metaphorically transferred from bodily beings to spiritual ones) implies the imposition of necessity. Indeed, he who is bound necessarily must remain in the place where he is bound, and the power of turning away to some other place is taken away from him. Thus, it is clear that binding has no role in those things that are necessary of themselves, for we cannot say that fire is bound to being carried upward, although it is necessary for it to rise upward. Binding, by contrast, has a role only in those necessary things upon which the necessity is imposed by another.

"Two kinds of necessity, however, can be imposed by another agent. One is coercive, through which something [*reading aliquis* for *omnis*] must, in an absolutely necessary manner, do that to which it is determined by the action of the agent [acting upon it]. Without this absolute necessity, it is not called coercion, properly speaking, but rather is a case of inducement. The other kind of necessity, however, is conditional, that is, necessity holding on the supposition of a given end. According to this manner of speaking, necessity is imposed on someone so that if he does not do this, his reward will not follow.

"Indeed, the first kind of necessity, namely, coercion, does not take place for the movements of the will, but only for bodily things, because the will by its very nature is free from coercion. The second kind of necessity can be imposed, namely as it would be necessary to choose X if this given good Y should be acquired or if this evil Z should be avoided. Indeed, in such things, the avoidance of evil is reckoned the same as the achieving of a good, as is clear in *EN* 5.1 concerning the means. However, just as such coercive necessity is imposed on bodily things through some action, so too is conditional necessity imposed upon the will through some action. The action by which the will is moved, however, is the command of the ruler and governor.

"Thus, the Philosopher says in *Metaphysics* Δ that the king is the principle of motion through his command. So too, the command of a given governor binding things pertaining the will is similarly related to the kind of binding that can be applied to the will, just as bodily action is related to the binding of bodily things by a coercive necessity. The bodily action of the agent, however, never induces necessity upon another thing except through contact between its very coercive action with the thing on which it acts. Hence, someone is not bound by the command of a given king or lord unless the command reaches the person who is commanded. It reaches such a person, however, through knowledge [*scientia*].

"Thus, nobody is bound through a given command except through knowledge of that command. Therefore, he who is not capable of knowledge is not bound by the command, nor is someone who is unaware of God's command bound to the doing of that command except inasmuch as he is bound to know the command. Now, if he is not required to know it, and indeed does not know it, he is in no way bound by the command. Just as in bodily beings, however, the bodily agent acts only through

From this we can infer the following three points.

First: Right conscience binds and obligates more than any other human law whatsoever. As St. Thomas teaches[39]:

> Conscience obligates, not on its own strength, but instead, on the strength of the divine command, for conscience does not declare that something is to be done because of how matters seem to it, but rather, because it has been commanded by God. Hence, it obligates *per accidens* [*sic*] on the strength of the divine precept, inasmuch as it declares that this is commanded by God. Therefore, *the dictamen* of conscience obligates more than the command of a superior, as does the divine precept in virtue of which it binds.

What St. Thomas says here is also handed on in Scripture itself: "We ought to obey God rather than men."[40]

Second: Right conscience never can be set aside, for it binds and obligates in an unqualified manner, *per se*, absolutely, and in every case, since it is the natural law [*lex naturae*], or the expression and communicating of the natural law, as St. Thomas teaches: "The natural law [*ius naturale*] is principally contained in the Eternal Law; however, it is secondarily contained in the natural judgment of human reason."[41]

Third: For the same reason, he who acts against right conscience *sins*, namely, because he acts against the Eternal Law.

Sub-question 1: *Does he who acts against right conscience commit two sins at once?*

In other words, does such a person commit one sin against the Eternal Law and another against the *dictamen* of conscience?

contact, so too in spiritual beings, a command does not bind except through knowledge. And therefore, just as both touch and the power of the agent act by the same power (since touch acts only through the power of the agent, and the power of the agent only through the mediation of touch) so too does the precept and conscience bind through the same power (for the precept binds only through the power of knowledge, and knowledge binds only through the power of the precept). Therefore, since conscience is nothing other than the application of knowledge to an act, it is obvious that conscience is said to bind on the strength of the divine command."

39. *In II Sent.*, d. 39, a. 3, ad 3.

40. Acts 5:29 (DR). See Concina, op. et edit. cit., *De conscientia*, diss. 1, ch. 2, no. 6, p. 6.

41. *ST* I-II, q. 71, a. 6, ad 4.

Response. He commits only one sin, for right conscience is not, properly speaking, a law which is distinct from the Eternal Law but, instead, is its expression and manifestation. For the same reason, although theft is prohibited by the natural law, divine law, and human law, he who steals still commits one sin, not three.

Sub-question 2: *Does he who acts against right conscience sin mortally or venially?*

Response. He sins mortally or venially depending on whether the conscience against which he acts presents something as a mortal or venial sin, for when reason "grasps something as being evil, it always grasps some reason for that being evil (for example, because it is contrary to a precept, or because it is scandalous, or for some other such reason). Thus, an evil will is reduced to the species of evil falling to that reason for the evil."[42]

Sub-question 3: *What if, however, acting against right conscience does not involve a unique species of evil? Does he sin gravely or venially?*

Response. This is a difficult matter to determine. If in acting against conscience he *at least vaguely* grasps that the act is contrary to the Eternal Law, he sins against prudence and obedience, more or less gravely depending on the gravity of his negligence and on the degree to which the will is virtually[43] moved to those things that are opposed to the divine precepts.

If, however, someone does *not vaguely heed* the gravity or lightness of the matter, we believe (here agreeing with Billuart[44]) that if such a person's disposition of soul would lead him to commit it if he were to actually think that what he is doing is a mortal sin, he would not be excused from mortal sin. He would, however, be excused if he would not will it [if it came to his mind], for given such a habitual disposition, it is fair to presume that he does not grasp the mortally sinful character of what he is doing.

42. Concina, op. cit., *De conscientia*, ch. 2, no. 3, ed. cit., p. 5.

43. Translator's Note: For a discussion of virtual intention see Reginald Garrigou-Lagrange, *De Beatitudine* (Turin: Berruti, 1951), pp. 60-62. The Latin must be consulted, not the English translation, for the latter (in its current form at the time of this volume's publication) is a paraphrase, not a full translation.

44. Billuart, *Summa sancti thomae, De actibus humanis*, diss. 5, a. 3, *dico* 3.

Article 2: *On Erroneous Conscience and the Obligation to Follow It*

§1. ON ERRONEOUS CONSCIENCE

Sub-question 1: *What is erroneous conscience?*

Response. As was said above, erroneous conscience is that which *declares falsehood as though it were something true* or which declares that something is conformed to right appetite when it is not truly and really conformed to it. And this occurs in two ways: (1) either someone believes that something is evil when, in reality and of itself, it is good or indifferent; or (2), someone may believe that something is good when, in reality and of itself, it is evil.[45]

Sub-question 2: *What are the causes of errors of conscience?*

Response. Such errors of conscience arise from two causes, namely (1) because someone *neglects to use a due form in reasoning* and (2) because *one makes use of falsehoods.* Indeed, as has been said, conscience designates a kind of gathering together, since it is nothing other than an application of knowledge [*scientiae*] to some particular act. Now, error takes place in this application either because that which is applied has an error in itself or because it is not applied well, just as in discursively reasoning [*syllogizando*] an error arises in two ways: either from the fact that falsehoods are used, or from the fact that one does not discursively reason in a valid syllogistic form.

Thus, *in the first way,* error in conscience takes place because of the misapplication of knowledge to an act. When we discursively reason concerning speculative things, we can neglect to use a valid form of argumentation, with this omission giving rise to falsity in the conclusion. Similarly, this can take place in the syllogism that is required in actions [*operabilibus*].

In a second way, error in conscience takes place because falsehoods are utilized. This does not take place on the part of the universal judgment of synderesis such as, "The good is to be done, and evil avoided," but rather, on the part of the minor premise subsumed under it. For by

45. See *ST* I-II, q. 20, a. 5.

means of the judgment of conscience, the knowledge had through synderesis is applied to an act through the subsumption of some particular act, which is sometimes supplied by superior reason and sometimes by inferior reason.[46] Now, it can happen that an error [*peccatum*] takes place in the judgment of superior reason and of inferior reason, leading to an error in conscience because of an error or falsity in the superior part of reason or in its inferior part. An example of an error in the superior part of reason is seen when someone believes that something is in accord with the divine law (or against it) when it, in fact, is not (e.g., heretics who believe that the making of an oath is prohibited by God). An example of the second (i.e., of an error in the inferior part of reason) takes place when someone errs concerning the civil notions of justice or injustice, the fitting or unbefitting (e.g., as when someone, judging that a given contract is licit, although it is not, forms an erroneous judgment of conscience to actually enter into such a contract).[47]

Sub-question 3: *How many forms of erroneous conscience are there?*

Response. Since we are accustomed to name causes and effects by means of each other, erroneous conscience is divided along the same lines as is the ignorance that is a cause of error in practical reason.[48] Thus, erroneous conscience is designated *involuntary* and *voluntary*, depending upon whether the error that is found in it is willed. It is designated *antecedent* and *consequent* depending on whether that error precedes or follows the will. And it is designated *invincible* and *vincible* because error, since it is not in our will, either can or cannot *morally* be overcome.

We also describe erroneous conscience as being *erroneous* of a right or of a fact,[49] *affected*, *crass*, and *supine*,[50] in the same manner as one speaks

46. Translator's Note: Note also that a developed discussion of the cogitative power needs to be introduced into this discussion as well.
47. See St. Thomas, *De veritate*, q. 17, a. 2.
48. *ST* I-II, q. 6, a. 8.
49. Translator's Note: The expression "erronea *juris*" and "erronea *facti*" is akin to language used below for probability: "probability of right" and "probability of fact." After considering several less clunky options for this semi-technical terminology used by various authors, I have chosen to render the genitive form directly in the English.
50. Translator's Note: *Crassa* and *supina* are used in a generally technical sense in this era, especially canonically, to refer to ignorance of something that one should have known but did not bother to look into. One might translate it somewhat loosely as "stupid and lazy," although that potentially runs the risk of equivocation. Thus, I have chosen to

of ignorance.[51]

§2. ON THE OBLIGATION IMPOSED BY ERRONEOUS CONSCIENCE

Preliminary Remarks

First, in order to understand the question at hand and how it is to be resolved, we must first know what it means for conscience to bind and obligate. As St. Thomas remarks:

> Conscience is said to bind when one incurs a sin if he does not fulfill that judgment of conscience. This does not mean, however, that he who fulfills it acts rightly. Otherwise a counsel would be said to obligate. Indeed, he who fulfills a counsel acts rightly; however, we are not said to be bound to the counsels, for someone does not sin if he neglects a counsel. Now, we are said to be bound by precepts because we incur a sin if we do not keep them. Therefore, conscience is not said to bind on account of the fact that one would be good were he to act from such a judgment of conscience; rather, it is said to bind because he would incur a sin if he were not to do this act.[52]

Second, therefore, two interrelated questions arise concerning the obligation of erroneous conscience, namely:

* Does he who acts against erroneous conscience incur a sin?
* When someone acts in accord with erroneous conscience, is that person excused from sin?

Two conclusions correspond to these two questions.

maintain the somewhat awkward terminology of the era in English. For an example of this language's application, see *Code of Canon Law* (*CIC*) (1917), can. 2229, §3, no. 1: "Ignorance of the law (*legis*), or even of only the penalty if it was crass or supine, does not excuse an automatic penalty; if it was not crass or supine, it excuses from medicinal but not from vindicative automatic penalties." *The 1917 Or Pio-Benedictine Code of Canon Law, in English Translation with Extensive Scholarly Apparatus*, trans. Edward Peters (San Francisco: Ignatius, 2001), p. 708.

51. See ibid.

52. St. Thomas, *De veritate*, q. 17, a. 4.

Conclusions

Conclusion 1

Everything that is done against erroneous conscience is a sin. Or to put it another way: Erroneous conscience binds or obligates so that we must not act against it. Or, to put it yet another way: A will at variance with erring reason is always evil.[53]

First Proof. From Authority, as expressed above, from the Apostle in Romans 14:23.

Indeed, the same authority who shows that nobody can act against right conscience also proves that we cannot act against erroneous conscience. For we are not permitted to act against right conscience because such conscience is a law commanding something as being commanded by God. Now, the same is true of erroneous conscience. Therefore, the reason involved in both cases is the same. Indeed, in the same place, the Apostle says, "He that discerneth, if he eat, is condemned; because not of faith. For all that is not of faith is sin" (DR). In this chapter, St. Paul is speaking about the eating of foods that were not *per se* evil but which certain people believed to be unclean and prohibited by the Mosaic Law. Thus, he draws the conclusion in the aforementioned text that he who believes that a given food is unclean and eats it, sins, even as his belief is false, because he acts against his own conscience. This is how this text is understood by St. John Chrysostom, St. Ambrose, and Theophylact, and it is generally read in this manner by the Holy Fathers and the interpreters of Scripture. Such is the position held by St. Thomas[54] and the Scholastics who seize upon this opinion from [Ecclesiastical] Law, ch. 13 (*De Restitutione Spoliatorum*)[55]: "Everything that is contrary to conscience, leads one toward hell."[56]

Second Proof. From Reason.

(1) Goodness or wickedness of will is taken from the object, not according to its nature, but, rather, according to how it is grasped by reason

53. See *ST* I-II, q. 19, a. 5.

54. See ibid.

55. *Decretal. Greg.* IX, bk. 2, tit. 13, ch. 13 (Turin: 1588), col. 716.

56. Cf. S. Antoninum, *Summa theologia*, pt. 1, bk. 3, ch. 10, §3 (Verona, 1740), bk. 1, col. 181. Concina, op. et loc. cit, ch. 3, no. 2, p. 8.

Translator's Note: It is almost certainly the case that "S. Antoninum" refers to the Dominican St. Antoninus of Florence, the author of a *Summa theologica moralis*.

as being good or evil (and as to be done or to be avoided). Now, it happens that something that is *per se* good may, *per accidens*, be grasped and proposed as being something evil. Likewise, it can happen that something that is *per se* evil may be grasped and proposed as being something good. Therefore, if the will is moved toward an object that is *per se* good, although proposed to it by erring reason as being evil, this leads the will to take on the formal character of evil and, indeed, to become evil, for it wills evil, not indeed that which is evil *per se* but, rather, that which is evil *per accidens*, on account of what reason happens to grasp. Similarly, if it were to flee from an object that is evil *per se* but that reason proposes to it, *per accidens*, as something good and commanded, the will will be evil for the same reason.[57]

(2) He who acts against erroneous conscience draws back from God's law. Therefore, such a person sins.

Proof, taken from St. Thomas:

> It does not seem possible that someone could avoid sin if his conscience, however erring it may be, declares that something is commanded by God, even if that thing is indifferent or *per se* evil, deciding to do the opposite while such a judgment of conscience remains in force. For given how he is disposed in these circumstances [*quantum in se est*], he has willed to not observe God's law through such an action. Therefore, he mortally sins. Therefore, however much such erroneous conscience can be set aside, so long as it remains, it is binding, for he who acts against it incurs sin.[58]

Moreover:

> Although what erroneous conscience declares may not be in harmony with the Law of God, nonetheless the person who errs in this way does hold it to be the very law of God. Therefore, speaking essentially [*per se*], if he draws back from this, he draws back from the law of God, even though it may be the case, *per accidens*, that he does not in fact draw back from the law of God.[59]

57. See *ST* I-II, q. 19, a. 5.
58. *De veritate*, q. 17, a. 4c.
59. Ibid., ad 1. Cf. ibid., ad 2.

Hence, Cajetan writes:

> Erroneous conscience obligates so much so that if one were to hold in conscience that to spit in a church were a mortal sin and nonetheless, in opposition to such conscience would spit in a church, such a person would mortally sin, for given how he is disposed in these circumstances [*quantum in se est*], he would formally consent to a mortal sin.[60]

Sub-question 1: *What species of sin is committed when one acts against erroneous conscience?*
I respond that, in acting against erroneous conscience, he is made to be a transgressor of the law of God and, consequently, is guilty of a sin that is more or less grave in the same manner as is the person who acts against right conscience.[61]

Sub-question 2: *Does a sin against erroneous conscience differ in species from a sin against right conscience?*
I respond negatively, with more probable certitude, here agreeing with what the Salmanticenses say concerning this matter.[62] For the judgment of conscience is the mere application (or, promulgation) of the law. Now, various applications do not change the nature of a law or its species.[63]

Conclusion 2
Everything that is done in accord with erroneous conscience does not always excuse from sin.

In other words: *Invincibly erroneous conscience excuses, but vincibly erroneous conscience does not.*

Or, to put it another way: *An involuntary erring will in harmony with reason is good; however, a voluntarily erring will is evil.*

Proof. As St. Thomas observes,[64] this question depends on what was said above concerning ignorance, namely, that ignorance sometimes causes

60. *Summula*, Verbo: *Conscientia.*
61. See pp. 175–76 above. Also, Aquinas, *De veritate*, q. 17, a. 4, ad 3.
62. Salmanticenses, *Cursus theologicus moralis*, tract. 20, *De principiis moralitatis*, ch. 5, punct. 2, no. 18 (Venice, 1734), vol. 5, p. 16.
63. See Concina, op. cit., diss. 1, ch. 3, no. 12, p. 11.
64. See *ST* I-II, q. 19, a. 6.

an act to be involuntary, but sometimes does not. Now, as is clear from what has been said, because moral good and evil exists in an act inasmuch as it is voluntary, it is obvious that the ignorance that causes an act to be involuntary destroys the character of moral good and evil. This is not the case, however, when ignorance does not cause an act to be involuntary.

Now, antecedent and invincible ignorance causes an act to be involuntary, as when a given man is not aware of a given circumstance of his action and is not bound to know that circumstance. Consequent and vincible ignorance, however, which is willed in some manner (whether directly or indirectly), does not cause an act to be involuntary. Moreover, I say that ignorance is directly voluntary when the will is directly moved to it. As was said earlier, however, it is indirectly voluntary when it finds its source in negligence, when someone does not will to know that which he is bound to know.[65]

Therefore, if reason or conscience were to err in a way that causes an act to be involuntary, arising from invincible ignorance, then such an error of reason or of conscience would excuse such a person, meaning that a will in harmony with erring reason would not be evil. If, however, conscience errs through a voluntary and vincible error (be it directly or indirectly voluntary), then such an error of reason or of conscience does not excuse, since the will in harmony with reason or conscience erring in this manner would itself be evil.

Sub-question 1: *Does erring conscience bind and obligate in the same manner as does right conscience?*

No. Right conscience binds *without qualification*, *per se*, and in every case. It must never be set aside and cannot be set aside without falling into sin. Erroneous conscience, however, binds *in a qualified sense* and *per accidens*.

First, it binds in a qualified sense and conditionally [*sub conditione*]:

> For when someone's conscience declares that he is bound to steal,[66] he is not obligated in such a way that he will necessarily sin by not stealing, except on this condition: if such a conscience remains. Such

65. See *ST* I-II, q. 6, a. 3.

66. This is how the text is cited in the author's manuscript. (Editor's Note, Ambroise Gardeil) **Translator's Note:** The official text reads "fornicandum."

a person can, however, rid himself of such conscience without sinning. Thus, such conscience does not obligate from every perspective. Indeed, something else is possible: a change of conscience. Once such a change takes place, such a person is no longer bound [by the former erring conscience]. Now, whenever something is designated with a given qualification, it is said to be so only in a qualified sense [*secundum quid*].[67]

Second, it binds per accidens:

He who has an erroneous conscience, however, believing it to be right—otherwise, he would not err and would not cling to such erroneous conscience—on account of the rectitude that he believes to exist in it, indeed clings, *per se*, to right conscience, though he clings to erroneous conscience, as it were, *per accidens*, inasmuch as this conscience, which he believes to be right, happens to be erroneous. And thus, *per se*, one is bound by right conscience, but *per accidens* by erroneous conscience.[68]

Sub-question 2: *Can erroneous conscience be set aside?*

I respond in the affirmative. This follows from the response to the first sub-question, namely, that the person who labors under erroneous conscience (in both its invincible and vincible forms) can always set it aside and reform it by himself or through counsel given by others, thus being able to free himself from the obligation that it imposes.[69] Indeed, erroneous conscience does not bind absolutely, without qualification, and *per se*, but instead, does so only in a qualified sense, on the supposition that it be received and that it perseveres. For example, if an erroneous judgment of conscience were to declare that I am bound to hear Mass on the third weekday after Easter, I am not bound to do so except upon the supposition of the error of conscience, and when this is set aside, there is no obligation.

Sub-question 3: *Whether erroneous conscience not only can be set aside but, indeed, must be set aside?*

67. *De veritate*, q. 17, a. 4. Cf. *ST* I-II, q. 19, a. 5.
68. Ibid.
69. See Cajetan's commentary on *ST* I-II, q. 19, a. 5. Also, see his *Summula* cited above.

I respond that we must distinguish between *invincibly* erroneous conscience and *vincibly* erroneous conscience.

First, he who has *invincibly erroneous* conscience *is not always bound to set it aside.* Rather, sometimes he is bound to follow it and at other times to set it aside.

(a) *Sometimes he is bound to follow it,* for he does not sin in following it since it is involuntary and, on the other hand, as was said earlier, it obligates on the strength of the divine command.[70]

A Doubt

Is the act that is done in accord with invincibly erroneous conscience not only good but also meritorious?

I respond, with more probable certitude, in the affirmative. For, by acting in this manner, his action is prudent and, without a doubt, ought to be meritorious, at least on account of the good end for which he acts—for example, charity toward his neighbor (as, in St. Thomas's example, when one believes that he is bound by divine precept to lie so that he might save someone's life). As St. Alphonsus says: "So too, on the contrary, he would demerit who does an act that is good but is grasped as being evil, on account of the evil end for which that work is striven after."[71]

[*Returning to the main point of the sub-question:*]

(b) *Sometimes, he is bound to set it aside,* namely, *when the practical doubt arises from error.* For example, someone may invincibly believe that the swearing of an oath is absolutely prohibited by the law of God, likewise, when interrogated by a judge, knowing that by swearing an oath he can save the life of an innocent man. Hence, he remains in doubt on two heads: if he takes the oath, he will sin against the command of God prohibiting the taking of oaths; if he does not take the oath, he will sin against charity. I say that a person faced by this kind of doubt would be bound to set aside his erroneous conscience. Thus, St. Alphonsus says,[72] if he can suspend his action, he is bound to postpone it until he consults with wise

70. See St. Thomas, *In II Sent.*, d. 39, q. 3, a. 3, ad 1 and 2. *De veritate*, q. 17, a. 4, ad 1. St. Alphonsus, *De conscientia*, no. 5, H. p. 3; G. vol. 1, p. 4.
71. St. Alphonsus, *De conscientia*, ch. 1, no. 6, h., p. 3. Gaudé, vol. 1, p. 4.
72. See ibid., no. 10.

persons; however, if he cannot suspend it, he is bound to choose the less evil one, preferring to avoid a transgression of the natural law than that of a human law, or by preferring to avoid a transgression of the divine law. If, however, he cannot discern which is less evil, whatever side that he chooses, he will not sin, for in cases of this sort, the freedom needed for a formal sin is lacking.[73]

Second, he who *has a vincibly erroneous conscience is always required to set it aside,* for as we have said, he always sins whether he acts in accord with to it or against it. "For he sins," says St. Alphonsus, "in acting against it, by choosing an evil that he judges to be evil. He sins in acting in accord with it, however, because given that he must (and can) overcome the error, he acts rashly by not setting aside that vincibly erroneous conscience."[74]

Sub-question 4: *What must be done by the person who labors under a vincibly erroneous, perplexed conscience?*

Such a case of conscience arises when someone is faced with two possible courses of action and must do one of them, although it is impossible for such a person not to sin whatever course he chooses to take.

Response. The case of someone who is perplexed between two evils does not exist without qualification but, instead, of itself depends on the supposition of something, namely, on his foolish opinion and erroneous conscience, or on the presumption of obstinacy on his part. For example, imagine someone who swore that he would kill a man, forming for himself a judgment of conscience (albeit one that is erroneous) that if he does not kill this person he will be a liar in relation to that oath.If he kills that man, however, he will commit homicide. Thus, he is perplexed from his foolish valuation of the matter, for even were he not to kill that person, he is not a liar. When someone is [thus] perplexed, however, he is not so in an unqualified sense, but rather, is perplexed only in a qualified sense, for he can set aside erroneous conscience or do penance, since the ignorance is vincible and voluntary. Then, if he remains in error, this error changes from being vincible to invincible and involuntary, and in so acting he will not sin.[75]

---

73. See C. Marc, *Instit. Mor. Alphons.*, vol. 1, nos. 29-30.
74. Op. cit., no. 4.
75. See S. Antoninus, *Summa theol.*, pt. 1, ch. 10, §3, 6th ed., col. 183. St. Thomas, *ST* I-II, q. 19, a. 6, ad 3; *Quodl.* 3, q. 12, a. 2 [lit. a. 27]; *De veritate*, q. 17, a. 4, ad 8.

Sub-question 5: *From what signs can we discern that a judgment of conscience is invicibly or vincibly erroneous?*
Response. We can make this discernment in exactly the same manner as how we distinguish invincible ignorance from vincible ignorance.[76]

Sub-question 6: *How must a confessor conduct himself with a penitent whom he recognizes to be laboring under conscience that is either invincibly or vincibly erroneous?*
This will be discussed below when we treat of the confessor's duties.[77]

QUESTION 2: ON CONSCIENCE, SUBJECTIVELY CONSIDERED FROM THE PERSPECTIVE OF ONE'S ASSENT—ON CERTAIN CONSCIENCE

Preliminary Note

First: On the order being followed here. After speaking about conscience from the perspective of its object, we must now consider it from the perspective of its subject, namely, as regards the various states that it can have in an assenting and judging intellect.

Second: The division of this second part. From the perspective of its assent (i.e., the character of the subject's assent), in view of the certitude involved in one's assent, conscience is commonly divided into: *certain*, *doubtful*, and *probable* conscience.

Now, indeed, truth and falsity exists in the intellect's second operation, which composes and divides by affirming or denying. Since our intellect, however, is in potency with respect to all intelligible forms, it is related in various ways to the parts of a contradiction (i.e., of an affirmation and a negation). Now, according to St. Thomas, we can understand this variety in terms of three kinds of intellectual states. Certain acts of

76. See Concina, *Ad Theol. Christ. Dogmatico-moralem Apparatus* (Rome, 1751), vol. 2, *De conscientia*, diss. 1, ch. 3, no. 18, p. 13. Gury, no. 38.

77. See Billuart, *De actibus humanis*, diss. 5, a. 4. (Editor's Note, Ambroise Gardeil: Regarding the reference the taking up of this matter later, he is referring to the treatise *De poenitentia*, which can be found in a fully composed state among the author's [unpublished] manuscripts.)

Translator's Note: There is a discrepancy here in the footnotes in the body of the text. The citation of Billuart's text is only found in the footnote section, not in the body itself.

the intellect involve *firm assent without fear* [*of error*], as when someone considers those things that he knows or understands. Such an examination of affairs is already *formed, determined,* and *certain*. Some acts [of understanding], however, are not perfectly determined and lack *firm adherence*. In such cases, they either *incline to neither side of the contradiction*, as happens in *the person who is in doubt*, or they *incline to one side more than to the other*, as happens in *the person who opines* and adheres to one side of the contradiction, although he fears that the other may be true.[78]

Now, conscience is an act of the practical intellect,[79] since it is the judgment or application of knowledge [*scientia*] to an act. Thus, from the perspective of the assenting subject, it can exist in three different states. Thus, it is called *certain, doubtful,* or *probable*.

We must begin our consideration here by first reflecting on certain conscience.

Third: The definition of certain conscience in general, as well as its division. Certain conscience is a practical judgment of reason by which we judge *firmly and without fear* that something is to be done here and now as good or to be avoided as evil. To put it another way: certain conscience is that sort of judgment by which someone *firmly and without fear of error* judges that something is permitted or not permitted.[80]

As is obvious, although this definition adds something to the definition of conscience which is formulated from the perspective of the object, this addition is only something formally pertaining to the notion of the subject, namely: *firmly and without fear* of the other side of the contradiction. This is so because certainty in general is nothing other than the determination of the intellect to one side of a contradiction, and, abstractly considered, is defined: "The firmness of the intellect's inherence to a given knowable thing without fear of the opposite being the case." Thus, taken in itself, certitude designates this given state of the intellect. When it is applied to conscience, it designates the firmness of the assent or of the judgment which lacks fear of erring. This firmness and certitude in the

78. See *De veritate*, q. 14, a. 1. *ST* II-II, q. 1, a. 4; q. 2, a. 1.

79. **Translator's Note:** This is a good example of where clarification is needed—namely, how to use vocabulary in relation to that which is speculatively-practical and that which is fully practical. (In any case, however, Fr. Beaudouin here thinks that conscience is fully practical and prudential / imprudential in character.)

80. Cf. Marc, *Instit. Morales*, no. 35.

mind, however, is caused by objective certitude, which is nothing other than *the very intelligible object itself present to the mind and drawing to itself the mind's firm assent.* Thus, subjective certitude clearly depends upon objective certitude, and unless this is present, subjective certitude will not exist but, instead, will be merely specious in nature [*sed fucata*].[81]

Today, following St. Alphonsus of Ligouri, authors commonly distinguish morally certain conscience into conscience that is *perfectly, imperfectly,* and *indirectly* certain. This division will be obvious once we provide a definition for each kind of conscience.

Article 1: *On Perfectly Certain Conscience and Its Obligation*

§1. ON PERFECTLY CERTAIN CONSCIENCE

Sub-question 1: *What is perfectly certain conscience?*

I respond: Perfectly certain conscience is that which *proceeds from true, first, and proper principles.*

To understand this point, bear in mind that, given that conscience is an application of discursive knowledge [*scientia*] to an act, it finds its perfection in the same way as does discursive knowledge [in the speculative order, lit. *eodem prorsus modo ac scientia*]. Now, discursive knowledge is an effect of demonstration, which is knowledge through causes, and its perfection is produced from true and first and proper principles. Moreover, the perfection of discursive knowledge requires that, on the basis of its principles, the inferred conclusion be reached in accord with right syllogistic form, through the assumption of a middle term that is not outside the termini of the syllogism. Hence, conscience is called *perfect* when it proceeds from true, first, and proper principles. It is called *direct,* however, inasmuch as the practical syllogism involved is valid in form.

Sub-question 2: *Is perfectly certain conscience the same as right, true, and good conscience?*

I respond that, *per se,* these two kinds of conscience mutually imply each other because, as has been said, the subject's certitude depends upon the object's certitude, and consequently, if the assent of the judgment is

81. Zigliara, *Summa philosophica,* vol. 1, *Logica,* ch. 4, a. 1 (40), nos. 3 and 4.

certain, the knowable thing is essentially [*per se*] true and good in a determinate manner. *Per accidens*, however, namely from the perspective of the subject, they are not [always] convertible. This is so because it sometimes happens that an object that *of itself is certain* may appear to the subject as though it were only probable or doubtful and, vice-versa, that which *is only probable or doubtful of itself* is sometimes grasped as being certain. Right now, however, we are speaking formally, using the term "perfectly certain conscience" for that which is said of conscience because of the rectitude, truth, and goodness of the object, together with the determination of the subject.

Sub-question 3: *Is perfectly and directly certain conscience found in practical matters?*

I respond affirmatively, for (as was said above) conscience is a practical *dictamen* that is inferred from principles. Now, very often, the judgment of conscience is inferred perfectly and directly from true, first, and proper principles. Therefore, [perfectly and directly certain conscience is found in practical matters.]

Proof of the minor premise. Certitude is found in like manner in both practical and speculative matters. Now, just as in speculative matters one does not happen to err concerning a particular conclusion that is *directly* subsumed under universal principles having the same terms, so too in some practical matters, conscience cannot err because in either judgment (both in speculative matters and in things to be done) both premises are *per se nota*, the *major premise* existing in a universal judgment, as well as the *minor premise*, because one and the same thing is predicated of itself in a particular manner.[82] Let us take an example:

* [Major premise:] To take someone else's property is evil because it is prohibited by the divine law (as superior reason declares) or because it is morally unbefitting, against justice and the civil law (as inferior reason declares).[83]

82. See Aquinas, *De veritate*, q. 17, a. 2.

83. **Translator's Note:** The moral philosophy of the virtues needs to be included here as well. At times, Fr. Beaudouin does seem to recognize this (especially where he invokes prudence and also when he points out that the question of reflex principles actually calls for discussion in relation to the virtues discussed in *ST* II-II).

* [Minor premise:] Now, this is someone else's thing.[84]
* [Conclusion:] Therefore, it is evil to take it.

The major premise is morally certain. The minor is held with certitude and evidence on the basis of experience. Thus, the conclusion (which, as we have said already, is what conscience is, namely, the application of discursive knowledge to an act to be done here and now) is perfectly and directly certain in the moral order.

Sub-question 4: *How is the certitude of conscience distinguished from physical and metaphysical certitude?*

I respond that, just as a moral conclusion is distinguished from a physical and metaphysical one, so too the certitude of conscience is proportionally distinguished from physical and metaphysical certitude as has been said, when one is speaking of Moral Science.[85]

§2. ON THE OBLIGATION OF PERFECTLY CERTAIN CONSCIENCE

Conclusion

Perfectly certain conscience binds and obligates. To put it another way, it is the certain and perfect rule of morals, and everything that is done in opposition to it is a sin.

This is proven by means of the same arguments as above when we discussed right conscience, for since subjective certitude arises from objective certitude, the binding or obligation of conscience from the perspective of the subject depends on the binding of conscience from the perspective of the object. To demonstrate the conclusion, it suffices that one apply to subjective conscience what we have said concerning objective conscience.

First: A proof based on the authority of St. Paul to the Romans (14:23; DR): "All that is not of faith is sin," namely, everything that is not based upon the certain judgment of conscience leading the agent would be certainly determined concerning the goodness or wickedness of the act in

84. **Translator's Note:** Here is an example of where expansion to include the cogitative power is important.

85. The studious reader will recall that this elaboratate treatise on conscience is only the introductory part of the *Institutio moralis* that the author himself hoped to publish. (Editor's Note, Ambrose Gardeil)

question. Now, what is done on the basis of conscience that is not certain is not from faith [in the sense given here to the term]. Therefore, certain conscience is the rule of morals, binding so that we may not act against it and obligating us such that we must always follow it.

Second: *A proof from reason.* A law or command binds and obligates only if it reaches him of whom it is commanded. Now, we come into contact with the law through certain conscience. Therefore, [right and certain conscience is binding and obligating.]

Third: If perfectly certain conscience did not obligate, it would follow that no action would be determinately good or evil based upon a necessary process of reasoning. Instead, every morally right or morally wrong action (as well as every permissible or impermissible one) would be reduced to an arbitrary will. Thus, the entire moral order would be destroyed. Thus, the more rigid rigorists admit this conclusion, and it is not rejected except by pseudo-philosophers who deny the existence of goodness and wickedness in human acts.

First Inference: Perfectly certain conscience binds and obligates without qualification and absolutely, doing so in every case, just like right conscience. Moreover, it can never be set aside without thereby incurring sin. This makes it sufficiently clear what we should think concerning certain men's sincerity of conscience, something of which, today, so many rationalist and liberal philosophers boast. Indeed, by the witness of St. Thomas and the truth itself, a grave sin has been committed by those who were nourished on Catholic doctrine and then became apostates from the true faith (nay, even coming to deny God), having set aside their prior conscience. Thus, they labor under vincibly erroneous conscience and are not excused in their sins. Hence too, they do not have true, right, and pure conscience. Indeed, pure conscience, which lacks duplicity of intention, as St. Antoninus says,[86] proceeds from a pure heart (that is, one that is cleansed of sins)[87] and from good conscience (that is, according to Bernard, one that does not follow from a deceived reason or a perverse will).

Second Inference: The supereminence of the faithful Christian's conscience over the conscience of the philosopher or that of the unbeliever.

86. Loc cit., §V, col. 185.

87. 1 Tim. 1:5.

This is obvious, in light of the two things that are required for conscience to be perfectly certain, namely *certitude of principles* and *perfection of syllogistic form.*

(a) Indeed, nobody can err in the first, naturally known,[88] principles of things to be done, for example, "The good is to be done and evil avoided" (although, nonetheless, some reject this out of petulance). In other more particular principles, however, error can (and in fact does) occur in many ways. This is the opinion held by St. Augustine and of St. Thomas. Indeed, with great labor and after a long time, philosophers have discovered many truths of the moral order and have handed them on. In the writings of many, however, they are received as doubtful or are reputed as being false. Thus, the uneducated person, listening to the disputation of the learned, finds himself to be perplexed, is very often deceived, and cannot easily form right and certain conscience for himself. The Christian, however, making use of the principles of reason and of faith, supplies right and certain conscience for himself most easily. Indeed, faith (which cannot be false) commands, as things to be held, things which reason can investigate on its own. In this way, the intellect finds itself to be reinforced. This explains a number of things: the unanimous agreement among theologians concerning the first moral principles; the unity of doctrine handed on by all; and the light by which Christians can partake, with utter ease, in the Natural Law and Eternal Law, likewise forming for themselves right and certain conscience for acting virtuously, without doubt of error. Moreover (and lastly), faith teaches that reason, by itself, cannot discover the ultimate end of the whole of human life, to which we are ordered by Divine Providence, thereby summoning the mind to things that are loftier than what reason can attain in its present state. In this way, men learn to rectify their acts in relation to the end and to zealously tend toward something that exceeds their present state of life.

(b) In the case of error concerning particular principles, however, or of deception through one's manner of syllogizing, Christian conscience can have recourse to confessors, teachers and, in particular, to the supreme Magisterium of the Church, by which such an error is refuted or rendered certain. In this way, it wipes away every danger of practical error and of sin.

88. **Translator's Note:** Recall, however, the issue of the infused virtues as well. This is acknowledged in what follows, but also see the developments offered by Fr. Merkelbach.

Sub-question: *Does he who acts against perfectly certain conscience incur a sin?*
I respond: He does not sin against prudence, since conscience would be right.[89] He falls short in command or in the judgment of choice, however, and the sins that he commits are diversified according to the various species of acts that are chosen against the law or the virtues.

Article 2: *On Imperfectly Certain Conscience and Its Obligation*

§1. ON IMPERFECTLY CERTAIN CONSCIENCE

Sub-question 1: *What is imperfectly certain conscience?*
I respond: Imperfectly certain conscience is that which proceeds from human authority or from likelihoods [*verisimilibus*], not through things that are *per se nota*.

I. *Preliminary Note.* Before the definition is explained, I must declare what is meant by the adverb "imperfectly" qualifying "certain conscience."

First, take care to note that various authors do not speak in the same manner regarding these matters. Using words that are less apt to the task, they introduce a degree of obscurity into this question. Moreover, they do not seem to be in harmony with each other. Indeed, some of them, within the limits of this treatise, divide certitude into *perfect* and *imperfect.* They resolve perfect certitude into metaphysical certitude. They say, however, that imperfect certitude is that "which involves propositions which are not absolutely incompatible with error, although it would be very difficult for that to happen."[90] Others use the term "perfect conscience" for that which is had through *intrinsic* principles, whereas they use the term "extrinsic conscience" for that which is had through *extrinsic* principles (e.g., from human authority). Certain other authors, however, say that imperfectly certain conscience is that which is indirectly perfected by means of reflex principles.

89. Translator's Note: Here is something perplexing, for falling short in command is to fall short in that which perfects prudence fully. (Also, he seems to be distinguishing here between the judgment of choice and the judgment of conscience. This draws conscience closer to the final judgment of deliberation.)

90. Gury, *Compendium theol. Mor.*, n. 39, 3.

Now, although such declarations and definitions are partially true, nonetheless, they do not quiet the intellect, and in order to understand the definition, we need to accurately determine the logical *suppositio* for the subject, "imperfectly certain conscience."[91]

Second, imperfectly certain conscience is designated in relation to perfectly certain conscience in the same manner, though proportionally, as how one designates the relationship between an imperfectly certain conclusion and a perfectly certain one. Now, perfection and imperfection in the conclusions of a science are understood as being contraries (just as is the case for *more* or *less* in qualities, such as, for example, more or less white, and more or less cold). This takes place in two ways: *extensively* (although this way does not matter for our purposes here [*quod est extra propositum*]); and *intensively*, namely, depending upon how deeply rooted the form is in the subject. Now, we have the latter in mind here, since what we are concerned with is the certitude of conscience considered from the perspective of the subject.[92]

Third, the fact, however, that a subject happens to be more or less determined or certain arises from the condition of the object, inasmuch as, of itself, it is more or less determined or certain, consequently being more or less apt to move one to assent to it.

Now, a comparison can be brought about in two ways.

(1) *In one way, such a comparison can be relative to the conclusion of another science.* Thus, moral conclusions [*moralis*] are said to be less perfect than metaphysical ones and physical ones. This imperfection, however, is common to all the conclusions of practical morality [*moralis practicae*], as is admitted by all who distinguish the various degrees in moral, physical, and metaphysical certitude. Thus, it does not provide a foundation for the distinction between perfectly and imperfectly certain conscience [which must itself be wholly found in the domain of moral certitude, alongside perfectly certain conscience].

(2) *In a second way,* one conclusion is said to be more or less perfect *in relation to another conclusion within the formal character of the same science.* We are now, however, speaking about certitude in moral knowledge

91. Regarding the nature of *suppositio* see Jacques Maritain, *Formal Logic*, trans. Imelda Choquette (New York: Sheed and Ward, 1946), pp. 57-76

92. See *ST* I-II, q. 52, a. 2 and q. 54, a. 3, ad 3.

[*scientia morali*]. Thus, it follows that conscience is denominated as "imperfectly certain" in comparison with perfect conscience on account of the fact that the knowable object is less perfectly rooted in the subject and is less formally participated in by him.

II. *Exposition of the Definition of Imperfectly Certain Conscience. First,* it is said: "it does not proceed from *per se nota* principles."

Indeed, there are two causes involved in a knowable object being more or less rooted in a subject. *One is from the perspective of the subject,* due to the fact that someone is not well disposed, grasping things that are intrinsically certain as though they were only probable (or doubtful or even false) and, vice-versa, admitting those things that are false, doubtful, or probable as though they were certain. This, however, is a *per accidens* cause.

The *other* (and *per se*) cause, however, is involved *from the perspective of the object,* which is intrinsically indeterminate, not being absolutely known and certain, and consequently of its very nature insufficient for causing comprehensive intellectual certitude, as does the object of perfect conscience that proceeds from true, first, and proper principles. And this represents the fundamental difference between perfect and imperfect conscience. The first proceeds from things that are *per se nota,* whereas the second does not. Thus, in the works of more recent authors, the certitude of perfect conscience is called *strict,* whereas the certitude of imperfect conscience is called *broad* or *ordinary.*[93]

Second, it is said: "But [instead, it] proceeds from human authority or from likelihoods [*verisimilibus*]." Indeed, given that imperfect conscience does not proceed from things that are *per se nota,* it follows that it is concerned with a given practical conclusion, assumed on human authority or through principles that are not demonstrative but, instead, are dialectical, likely [*verisimilia*], or probable.

(1) "From human authority." This portion of the definition expresses the first way that conscience falls short of the perfection of certitude. In this case, it does not proceed from insight into principles but, rather, from testimony, and those things that it applies to the act are not seen (as is the case in perfect conscience) but, instead, are believed. When, however, on account of the weight of the testimony involved, this conscience has a

93. See Marc, op. cit., n. 31. St. Ligouri, tract. cit., passim.

firmness of assent without fear of the opposed position, it rightly merits being likened to perfect conscience and follows its rules. "Faith," says St. Thomas, "exceeds opinion in that the former has firmness of adherence, though it falls short of science in that it lacks vision."[94] If such testimonies, however, although perhaps weighty in nature, do not exclude every fear of the opposite being true, imperfect conscience is likened to opinion. Concerning this, Domingo de Soto writes:

> Therefore, in the end, we must say two things in conclusion about the nature of opinion. First, one must be aware that in the doctrine of Aristotle concerning the intrinsic nature of opinion, the fear spoken of does not have the same character as the fear spoken of by modern thinkers. For the judgment by which I now assent, 'Rome exists,' is an opinion. Properly speaking, however, it is not made with fear, unless we were to call "fear" the fact it is not contradictory to say that such an assent might be false, given that it is not evident. Second, I say that, although common use stopped positing an essential distinction between human faith and opinion, we must here make use of the distinction made by the logicians, namely that opinion is a *habitus* whose intrinsic character is to assent with fear [of the opposite being true], whereas human faith is a certain, though non-evident, assent (whether true or false). Nonetheless, although we may speak as do the many, let it be permitted for the wise to understand things with the few and to speak according in line with Aristotle's use of this terminology.[95]

(2) "Or *proceeds from likelihoods*": namely, from weightier motives, which make man sure and exclude anxiety, although they do not expel all fear. St. Thomas speaks of "probable certitude, which attains the truth in many cases, even if it falls short of the truth in a few."[96]

---

94. See *ST* I-II, q. 67, a. 3.

95. See Domingo de Soto, *In Dialecticam Aristotelis*, 1st Posteriorum, ch. 27, q. 8, *De scientia, fide, et opinione*, a. 2, concl. 2 (Salamanca, 1552), p. 128 recto, col. 1.

96. See *ST* II-II, q. 70, a. 2. The nature of opinion and faith (in accord with the mindset of this doctrine) was skillfully discussed, in the studium [*in conventù scientifico*] of Fribourg in 1897, by Fr. Marie-Benoît Schwalm, who had once upon a time listened to these lectures. See M.-B. Schwalm, "La croyance naturelle et la science," *Revue thomiste*, Vol. 4 (1897): pp. 627-645. (Editor's Note, Ambroise Gardeil)

In the writings of more recent authors, however, this is denominated "imperfect certitude" or "broad and ordinary certitude." Again, such certitude excludes the danger of error, not metaphysically, but morally. It admits, however, the possibility of fear, although this is light and prudently scorned as being of little worth.[97]

§2. ON THE OBLIGATION OF IMPERFECTLY CERTAIN CONSCIENCE

Conclusion
Imperfectly certain conscience suffices for acting in a permissible manner.

This conclusion is opposed to what is asserted by Rigorists, [be they] Jansenists or Calvinists, and is also opposed to certain Neo-Jansenist philosophers. It is admitted by all teachers of the Catholic faith and is supported, in a proportional manner, by the same arguments as the preceding conclusion concerning perfectly certain conscience.

First. Proof from authority. Indeed, in the text cited above (Rom. 14:23), the Apostle does not require another certitude when he speaks about the eating of foods that some believe they can permissibly eat, even though, in others' eyes, this seems impermissible.

In *ST* II-II, q. 70, a. 2, St. Thomas says:

> Certitude is not to be sought in a similar manner in every matter. Indeed, when it comes to human acts—over which judgments are rendered and about which testimony is required—one cannot have demonstrative certitude, given that they are concerned with contingent and variable things. Therefore, it suffices that one have probable certitude, which attains the truth in most things, even if it falls short in a few.[98]

St. Antoninus says:

> The third moral or [*seu*] civil condition is mentioned at the beginning of the *Nicomachean Ethics*, where it is said that he who is educated in a given topic is to seek certitude according to the requirements of the

97. See Concina, op. cit., diss. 10, ch. 2, §1.
98. *ST* II-II, q. 70, a. 2. See *ST* I-II, q. 94, a. 1, ad 3. *In I Ethic*, lect. 3. And in many other places.

> matter under consideration.... For moral certitude does not rise up from demonstrative evidence. Rather it comes from things that are more probably inclined to one side of an issue than to another. That which appears to be true in many cases and to those who are most wise is, however, called "probable." Consequently, in human things to be done, it is sufficient to have such certitude as does not remove all scruples, though it does suffice to lead us to scorn such concerns.[99]

Moreover, let us listen to what Albert the Great says concerning these matters. Indeed, although those things that he refers to pertain to probability in the [speculative] sciences, nonetheless, every proportion preserved, they can be applied to moral matters:

> The signs of likeliness [*verisimilitudinis*] may occur immediately on the surface and on the externals of a thing that a sensitive power receives by comparing sensed things to each other. And if such things are signs, it is probable that it will be seen by all. If the signs providing proof of likeliness are not on the surface but, instead, are in someway deep within it, not enduring in a necessary manner but also not being extrinsically upon the surface of the thing, then it is something that is seen by many because, with the sensation, they mix in something coming from reason. If, however, the sign of likeliness sinks down into the essential and convertible causes that are convertible as causes, then it is something seen by the wise... And that which is seen by the wise has degrees, for it is seen either by all, or by many, or by those of great knowledge—all to the degree that the sign and likeliness sinks down more greatly into the essential and intellectual necessities of the thing in question. Such things are seen only by those of great knowledge, who know how to grasp such things by the power of science and of art.[100]

---

99. *In I Post.*, tit. 3, ch. 10. See Gonet, *Clypeus theol. Thom.*, pt. 2, tract 3, *Dissert. De Consc. Probab.*, a. 6, no. 168 (Lyon, 1681), vol. 3, p. 297.

100. This is found in a more diffuse manner in Albert, *In I Topica*, tr. 1, ch. 2, edit. cit., vol. 2, p. 241. (Editor's Note, Ambroise Gardeil)

TRANSLATOR'S NOTE: This could be developed in interesting ways in relation to the development of our knowledge of the natural law. Interesting indicators in this direction can be found in Maritain, *Loi naturelle ou Loi non-écrite*, pp. 133-200.

Now based on what has been said, the skilled reader will understand that what is probable, based upon the authority of the wise, is always reduced to reason [for such authorities have based themselves upon reasoning and art, as explained above.] Thus, when one duly weighs out and ponders these matters, one sees how highly the authority of the most renowned wise men should be held, for example St. Augustine, the Holy Fathers [of the Church], St. Thomas, St. Bonaventure, and St. Alphonsus, especially when their doctrine is commended by the Church.[101]

Philosophers of some note agree on this matter: "The intelligent person," says Aristotle, "seeks as much certitude in a given genus as the nature of the thing requires." And Cicero says, "We follow probable things no further than where that which is likely occurs." In this remark "probable" and "likely" mean the same thing as "imperfect certitude." And this is the way we are to understand the time-honored teachers who, after St. Thomas, state that probable and likely knowledge suffice for the practical *dictamen* of conscience.

Second. Proof from reason. Conscience is a practical *dictamen* proceeding from the rules of prudence. Now, since prudence is a virtue that is concerned with individual, contingent, and fallible activities [*operationes*], and inasmuch as it is a virtue in the intellect, its *dictamen* must be morally certain and firm, not defective. Inasmuch, however, as it is concerned with individual contingent things that occur outside of speculation, (that is, when they cease to be seen and sensed through experience), it is impossible that it have this scientific and direct certitude which requires that the thing could not be other than what it is.[102]

Thus, when it is impossible for perfect certitude of conscience to be found, imperfect certitude suffices. "For God does not require from man more than is possible for the human condition because the Divine Wisdom disposes all things sweetly."[103]

---

101. One hears a reverberation of this teaching in the writings of Antonin Sertillanges, who at one time was present at the lectures upon which this book was based. See Sertillanges, *Saint Thomas d'Aquin* (Paris, 1910), vol. 2, p. 325. (Editor's Note, Ambroise Gardeil)

102. See St. Thomas, *In VI Ethic.*, lect. 3. John of St. Thomas, *Cursus Theologicus*, tr. *De Bonitate et militia act. Hum.*, disp. 12, a. 1, no. 29.

103. Cajetan, *Summula*, at the term "Opinion." Because certain people raised doubts concerning Cajetan's thought on this matter, let me here cite his words: "Indeed, for this reason something is not held as an opinion merely because various authors understand something in different ways, for even when there is contrariety of this kind, it stands that one [small]

This rule of certitude is made use of by men who are prudent in human actions (e.g., popes and rulers in the things to be administered in the Church or in the business of the Kingdom, generals of armies in the direction of the activities of war, doctors in the art of curing, and both ecclesial and civil judges in the lawsuits to be decided in both kinds of court).

Third. Proof from the unsuitable [consequences that would follow if the opposed position were true].

(1) Were the opposed position true, it would follow that someone would not be permitted to follow the most probable opinion. Now, this was condemned by Alexander VIII, in the 1690 decree of the Holy Office against the Jansenists: "It is not licit to follow a [probable] opinion, even the most probable among the probable ones.[104] Indeed, the most probable proposition remains within the limits of opinion, and while it reaches the borders of certitude, it does not enter within them.

(2) It would follow that, in many cases, the agent would labor under perplexed conscience, and one cannot act in this way without sinning. Indeed, it is impossible for the human mind to determine all contingencies or to weigh up all activities, circumstances, and intentions as they hold in reality, a task properly pertaining to God alone. Thus, it would be necessary to suspend activity or to commit oneself to the danger of sinning, "and one would need to absent oneself from life in the world [*exeundum esset de mundo*]."[105]

Sub-question 1: *Can imperfectly certain conscience be set aside?*

I respond as follows.

First, per se, no, for, of itself, such conscience approaches the certitude of science. Such certitude is not destroyed if scientific certitude is reached when the matter becomes more fully known. Instead, it is perfected and made absolutely certain.

---

bit [of information] could be a sufficient reason for moral certitude and already is not an opinion for those who grasp that reason. Because many do not know, however, how to discern between moral and mathematical certitude, they lump everything together as though they were all opinions." See Concina, op. cit., vol. 3, diss. 10, ch. 2, §1, nos. 2 and 3, edit. cit., vol. 2, p. 671.

104. Denzinger, no. 2303 (43rd ed.).

105. Cf. John of St. Thomas, op. et tract. cit., disp. 12, a. 3, no. 8, and Concina, who describes this argument in some detail, op. cit., bk. 3, diss, 10, ch. 2, §v, nos. 8 and 9 (p. 680).

Second, per accidens, however, *it can and must* be set aside, namely when conscience is not truly and really imperfectly certain, but, rather, is in this state because one has falsely assessed the matters at hand, or because one was listening to authorities whose weight was not very great, or because one had motives were then discerned to be false or doubtful.

Sub-question 2: *Can conscience which is indeed imperfectly certain be subsequently perfected, in an indirect manner, by means of reflex principles?*
The response to this will be found in the next, third article.

Article 3: *On Indirectly Certain Conscience and About Its Obligation*

§1. ON INDIRECTLY CERTAIN CONSCIENCE

Sub-question 1: *What is indirectly certain conscience?*
Response. Indirectly certain conscience is that which is formed by the addition of some reflex principle, thereby communicating moral certitude to the action.[106]

The definition is explained as follows.

First, indirectly certain conscience.

The word, "indirectly," must be understood in relation to the syllogism's matter, not its form, which, as logicians teach, is perfected indirectly through the resolution of one syllogistic figure into another or through a reduction (by means of another principle) to the principle of all syllogisms, namely to "Dici de omni" or to "dici de nullo."[107] Indeed,

106. See St. Alphonsus of Liguouri, *Dissertatio de usu moderato opin. Prob.* Cf. *Theol. Moralis*, edit. Heilig, bk. 1, no. 57, vol. 1, p. 27.

107. **Translator's Note:** Some light will be shed here by considering the following explanation from Édouard Hugon, *Cursus Philosophicus Thomisticae*, vol. 1 (Logica) (Paris: Lethielleux, 1927), pt. 1 (*Logica Minor*), tract. 3, q. 1, a. 2, no. 7 (pp. 173-74):

> "Based on what has been explained up to this point, it is clear, therefore, that the foundation for syllogisms, in which two extremes are compared with a middle term, is the principle of identity ("Those things that are one and the same with a third term are the same as each other") and the principle of discrepancy ("When two things are compared to a third and one is the same as that thing and the other is not, then those two things are themselves diverse"). Thus, the termini in a syllogism have this sort of relationship: *spiritual substance = immortal; the human soul = spiritual; therefore, the human soul =*

we make use of the same modes of the syllogistic figures in forming conscience (whether it be perfectly or imperfectly certain), and if needs to be perfected, it either must be logically resolved into another figure by means the same syllogistic art or must be reduced by means of another principle to the first principle, "Dici de omni," or "dici de nullo." Therefore, this is common to either kind of conscience and cannot be the cause of them being distinguished from one another.[108]

As has been said, however, perfect and imperfect conscience differ from the perspective of their matter (that is, of their principles) inasmuch as, on the one hand, perfectly certain conscience is inferred directly from

---

immortal. And, by way of contrast: *material substance ≠ immortal; the souls of brute animals = material; therefore, the soul of brute animals ≠ immortal.* However, already, a comparison with a middle term cannot be brought about unless the middle term has *suppositio* universally [*generaliter*] and distributively, in accord with the rule that will soon discuss: 'The middle term must be general [*generaliter esto*] in at least one premise.'

"Now, the comparison with the middle term is made by virtue of the principle: *Dictum de omni, dictum de nullo.* (Euler expresses this principle thus: '*Everything* that is in the containing is in that which is contained. Everything that is outside of the containing is outside of the content.') The sense of the principle, 'Dictum de omni,' is: whatever is affirmed universally [*generaliter*] and distributively of a given subject must be affirmed of all those things contained under it. For example, we may say: *every animal is sensate; every man is an animal; therefore, every man is sensate. Man*, the less universal subject, is contained under *animal*, which is more universal. Therefore, if *sensate* is said of *animal*, it must also be said of *man* which is contained under *animal.* In this respect, a syllogism is defined: *an argument in which the conclusion is reached so that all the predicates that belong under the more universal subject likewise belong to all the particular [subjects] contained under it.*

"The sense of the principle *Dictum de nullo* is: whatever is universally [*generaliter*] and distributively denied of a given subject must be denied of all those that are contained under it. For example, we may say: *no living thing is a stone; every plant is a living thing; therefore, no plant is a stone. Plant* is contained under *living thing* as something inferior under something more universal. Therefore, whatever is opposed to *living thing* is opposed to *plant.* In this case, a syllogism is defined: *an argument in which the conclusion is reached that all the predicates which are opposed to the more universal subject are opposed to all the particulars contained under it.*

"Therefore, there are four principles. Affirmative syllogisms are founded upon the principle of identity and the principle *Dictum de omni.* The negative syllogism is founded upon the principle of discrepancy and the principle *Dictum de nullo.* Indeed, the structure of the syllogism is founded upon the principles of identity and of discrepancy, whereas the rectitude of the syllogism is founded upon the principles *Dictum de omni* and *dictum de nullo.*"

Regarding the nature of *suppositio*, see Maritain, *Formal Logic*, pp. 57-76.

108. **Translator's Note:** Fr. Beaudouin does liken the practical syllogism a bit too closely to a purely speculative syllogism, although he is aware of the role of rectified appetite in reaching the terminal judgment in the prudential discursus. This is an example of something often underappreciated by Thomist rhetoric, although, as shown above, many following in Cajetan's line were careful to emphasize the mutual causality involved in practical ratiocination. Fr. Beaudouin himself will cite an important passage soon below.

per se nota principles and, on the other, an imperfectly certain conclusion of conscience is inferred from likely (not *per se nota*) principles. And a directly imperfect conclusion can be indirectly perfected through the subsumption of one or another reflex principle which is extraneous to the prior, valid syllogism, such that, on the strength of this reflex principle and by the aid of a subsidiary and indirect syllogism, it can and must be admitted as morally certain.

Second, the definition says, "indirectly *certain*," meaning that it involves moral certitude *concerning* the moral fittingness of the action, a certitude which we must have in order to act in a permissible way, as St. Alphonsus explains, in the text cited above.

Thus, the indirectly inferred conclusion does not have metaphysical or perfect moral certitude, as some have thought, for the direct propositions from which the first practical *dictamen* is elicited are likely [*verisimiles*] but non-evident. Without any artifice or aid of extraneous principles, such propositions cannot, of themselves, emerge as infallible and evident. Consequently, they cannot generate a perfectly certain conclusion or conscience.

Nonetheless, certitude, which is required for acting…

Third…can be had through the use of reflex principles. The reason for this is that the intellect is determined to totally and firmly adhere to only one of the two options either because it is moved by the intellect or by the will. Indeed, it is moved by the intellect either immediately or mediately. It is moved immediately when the truth of the understood propositions is infallibly clear, whereas it is moved mediately when, by the strength of first principles, it firmly adheres to demonstrative conclusions. When the intellect cannot determine itself to one side of a contradiction, however, neither immediately through evidential knowledge [*evidentiam*] of first principles, nor even on the strength of the principles as known in conclusions, it is determined by the will, which chooses to assent to one side determinately and precisely *on account of something that is sufficient for moving the will*, although not for moving the intellect, inasmuch as it seems good and befitting to assent to this [particular] option.[109]

The will, however, is not sufficiently moved to choose a befitting good unless it is first moved by reason. Indeed, the will follows the lead

109. See St. Thomas, *De veritate*, q. 14, a. 1. *ST* II-II, q. 1, a. 4.

of reason, and every human choice proceeds from deliberation and counsel. Therefore, when the intellect is not sufficiently determined and is not assured through the inference of a direct syllogism, it turns itself to those principles that, in relation to the first, are called indirect or reflex. Thus, it sets up another process of practical reasoning and indirectly infers the morally certain ultimate practical judgment that is the *dictamen* of conscience.[110]

A Corollary

Hence, it follows that two reasoning processes are found in indirectly certain conscience. The first is that which proceeds directly, upon which the imperfect (or, probable) judgment concerning the morality of the act follows. Then, presupposing this first process of reasoning, a second process intervenes, proceeding indirectly from reflex and extrinsic principles. After this process of reasoning, there follows the ultimate, practically certain judgment concerning what is to be done here and now.

The judgment inferred from the first process of reasoning is called *speculative* or *speculatively-practical*; however, the second judgment is called *practical* or *practically-practical.* And in these cases, conscience is denominated *speculatively probable* or *practically* (that is, *morally*) *certain.* In the works of more recent authors, this latter is more often called *imperfectly* or *indirectly certain.*

§2. ON THE OBLIGATION OF INDIRECTLY CERTAIN CONSCIENCE

Conclusion

When directly certain conscience cannot be had, indirectly certain conscience suffices for one to act in a permissible manner.

I said, "When directly certain conscience cannot be had," because prior to acting, the agent must diligent inquire into the truth and can form indirectly certain conscience for himself only if directly certain conscience is lacking.

Proof of the conclusion.

First, from authority: St. Augustine said: "Even if the just man were to serve under an ungodly king, he may morally go to war for the pres-

110. Translator's Note: He will comment that this process is often implicit.

ervation of the order of civic peace, to which he is commanded, whether or not it is certain that this is not contrary to the command of God."[111]

St. Alphonsus expressly teaches the same thing: "Before all things," he says, "We must hold two points as certain. First, moral certitude concerning the moral fittingness of an action is required for acting in a permissible manner. Second, this certitude can be had not only directly but also from a reflex principle, by which that moral certitude is communicated to the action."[112]

This is commonly taught by more recent authors.[113]

Second proof, from reason. He who acts prudently does something that is morally good. Now, he who acts from indirectly certain conscience acts prudently. Therefore, he does something that is morally good.

Proof of the minor premise. The certitude of prudence is twofold, as Cajetan notes[114]:

> There is one kind of certitude, consisting only in knowledge, and this in the universal indeed is the same as the certitude of moral science whose universal is true in most cases. In particulars, however, it does not exceed the certitude of an opinion, since it states a conclusion concerning things that are in the future or are absent *and this is not [the kind of certitude] proper to prudence.*
>
> There is, however, another kind of certitude of practical truth, consisting in conformity to right appetite; and *this is proper to prudence*, which does not consist solely in reason. And such certitude is always present to prudence, even with respect to particular absent and future things.[115]

This means that *speculatively speaking*, moral certitude is not always had from a direct syllogism, as is clear from so many opinions that are found *for* and *against* [a given course of action] in the writings of [recog-

111. **Translator's Note:** The original cites "In decreto, p. 2, can. 4: *Qui culpatur*, causa 23, q. 1, ch. 4. The text is found in Billuart, *Summa sancti Thomae*, vol. 2, diss. 5 (*De conscientia*), a. 3, incidental question. There it is cited as being from *Contra Faustum*, bk. 22, ch. 75.

112. Op. tract. et ed. cit., bk. 1, no. 57.

113. Cf. Marc, op. cit., no. 38. Gousset, *Théol. Morlae*, tr. *De la conscience*, ch. 1, no. 59, p. 25.

114. *In ST* II-II, q. 47, a. 3, no. 1.

115. **Translator's Note:** This is an example of an important point from Cajetan, useful for balancing out the weakness noted above.

nized] teachers [*apud Doctores*]. *Practically speaking*, however, this moral certitude is never lacking for action because, without a doubt, through the intending of the end of virtue the desire of the will is rectified, and reason is assured through a reflex principle. Therefore, conscience, thus inferred from the principles of prudence, declares the practical, true, best, and certain judgment, inasmuch as it is in harmony with reason and right appetite.

Augustine's example of the soldier furnishes a clear example of this.[116] The soldier's [rational] appetite is right on account of the fact that he wills to preserve the order of civic peace. Not having direct knowledge, however, whether a war is just, he assures his reason for acting by means of a reflex principle, namely, that he is bound to obey a command unless that which is commanded is clearly unjust. Now, in this case, he is not certain concerning the injustice of the war. Therefore, he practically forms for himself an indirectly certain conscience, concluding that he can and must comply with his commander's orders.

Third, another proof. Indeed, nothing unbefitting follows from this position. Indeed, by prudently judging (that is, by bringing to bear all [necessary] diligence) that a something is to be done for the good of a virtue, although error could occur concerning the real goodness of the action, nonetheless, such an error will be *per accidens* and will not be imputed as a sin to the person thus acting, since the ignorance from which he proceeded would be antecedent, involuntary, and invincible.

Sub-question 1: *Does imperfectly certain, direct conscience need to be perfected indirectly through reflex principles?*

I respond: Moral theologians [*Doctores*] do not agree among themselves concerning this matter. This seems, however, to be more of a verbal disagreement than one concerning the reality in question. Indeed, those who teach that imperfectly certain (or broad) conscience is sufficient for a right informing of morals say that it is sufficient *practically*, not speculatively, from which it follows that they presuppose something else in the demonstration of the truth. Those who assert, however, that imperfectly certain conscience is indirectly perfected by reflex principles require implicit (not necessarily explicit) use of principles of this sort.

116. See above.

Sub-question 2: *How many reflex principles are there by which imperfectly certain conscience is indirectly perfected?*
I respond, in general [*in univerali*], that principles of this kind are the means by which it is demonstrated that imperfectly certain conscience is morally certain and suffices for acting in a morally befitting manner. For example, "God does not require from man more than is possible for the human condition" (Cajetan).—Prudence does not require unqualified [*majorem*] certitude.—Where absolute certitude is lacking, it suffices to approach the truth.—In obscure matters, the things that are more likely are to be chosen.—There is no risk of sin [*nullum est periculum peccandi*].—And other things of this sort that are explicitly or implicitly brought forth.

Corollaries
Corollary 1. The form conscience that more recent authors call imperfectly or indirectly certain is called *probable*, *likely*, and *probably certain* by time-honored authors.[117] Hence, the terms *probable* and *opinable* are used more broadly in their writings than in the writings of modern authors.

In order to avoid equivocations, however, let the theologian follow the new practice of calling this certitude *imperfectly* or *indirectly* certain. One should note well, however, that this doctrine is neither new, nor subversive to moral science, as certain Neo-Jansenists bandy about today. Indeed, if there has been something new added in this modern way of speaking, perhaps it is a more accurate method in these utterly difficult questions which stand in need of further discussion and resolution, so that there might be a clearer determination, following the path blazed by St. Alphonsus, concerning the safe and middle path to be taken between the Laxists and Rigorists.

Corollary 2. Even as regards imperfect conscience, the excellence of Catholic Teaching over the pleadings of the philosophers and erroneous dogmas of false religions is clear, for as St. Thomas teaches, when absolute certitude is lacking the intellect is determined by the choice of the will.[118] Now, it is presupposed that the will of the faithful Christian is rectified through charity, as well as by natural and supernatural justice and is always

117. See *ST* II-II, q. 70, aa. 2 and 3.

118. Translator's Note: Here is an example of where he clearly does see the role of the mutual causality of intellect and will as important.

directed in its choices by reason or faith. If the will, however, becomes corrupted by turning aside from the true and ultimate end and does not in choice turn itself toward reason or the true faith, it is preoccupied with its own error, envy, hatred, anger, pride, and other sorts of affects, by which the mind is blinded and inclined to a false judgment through one's perversity of heart. Here, we have the wellspring of the errors of various philosophical sects, as well as those held by other religions, to which the intellect firmly adheres on account of the will's obstinacy and not out of the truth of knowledge [*scientiae*] or of faith.

Corollary 3. And lest someone were to overlook the present doctrine or, looking upon so many opinions *pro* and *con* disputed in moral theology, would report that he experiences offense or scandal, one should take care to distinguish between science and conscience.[119] Indeed, the theologian speculatively treats of the goodness or wickedness of the act and of the object. He teaches many rather important things as being absolutely certain, so that, as experience so deigns, perfectly certain conscience may then be formed. When absolute certitude is lacking, however, then he hands on probable, more probable, or likely judgments, and since he cannot attain the essence of the object in itself, he teaches what seems to approach more closely to truth and science.[120] And let me repeat myself: this consideration is speculative and, consequently, the inferred judgment is not conscience, properly speaking, and does not suffice for directing one's actions. Thus, it is moreover required that he who acts, making use of direct and reflex principles, must set up a new process of reasoning by which he may practically conclude what can be done here and now, thus forming morally certain conscience for himself. In what follows, however, we will discuss how and when this may permissibly be done, as well as how and when it is impermissible to do so.

QUESTION 3: ON DOUBTING CONSCIENCE

Preliminary Note

119. Translator's Note: Here is a clear example of how he is not seeing conscience as being a judgment rendered in moral science.

120. Translator's Note: By this, he may mean quite literally, not "knowledge" but "scientific knowledge," which would mean, "inferentially demonstrative knowledge."

First of all, the very term "doubting conscience" must be explained. Strictly speaking, doubting conscience really does not exist, for conscience is the ultimate practical judgment (or, the application of science to an act). Now, a doubt is not a kind of judgment, since strictly speaking, a doubt is a suspension of judgment or of assent, or according to Albert the Great (as reported by St. Antoninus),[121] an unterminated movement of reason.Taking the expression "doubting conscience" in a broad sense, however, conscience is said to be doubting in the sense that the doubting person suspends his assent on account of a tacit or expressed judgment concerning the object. Likewise, it can be so called doubtful inasmuch as he has various speculatively-practical judgments on both sides concerning the matter in doubt, suspending a definitive judgment concerning the same thing. If, however, on account of trifling motives he turns toward either part of the contradiction, it is called *lax* or [*et*] *scrupulous* conscience. Thus, we will discuss this question in three articles:

1. Doubting conscience in general;
2. Lax conscience;
3. Scrupulous conscience.

Article 1: *On Doubting Conscience in General and Its Obligation or Reformation*

§1. ON DOUBTING CONSCIENCE IN GENERAL

Sub-question 1: *What is doubting conscience?*

I respond that doubting conscience is that which turns toward neither side of a contradiction, or, as St. Alphonsus Ligouri states, one that suspends its assent for either side of a doubt, remaining undecided and hesitant.

The definition flows from what was said above.

Sub-question 2: *How many kinds of doubting conscience are there?*

I respond that doubting conscience is twofold, namely *negative and positive*. Indeed, our intellect is not inclined more toward one side of a contradiction than to the other either "on account of a defect of evidence that would move it, as in those problems for which we have no reasons [for

121. See *Summa theolog. Mor.*, pt. 1, tit. 3, ch. 10, §9, edit. cit., col. 193.

either side of the argument], or on account of the apparent equality of those things that would move us to assent to either side."[122] In fact, just as a scale does not tilt toward either side if it no weight presses on it or if each side is equally weighed down, the same is also true of doubting conscience, which by its very nature is marked by hesitation, when considered from the perspective of reason and the motives that produce hesitation in the mind. It is said to be "*negatively* doubting" when no sufficient or probable reasons (which would be strong enough to bend the mind's assent toward one of the two sides) are met with on either side of the argument. It is said to be "*positively* doubting," however, when there are sufficient and probable reasons present, presenting the mind with equally strong reasons for assent. Note that I said, "sufficient or probable reasons," namely those that are such that a prudent soul would be moved by them, for trifling reasons move pusillanimous men, not prudent ones.[123]

Sub-question 3: *How may both negatively and positively doubting conscience be distinguished?*

I respond that negatively doubting conscience is distinguished into *speculative* and *practical.*

Speculatively doubting conscience is that by which one is in doubt concerning the rectitude or befittingness of the act in general. *Practically doubting* conscience, however, is that by which one is in doubt concerning the rectitude or moral befittingness of the act to be exercised here and now.

This division is clear, for as I have said, the ultimate practical judgment (or, more rightly, in the case of a doubt, the suspension of an ultimate practical judgment) supposes a tacit or express judgment concerning the speculative rectitude of the act. Now, from both of these judgments, conscience is denominated *speculatively* or *practically* doubtful. For example, in the writings of St. Alphonsus,[124] speculative doubt will be that by which someone doubts whether a baptism with rose water[125] would be

122. Aquinas, *De veritate*, q. 14, a. 1.

123. See Zigliara, *Logica*, (40) no. 10.

124. Op. cit. *De conscientia*, no. 20, H. p. 10; G. p. 11.

125. Translator's Note: Literally "aqua distillata," referring to the "distilling" of water from something water containing, though leaving some infusion from the source. The example of rose-infused water is quite normal in treatments of the sacrament of baptism. See

valid (and other such things). A practical doubt, however, will be that by which one doubts, "Is it permitted for me to baptize *this* boy with rose water?"

Certain writers, however, distinguish doubt in three ways, namely into *speculative*, *speculatively-practical*, and *practically-practical*.

The first is concerned with the truth of the thing, the second with the permissibility of the act in general, and the third with the moral befittingness of the same thing inasmuch as it is to be done here and now. For the sake of example, in the example related above, we find: (1) speculatively doubting conscience ("Is baptism with rose water valid?"); (2) speculatively-practical doubting conscience ("Is it permissible to baptize with rose water?"); (3) practically-practical doubting conscience ("Is it permitted for me, here and now, to baptize this boy with rose water?"). Each of these propositions has its own unique character. Indeed, presupposing that there is a doubt concerning the validity and liceity of baptism with rose water, it can nonetheless be certain that it is here and now permitted for me to baptize him, if the peril of death urges it and there is no natural water at hand.

In order to avoid an endless proliferation of distinctions and terms, however, doubts or judgments that precede the ultimate practical judgment (whether they be concerned with the truth of the matter or the permissibility of the act in general) are called speculative. And, in the text cited above, St. Alphonsus speaks in this sense, saying: "Truth must always be distinguished from permission, for although a speculative doubt (in whatever sense it is taken, either as being merely speculative, or as being speculatively-practical) considers the permitted thing *in obliquo* and, rather, consequently, it nonetheless considers a speculative truth *in recto* and principally. A practical [doubt], however, considers the permitted thing."[126] Nonetheless, according to the requirements of the matter, authors sometimes make use of this threefold distinction.

§2. ON THE OBLIGATION OF DOUBTING CONSCIENCE

Alphonsus di Liguouri, *Homo apostolicus*, 9th ed., vol. 2 (Regensburg: George Joseph Manz, 1862), tr. 14, ch. 2 no. 8. Understandably, this has been rendered in a literal fashion as "dripping" or "trickling" water by some, however.

126. Ibid., n. 21; H. G. p. 11.

Conclusion

One is never permitted to act with practically doubting conscience. Instead, such conscience must be set aside and reformed, or if it cannot be set aside, the safer path is to be chosen.

Proof of the first part of the conclusion. It is never permitted to act, etc...

First, indeed, everything that is not from faith (that is, from certitude of science [i.e., discursive knowledge]) is a sin, as was shown above.

Now, he who is practically in doubt concerning the goodness or wickedness of the act to be done here and now does not have the certitude of science and does not act out of faith. Therefore, he acts in an impermissible manner.

Second, then: He who acts while doubting exposes himself to a proximate danger of sinning, since he does not know whether or not the act in question is a sin...

Now, as Scripture witnesses: "he who loves danger will die in it." For the will thus approaches a deed, ready to perform it, no matter whether or not it is contrary to God's law, and such a willing is evil by its very nature and offensive to the divine majesty.

Thus, such a willing and such conscience must be set aside and reformed.

This doctrine is certain and is admitted by all Catholic theologians and moral philosophers.

Proof of the closing part of the conclusion. If it cannot be set aside, the safer path is to be chosen.

I said, first: "*If it cannot be set aside*," meaning: if it happens that someone does not know how, on his own, to resolve and set aside the practical doubt and does not know other, more learned men whom he may consult, and likewise cannot not act, *then* in order to act in a permissible manner...

I said, second: the safer path is to be chosen. Before proving this, the terms must be explained:

(a) "The safer path" is designated relative to "the less safe path." Now, in general, something is called "safe" because it draws someone back from danger of sinning, and the more that someone draws back from the peril of sinning, the more does that person incline toward the law and restrain his freedom. Thus, the "safer path" is that which more greatly favors the law and favors freedom less, whereas, the "less safe" is that which favors freedom more and the law less.

(b) The safer path *must be chosen.*

The safer path can be chosen either from a counsel or on the strength of a precept. We are not here speaking of counsels, for no Catholic denies that it is a counsel that the safer path is to be chosen in doubtful matters.[127] In the question, however, it is asked, "Whether in a doubt the choice of the safer path *would be necessary on the strength of a precept?*"

The affirmative opinion is commonly held to be true.

Proof. This rule, "In doubtful matters the safer path is to be chosen," is taken from the Sacred Canons, and is found in the chapter *Illud Dominus, de Cleric. excommun. deposito,*[128] and the same is said in the chapter *Ad audientiam de homicid.*[129]: "Since in doubt, we must choose the safer path, it is appropriate for you to enjoin the aforementioned [*memorato*] priest that he not minister in sacred orders."

"From the letter alone," as Concina notes, "It is clear that the doctrine is universal, applied to a particular case."[130] Thus, teachers commonly accept this principle, at least with respect to every practical doubt. Indeed, it is clear, according to both the divine and natural law, that one must abstain from a given act when in doubt whether it is offensive to the divine majesty. He who, faced with such doubtful matters, instead chooses to neglect the safer path (or [*seu*] the only safe path), thus taking the doubtful path, thereby sets himself in such a disposition of soul, that he would will to act in this way whether or not it were a sin. And no reasonable person could deny that this is a sin.[131]

Confirmation

This is so because the action of a person acting in this way would not be from faith, that is, from certitude of science [i.e., discursive intellectual certitude]. Hence, Cicero says, in *De officiis,* bk. 1: "A good command is

127. **Translator's Note:** As already noted, it is normal to impugn this sort of outlook as being a kind of minimalism. It is important, however, to make room for articulating the domain of imperfection in the domain of that which is "not commanded" in a given set of circumstances. A lack of appreciation for the unique case of the less good can lead one either into tutorism or laxism. On this topic, see Reginald Garrigou-Lagrange, "Imperfection." In *The Love of God and the Cross of Jesus,* vol. 1, translated by Jeanne Marie (St. Louis, MO: B. Herder, 1948), pp. 318-44.

128. *Decretales Gregorii,* IX, bk. 5, tit. 27, ch. 5.

129. Ibid., tit. 12, ch. 12.

130. Op. cit., *De Consc.,* bk. 2, diss. 1, ch. 7, no. 4, ed. cit., vol. 2, p. 70.

131. See Concina, loc. cit.

uttered to you by those who forbid you to do something when you are in doubt concerning whether it is just or unjust."

Sub-question 1: *Does he who acts with a doubting conscience about a sin thus incur a sin?*

I respond affirmatively, and this is obvious in light of the thesis discussed above. St. Augustine says, "For it is certainly a sin to do something whose sinful character is in doubt to the person doing it."[132]

All moral theologians [*Doctores*] are in agreement on this point.

Sub-question 2: *Does such a person commit a mortal or a venial sin [grave vel leve], and what is its species?*

I respond with St. Alphonsus: "He sins, indeed by a sin of the same species and gravity as that concerning which he is in doubt, for he who exposes himself to the danger of sinning already sins, according to the words of Sirach 3:27: 'He who loves danger will die in it.' Therefore, if one doubts whether it is a mortal sin, he mortally sins." So too, Billuart says, "If one doubts whether one bears false witness or has committed detraction, or is in fear concerning this, such a person sins by the sin of perjury or detraction." And so too for other cases.[133]

Article 2: *On Lax Conscience and Its Obligation*

§1. ON LAX CONSCIENCE

Sub-question 1: *What is lax conscience?*

I respond that lax conscience is that which, on account of light motives and without a rational foundation, thinks something is good when, in reality, it is evil, and likewise judges that a sin is venial [*leve*] when it is, in fact, mortal [*grave*].

---

132. Augustine, *De baptism contra donatistas*, bk. 1, ch. 6, no. 6 (*PL* 43:113).
The genuine text speaks thus: "And thus, if it is uncertain whether it is a sin to receive baptism from the party of Donatus, who may doubt that it is a particular sin not to prefer to receive it where it is certain that it is not a sin?" Cf. *CSEL* 51 (Vienna, 1908), p. 152. (Editor's Note, Ambroise Gardeil)

133. St. Alphonsus, op. cit., bk. 1, no. 22, H. G. p. 11. Cf. Billuart, op. cit., diss., 5, a. 6, §2, *dico* 1. Marc, op. cit., no. 36.

Sub-question 2: *What are the causes of lax conscience?*

I respond that, in general, lax conscience belongs to the imprudent person and arises from causes that are reducible to vincible ignorance (on the part of the intellect) and perversity of will (on the part of the will). Now, this all takes place in many ways. Indeed, since the intellect moves the will and, in turn, the will moves the intellect, a defect in one power reverberates upon the other. And, indeed, since the act of both the intellect and of the will depend on the imagination and sense appetite, which can be deficient in many ways, it is clear that the path that leads to perdition is wide. In many people, however, it is caused by presumption, vainglory, arrogance, the corruption of one's earlier life, fickleness of soul, and ignorance that is crass or supine.[134]

Sub-question 3: *What are its effects?*

I respond that the effects of lax conscience are sluggishness of senses, blindness of mind, and folly as regards the intellect, whereas with regard to the will, it causes hardness of heart.[135]

This kind of conscience is called "hardened" when, from the habit of sinning, one pays no heed to grave (or even very grave) sins, and drinks iniquity as if it were water.[136]

Lax conscience is called "pharisaical" when one reckons small faults as being great ones and, in turn, great ones as being small. The Pharisees were men of this sort, who, "strain out a gnat and swallow a camel" (Mt. 23:24; DR).[137]

§2. ON THE OBLIGATION OF LAX CONSCIENCE

Conclusion

He who labors under lax conscience must set it aside and reform it. Or, to put this another way: one is never permitted to act with a lax conscience.

Proof. This is so because such a judgment of conscience proceeds from vincible ignorance, and we must apply to it what we already have said

134. See note 50, Question 1 above, for details regarding this terminology.

135. See *ST* II-II, qq. 15 and 46.

136. **Translator's Note:** See Job 15:16 (DR): "How much more is man abominable, and unprofitable, who drinketh iniquity like water?"

137. See Marc, op. cit., no. 24.

concerning vincibly erroneous conscience, along with affected, crass, and supine ignorance.

All hold this position. [*Ita omnes.*]

Sub-question 1: *How is it set aside?*

I respond that it is set aside by the influence of true faith and purification of the heart, through the profession and exercise of the true religion. The remedies for this kind of conscience are related to the errors involved in it, both on the part of the intellect and that of the will. They are proposed throughout moral science [in relation to the various virtues and vices involved].

Sub-question 2: *What sin is committed by the person who acts from lax conscience?*

I respond that such a person sins in the same way as does the person who acts from doubt.[138] Nay, he can gravely sin *in a[n otherwise] venial matter* if his rashness impels him to act in this way, having overlooked and scorned any *dictamen* whatsoever.[139]

Article 3: *On Scrupulous Conscience and Its Obligation*

§1. ON SCRUPULOUS CONSCIENCE

Sub-question 1: *What is scrupulous conscience?*

I respond that scrupulous conscience is that which, on account of trifling motives and without a reasonable foundation, often fears that an occasion of sin is present, even though, in reality, it is not.[140]

Indeed, the etymological derivation of the term "scrupulous" is based on a metaphor taken from the Latin word, "*scrupo*," which refers to a small, rough stone that finds its way into the shoe of someone walking, both injuring and grieving that person, slowing his step. Thus, scrupulous conscience is nothing other than the trifling and vacuous apprehension and insignificant reasoning that occur in relation to some worrisome action

138. See the response to the second question in the preceding article.

139. See Gury, op. cit., vol. 1, no. 50. Marc, op. cit., no. 25.

140. See St. Alphonsus, op. cit., no. 11, H. p. 5; G. p. 6. Cf. Marc, op. cit., no. 27 and no. 1835.

for which no solution has yet been found. And thence, the soul opines, suspects, or is filled with anxious doubt, that one's action may be evil. The term "scrupulous conscience" is commonly used to refer either to the very anxiety caused by scruples, or to the disposition of a soul with a propensity to scruples, or to the scruple itself (a quasi-*dictamen* of the scrupulous intellect). Our discussion concerning scrupulous conscience will focus on these understandings of what scrupulous conscience is, especially the final sense.

Sub-question 2: *From what causes does scrupulous conscience arise?*

I respond that scrupulous conscience is caused by pusillanimity of heart, as St. Antoninus says.[141] As St. Thomas says:

> According to its proper formal character, however, pusillanimity is opposed to magnanimity, from which it differs as greatness and smallness differ in relation to one and the same thing. For just as the magnanimous man, through his greatness of soul, tends to something great, so too does the pusillanimous man, through his smallness of soul, draw back from great things.[142]

Briefly stated, the prudent and grave man is great, judging and acting on account of grave and great things; however, the pusillanimous man is small and is moved to choose one side of a contradiction by motives that are trifling and small or of no moment.

Sub-question 3: *What are the causes of pusillanimity?*

I respond that the causes of pusillanimity are either intrinsic or extrinsic.

(a) The intrinsic causes are the following.

First, *ignorance on the part of the intellect.* Ignorance indeed has many, various causes. As regards this point, however, note that scruples arise especially from the kind of ignorance which makes it impossible for one to distinguish between what is permitted and what is not permitted. Likewise, it arises from the inability to distinguish between a temptation and personal consent. It also can arise from a mind that is subtle enough to think up reasons for doubting, though not subtle enough to resolve such

141. Loc. cit.

142. *ST* II-II, q. 133, a. 2.

doubts. It also can arise from weakness and inconstancy in a soul which does not adhere firmly to things once they are determined or to sufficiently known practical principles, due to the power of one's imagination and a multiplicity of phantasms (for which reason women are more frequently scrupulous than are men).[143] And what is graver still, the pusillanimous or scrupulous person often does not know his condition and thus, not perceiving his defect, thinks himself to be prudent and other men imprudent.

Second, *inordinate pride and fear on the part of the appetite.*

Pride. Indeed, as St. Thomas observes, "Pusillanimity can, in some manner, arise from pride, namely when someone relies too much upon his own insight, thereby thinking he that is not up to the task of doing things which he, in fact, is capable of doing."[144] Indeed, he has sufficient motives for rightly and firmly judging on his own or on the counsel of others, but as is said in Proverbs 26:16 (DR): "The sluggard is wiser in his own conceit, than seven men that speak sentences." In fact, nothing prevents one from deriding oneself concerning some things, while extoling oneself to the heights as regards other matters. Hence, Gregory the Great, in his *Pastoral Rule*, says of Moses: "Perhaps he would have been proud, if he were to take up the leadership of his people without trepidation; and again, he would have been prideful if he refused to obey the command of the God [*Auctoris*]."[145] Hence, St. Alphonsus says, "Scruples often have their source in the vice of pride."[146] And Billuart: "He wishes to submit to nobody's counsel on account of a hidden pride which leads him to place far too much faith in his own judgment."[147]

Inordinate fear. Such fear is operative, given that the soul flees that which ought not to be fled if it were considered in itself and likewise fears things which should not be feared according to the right judgment of reason, as the psalmist says in Ps. 13:5 (DR), "There have they trembled for fear, where there was no fear," that is, where there was no reasonable cause for fearing. Inordinate fear, however, is sometimes caused by one's

143. Billuart, *De act. Hum.*, diss. 5, *De conscientia*, a. 5, quaeritur 4.

Translator's Note: It surely goes without saying that the translator does not endorse the final point of dated psychology.

144. *ST* II-II, q. 133, a. 1, ad 3.

145. Gregory the Great, *Regula pastoralis liber*, pt. 1, ch. 7, *PL* 77:20.

146. Op. cit., n. 12, H. p. 5; G. p. 6.

147. Loc. cit.

natural dispositions and temperament (e.g., by a manic sickness and by melancholy that confines and freezes the heart, with such confinement moving, perturbing and disposing the imagination toward conceiving that something will be evil and, consequently, must be fled by the appetite).[148]

This is sometimes caused, however, by negligence of one's bodily needs, namely through excessive abstinence, vigils, and other such things. Thus, Blessed Jerome said, "Surely, a reasonable man loses his dignity when he prefers either fasting to charity or vigils to the integrity of his senses, so that madness or sadness (i.e., melancholy) would befall him on account of abstinence and indiscrete recitation [*decantationem*] of psalms or of offices."[149]

(b) Extrinsic causes.

The first extrinsic cause of scrupulous conscience is shared company among scrupulous people, for one scrupulous person makes another scrupulous, just as one fearful person makes another fearful. And the direction of a scrupulous confessor is to be counted as belonging to such gatherings of scrupulous people, as well as the reading of cases of conscience by someone who is not fit to be discerning in the matters discussed therein. For just as the person who is not expert in the art of medicine, pouring over the words of doctors and stirring up an overly active imagination, comes to believe that he is suffering from the illnesses described in such texts, so too the unlearned or incautious person, pouring over cases of conscience, often believes that he has discovered that he is guilty of a mortal sin.

The second [extrinsic] cause is a demon who by this artifice tempts men to turn aside from the exercise of the virtues. Indeed, as St. Thomas teaches, although a demon cannot directly move the intellect or the will, he nonetheless can directly influence the senses and imagination and can indirectly influence the intellectual powers. Thus, from the disturbance of the imagination and the heart, he induces ignorance, pride, and fear.

Finally, *the third* [extrinsic] cause is God, who sometimes permits scruples either as a punishment for prior sins, or for the exercise of humility and patience, or for stirring up appropriate ardor [*teporem*] in His service.[150] And sometimes, the souls of the saints who are called to a superior

148. See St. Anoninus, ibid., col. 194, who cites Galen and Avicenna.

149. *In Decreto*, pt. 3, *De consecration*, dist. 5, ch. 24, cited in St. Antoninus, loc. cit.

150. See Billuart, ibid.

state, by God's mercy, find themselves overshadowed by an extraordinary kind of darkness of conscience, being disturbed by torments or great anxieties of fear, as can be read in the various lives of the saints.

Sub-question 4: *What are the effects of scrupulous conscience?*

I respond first, *in general* [*in universali*]: *because of pusillanimity*, someone may draw back from virtuous deeds out of a fear of sinning. Nay, sometimes, in order to avoid minor sins, one is thereby led to commit graver ones. This happens in particular to those suffering from scrupulous conscience concerning a specific matter (e.g., concerning the recitation of the hours, the celebration of the Mass, and so forth). Indeed, other deeds are often reputed as being of no importance, and thus, lax conscience is nourished right alongside the scrupulous conscience. And this should not be surprising, given that they come forth from the same root, namely from a smallness and fickleness of soul. For example, it is not a rare occurrence for someone who anxiously feels the need to repeat the words of consecration not, however, to take care in the ablution of the [sacred] vessels or of the corporal and, likewise, does not see to the other duties of his state of life.

I respond second, *as regards particular points* [*in speciali*]:

(a) *Ignorance* gives rise to *disturbance and inconstancy of soul.* The scrupulous person frequently changes his judgment and is disturbed in mind, especially in his external deeds, (e.g., in the celebration of the Mass, in the recitation of the hours, or in the administration or reception of the sacraments). He recites his prayers with a fastidious slowness, frequently repeating them, and halting so that he may recall his intention.[151]

Facing things that must be done, he is slow in coming to a decision. He consults with the learned and the prudent, but he does not place his trust in them. With anxious fear, he delays his judgment, repeatedly going off to consult the same people, as well as others, believing nobody and forever seeking a maximum amount of security.

Looking back over things that he has done, especially in his examination of conscience and confession, he investigates, discusses, and explains everything with precision. Deploying subtle cleverness, he discloses minor circumstances (nay, utterly inconsequential ones), does not omit ones that are not pertinent, and repeats himself *ad nauseam*.

151. See ibid., quaeritur 2.

Thinking of past confessions which were made with moral sufficiency, he forever remains in practical doubt, never letting go of his concern about them, believing that he did not explain himself in detail about everything, and the more he is given a hearing, the more is he disturbed with many forgotten or neglected things which pop into his mind.[152]

(b) *Hidden pride* gives rise to *an obstinacy of judgment*, leading him to experience difficulty in being subject to the counsels of a prudent confessor. He approaches other people, and his perplexity only increases as he listens to others. If there are various responses to his questions (which is not a rare occurrence) he takes delight in his prudence and is hardened in his own self-estimation. But, if he is given counsels which unanimously agree with each other, he doubts their truth and rectitude because they are opposed to his own estimation and judgment. Therefore, he once more goes forth to see if he might perhaps find someone who fully shares his own opinion concerning this matter, thus remaining restless.

(c) *Fear* begets *sadness and weariness* in his soul, which is weighed down by these feelings so that it finds itself unable to do anything good, and his vigor of mind and strength of body are consumed by all this concern. Sadness, however, produces disturbance, disturbance produces desperation, and desperation is utterly destructive [*interimit*]. Sometimes, his imagination and senses are so vehemently disturbed that he comes to suffer from madness.

Then, by his own example, the scrupulous person diminishes the boldness of others, along with his own readiness to perform virtuous acts, for as we said above, the shared company of scrupulous people begets scrupulous people.

§2. ON THE OBLIGATION OF SCRUPULOUS CONSCIENCE

Conclusion
Scrupulous conscience must be set aside and reformed.

Proof. This is so because such conscience is erroneous and, therefore, must be shunned. It makes what is good to be evil and what is a mere straw to be a great wooden beam. That is, from a light sin, the scrupulous person fabricates a grave one, generates desperation, and damns himself

152. See Billuart, loc. cit.

from salvation. Whence, in the law it is said: "Every suspicion must be cast aside rather than accepted."[153]

In that case, it is very dangerous, as is clear from its effects. Nay, as St. Alphonsus adds:

> Wisely do Sanchez, St. Antoninus, Gerson, Valentia, the Salmanticenses, and Cajetan teach that the scrupulous person is sometimes bound by a grave obligation to act against his scruples since, from anxiety over scruples, he can fear a grave loss in spiritual progress or in health of body or mind. Thus, as Gerson said, scrupulous people must act against their scruples and struggle against them with a sure and certain step in their efforts. We cannot check scruples better than by holding them in scorn.[154]

Sub-question 1: *How is one to set aside scrupulous conscience?*

I respond that, of itself, it is set aside by scorning the trivial motives on which it is founded. As a rule, however, it is not reformed without counsel from someone else, especially from a superior. And the reason for this is obvious, for scrupulous conscience arises from a fickleness or smallness of soul, which is an infirmity and must be cured with the help of spiritual (and sometimes even bodily) medicine. "Nay," says St. Alphonsus, "It can be said that the only remedy for those who are sick in this way is for them to submit to the judgment of their superior or confessor, as all the Fathers, theologians, and spiritual masters teach."[155]

Sub-question 2: *How ought a confessor conduct himself with scrupulous people?*

I respond that *a prudent confessor* must *first* strive to discover *through signs*, as well as the available evidence, whether his penitent is truly scrupulous and what may be the cause of such scrupulosity. *Second*, when he discovers this, he can, by means of appropriate remedies, cure the person who is vexed by scruples.

---

153. See *Decretum*, pt. 3, causa 6, q. 1, ch. 9, *Oves*; Cf. S. Antoninum, loc. cit., col. 193.

154. Op cit., no. 17, 18, and 19; H. pp. 8-9. See the places from which those authorities are drawn at the beginning of edition of the works of St. Alphonsus edted by P. Gaudé, vol. 1, p. 9 and 10. (Editor's Note, Ambroise Gardeil)

155. Op. cit., no. 12; H. pp. 5-6; G. pp. 6-7.

(1) *Signs and evidence of a scrupulous conscience.* The signs and evidence of a scrupulous conscience are obvious from the effects that were described above. Now, having performed this inductive work, such signs and evidence can help one disclose and discover the hidden sickness and its cause. Let a confessor take care, however, as Billuart advises[156]—and in this there is a danger of deception—lest he fail to rightly distinguish between a scrupulous conscience and one that is God-fearing, which proceeds from *servile* or *filial* fear with rectitude of judgment.

Indeed, some people, at last looking back over a more unrestrained life, are for some time uneasy about confessions that they made in the past. Out of their habit of sinning, they perpetrated many sins from an erroneous conscience and, having scorned that past life, they fear that they may not have sufficiently and accurately reprimanded all the things that they did or that they may err in the future concerning things to be done. This anxiety is reasonable, and solicitude necessarily must be employed in examining and cleansing a conscience that has become entangled through a very long habit of sinning.[157] In contrast, the confessor must remain vigilant, lest such fear may be contrary to reason and may degenerate into scrupulous conscience.

Some people, however, have professed the perfection of the counsels, thus prudently and reasonably watching over their purity and cleanness of conscience, employing care lest they offend God even in the least of things. As St. Augustine said, "He who scorns small things, little by little falls away." Such a conscience, which proceeds from filial fear, is not to be set aside nor reformed. Rather, it must be forever perfected.[158]

(2) *Remedies.*

(a) *In general.* First, above all, a prudent confessor may require the obedience and subjection of humility. As St. Alphonsus writes:

> Let him earnestly take care to persuade penitents who are vexed by scruples that one acts in an entirely safe manner when he submits to the counsels of his director and obeys him in all things which are clearly not sins, for then he does not obey man but God Himself,

156. Loc. cit.
157. See Billuart, loc. cit., quaer. 2, no. 2.
158. See *ST* II-II, q. 19, a. 2, 7, and 12: On filial fear.

who said, "He that heareth you heareth me: and he that despiseth you despiseth me" (Lk. 10:16; DR)."[159]

Second, on the contrary, however, let him insist that he who refuses to furnish obedience to the commands of his confessor and does not scorn his scruples thereby places a great hazard in the way of his salvation. For just as presumption leads someone to exceed the proper dimensions of his power when he strives to do more than he is capable of, so too the pusillanimous person lacks proper proportion to his power when he refuses to tend toward that which is commensurate to his power. And therefore, pusillanimity is a sin. For this reason, the servant who, having received his master's money, buries it in the ground, refusing to apply it in his labor, is punished by the Lord on account of a kind of fear coming from his pusillanimity (Mt. 25 and Lk. 19). Hence, Gregory the Great, in his *Pastoral Rule*,[160] says that if we strictly judge those who flee from going forth to preach as is useful to their neighbors, their guilt is as great as what they could have accomplished by going out into the public [to do such preaching].[161]

Third, moreover, a prudent confessor must strive to give general, not particular, rules to penitents of this kind. Indeed, when such scrupulous people only have particular rules at hand, they almost never can reach a resolution regarding how they should act, for they forever remain in doubt as to whether the prescribed rule can apply to the case under consideration, which they will think is different in comparison to the case discussed with their confessor in the past. Hence, Concina rightly says, "Once they have accepted the rules of direction, [penitents] must not annoyingly address a director and vex him with the most annoying of questions. Rather, they must drive away their scruples with the help of the rules that they have received."[162]

(b) *Particular remedies* (namely, those derived from the various intrinsic or extrinsic causes from which scruples arise).

If the scruples arise from *intrinsic causes*, let the prudent confessor

159. St. Alphonsus, op. cit., no. 13; H. p. 7; G. p. 7. See also, nos. 12-19. Billuart, loc. cit.

160. See Gregory the Great, *Regula pastoralis liber*, pt. 1, ch. 5, *PL* 77:19.

161. See *ST* II-II, q. 133, a.1c and ad 1.

162. See St. Alphonsus, op. cit., no. 13; H. G. p. 8.

know that fear and ignorance excuse one from sin, whereas pride is a cause thereof. Thus, [we have the following advice.]

First, when scruples proceed *from ignorance*, let him teach the penitent with the greatest of charity. Let him not permit the penitent to repeat past confessions except when the following two conditions hold: (1) he must be certain that the things that he is in doubt of are mortal sins; (2) he must be equally certain that they had not been duly confessed in the past. Similarly, let the confessor not permit presently doubtful sins to be confessed but, rather, only certain ones (and have him do so simply, speaking only about those circumstances which are absolutely necessary), and let the confessor admonish such a penitent not to be anxious and utterly detailed in his examination of conscience but, instead, to be moderate in performing it. And when the penitent has only a doubtful sin, enjoin him to celebrate a private Mass [*inauditum celebrare*] or [if he is not a priest] to go to the Holy Sacrifice, for the positive law concerning the integrity of confession does not obligate with great inconvenience.[163] Let him admonish the penitent that he must not delay much in whatever it is that he must do. Let the confessor also make clear that if something does not at first glance appear to be impermissible, he may certainly believe that it is permissible and may act in accord with it. And if it were perhaps to be the case that it is a sin (which is rarely the case), he will be excused from formal sin on account of invincible ignorance because there is nothing more that he could morally do in order to know that it is not permitted… Hence, let the confessor forbid the repetition of the Divine Office by the scrupulous person who is continuously anxious in its recitation and always fears that he omitted something or was distracted. Nay, if he were so scrupulous that there would hardly be an end to his repetition, thence leading him to suffer from grave and continuous troubles, the recitation of his breviary would need to be completely forbidden as something morally impossible.[164]

Second, when scruples proceed from *hidden pride*, "If it is necessary, let the confessor be somewhat harsher with his penitent, not however, so that he may drive him to desperation but, rather, so that he may mix some oil in with the wine."[165] In particular, let him call the penitent back to a

163. See Billuart, a. 5, cit., quaeritur 5, no. 5.

164. See ibid., no. 3.

165. Ibid., pro coronide.

consideration of God's greatness, of his own weakness and imperfection, and especially of the smallness of the intellect, which forever fluctuates on account of light matters. Above all, let the confessor impress upon the penitent the need to be humble before God, something which is brought about through subjection to men and to God's ministers.

Third, when scruples arise *from fear*, one must cultivate an awareness that perfect charity casts out all fear. Therefore, to the degree that someone progresses in charity, to the same degree does he have less fear. Let him cultivate awareness of the mercies of the Lord, the mystery of the Incarnation, and the economy and worth of the Redemption. Let him have confidence in God's grace, saying, "I can do all things in Him who strengthens me."

With the fearful man, let the confessor remember "that he must not vacillate in his resolutions, as if he were doubting or only opining. Instead, let him define and command with certitude what is to be done, for otherwise the penitent's anxiety will not be allayed but, instead, will grow greater. With meticulously fearful persons, let him proceed in a spirit of leniency."[166]

Fourth, if the scruples are caused by *bodily illness*, let him consult a doctor, make use of a remedy, and if nothing is accomplished, let him patiently bear with the infirmity and scorn it in a prudent manner. If it arises from negligence of his bodily regimen, let the confessor impose moderation and the virtuous mean, doing so with all spiritual discretion, lest perhaps after too much abstinence he may fall into laxity and no longer fast at all.

If the scruples arise from *extrinsic causes*, [then I have the following advice].

First, the confessor may forbid his penitents to share company with scrupulous people and prohibit them from reading cases of conscience. Let him never permit the penitent to consult many confessors separately, now going to one and then to another. If the gravity of the matter requires many opinions, however, they are to be consulted together and not separately.

Second, if the penitent's scrupulosity arises from the art of a demon, let the confessor make use of the Church's approved remedies and consult

166. Ibid.

the other things that are found variously in the writings of teachers regarding the matter of demonic vexation.

Third, if the scrupulosity is caused by the divine permission, let the penitent prepare himself as much as he can by keeping the precepts. Let him solicitously read the Sacred Scripture and continue in devout prayer. If the scrupulous person is in those states of soul [*viis*], however, which the Mystics call extraordinary or supernatural, let the confessor apply the greatest of prudence lest he impede God's work as well as the perfection of the penitent. Let him have recourse to approved works by the Doctors and experts in mystical theology.

Let the prudent confessor make use of these remedies together or separately in accord with the natures and causes of the penitent's scruples, as well as the other remedies commended by St. Alphonsus,[167] St. Antoninus,[168] John Gerson,[169] and other proven authors who specifically treat of this subject.

QUESTION 4: ON PROBABLE CONSCIENCE

Preliminary Note

As regards this question's title, take care to note that [morally acceptable] conscience, properly speaking, is not probable, since every action that is not from faith or from certain conscience is illicit. Conscience is called "probable," however, on account of the speculatively probable opinion that can become indirectly certain by means of a reflex principle.

Now, the speculatively probable opinion involved in the formation of practically certain conscience can be considered from two perspectives: first, ***absolutely***, in itself or [*vel*] in the state of solitude,[170] and second, ***comparatively***, that is, alongside another probable opinion.

167. See St. Alphonsus, op. cit., no. 11-20 (H. G. pp. 5-20).

168. St. Antoninus, *Summa*, pt. 1, tit. 3, ch. 10, §10, V.

169. See *Tractatus de praeparatione ad missam et poll. noct.*, consid. 3. (Cf. St. Alphonsus, op. cit., Gaudé, vol. 1, p. 7.)

170. **Translator's Note:** Concerning this expression, "the state of solitude," see John of St. Thomas, *The Material Logic of John of St. Thomas*, q. 3, a. 1 (p. 92): "Both universality and particularity pertain to the kind of state enjoyed by the nature, which can receive a denomination either from universality or from singularity. Therefore, every nature can be in a threefold state. (See *On Being and Essence*, ch. 3 and Cajetan's commentary.) The first is the state of the nature taken in itself. Here, we consider only the characteristics which make up the nature or quiddity itself. This state is also called [the] 'state of indifference,'

First, we must speak about that kind of conscience which can be formed from a probable opinion, absolutely speaking. Then, we will speak about that kind of conscience which is formed from a probable opinion, comparatively speaking, both in general and then specifically, as will be clear below.

Article 1: *On Conscience Formed from an Absolutely Probable Opinion, or [seu] in the State of Solitude, and Its Obligation*

§1. ON CONSCIENCE FORMED FROM AN ABSOLUTELY PROBABLE OPINION

Sub-question 1: *What is probable conscience?*

I respond: "Probable conscience is that form of conscience *by which someone, relying upon a given probable opinion, forms for himself the dictamen of [practico-moral] reason on the basis of certain principles, whether reflex or accompanying, so that he may act in a permissible manner.*"[171]

Two points are touched on in this definition, namely *the probable opinion* itself and *the formation of conscience*. Indeed, since opinion intrinsically involves fear that one's opinion may not hold as true, it does not have the certitude that is required for acting in a morally upright manner. Relying upon such an opinion, however, someone can, in practice, form an indirectly certain conscience for himself by means of reflex principles, doing so in the way we mentioned above and will immediately discuss in greater detail [in the remainder of this text]. In order, however, to see the sort of opinion that someone may utilize in the formation of an indirectly certain conscience, we must first accurately explain what a probable opinion, absolutely speaking, is.

because the nature is, in itself, indifferent to accidental predicates. It is also called [the] 'state of solitude' because here the nature is alone and free from all predicates extrinsic to it. It is also designated as negatively common because here the nature is not understood as multiplied. The second state is connected with the existence that the nature has in singular things; it is the 'state of singularity.' The third state is connected with the existence that the nature enjoys in intellectual abstraction: this abstraction can also be described as a state of solitude, but here solitude does not imply isolation from every extrinsic predicate; it only signifies that the nature, in this state, is abstracted from individuals."

171. St. Alphonsus, *Tr. De Conscientia*, no. 40, H. p. 20; G. p. 21.

Sub-question 2: *What is a probable opinion, absolutely speaking?*

I respond that "absolutely speaking, a probable opinion is one which is considered in itself and not in relation to another [opinion]. 'Opinion,' however, signifies the act of the intellect that is concerned with one side of a contradiction while fearing that the other side may be true."[172] Thus, an opinion differs from a doubt because the former it is a determinate judgment concerning the truth of one side of a contradiction, whereas a doubt is the suspension of judgment. It is distinguished, however, from the certitude of science [or also discursive certitude in a quasi-scientific manner that is analogically applied to the case of prudence] because the intellect is not moved by a given certain and evident principle but, rather, by a likely or probable motive. And therefore, such a judgment is accompanied by fear of the other side of the contradiction. Now, this fear, which is connected to opining assent, does not involve a movement or drawing backwards from the side to which assent is given, for in that case the intellect would act with opposed motivating factors. This fear is, however, a defect, or to put it another way, a deficiency in scientific firmness in judgment [with the qualifications stated above concerning the prudential sense of science as well]. Indeed, the principle or motive inclining the intellect in an opining judgment is the very likeliness and appearance of truth. And because the motive is infirm and weak, it thus gives birth to a judgment accompanied by fear that the other part of the contradiction may be true.[173]

Now, a probable opinion can be described either from the perspective of the *subject* or from the perspective of the *object.*

From the perspective of the *subject,* it is said to be *an assent to one side of a contradiction with fear concerning the other side.*

From the perspective of the *object,* it is an assent *on account of a motive or weighty foundation that succeeds in drawing to itself the assent of a prudent man,*[174] with fear of the other side being true.[175]

172. *ST* I, q. 79, a. 9, ad 4.

173. See Concina, op. cit., bk. 3, diss. 2, ch. 1, pp. 359-360; Marc, op. cit., no. 61.

174. Translator's Note: Note carefully the handoff to prudence here. This is important, for Fr. Beaudouin's sense of "conscience" is not fully able to be "written down on paper," given that the ultimate weighing of opinions and possible choices must be undertaken precisely by the person who has the virtue of prudence.

175. See St. Alphonsus, op. cit. no. 40.

Sub-question 3: *On what foundations or motives does probable opinion rest?*

I respond that probable opinion rests on two foundations, namely *an intrinsic one* and *an extrinsic one*. Its *intrinsic* foundation is sought from the formal notion of the very thing at hand, its nature, properties, causes, effects, and even from the unbefitting characteristics of the opposite side of the contradiction. Its *extrinsic* foundation, however, is taken from the authority of the teachers who hold (or have held) this opinion. Yet this authority is motivating only inasmuch as it is presumed that these teachers teach (or taught) this opinion for good reasons. Hence, extrinsic probability must be assessed more with regard to the merit and erudition of the teachers and as regards their zeal and diligence in their examination of the matter than as regards the number of teachers holding an opinion.

Doubt 1: *Does extrinsic probability constitute a truly and solidly probable opinion?*

I respond affirmatively. Indeed, extrinsic probability is [ultimately] resolved into intrinsic probability, and teachers think that an opinion is probable only on account of weighty and likely motives. Thus, the Angelic Doctor says that someone of little science is more certain about what he hears from someone having scientific knowledge than he is about what seems to be the case according to his own reason. And a man is much more certain about what he hears from God, who cannot be deceived, than about what he sees through his own reason, which can be deceived.[176]

This point is confirmed by the authority of the Church which often recommends to us proven authors and Holy Doctors.[177]

Doubt 2: *What authority is required and suffices for establishing that some opinion is absolutely or of itself probable?*

I respond that one must place the authority of the Church above all others. Indeed, the decisions of the Holy Fathers and of the Sacred Congregations respectively suffice so that a probable opinion may be established and held safely in practice.

176. See *ST* II-II, q. 4, a. 8, ad 2.

177. See Marc, op. cit., no. 64. Gury, op. cit., no. 78, quaer. 3; Scavini, *Theol. Mor. Univ.*, bk. 1, no. 93.

After this, one must respect the authority of the Holy Fathers of the Church and of the Doctors in Sacred Theology who, with the Church's toleration, commonly hand on that a given opinion is probable. As regards the authority of theologians, it suffices (following Scavini[178]) to take heed of the following brief points drawn from Melchior Cano, who outstandingly worked through the details of this argument.

First, the constant and unanimous opinion of theologians teaching that something is permitted must be esteemed as holding such authority that it would be right to say that someone approaches toward heresy in wishing to depart from such an opinion.

Second, the testimony of many (if other learned men feel the case to be the opposite) calls for one to do no more than is persuaded by their reasoning or an even weightier authority… Among such authors, however, those are to be preferred who treat the matter expressly, for they are estimated to have weighed out the reasons at play more diligently. Next, one is to follow those who have proven their doctrine by experience, for experience is the best teacher of things. Finally, we have those who hold all the passions in a subordinate place and write only out of a love for the truth, as is done by holy authors.

Third, both ancient and more recent authors must be considered at length [*evolvendi sunt*], nay even the most recent, must be consulted, for they alone can propose recently given decisions.

Doubt 3: *Does the authority of one teacher ordinarily suffice for establishing that a given opinion is truly probable?*

I have two responses. First, speaking in a universal sense, I respond negatively.

This is clear from the 27th proposition condemned by Pope Alexander VII: "If a book is published by a younger or modern person, its opinion should be considered as probable, provided that it has not been established that it has been rejected by the Holy See as improbable"[179] And St. Thomas: "In those things that pertain to faith and good morals, nobody is excused if he follows the erroneous opinion of a given teacher."[180]

178. Ibid., no. 93; Cano, *De locis*, bk. 8, ch. 4.

179. Denzinger, no. 2047 (43rd edition, translation slightly altered).

180. *Quodlibet* III, q. 4, a. 2.

This is also clear if one reasons through the matter, for the opinion of a given teacher is not probable on account of his authority but on account of his reasons, which are likely and weighty. Thus, if there is no reason for the opinion, no faith is to be placed in such an authority. Otherwise, as Billuart notes, one would consider as being safe so many wicked opinions asserted by the laxer of the probabilists who mutually flattered each other and elevated themselves, by means of the reciprocal praise that they offered to each other, to the self-proclaimed status of being weighty and learned authors.[181]

As noted above, I have two responses. Now, second, *in specific matters*, I say, "If there were a given Doctor in the Church whose authority would outweigh or even equal the reasonings and authority of many teachers, it would suffice that his opinion be held to be absolutely probable and safe in practice except, perchance, if someone of the same weight and authority would contradict what he says on the matter."[182]

In this sense, we have said that one is permitted in practice to follow the opinions of St. Thomas and St. Alphonsus of Liguouri, so long as they have not been rejected or altered by the Church. As regards St. Thomas, his authority in the Church is so great that he has no need of commendation. As regards St. Alphonsus, who always declared that he followed the Angelic Doctor as his Master, his authority is clear from the authoritative statements of the Sacred Penitentiary. Indeed, when the Sacred Congregation was asked whether a confessor who follows St. Alphonsus's teaching ought to be troubled that he has not weighed out his reasonings but has only taken into account the authority of his great name, the Congregation responded negatively that such a confessor need not be troubled in mind. And this response was confirmed by Pope Gregory XVI on July 22, 1831.[183]

Doubt 4: *What diligence is required and sufficient for judging that a given opinion is truly and solidly probable?*

I respond with three remarks. First, the illiterate can safely follow the opinion or counsel of a pastor or confessor whom they hold to be a prudent

181. See Billuart, [*Summa sancti thomae, De conscientia*], diss. 4, a. 4, *petes* 5, op. et tract. cit.

182. B:llart, loc. cit.

183. See the full text in Marc, op. cit., §Praecipua S. Sedis testimonia, edit. 9a, p. xiii.

and learned man or that of another equally prudent and learned man, for there is nothing better that they can do.

Second, the semi-learned can consult more learned persons or pursue the teaching found in books.

Third, learned men may hold that an opinion is probable and may persuade others that it is such when, having set aside passions and prejudices, and having carefully assessed in a mature and timely manner the reasons of importance on both sides and being attentive to the gravity and weight of authors for and against the matter, they sincerely judge before God that it is probable.

Sub-question 4: *How many forms of probable opinion, absolutely speaking, are there?*

I respond that authors commonly distinguish opinion, absolutely speaking, into *barely probable, only probable*, and *very probable*. And these degrees of probability are understood inasmuch as they exhibit a lesser or greater proximity to the truth in itself, not through a comparison to the opposed proposition. The reason for this is that opinion in the state of solitude[184] is distinguished, of itself, in relation to scientifically certain knowledge and or certain assent (i.e., depending on whether the opinion more or less recedes from or approaches toward science[185] and to the attaining of truth based on the very things that are proper and essential to the thing at hand). If probability of opinion, however, arises from human authority, its degrees are taken from the greater or lesser number and weight of testimonies. For, as St. Thomas says, "It is probable that the dictum of many contains a greater amount of truth than does that of one person."[186]

Sub-question 5: *What are slightly probable opinions, only probable opinions, and very probable opinions?*

I respond on three heads.

First, *a slightly probable opinion or one that is dubiously probable* is one relying on some minor foundation, namely in such a manner that it does not succeed in drawing to itself the assent of a prudent man. It is not a true

184. **Translator's Note:** See note 170 above.

185. **Translator's Note:** Realizing that this is being analogically used here as regards prudence's discursive knowledge.

186. See *ST* II-II, q. q. 70, a. 2.

opinion, since it implies only the shadow of probability. And a probably probable opinion is similar to this, for probability concerning the probability of an opinion does not change probability into an opinion.[187]

Second, *opinion that is only probable* has the same definition as opinion simply speaking, namely, *it is an assent of the intellect to one side of a contradiction with fear that the other side may be true.* One must, however, make a qualification in the case of opinion that is only probable, namely, that the fear that is part of its intrinsic formal character [*ratione*] is not taken from weighty motives that militate for the opposed opinion but instead is taken from the intrinsic nature of the motive which moves a prudent man while of itself not managing to draw firm and certain assent. In venerable authors, it is called "vehement opinion," and "probable certitude," whereas in the later scholastics and more recent authors, it is called "speculatively probable and practically certain," or, "practically certain," without an addition. Indeed, in such authors, it is sometimes called "morally certain."[188]

Third, *a very probable opinion* is one that relies on the weightiest foundation and approaches most closely to the truth of scientific certitude. It occupies the highest degree of probability, although it does not pass beyond the limits of probability and does not exclude every prudent fear that it may be false, in contrast with certain scientific knowledge, which excludes every prudent fear of this sort.[189]

§2. ON THE OBLIGATION OF CONSCIENCE THAT IS FORMED FROM AN OPINION THAT IS ABSOLUTELY AND OF ITSELF PROBABLE

Conclusion 1

One is never permitted to act by following a barely probable opinion.

This conclusion is stated against the *Laxists*, who taught that one is permitted to follow any opinions whatsoever, in accord with their axiom: "The more generous opinion can be chosen, so long as it is in some way probable. [*Benignior dummodo aliqualiter probabilis.*]"

This is proven, first, on the authority of Innocent XI who condemned this proposition (the third such condemned proposition): "In general,

187. See Marc, op. cit., no. 61, 3.

188. Cf. Marc, op. cit., no. 61 and 72.

189. See St. Alphonsus, op. cit., no. 40, H. G. p. 20, and no. 82, H. p. 72 (G, no. 81, p. 60); Marc, ibid., no. 71.

when we do something confidently according to probability, whether intrinsic or extrinsic, however slight, provided there is no departure from the bounds of probability, we always act prudently."[190]

This is also proven, second, by reasoning the matter out, for it is obvious that what is barely probable is not probable and must be scorned by a prudent man. Thus, a barely probable opinion can rightly be excluded precisely on account of the very notion of opinion which is always supported upon a weighty foundation, and the doubt which can be provoked concerning this barely probable or probably probable opinion is resolved after the manner that we discussed in the preceding question concerning doubting conscience. Indeed, light motives, as we have said, succeed at moving the presumptuous or pusillanimous man to action, but not the prudent man.[191]

No more time needs to be spent in refutation of this position since it is held by no Catholic today.

Conclusion 2

One is permitted to act by following a very probable opinion, as well as one that is only probable.

This conclusion is stated against the *Rigorists*, who required direct and absolute certitude in order for one to act in a permissible manner.

The conclusion is proven in two ways, namely universally and, then, with regard to each in particular.

First, *universally* speaking, an opinion that is only probable or one that is very probable approaches toward the truth of scientifically certain knowledge and does not face an opposed proposition by which its probability would be shattered. Thus, according to St. Thomas's judgment, it is probably certain. More recent authors say that it is imperfectly and morally certain. Therefore, those things that are said concerning imperfectly certain conscience are proportionally applied to very probable opinion and to opinion that is only probable.

As was said above, we can also render proofs in this matter with regard to each of these specific kinds of probability:

190. Denzinger, no. 2103 (43rd edition).

191. TRANSLATOR'S NOTE: See the earlier comment about the role of prudence and the importance of this qualifier in Fr. Beaudouin's text. (It is tempting for readers to dismiss this as merely a flourish. As already noted, it is likely more than that, ultimately limiting the degree to which casuistry can be written out in detail.)

(1) As regards *very probable* opinion, it is certain that one is permitted to follow it. Indeed, this proposition is contradictorily opposed to the 3rd proposition that was condemned by Pope Alexander VIII, which said: "It is not licit to follow a [probable] opinion, even the most probable among the probable ones."[192] And today, among Catholic authors, this conclusion is not brought forward in controversies.

(2) It is commonly held that one may follow an opinion that is only *probable*, a claim expressed in the writings of venerable teachers as well as more recent ones. As Billuart writes:

> We do not deny that a solidly probable opinion, considered separately, could be safely chosen so long as nothing appears to the contrary and so long as it is not obviously lax. This is so because man cannot always have utter certitude in moral matters, and he acts prudently who acts according to weighty reasons which are diminished by no solid considerations."[193]

Next, this is proven by St. Thomas, who says: "He who, in spite of contrary opinions, is not led to a state of doubt does not place himself in danger and does not sin."[194] Now, someone relying on an opinion that is only probable is led to no doubt. For, on the one hand, according to what the weight of the matter demands, he looked into things and has investigated the truth of the matter to the degree that this was possible. On the other hand, no motive leading to doubt militates for the opposed proposition. Thus, temerity and imprudence are precluded. Therefore, acting in such a matter, he does not put himself in danger and does not sin.

This is confirmed on the basis of St. Alphonsus's authority. He wrote:

> I do not have the spirit of prophecy. I do not feel, however, that the Church will ever declare that my adversary's (Vincenzo Patuzzi's) opinion is true, namely that without a doubt one is not permitted to follow opinions outside of those that are morally certain on the basis of a direct judgment of conscience. I do not say, however, this based on my

192. Denzinger, no. 2303 (43rd ed.)
193. Billuart, op. cit., diss. 6, a. 1.
194. St. Thomas, *Quodlibet* VIII, q. 6, a. 1.

> own considerations alone, nor by relying upon my own weak capacities, but do so based upon what has been written by great theologians, especially the Angelic Master, a man so greatly illuminated by God and already declared to be a Doctor of the Church.[195]

Likewise, St. Alphonsus's disciple Marc felt the same in this matter:

> An opinion of this sort already has a morally certain foundation that it is true. Thus, St. Alphonsus likens such an opinion, in the practical order, to a morally certain judgment [*sententiae*], saying: "When there is so probable a case on behalf of the law, then a kind of moral certitude would defend the law."[196]

Sub-question 1: *Must someone relying on an only-probable or very probable opinion make use of reflex principles in order to form a practically certain conscience for himself?*

I respond affirmatively. Indeed, since very probable opinions or opinions that are only probable do not exceed the level of probability, they include a fear that the other side may be true. Thus, such an opinion is not a morally certain judgment [*sententia*]. Therefore, by means of reflex principles, a prudent man must make up for what is lacking in the certitude of such judgments. He does not need, however, to explicitly bring forth reflex principles of this sort.[197] Instead, it suffices that they be implicitly presupposed, as was said in the question above concerning indirectly certain conscience.

Sub-question 2: *What are the reflex principles which can be implicitly or explicitly used by the prudent man in such a case?*

I respond that they are the same principles by which imperfectly certain conscience is perfected.

195. See *Vindicias vindiciarum*, pt. 1, ch. 1, §IV, no. 3, vol. 1, p. 64.

196. Op. cit., no. 76. Cf. St. Alphonsus, op. cit., bk. 1, no. 71, and 76. V. Caeterum. H. pp. 46-58, G. no. 68.

197. **Translator's Note:** It is important to note this qualification, which perhaps points to the way that the interrelation between will and intellect are involved in prudence's discursus. (A parallel example here is the way that certain philosophical truths are *objectively implied* in what is revealed, even if they are not the direct object of a given revealed datum.)

Article 2: *On the Conscience That Is Formed from an Opinion That Is Probable, Comparatively Speaking, Considered in General, and Concerning Its Obligation*

§1. On conscience that is formed from an opinion that is probable, comparatively speaking, considered in general

Sub-question 1: *What is an opinion that is probable, comparatively speaking?*[198]

I respond that such an opinion is one that is formed from a probable opinion that is not only considered absolutely and in itself but also *in relation* to another opposed position which itself has probability. Such an opinion is based on a weighty foundation, although not one that is certain. Consequently, it includes fear of the opposed position, absolutely, from its intrinsic character, like probable opinion considered in the state of solitude.[199] In addition, however, the opposed position itself is also based upon a weighty foundation, and thus the fear that is found in the assent to the other position is caused both absolutely (from the probability of its motive force) and relatively (from the probability of the opposed position). Thus, it is distinguished from opinion absolutely considered, whose fear of the opposite position is solely caused by its intrinsic motive force and not by some extrinsic motivation.

Sub-question 2: *How many kinds of comparison may be performed among probable opinions?*

198. On this matter, see what is written in Mandonnet, "De la valeur des theories sur la probabilité," *Revue thomiste*, Vol. 10 (1902): p. 314. Fr. Mandonnet, a professor at the University of Fribourg, was present at the lectures on which this text is based and indeed was a diligent note-taker for them. And he does not differ from his master as regards his opinions on these matters (besides what he thinks about equiprobabilism, cf. p. 334) but, rather, as regards the possibility of the hypothesis, namely, "that mutually contradictory or evictive propositions can indeed be found in the moral domain." See Mandonnet, "La position du probabilisme dans l'Eglise Catholique," *Revue thomiste*, Vol. 10 (1902): pp. 5-20; "Le décret d'Innocent XI contre le probabilisme," *Revue thomiste*, Vol. 9 (1901): pp. 460-481, 520-539, 652-673. Also, see ibid., "Encore le décret d'Innocent XI," *Revue thomiste*, Vol. 10 (1902): pp. 676-698. Note well that the so-called Probabilist master who is mentioned on p. 316 of the 1902 article ought not to be identified with Fr. Beaudouin but perhaps with the author (with regard to moral matters) of the Clermont [or, Jasna Góra, Czestochowa, *Claromontana*] edition of *Institutiones Theologiae* said to be by Vincentio, whom the renowned professor had previously heard. (Editor's Note, Ambroise Gardeil)

199. **Translator's Note:** See the first footnote in this question.

I respond that in the writings of authors in general, two kinds of comparison can be performed between opinions, namely a comparison with regard to *security* and one with regard to *probability*.

Sub-question 3: *How are opinions compared in terms of security?*
I respond that, *on account of the security involved*, one opinion is said to be "safer" in relation to the other, which is said to be "less safe," because it more or less withdraws one from the danger of sinning and inclines one toward the law or toward freedom.[200] We already discussed this comparison above when we discussed doubting conscience.

Sub-question 4: *How are opinions compared in terms of probability?*
I respond that, on account of the probability involved, one opinion is called "more probable" in relation to another that is called "less probable," and one is called "probable" in relation to another that is called "equally probable." Indeed, an opinion that is in contest with another ([speaking] most properly and reduplicatively, precisely inasmuch as it is relative) is distinguished in relation to the opposed opinion. Now, only two kinds of consideration are found in probable opinions. Indeed, one opinion is said to be (and is) equally probable as the other opposed to it or it is more probable than that which is said to be (and is) less probable in comparison to the opposed opinion. Thus, only two kinds of pairings are possible in terms of the probability involved, namely: a more probable opinion in contest with a less probable one and a probable opinion in contest with one that is equally probable.

Corollary
From what has been said, one can infer that a "safer" opinion is one thing and a "more probable" opinion is another. Likewise, the "less safe" is different from the "less probable." Indeed, an opinion is called more and less probable on account of greater or lesser truth concerning the matter at hand. An opinion is called more or less safe, however, inasmuch as it involves a greater or lesser danger of sinning. Thus, the less safe opinion and the less probable opinion are not necessarily the same thing, nor are the

200. Translator's Note: Note the law vs. freedom motif, which Fr. Labourdette rightly critiques from this period. However, see remarks above, in note 127.

safer and the more probable. Indeed, a safer opinion does not always have for itself a more likely or graver motive. Nay, sometimes, it has only a slight foundation or none at all, and consequently, although it may be safer, it nonetheless is less probable, not more so, than the opposed opinion. And for the same reason, that which is less safe can be more probable. This point is clear in the opinion expressed by St. Bonaventure when he teaches that the person who has fallen into mortal sin is bound immediately, under force of precept, to go to confession (so long as there is an abundance of confessors). This is safer, although less probable than the contrary opinion held by St. Thomas which is less safe and certainly more probable.[201]

Consequently, the measure of severity and rigorism is taken in moral matters on the basis of the greater or lesser distance that there is from the danger of sinning. The measure of probability is taken, however, from the greater or lesser appearance of truth.[202]

§2. ON THE OBLIGATION OF CONSCIENCE THAT IS FORMED FROM AN OPINION THAT IS PROBABLE, COMPARATIVELY SPEAKING, CONSIDERED IN GENERAL

Universal Conclusion

One is never permitted to act with a speculatively-practical conscience, comparatively understood, which is only probable or more probable. Instead, such conscience must be set aside and reformed.

This conclusion is certain and commonly held, even in the writings of probabilists,[203] and is proven as follows.

Indeed, everything that is not from faith (i.e., certain conscience) is a sin. Now, speculatively-practical conscience which is only probable or more probable (comparatively understood) is morally certain neither in itself (since it includes fear of the opposite position in its character) nor in relation to the other side (since the opposed side is probable and causes a grave doubt concerning its truth). Thus, one who acts with such conscience does not act prudently and would commit oneself to the danger of formally sinning.

201. See Billuart, *Summa sancti thomae, De conscientia*, diss. 6, a. 1.

202. See Gonet, *Clypeus*, loc. cit., a. 2. Billuart, tr. cit., diss. 6, a. 1. St. Alphonsus, passim. Scavini, op. cit., no. 95.

203. See Billuart, tr. cit., diss. 5, a. 6, §II.

Therefore, one is never permitted to act with a speculatively-practical conscience (comparatively understood) which is only probable or more probable, and such conscience must be set aside and reformed so that it may come to be indirectly morally certain by means of a reflex principle.

Sub-question 1: *What ought to be done by someone who cannot prudently set aside such conscience on one's own or by means of a further aid?*
I respond that someone faced with this situation must choose the safer path and that what was said in question three above concerning negative doubt must be proportionally applied to positive doubt.

Sub-question 2: *Does someone sin by acting with a conscience that is only probable or more probable in a speculatively-practical manner?*
I respond affirmatively. Indeed, he sins by the same species and gravity of sin involved in the fear in question because he virtually wills the sin to which he exposes himself.[204]

Sub-question 3: *How or by means of what reflex principles is conscience that is comparatively speaking only probable or more probable in a speculatively practical manner indirectly reformed and rendered practically (or, morally) certain?*
I respond as follows. *Venerable* authors briefly resolved this difficulty by saying, with St. Thomas, that since the person who has two contrary opinions finds himself to be entangled, he would dangerously determine the path to be taken unless, having diligently looked into the matter, he were to choose the more probable option.[205] And in resolving doubts of this

---

204. Billuart, tr. cit., diss. 5, a. 6, Dico 2.

205. The author refers to St. Thomas's comments in *In III Sent.*, dist. 25, q. 1. Such an opinion is not found, however, in that text. Perhaps this is nothing more than a gloss of some other texts such as *Quodl.* VIII, q. 6, a. 3 and *Quodl.* IX, q. 7, a. 2. Indeed, the first text is interpreted by the author in an earlier version of his lectures which (in 1885, taken from the notes of Fr. V. Scheil, then his student, now an associate of the *Collegium Academicum pro Inscriptionibus colendis et explicandis*) which I have at hand [*in manibus verso*]. One sees in this text, taken from p. 84 of a copy made in 1885: "Based on what St. Thomas says, he who finds himself in a state of doubt because of a contrariety of opinions, and if he acts while remaining such a state of doubt he places himself in danger of sinning and thus, without a doubt, sins (*Quodl.* VIII, q. 6, a. 3). Now, he does not, on the strength and efficacy of certainly more probable motives, overcome and conquer motives that are less safe and less probable. Therefore, the doubt remains, and when he acts in this manner, he places himself in danger of sinning and without a doubt sins." (Editor's note, Ambroise Gardeil)

sort, they made use of this legal axiom: "When matters are not clear, we are to follow that which is more likely." They understood "more likely" or "more probable," however, in a practical manner, namely the kind of certitude that is had after having undertaken a diligent inquiry into the goodness or wickedness of an act to be performed here and now, according to the formal character of both the object and all the circumstances, and they left this judgment to the prudent man.[206]

More recent authors, however, brought this argument back into question, fiercely disputing among themselves from the sixteenth to the seventeenth century, expressing various opinions that, for the sake of brevity, can be reduced to four headings.[207]

First, *the tutiorists* very easily and simply resolve the question by saying, "In order to act in a permissible manner when there is a conflict of probable opinions, the safer option must always be followed." Their rule is, "Always do what is safer"—*semper tutius*. This opinion is true if one is concerned with a practical doubt that someone cannot manage to prudently set aside, as we said in response to the first question above. When it is universally applied, however, to every speculatively-practical positive doubt, it has the savor of Jansenism and cannot be squared with the words of venerable authors. Therefore, Catholic teachers partly reject it and, having posited the distinction between probability *of fact* and *of right*, admit that the safer option must be followed when it is a question

206. **Translator's Note:** Heed again the role of prudence in this. To a degree, Fr. Labourdette's account of casuistry and the theology of conscience seems to be fighting against a certain popularized notion of them (often imputed to Jesuits, whether fairly or unfairly). This is perhaps a bit too unfair to the overall thrust of what moral theologians were trying to articulate over a multi-century period of time. A very fair example of trying to integrate *and* critique the theology of conscience into the framework of prudence can be found in Fr. Garrigou-Lagrange's work. See Garrigou-Lagrange, "Remarks Concerning the Metaphysical Character of St. Thomas's Moral Theology," pp. 245–270 (substantially the same as his *The Order of Things*, pt. 2, ch. 6); "Prudence's Place in the Organism of the Virtues," *Philosophizing in Faith*, pp. 153-70; *De beatitudine, de actibus humanis, et habitibus*, pp. 373-96.

207. The opinions that are enumerated here are not always found in a strictly determinate manner in the writings of authors. Indeed, there are many, various manners of speaking, and in such heated disputations, it is not immediately clear what each person genuinely holds. Moreover, it seems to be of little use for beginners in moral theology and would involve discussions of too great a length and too exacting a nature were we to pass through the various opinions that have been thought about this question. He who is interested may consult the theologians and writers of ecclesiastical history who professedly discuss this argument. See the citations of Müller and Jos. D'Annibale referred to in Marc, op. cit., no. 86. Also, see Concina, *De conscientia*.

of *probability of fact* but, however, deny that this is so when it is a case of *probability of right*. And thus dividing moral matters, they hold on to half of the Tutiorists's position (i.e., in matters of *probability of fact*) but claim the other part for themselves, teaching with one voice: "When it is a question of *probability of right*, one is not necessarily bound to choose the safer path."

One must determine, however, when and how one would be permitted to follow the less safe, probable opinion in contest with the safer one when it is a probability of right. Here, one is faced with great exertion and pressure! The difficulty grows, authors and various people opining are divided, and various systems of thinking can be held without falling under the Church's condemnation.[208]

Second, *the probabiliorists* teach that one would be permitted to follow the less safe opinion which is certainly more probable in contest with the less probable but safer opinion, and with the approval of all the probabilists, they quite invincibly demonstrate this proposition against the tutiorists. They stop here, however, and if one is concerned with something equally probable that is less safe, they contend that one is not permitted to follow the equally probable [but less safe option] in contrast to what is safer. Their axiom is, "Choose what is safer or more probable"—*Tutius vel probabilius*.

Third, *the equiprobabilists* go further and teach in favor of freedom of choice, following St. Alphonsus, that one would be *sometimes* permitted to follow that which is equally probable but less safe in contest with what is safer.

Fourth, *the probabilists*, however, looking to be even more generous, say that one is always permitted to follow that which is equally probable

208. To understand the formal character guiding this division and enumeration, the student must heed that the hinge of the disputation turns on the comparison of the parts of each comparison, namely of (1) the more or less safe on the one hand, in relation to (2) that which, on the other hand, is more probable, equally probable, or less probable. If the safer option (whether it be more probable, equally probable, or less probable) is compared to the less safe, it is utterly clear that one would be permitted to follow that, at least with regard to counsels. However, is one always bound, in matters of precepts, to choose the safer option? This is the point of controversy, and to resolve one's doubt, one must compare the less safe that is more probable, equally probable, or less probable with that which is safer.

And thus, upon an attentive consideration, one can clearly see the various opinions by which Catholic authors either agree or disagree with each other.

but less safe in contest with what is safer. Nay, some of them hold that one is always permitted to follow that option which is less safe and less probable in contest with one that is safer and more probable.

Sub-question 4: *What ought one to think about the opinions named in the previous sub-question?*

We will discuss this in the following four articles.

Article 3: *On Conscience Formed from an Opinion That Is Probable, Based on a Probability of Fact, Comparatively Understood, and Concerning Its Obligation*

§1. ON CONSCIENCE THAT IS PROBABLE, BASED UPON PROBABILITY OF FACT

Sub-question 1: *What is an opinion that is probable based on a probability of fact and on a probability of right?*

I respond, in general, that when authors set forth this definition and distinction, they do not use their terms in the same way as each other and do not seem always to agree with each other. The reason for this is that, since a probable opinion is a likely judgment of reason concerning the goodness or wickedness of the act to be done and since the activity is subject to various rules of morals (i.e., to the end, to law, and to reason), this distinction can be explained in various way. Therefore, lest the question be obscured by a dense terminological crust, one must first refer to what authors have thought concerning this matter.

Sub-question 2: *What do teachers hold concerning the distinction of probability into probability of fact and probability of right?*

I respond that there are various opinions (or ways) for explaining this matter.

First, some authors, admitting the distinction in itself, reject it inasmuch as it is applied to the current matter. They do so because the venerable authors clearly did deploy it in solving morally practical doubts, and to their mind, the common utterance, "When matters are not clear, we are to follow that which is more likely," seems to run through the entirety of moral matters and to be sufficient. Hence, as Concina said: "There is no question of fact into which we may not [also] mix some question of right."[209] Nay, he says that, "One substantially makes use of the same rule in confecting the Sacraments of the Church, in caring for the sick, in wars, and in other matters of weightier importance."[210]

Second, others, restricting the aforementioned opinion, distinguish between those things that are necessary with a necessity of precept or with a necessity of means. They say that in those things that are necessary with a necessity of means, the safer option must always be embraced. And, in general, many more recent authors make use of this manner of speaking, although by using various terms. Gury writes, "For as long as there is an absolute obligation to determinately obtain a given end, which would be put into danger by the use of means that are probably not apt for achieving that end, one is not permitted to follow the probable opinion nor the more probable opinion, setting aside the safer one. Therefore, in that case, the safer path must be followed."[211] And Marc, a disciple of St. Alphonsus, in proof of this thesis says, "One is not permitted to expose the end which absolutely must be sought (which is that which is being considered here [*qualis est ille de quo agitur*]) to the danger of being frustrated."[212] What kind of end, however, is being considered here? What is the apt means for achieving the end, in itself and necessarily to be chosen so that the activity may be right? This is not sufficiently clear. Indeed, the means are said to be necessary as ordered either to the proximate end or to the remote end. Now, the acts of the virtues are the proximate ends [of moral actions],[213] as St. Thomas teaches, and since all the virtues are interconnected and also are related as ordered to the ultimate end, we have the precepts in the Decalogue which, whether they are more proximate or more remote, necessarily are required for the perfection of virtue and for the achieving of beatitude. Indeed, he who said, "Do not kill, and do not steal," also said, "Do not commit adultery" (Deut. 5:17–19). And the Apostle wrote in 1 Cor. 6:9–10 (DR): "Know you not that the unjust shall not possess the

209. Concina, *De conscientia*, bk. 2, diss. 1, ch. 6, §unico, no. 10, ed. cit., bk. 2, p. 67.

210. Ibid., bk. 3, diss. 5, ch. 4, §II, *in titulo*, p. 480.

211. Gury-Ballerini, *Compendium*, *Tr. de conscientia*, no. 50, ch. 6, a. 2, thesis 1 (1882), vol. 1, p. 52.

212. Marc, op. cit, no. 81.

213. Translator's Note: This is an important observation for integrating the philosophy / theology of conscience into a full virtue ethics.

kingdom of God? Do not err: Neither fornicators nor idolaters nor adulterers. Nor the effeminate nor liers with mankind nor thieves nor covetous nor drunkards nor railers nor extortioners shall possess the kingdom of God." Thus, since the precepts are proposed as necessary means required for beatitude, using the distinction between necessity with a necessity of precept and of means, it is not clear in what cases it would or would not be permitted to make use of probability.

Third, it is not made any clearer according to their manner of speaking by distinguishing probability concerning the objective moral fittingness of the act (or, its permissibility) in contrast to *probability of fact*. One would need to determine what is the moral fittingness or permissibility of the act in the given case, for all the acts of the virtues are called morally fitting (or permitted). Indeed, the virtuous man proposes to himself that he is to act according to virtue, and if he acts contrary to them his act will be unbefitting and unpermitted.[214] For example, to break a fast, to omit the recitation of the liturgy of the hours [*omittere horas*], and so forth, are all just as unpermitted acts as are acts of stealing or of injuring one's neighbor, and although they are more or less grave on account of the matter of the act, they nonetheless remain (and indeed are) sins. Thus, to bolster the aforementioned exposition, they add: or when it is a question concerning *probability of right*.[215] And thus we have what is intended: more recent authors divide *probability of right* against *probability of fact*, and St. Alphonsus follows Billuart in this matter.

Sub-question 3: *What does probability of fact and probability of right mean for St. Alphonsus?*

I respond that the Holy Doctor, in no. 41, says:

> *Probability of fact* is that which is concerned with the truth of the matter or the substance of the thing (e.g., whether a sacrament confected with a given matter would be valid or would be null or whether a contract entered into based upon a given agreement would be usurious). *Probability of right*, however, is concerned with the moral fittingness

214. Translator's Note: This should be read in combination with what was said just above concerning the ends of the virtues, as well as the occasional remarks regarding the importance of prudence.

215. See Billuart, *De consc.*, diss. 6, a. 3.

of the action, that is, whether one would be permitted to confer a Sacrament with a given matter or whether one would be permitted to enter into a contract based upon such an agreement.[216]

This doctrine is very true. As regards *the application to the use of probability*, however, the distinction proposed seems to struggle with the same obscurity as that which was proposed by Billuart, and it adds its own difficulty unique to the way set forth by the Holy Doctor [*et addit difficultatem propriam in viâ S. Doctoris*]. Indeed, he said above in no. 21:

> A *speculative* doubt is that had when someone doubts the *truth of the matter* (e.g., when one doubts whether a given war is just or unjust, whether painting on a feast day would be a servile or liberal activity, whether baptism with rose water would be valid, and other such things). *Practical* doubt, however, occurs when there is a doubt concerning *the moral fittingness of the matter at hand.* One has such doubt, for example, when one wonders whether it would be permissible for me to serve as a soldier in a given war whose justness is in doubt, whether I should paint on this feast day, or whether I should baptize this child with rose water. The *true* must always be distinguished from the *permitted*, for although a speculative doubt considers the permitted thing *in obliquo* and, rather, consequently, it nonetheless considers a speculative truth *in recto* and principally. A practical [doubt], however, considers the permitted thing.[217]

Based on this, one might be tempted to infer that the foundation of the distinction is reduced to the difference between speculative (or speculatively-practical) opinion and practically-practical opinion. This distinction, however, is found in every moral matter. Indeed, we saw above that someone relying on an imperfectly certain opinion can fashion an indirectly certain practical *dictamen* for himself. And from St. Augustine, we brought up the example concerning the soldier who can serve as a soldier for his king practically with certitude of moral conscience, although he speculatively has doubts concerning the justice of the war. And the judge,

216. St. Alphonsus, op. cit., no. 41; H. G. p. 21.
217. Ibid., no. 21. H. p. 10, G. p. 21.

having weighed out the reasons and importance of the matter equally on either side, can and must adjudicate the matter for the owner. Hence, this manner of speaking does not still the intellect and does not completely explain in what matters one is permitted to make use of probabilism and in what matters one is not permitted to do so.[218]

Sub-question 4: *What must be said by way of resolution [resolutorie], or what is a probable opinion having probability of fact and probability of right?*

I respond[219] that an opinion that is probable with *probability of fact* is one that seems true *not only based on its relation to the agent* but also *based on its relation to the truth of the thing in itself.* An opinion, however, that is probable with *probability of right* is that which seems true *based on its relation to the agent.*

This definition is in agreement with St. Thomas's thought[220] as well as that of Suarez, who says that, "A judgment concerning right designates a relation to the agent."[221]

We will now simultaneously explain and prove this definition and distinction. (a) *First, we do so indirectly*, by setting aside the sense in which *fact* and *right* can be falsely understood.

---

218. Marc, no. 59, following St. Alphonsus, says, "On account of the object, probability is either of fact or of right, inasmuch as it is concerned with the truth of the matter or with the moral fittingness of the action," and he refers to no. 32, 2, where he says that doubt *of fact* is concerned with the essence or existence of the thing, whereas doubt of right is concerned immediately and essentially [*per se*] with the law or obligation and, consequently, with the moral fittingness of the action. Then, he notes that doubt of right arises from probability of fact doubt and adds other things that seem quite obscure, especially if you compare them with what follows in nos. 48 and 51 where he discusses the principles that are concerned with the substance of a fact and the conditions of a fact.

    Also, see no. 80, in which a threefold distinction is offered for an easier understanding of the question, namely a threefold danger in use of a probable opinion: the danger of *error*, the danger *of sin*, the danger *of an evil effect*.

    I do not make these comments so as to destroy this doctrine, which is very true, and I do not find fault with the teachers who advantageously and cautiously restrict the use of probability. Instead, I make these remarks in order to arouse the mind of students so that they may understand with certitude what is rightly advanced.

219. **Translator's Note:** What is said here, above all concerning the use of the distinction between a *medium rationis* and a *medium rei*, was pointed out as being of great importance by Fr. Garrigou-Lagrange.

220. See *ST* I-II, q. 60, a. 2.

221. Suarez, *In ST* I-II, tract. 3, disp. 12, sect. 6, no. 10 (Vivès edition, vol. 4, 1856, p. 452).

Fact. As we have noted, a probable opinion is a judgment concerning the goodness or wickedness of an act to be done. Now, an act can be compared to a virtue as an effect is compared to its cause, and thus, the acts of all the virtues can be called *facts* because every moral virtue has a given good for which that virtue is the productive cause. Hence, *fact,* thus taken in this general sense [*sic universaliter sumptum*], is not divided against *right.*[222] In another way, an act can be compared to a moral virtue as the *matter about which it is concerned* [*materia circa quam*]. And in this manner, an activity is not considered as an effect proceeding from its cause but, instead, as a subject with which a *habitus* is concerned, namely a contingent doable thing or that which must be done as being good or fled from as being evil.

Right. If, however, the contingent thing to be done is considered according to its relation to reason directing and judging concerning the goodness or wickedness of the act, "Thus, there is one truth in all moral matters, which are contingent things to be done. Hence, there is only one virtue for directing them, namely prudence."[223] Therefore, conscience also, which emanates from prudence, directs human acts by the same notion of truth and judges concerning things to be done inasmuch as they are here and now consonant or dissonant with reason, being in harmony with it or not. And in this sense, it is true to say that there is no fact with which a question of right is not associated and vice-versa. Indeed, when it is understood in a general sense, "right" is not taken as pertaining to the object of justice but universally signifies the ruling and equaling of the act with the principles of morality (whether proximate or remote), namely human reason or the eternal, natural, or positive law.

Thus, in the proposed definition, *fact* and *right* must not be understood in a general sense [*universaliter*] but, instead, must be specifically understood, inasmuch as "fact" designates a relation to the thing in itself, and "right," a relation to the agent.

(b) Now, we will directly explain the definition, namely, that *probability of fact* is derived *in relation to the truth of the thing in itself* and *probability of right in relation to the agent.*

In order to understand this definition, one must note that although the act (i.e., the contingent thing that can be done) is related to reason,

222 See *ST* I-II, q. 60, a. 2.

223. *ST* I-II, q. 60, a. 1, ad 1.

which directs and judges, nonetheless the act does not receive the rule or measure of reason in the same manner *on account of the various proportions of matter*, or, in other words, "on account of the various relations of the receiving matters," as St. Thomas says.[224] The reason for this is that good and evil are attributed to certain activities precisely on account of what they are, no matter how a man is affected toward them, namely inasmuch as the good and evil found in them is taken in accord with the notion of *commensuration to another*, which consists in a kind of equality of proportion of an external thing to an external person.[225] In such matters, there must be some virtue directing the activities in accord with what they are (e.g., buying and selling and activities of this sort in which one encounters the notion of what is owed and not owed *to another*). For this reason, justice and its parts are concerned with activities as their proper matter. In certain activities, however, good and evil are applied only according to a *commensuration to the agent*. And therefore, in these matters, good and evil must be considered according to how the man performing them is affected in a good manner or an evil manner by things of this sort, "in themselves and not as related to another, and for this reason virtues in such matters must be principally concerned with interior affects, which are called the passions of the soul, as is clear for temperance, fortitude, and other such virtues."[226]

Thus, based on the reasoning offered by St. Thomas, it follows that the entire moral domain is divided into two parts and that there is a twofold rule and measure for judging whether an act or contingent doable thing is good or evil. And lest there be a confusion between the two genera, St. Thomas calls those things that are commensurated in relation to the truth of the thing "activities" [*operationes*], whereas he calls those that are commensurated in relation to the agent "passions."[227]

Cajetan seems to distinguish between things which are made by art [*factibilia*] and moral actions [*agibilia*].[228] This is of little consequence, for

224. *ST* I-II, q. 60, a.1, ad 2.

225. See *ST* II-II, q. 58, a. 10.

226. *ST* I-II, q. 60, a. 2; II-II, q. 57, a. 1; q. 58, a. 10.

227. See Cajetan, *ST* I-II, q. 60, a. 2, no. 1, *De titulo*.

228. See ibid., a. 1, no. 8.

Translator's Note: This point of terminology, and how Fr. Beaudouin is relating it to the distinction between "of fact" and "of right" remains opaque to me after several readings. As will be seen below, however, the moral application of certain arts (*factibilia*)

our dispute is not about terms. Thus, we can make use of the words "of fact" and "of right" in accord with more recent authors, provided that we understand that *probability of fact* is taken in relation to the truth of the thing in itself according to a commensuration of the activity to another [party], whereas *probability of right* is taken in relation to the agent in accord with a commensuration of the act to the agent himself. In accord with these two commensurations, something is judged to be morally befitting or not, as well as permitted or not.

§2. ON THE OBLIGATION OF CONSCIENCE THAT IS FORMED FROM AN OPINION THAT IS PROBABLE THROUGH PROBABILITY OF FACT

Conclusion

When it is a question of probability of fact, the safer option must always be chosen.

This conclusion is commonly held and admitted as being certain.[229] On this point, the probablists and the tutiorists both agree with each other. In the exposition, proof, and extension of this thesis, however, they seem to diverge from each other a bit. But, if beneath the husk of words, we consider the reality that they both perceive, we will discover that there is no great difference between them, indeed, perhaps none at all.

(1) *The tutiorists and some probabiliorists* apply the universal principle, "The safer option is always to be chosen," to all things which are *factibilia and allow for no exception.* And this position, according to how they mean things, is not utterly untrue. Indeed, they do not understand *that which is safer* or *the safer option* in exactly the same sense as do the Probabilists. Therefore, they say that a "safer" proposition can mean, first, security from sin and, second, security from falsity. Now, in the current matter concerning *factibilia* or concerning *activities related to another* [person or institution],[230] security from sin exists only *if security from falsity*

follows rules similar to the determination of actions related to the various species of justice (which are *agibilia* dealing with a relation to others).

In some readings below, it seems like he is combining these two types of actions together under the rubric of "that which is probable through a probability of fact."

229 See Gonet, Billuart, St. Alphonsus, op. cit., bk. 1, no. 41ff and bk. 3, no. 700 (ed. Gaudé, vol, 2, p. 167), Scavini, Gury, Marc, etc.

230. TRANSLATOR'S NOTE: Notice that *factibilia* are quite different from *activities in relation to others* (which are acts of *justice / injustice*).

simultaneously exists, since an activity is good not only in relation to the agent but especially through a commensuration to the truth of the thing in itself. Hence, they universally conclude that the safer option is always more probable and must be followed. And this is not something outside of St. Alphonsus's thought, for he says, "In the use of medicines, the more probable course and the safer course are the same."[231]

This is proven in two manners.

First, indeed, if the commensuration of the activity to the thing as it is due is certain, no probability holds for the opposed option. When the law is certain in things to be done, there is no probability for freedom against the law. Therefore, *a fortiori* there is not probability in *factibilia*.

Second, if there is not certitude in the commensuration of the activity to the thing in itself and nonetheless *one must necessarily act*, they say that the same rule rules the activity. Indeed, the designation *more probable* is designated here not in relation to the agent but in relation to the truth of the thing at hand. Thus, the more probable course is always the safer one. And as regards the fact, as Concina says:

> It is clear that, when there is a dispute concerning the right of the parties involved, a judge can render a judgment in the tribunals on the side of the opinion that, after a lengthy and diligent examination, he discerns either to be probable or far more probable, judging on the side of possession. Otherwise, judges could never render a sentence in debatable lawsuits, since in such matters they cannot discover the truth with absolute evidential certitude.[232]

Likewise, when confecting the sacraments, if necessity urges one to perform the rite when a certainly valid matter is lacking, it is always necessary to choose the safer option (i.e., that by which it is more probably the case that in the matter at hand the sacrament will be confected); nay, sometimes in the case of necessity one is permitted to use a matter that is only probably valid if one does not have at hand a more probable and safer one. The same reasoning holds for activities which would lead to the danger of injuring one's neighbor. It is clear that it is never, of itself,

231. Op. cit., no. 33, H. G. p. 22.

232. Concina, *De conscientia*, bk. 3, diss. 10, ch. 1, §3, no. 5 (op. cit., vol. 2, pp. 666-67).

permitted that one act in such a way as to injure one's neighbor. If one must act, however, one must always choose that which more safely and more probably removes the possibility of injuring a neighbor in the given matter. The same holds for other cases, namely in the waging of wars, in caring for the sick, and in deeds of dealing with importance.

Thus, according to those authors, the same rule, "The safer option must be followed," holds for all things that are *of fact* [*per omnia factibilia*] and is only diversified from the perspective of the matter. Our current concern, which is universal in bearing, is not to explain this diversity. Otherwise, we would wander through all the topics that involve activities undertaken in relation to others. What is proper to each of these topics is treated when one discusses charity, hope, faith, justice, religion, the Sacraments (both with regard to their confection and their reception), and so forth.[233]

Therefore, the question may be brought to a conclusion from this universal perspective by saying: in the case of *probability of fact*, the safer path must be chosen. Or, one may say with venerable authors: "In doubts, we follow that which is more likely," provided that one understand the notion "more likely" in accord with the subject matter, namely, in things that are *of fact*, in accord with the intrinsic truth of the matter at hand.

(2) *Probabilists* proceed along another path. Indeed, they take care to delimit their probabilism, and they were led to this moderation for two reasons: first, so that they may avoid laxity on certain opinions and

233. On this matter, St. Thomas says in *ST* I-II, q. 60, a. 3: "In external activities, the order of reason is established, as has been said, not according to a proportion to a man's affects, but according *to the very moral fittingness of the thing in itself.* From this fittingness we take the notion of what is owed, from which the formal notion of justice is constituted. Indeed, we see that justice involves rendering to another that which is owed to him. Hence, all these virtues, which are concerned with activities, in some manner contain the notion of justice. There is not, however, one single notion of what is owed that would be found in all things, for something is owed to an equal in one way, in another way to a superior, and in yet another way to an inferior. Moreover, what is owed differs when it is from a contract, from a promise, or from a favor that has already been received. Thus, various virtues arise in accord with these various formal notions of what is owed. For example, through religion we render to God what is owed to Him; through piety, we render to our parents and our country what is owed to them; through gratitude we render to our benefactors what is owed to them, and so forth for the other [species of justice]."

Translator's Note: This is an *immensely* important point regarding the limited scope of discussions of conscience and arguably, also, points toward the role for a partial but important role for casuistry in the various treatises on the virtues. If appropriately integrated into the overall Thomist framework, this could be seen as a way to incorporate the important insights expressed in Besong, "Reappraising the Manual Tradition," pp. 557-584.

second, so that they may escape the condemnations that were deservedly written by Popes Alexander VII and Innocent XI.[234] Thus, they distinguish *probability of fact* and *probability of right* in order to thereby restrict the thesis of probabilism, judiciously saying, "In a doubt or in the case of *probability of fact*, the safer path is to be chosen." They prove this position and, then, afterwards multiply exceptions to the rule.

(a) *Proof* that in the case of a *probability of fact the safer path is to be chosen.*

First, St. Alphonsus writes:

> We say that one is never permitted to make use of a probable opinion in the case of *probability of fact* when there is danger of harming another person or oneself, for probability of this kind does not suffice for removes the danger of doing harm. Indeed, if that opinion is *false*, one will not avoid harming one's neighbor or oneself [*damnum operantis*], for if, for example, baptism confected with saliva is in reality nothing, thus meaning that the infant would remain unbaptized, the probability that he would be baptized assuredly cannot make it be the case that it would be valid.[235]

234 See proposition 26 condemned by Alexander VII and propositions 2, 5, 6, 16, 17, 22, and 29 condemned by Innocent XI. [**Translator's Note:** Alhough not provided in the original, the text of these propositions is included here.

Alexander VII, 26th condemned proposition: "When litigants have equally probable opinions in their defense, the judge can accept money to bring a sentence in favor of one over the other." (Denzinger, no. 2046)

Innocent XI, 2nd condemned proposition: "I think that probably a judge can pass judgment according to opinion, even the less probable" (Denzinger, no. 2102, 43rd ed.).

Innocent XI, 5th condemned proposition: "We dare not convict of mortal sin one who has produced an act of the love of God only once in his life" (Denzinger, no. 2105, 43rd ed.).

Innocent XI, 6th condemned proposition: "It is probable that the precept of love toward God is not initself absolutely obligatory even every five years." (Denzinger, no. 2106, 43rd ed.).

Innocent XI, 16th condemned proposition: "Faith is not considered to fall by itself under a special precept" (Denzinger, no. 2116, 43rd ed.).

Innocent XI, 17th condemned proposition: "It is enough to utter an act of faith once during life" (Denzinger, no. 2117, 43rd ed.).

Innocent XI, 22nd condemned proposition: "Only faith in one God seems necessary by a necessity of means, not, however, the explicit <faith> in a Rewarder" (Denzinger, no. 2122, 43rd ed.).

Innocent XI, 29th condemned proposition: "A grave, pressing fear is a just cause for simulating the administration of sacraments" (Denzinger, no. 2129, 43rd ed.).]

235. *De conscientia*, no. 42, H. G. p. 21.

Second, it is also proven because, properly speaking, there is no probability present on behalf of freedom in the aforementioned circumstances. Indeed, probability of whatsoever degree is destroyed in a contest with an entirely certain contrary [opinion]. Now, when an act threatens to cause temporal or spiritual harm to another [person or institution], the law of justice and of charity is not doubtful but instead is certain (and certainly known). "For in such a case," writes St. Alphonsus, "The law not only obligates us to observe it, but also that we not expose ourselves to a proximate danger of violating it."[236] Therefore, there is no probability present in favor of freedom, the law is certain in this case, and we are bound to follow the safer path. Also, see Scavini[237] and Gury-Ballerini, no. 56, who says in *note a*: "It must be denied that any probability remains for one's opinion in these circumstances."[238]

Third, this is proven from the fact that "*probability of fact* insufficiently removes the danger of harm and of sin."[239] This is clear from the difference between right and thing [*de iure vel de re*]. "For," as Suarez says:

> The first designates a *relation to the agent* and entirely destroys the danger of wickedness, whereas the second designates a *relation to the thing itself* and does not destroy the danger of harm that exists therein. Hence, in the former case one has a sufficient excuse in following a probable judgment because the law is not yet sufficiently proposed. In the latter case, however, there is not a sufficient excuse since it is clear enough that danger remains in the thing itself.[240]

Thus, according to the *Doctor Fundatissimum*,[241] who speaks after the manner received in the writings of venerable authors, one must distinguish between probability *in relation to the agent* and probability *in relation to the thing itself.* One is permitted to follow a probable opinion in relation to the agent but not in relation to the thing itself. Indeed, the act in each

236. St. Alphonsus, *Homo apostolicus*, no. 58.

237. Scavini, op. cit., no. 99.

238. Gury-Ballerini, *compendium ed. cit.*, vol. 1, p. 52.

239. St. Alphonsus, no. 42, H. G. p. 21.

240. Suarez, *In ST* I-II, tr. 3, disp. 12, sect. 6 (Vivès, vol. 4, p. 452).

241. By this name, the author seems to name Suarez, as is clear from the context, although it is generally attributed to Giles of Rome. On Suarez's titles, see Hurter, *Nomenclator*, vol. 3, no. 163 note 1, col. 379. (Editor's Note)

of the aforementioned matters is not measured by the same rule, and thus rightly and fairly does probabilism set limits and boundaries for itself.

If setting aside *probability of fact* (i.e., probability in relation to the agent), we ask whether it is ever permitted that one act based upon *probability of fact*, the probabilists will respond by bringing forth exceptions, which are nothing other than the broadening measures [*ampliationes*] used by the tutiorists. And thus they all agree.

(b) *Exceptions.*

The first exception is: "Unless one necessarily must act."[242] When the need to act does or does not press on one, however, can we also permissibly make use of a *probability of fact*? As we have already said, this depends on the subject matter and must be accurately weighed out based upon what properly pertains to the precepts or virtues that are related to others[243].

Yet they immediately propose certain exceptions regarding particular matters.

The second exception is found when it is a question of confecting the Sacraments: "Unless it may be reasonably thought that the Church can supply in this circumstance." But when does this occur? St. Alphonsus refers to what is said concerning the jurisdiction of confessors.[244]

And, one must resolve in a like manner the other exceptions that are variously found in the writings of authors. Indeed, they are not determined in accord with the common and general principles being handed on here [in this theological treatise *De conscientia*] but, instead, are determined based on proper principles drawn from those belonging to the various parts of justice [*treated in the later treatises of theology*].[245]

Corollaries

Several things are inferred from these points.

First, it is inferred that the theologian making use of probability must carefully and cautiously distinguish a twofold order of things to be done,

242. See Gury, loc. cit., no. 57, 4, §Dixi secundo, p. 54. Marc, op. cit., no. 82, Excipe 1; St. Alphonsus, ibid., no. 49.

243. **Translator's Note:** This is another important qualification akin to those noted above, showing the connections between casuistry, conscience, and the virtues.

244. St. Alphonsus, no. 50, H. G. p. 23. Marc, no. 80.

245. **Translator's Note:** This also is a very important remark to be noted as part of the path forward in these matters. See also the remark wth which this article closes.

namely of fact and of right (or of things to be made and to be done) and thus in every case he will judge what must be done.

Second, furthermore, one infers that those things that are variously found in the writings of teachers as corollaries and examples are excellently expressed both in themselves and as regards the limits placed on the use of probability. They do not, however, exhaust the entire matter.

Third, nonetheless, lest the youthful student be tempted to give up, looking for brevity, the following assertions universally hold true:

1. In matters of faith and in in all things having a necessity of means for eternal salvation, one is not permitted to follow a less probable opinion (as was foolishly said in proposition 4 proscribed by Pope Innocent XI)[246]; nor in such matters can one follow the more probable opinion. Instead, we must follow the safer path.[247]
2. In the confecting of the sacraments, the minister cannot make use either of a probable or a more probable opinion concerning their validity but is bound to follow the safe opinion that that has the character of being safer or morally certain. This is clear in light of the first proposition proscribed by Innocent XI.[248] This holds unless, as was said above, some kind of is a necessity at hand.[249] And, proportionally, the same must be said in general regarding the reception of the Sacraments. "I think this," says St. Alphonsus, "not so as to rescind the first opinion I expressed (which affirms with certitude that one is not permitted to make use of probability in cases of the reception of the Sacraments) at least because the second conclusion almost never can be reached in practice by those receiving the sacraments without a detriment to one's soul."[250]

246. See Denzinger, no. 2104 (43rd ed.): "An infidel who does not believe will be excused of infidelity, since he is guided by a less probable opinion."

247. See St. Alphonsus, no. 43 (p. 22).

248. See Denzinger, no. 2101 (43rd ed.): "In conferring the sacraments, it is not illicit to follow the probable opinion with respect to the validity of the sacrament, disregarding what is more certain, unless it is forbidden by law, convention, or the danger of incurring grave harm. For this reason, it is only in the conferral of baptism <and> priestly or episcopal ordination that the probable opinion is not to be held."

249. See St. Alphonsus, ibid., nos. 49-50 (p. 23).

250. St. Alphonsus, ibid., no. 51 (p. 24).

3. "A doctor must employ safer medicines that would be advantageous for the sick people in their care and cannot make use of less probable ones, forsaking more probable for safer ones. Indeed, in medical matters the more probable course is that which is safer for the healing of the sick person."[251]

   Note, however, that when there is little hope of healing the sick person, a sufficiently probable opinion (and perhaps a more probable one) holds and affirms that one is permitted to apply a probable or doubtful remedy in the way that will be discussed below.[252]
4. The judge is bound to judge in accord with the more probable opinion. Indeed, he is bound by divine and human precept to measure out his justice to each according to the greater weight of reasons that favor each party.[253]
5. Universally speaking, one is never permitted to make use of probability when there is danger of spiritual or temporal harm to one's neighbor. Note, however, that this holds when one's neighbor certainly possesses his right.[254]

   Hence, "If someone doubts whether what he sees in a forest is a wild animal or a man, he cannot kill it, even he judges in a probable manner (or even in a more probable manner) that it is a wild beast, for if in reality that animal were a man, that probability (or even a great probability) would not free the man from death...." Finally, "if one is not permitted to make use of a probable opinion *without just cause* when there is danger of spiritual or temporal harm to another [person or institution] (a point that is held as being certain in the writings of all), how much more will it not be permitted to make use of one when there *is an imminent danger to one's own soul*... We said, 'without just cause', for when a just cause presents itself, there is no obligation to

251. Ibid., no. 44 (p. 22).
252. See ibid., no. 46 (p.22).
253. See ibid., no. 46 (p. 23).
254. See ibid., no. 52 (p. 24); *Homo apostolicus*, bk. 1, 28; cf. bk. 3, no. 700.

> avoid such danger unless one foresees, in a morally certain manner, that it will lead one to sin."[255] Marc applies this rule concerning the *proximate occasion* of sinning in a general manner to every probable danger of formally sinning...[256] [A]nd he adds, third, that in danger *to one's life* one is not permitted, without [some other] necessity, to expose oneself to probable death (e.g., by eating food that has the probability of being either harmless or poisonous).

These suffice by way of example. It cannot, however, replace the full account that is handed on in the specific parts of [moral] theology.

Article 4: *On the Conscience Formed from an Opinion That Is Certainly and Notably More Probably Less Safe in a Contest with a Safer Path That Is Less Probable, and Concerning Its Obligation*

§1. ON THE CONSCIENCE THAT IS FORMED FROM AN OPINION THAT IS CERTAINLY AND NOTABLY MORE PROBABLY LESS SAFE, IN A CONTEST WITH A SAFER PATH THAT IS LESS PROBABLE

Sub-question 1: *What is a more probable opinion?*

I respond that an opinion is called "more probable" when it rests on a foundation that is weightier than is the foundation of the opinion that is opposed to it.

Sub-question 2: *How many forms of more probable opinions are there?*

More probable opinion is sub-distinguished in two ways in the writings of authors. First, one is called "slightly" (or, dubiously) more probable. Second, the other is called "certainly," "notably," "truly," and "absolutely" more probable. Following St. Alphonsus, we indiscriminately make use of terms of this kind. Indeed, the foundation on which that which is more probable is based can be "slightly" or "notably" weightier, and the

255. See Billuart, *Summa sancti thomae, De conscientia*, diss. 6, a. 3. St. Alphonsus, op. cit., bk. 5, no. 63 (ed. Gaudé, vol. 2, p. 750). *Vindiciae*, no. 137.

256. See Marc, op. cit., no. 83, 2.

distinction is based on this. According to St. Thomas, however, "Reason considers what is slight as if it were nothing."[257]

St. Alphonsus accepts this maxim, saying, "What is slight is, however, reputed as being nothing."[258] And he quite rightly infers: "When between both opinions the preponderance is slight, such that the excess is quite slender or doubtful, then both opinions are held to be equally-probable."

Below, we will discuss opinions that are barely or doubtfully more probable. Our concern here is with truly and solidly more probable opinion, which is defined: "An opinion that is based on a foundation that is certainly and notably weightier than the opposed opinion." Or, following Marc's manner of expressing it, "A certainly more probable opinion is one that, after having established the weight of reasons militating for each opinion, is judged without hesitation to be of greater weight." St. Alphonsus himself opposes certainly more probable opinions to those that are slightly more probable, dubiously more probable, not solidly probable, and those that are practically improbable.[259]

Sub-question 3: *What sort of excess should exist in an opinion so that it may certainly be more probable than the opposed one?*

I respond that not just any minor excess suffices for probability. Instead, notably- and morally-weighty probability is required. That is, it must be a probability that is so great that, morally speaking, it would cast off one's doubt and move a serious and prudent man[260] in such a way that he would assent to that side rather than to the other one, as Billuart says. And for this, as St. Alphonsus says, one degree of excess suffices for him to be certain in this way:

> When an opinion is certainly more probable, even by *a single degree*, then it is notably more probable. This is so because such certitude concerning

257. *ST* I-II, q. 14, a. 4.

258. St. Alphonsus, tr. cit., no. 55 (H. p. 26). It is not found in Fr. Gaudé, who follows the 7th edition.

259. See Marc, op. cit., no. 70 and 71. Also, see no. 73.

260. **Translator's Note:** This emphasis on the role of prudence in conscience, something found in a number of the members of the Thomist school, would have inspired someone like Merkelbach to undertake the expansion of the treatise on conscience which can be found in his *Summa theologiae moralis*, discussed in the article by him included in this volume. The first part of this expansion is presented after Fr. Beaudouin's text.

> greater probability proves that this probability is indeed preponderating in such a way as to suffice for moving the scales, and I assert that a certainly more probable opinion is the same as one that is notably more probable because if it were not notable, it could not move the scales.[261]

And [the notion of] *certainly* more probable opinion has some latitude. Indeed, one thing can exceed another by many and various degrees, thus ascending all the way to the ultimate degree of probability that one finds in a most [or, very] probable opinion.[262]

As Marc observes,[263] however, St. Alphonsus very rarely makes use of the term "most probable" [or, "very probable"] in a comparative sense. Indeed, properly speaking, as we have said, that which is most [or, very] probable is designated as such in itself, in the state of solitude[264] and absolutely taken.

Corollary

From what has been said, one may infer that comparatively understood propositions mutually infer each other. Indeed, relatives are designated conversely. In other words, of themselves, each of them is predicated as coupled with the other, expressing the relation *in obliquo*. Indeed, a more probable opinion is one that is based on a weightier foundation than the opposed, less probable opinion which is based on a less weighty foundation. And, conversely, a less probable opinion is one that is based on a less weighty foundation than the more probable one which is based on a weightier foundation.

§2. ON THE OBLIGATION OF THIS KIND OF CONSCIENCE

Conclusion

One is permitted to follow an opinion that is certainly and notably more probably less safe in a contest with an opinion that is safer but less probable when it is a question of probability of right.

---

261. See St. Alphonsus, *Theol. Mor.*, 7th ed. (1773), vol. 3, *in fine. Auctoris monitum*, cited in *Vindicias Alph.* 1874, vol. 1, p. 81; diss. no. 90. Cf. Marc, op. cit., no. 73.

262. See Billuart, *Summa sancti thomae, De conscientia*, diss. 6, a. 3, *Prob. Concl.* 1.

263. See Marc, *op. cit., no.* 71

264. TRANSLATOR'S NOTE: See the first footnote in this question.

Note. We said, "one is permitted." In other words, it is permissible but not commanded. Accordingly, on account of a counsel someone can follow a precept that is safer but less probable.

This conclusion is stated against the tutiorists who teach that a given person is always bound to follow the safer but less probable opinion in a contest with that which is less safe but more probable. Thus, we find this matter articulated once upon a time by Sinnichius, Vendrochius, Faganus, and Henry of St. Ignatius. Mercorus, Contenson and Baronius embraced the safer opinion but did not officially [*ex instituto*] dispute this.[265]

Today, however, this opinion is no longer popular, and the Probabilists' conclusion is commonly admitted.

This is proven on the basis of authority, from reason, and from certain unbefitting things that would follow if it were not the case.

First: *Proof from authority*. There is agreement on this opinion among more recent authors who are probabiliorists as well as equiprobabilists and probablists. Moreover, time-honored authors always taught it, as did Ss. Thomas and Bonaventure, relying upon Rule 45 in Canon Law and in Civil Law 114: "In unclear matters, we observe what is more likely or what people are generally accustomed to do."[266]

This rule is found in other places in the civil law where that which is more likely though less safe is not commanded but, instead, is permitted as being legal.[267]

Second: *Proof from reason*.

(a) Something is permitted when it seems prudently true and morally befitting after all earnest observations have been made. Now, in a contest with that which is safer but less probable, a more probable opinion certainly presents a foundation for prudently judging that something is true and morally befitting. Therefore, one is permitted to follow it.[268]

Proof of the minor premise. Indeed, the opposed safer but less probable opinion is also less likely. Therefore, it cannot draw to itself the assent of a prudent man.

---

265. See Concina, op. et loc. cit., bk. 3, diss. 10, ch. 1, §2, no. 2.

 Translator's Note: Upon consulting Concina, it seems that here Fr. Beaudouin is merely referring to the point of history concerning the figures listed.

266. *Sextus liber decretal*, ed. cit., col. 898-899.

267. See Concina, loc. cit., no. 6, vol. 3, p. 665.

268. See Concina, loc. cit., no. 5, p. 664.

(b) One does not sin formally by doing what he prudently, reasonably and in good faith judges is indeed not a material sin against the law. Now, by following an opinion that is certainly and notably more probable, he does that which he prudently, reasonably and in good faith judges indeed is not a sin. Therefore, he does not sin.

The minor premise is proven as follows. In so judging concerning a more probable opinion of this sort, he judges according to the merits of the case in all judgments, whether public or private. Thereupon, he is determined to judge on the basis of weightier and more solid motives, unable to choose on behalf of the less probable opposed opinion except by being imprudent.[269]

Third: Proof from certain unbefitting things that would follow if it were not the case. As Billuart observes, if one always were to follow the safer path three things would follow. First, the study of moral theology would be utterly useless… Accordingly, before all study, and before every inquiry and consultation, all would recognize what is safer and that the only safe path would be to abstain from anything else [*et solum tutum esse ab his abstinere*].

Second, it would be necessary to forbid the reading of all books of moral theology and of law (even those written by Sts. Thomas, Bonaventure, Antoninus, Raymundus, and so forth) and to cast them aside as being scandalous and likely to lead one into sin, given that hardly a single author exists who does not often teach that there are more probable opinions allowing freedom of choice, ones which may be followed against safer ones that stand on the side of the law. Above all, one would need to acknowledge that the Holy Doctors gravely sinned in teaching these less safe but more probable opinions.

Third, it increases the weight of Christ's yoke beyond measure and thus makes it utterly intolerable.[270]

Sub-question 1: *Are reflex principles required for one to form a judgment of conscience from a less safe probable opinion?*

I respond affirmatively. Indeed, since an opinion that is certainly more probable does not pass beyond the boundaries of probability, given reflex

269. See Billuart, *Summa sancti thomae, De conscientia*, diss. 6, a. 3, prob. 3, *Ratione.*
270. See ibid.

principles are required, and by relying upon them, one can form for himself a practically certain *dictamen*. As we have said, it is certainly the case that probability of whatsoever degree is never a sufficient rule in moral matters. And Billuart admits this saying, "(Thus, more probable opinions) that are concerned with an action's right [*ius*] or permissibility are speculatively-practical and influence the practically practical *dictamen, by the mediation of a reflex judgment*."[271]

Sub-question 2: *What are these reflex principles?*

I respond that since a certainly more probable opinion is morally certain, we make use of the same principles as when we are faced with an opinion that is only probable or very probable, namely: "In obscure matters, we follow that which is more likely." In contingent and moral matters, when scientific certitude is lacking [*certitudo scientiae*],[272] we embrace that which more closely approaches toward the truth. And there are other such principles that are used implicitly or explicitly.

Objections

Since the contrary opinion has no partisans today among Catholic teachers, it is not useful to refer to arguments of Henry of St. Ignatius and others. Consult Concina, Gonet, Billuart, and other esteemed authors. But let the faithful person be careful in practice and let him avoid those who boast that they are teachers of safe doctrine.

Article 5: *On Conscience Formed from an Equally Probable but Less Safe Opinion in Contest with One That Is Safer and More Probable*

§1. ON CONSCIENCE FORMED FROM AN EQUALLY PROBABLE BUT LESS SAFE OPINION IN CONTEST WITH ONE THAT IS SAFER AND MORE PROBABLE

271. Ibid., diss. 6, a. 3, at the end of the beginning section starting "Dixi."

272. Translator's Note: I see here a kind of latent equivocation in Fr. Beaudouin's use of *scientia*, a point that has at times necessitated parenthetical remarks for the sake of clarifying his comments.

Sub-question 1: *What is equally probable opinion?*
I respond that it is an opinion that is based on a foundation that is of equal weight to that which is opposed to it (or having a weight that is nearly equal to it). I said that it is equal or nearly equal in weight because, as is clear from the preceding article, when the excess in question is slight and dubious, such a minor difference is considered to be of no import and of small weight, thus not deserving to be taken into account. Hence, in St. Alphonsus's writings, an equally or dubiously more probable opinion is the same as one which is called *certainly, resolutely [graviter], and solidly* probable, and the opposed opinion is called *equally, nearly,* and *sufficiently* probable.[273]

Sub-question 2: *What is the property of equally probable opinions?*
I respond that equally probable opinions struggle with each other in order to draw the assent of a prudent man. And this property arises from the nature and logical relations of the mutually opposed propositions. This is admitted not only by the equiprobabilists but also by the probabiliorists. As Billuart writes, "When either side of a contradiction is equally probable, the motives of both mutually struggle with each other and have equal weight so that the motives for one opinion strives to obtain assent to the same degree as do the motives for the other opinion. Thus, the intellect remains in suspense and truly in doubt between the two sides, like a scale in suspense when there are equal weights on either side of it or like a stone remaining unmoved when pulled in two directions by two equal powers."[274]

Sub-question 3: *In how many ways does the struggle between equally probable opinions take place?*
I respond that such a struggle between equally probable opinions happens not only when the motives of each proposition are *contrary* but also when they are *disparate*. Indeed, a contradiction can exist either in the reasons taken together with the conclusions or in the conclusions by themselves. The point I am making will be clearer if I give an example. I could ask myself, "Is it permissible for one to paint on a feast day?" Some deny that

273. See Marc, no. 73.

274. Billuart, op. cit., diss. 2, a. 2. See St. Alphonsus, op. cit., H. no. 71, p. 46, G. no. 68, p. 39; Marc, ibid., no. 74.

it is permitted, for it *is servile work*. Others, however, affirm that I can do it because *it is not servile work*. These two propositions are contradictory both in themselves and in the reasons on which they are supported. Now, to take a different example, I may ask myself, "Is one permitted to hunt on a feast day?" Some people respond to this that one is not permitted to do this because i*t is servile work*. Others, however, say that it is permitted because *customs excuse*. In this second case, as is clear, the reasons are disparate and only the conclusions are contradictory.[275]

Sub-question 4: *In what state does the intellect remain when equally probable propositions cancel each other out?*

I respond that the intellect remains in doubt, not in a *broad sense* but *strictly speaking*. Indeed, a *broad* doubt (which, really, is improperly called a doubt) signifies an imperfection of assent to one side of a contradiction, namely with fear that the other side may be true. It may be concomitant with imperfect (or, broad) moral certitude and is found in the mind's adherence to opinions that are very probable, only probable, or certainly more probable.

As St. Thomas says, however, *strict* doubt is nothing other than the suspension of assent on account of the *apparent equality* of the reasons on either side of a contradiction. Thus, precisely speaking, when one proposition overrides another this is not because one would be destroyed by the other. In that case, such overriding would be absolute. Instead, this happens because the other has the power of moving the intellect to a prudent assent.[276] From these facts, one can quite easily understand St. Alphonsus's manner of speaking[277] throughout his moral work[s]: "Each is probable and neither is probable, but only doubt remains." In other words, each is probable in itself but each is doubtful relatively speaking.[278]

Sub-question 5: *What is the genuine opinion of St. Alphonsus in this matter?*

275. See Marc, no. 74.

Translator's Note: Fr. Beaudouin ends with a quote, although the opening is not clear.

276. See *Vindiciae alph., diss apol.*, no. 86, ed. cit., vol. 1, p. 487.

Translator's Note: Fr. Beaudouin ends with a quote, although the opening is not clear.

277. See op. cit., bk. 1, no. 78, H. p. 62; G. no. 76, p. 52.

278. See Marc, no. 74, *in fine*, §Exinde.

I respond that St. Alphonsus takes a middle path between the probabiliorists, who defend the law too much, and the probabilists, who favor freedom too greatly. Indeed, the probabiliorists teach that one is never permitted to follow an equally probable but less safe opinion in a contest with a safer opinion, whereas the probabilists say that one is always permitted to do so. St. Alphonsus's position stands between the two. Against the probabiliorists, he asserts that one is permitted to follow the equally probable but less safe opinion in a contest with a safer one. In contrast, against the probabilists, he shows that one is not always permitted to do so but can only favor such a less safe opinion sometimes, namely when possession favors freedom.[279]

We embrace this opinion and will defend it by way of two conclusions.

§2. ON THE OBLIGATION OF CONSCIENCE THAT IS FORMED FROM AN EQUALLY PROBABLE OPINION.

Conclusion 1

One is permitted to follow an opinion that is less safe and equally (or nearly equally) probable in contest with a probable and safer one.

This conclusion[280] is drawn in opposition to the probabiliorists inasmuch as they teach that one is not permitted to follow an equally probable but less safe opinion.

This is proven based on the basis of authority and by reasoning the matter out.

First: Proof from authority. Without even discussing the Church Fathers and Holy Doctors who teach that the safer option need not be always followed in doubts, one has a sufficient authoritative basis for this conclusion based upon the authority of St. Alphonsus, whose works have been approved by the Holy See. Quite clearly Pope Pius IX said: "Moreover, as is the case for those of other Doctors of the Church, we will and declare that the works, commentaries, shorter works, and indeed all the

279. TRANSLATOR'S NOTE: As will be seen, the awkward expression comes from the reflex principle: "*Melior est conditio possidentis.*"

280. Note well that the response to the question is not expressed here in a fully integral manner but must be modified by the second conclusion on p. 281 below. The conclusion is divided because of the different adversaries to which each conclusion is opposed. (Editor's Note)

writings of this Doctor should be not only privately but publicly cited, advanced, and consulted when matters call for it."[281]

Thus, as is clear from the Response given on December 19, 1855, by the Sacred Congregation of the Penitentiary, professors of Sacred Theology can permissibly follow and publicly hand on the teaching of the Blessed Doctor, notwithstanding the oath that was promulgated upholding the doctrine of the University which followed *probabiliorism* or the *positions of the probabilists.*

This is confirmed, first, from *The Letters given by Pope Leo XIII to Frs. Leopold Dujardin and Julius Jacques C.SS.R. Aug. 28, 1879:* "Indeed, we also render thanks to you by name for your undertaking, given that the Holy Author often in his own writings took pride in the fact that he followed the teaching of the Angel of the Schools. From the deference shown toward him by a more recent Doctor of the Church of his character [*huiusmodi*], may new praise of St. Thomas's Doctrine spring forth as well as new glory, which would even more seriously recommend the renewal of Christian philosophy that we have most insistently urged through Our recent encyclical letters calling for the examination of the Angelic Doctor's thought."[282]

Likewise, confirmation is found, second, by considering *the authority of St. Thomas in St. Alphonsus's writings*. With regard to the question currently facing us, St. Alphonsus explicitly declares himself to be a disciple of St. Thomas. "This is St. Thomas's opinion," he says, "which I follow and which seems certain to me…and also on account of the intrinsic reasons that have not yet been presented but are certain and evident, as we will demonstrate."[283]

Second: Proof from reason. A law that is in doubt does not obligate, for an uncertain law cannot introduce a certain obligation. Now, in a contest between two opinions that are equally (or nearly equally) probable, the law remains doubtful and uncertain. Therefore, it does not obligate.

The major premise is proven as follows. Let us begin by considering *its first part*, namely "A law that is in doubt does not obligate." Then, we will consider the second part.

281. Pius IX, Apostolic Letter of 1871, conferring the title of "Doctor of the Church" on St. Alphonsus of Liguouri. See Gaudé, vo. 1, p. 50.

282. In Marc, op. cit., preface.

283. St. Alphonsus, op cit., pp. 59-60, H. p. 28; G. no. 56 (p. 25).

First, a sufficiently promulgated law obligates. Now, a law that is in doubt is not *sufficiently promulgated.* Therefore, a law that is in doubt does not obligate. St. Alphonsus[284] proves the major and the minor premises of this defense by use of St. Thomas's own argument:

> The law is a kind of rule and measure of acts inasmuch as it leads someone to act… Now, a rule and measure is imposed on account of the fact that it is applied to those things that are ruled and measured. Thus, in order for the law to obtain obligatory force (which is a property of the law) it must be applied to men who must be ruled by it. Such an application, however, is brought about by one being led to know of it precisely because of its promulgation. Therefore, promulgation itself is necessary so that the law may have its force.[285]

Second, "A law that is not promulgated as something certain does not obligate." Now, a law that is in doubt is not promulgated as certain. Therefore, a law that is in doubt does not obligate.

The major and minor premises are proven by St. Alphonsus as follows:

> Indeed, given that a law necessarily must be promulgated in order for it to have obligatory force, if a doubtful law is promulgated, it will be promulgated only as a mere doubt, opinion, or question. One will ask, "Is there a law present that prohibits this action?" [In such a case], however, a law will not be [truly] promulgated. Hence, all agree that in order for a law to obligate it must be certain and manifest and must be certainly manifested or made known to the man to whom it is promulgated. In speaking about the Eternal and Natural Laws, St. Thomas teaches that for these to be a measure for us they must be most certain and made known to us. Let us heed the words of the Holy Doctor. In *ST* I-II, q. 19, a. 4, obj. 3, he objects to himself, "The measure must be most certain. The Eternal Law is, however, unknown to us. Therefore, it cannot be the measure of our will such that the goodness of our will would depend upon it." And he responds as follows: "Although the Eternal Law is unknown to us as it is in the divine mind,

284. Ibid., H. no. 26 and 60; ed. Gaudé, no. 26 and 57.

285. *ST* I-II, q. 90, a. 1.

> it is nonetheless made known to us in some manner through natural reason, which is derived from it as an image of the Eternal Law or it is made known to us through some super-added revelation." The reason why the law must be certain is obvious, for given that (according to the Holy Doctor) the law is the measure and rule by which man must be measured and ruled in his actions, by no means can he be rightly measured and ruled unless the measure and rule were certain for him so that it may obligate him and indeed be known by man.[286]

Then, St. Alphonsus confirms his reasoning based upon the authority of D. Collet, Jean Gerson, Jean-Baptiste Gonet, Sylvius, and others.[287]

Now we move on to the proof of the second part of the major premise of the main argument presented above, namely: "an uncertain law cannot introduce a certain obligation."[288]

Nobody is bound by a given precept except by means of certain knowledge [*scientia*] of that precept. Now, an uncertain law is not certainly known [*non est scientia*]. Therefore, an uncertain law cannot introduce a certain obligation.

The major and minor premises are together proven by St. Thomas, whose argument St. Alphonsus pursues in the following manner.[289] He says that the metaphor presented here by St. Thomas could not be more enlightening and suitable for proving our position or principle, namely that an uncertain law cannot introduce a certain obligation. The Holy Doctor says that certain knowledge [*scientia*] of a command is akin to a bond that binds the will. Thus, just as in order to bind something a rope must actually be tied to it, so too in order for man's will to be bound so that he would be bound to do or not do a given action, he must have certain knowledge concerning the command. Otherwise, that man would remain in his freedom. Now, "all philosophers, with St. Thomas, teach that there is a distinction between opinion and certain knowledge. Opinion denotes doubtful and probable knowledge of a given truth, whereas they use the term *scientia* to designate knowledge that is certain and accessible.

286. St. Alphonsus, op. cit., H. no. 63, 64ff. Gaudé, no. 57, 58ff.

287. In particular, see ibid., H. no. 70, Gaudé no. 66. In this text, the same argument is treated in a brief fashion.

288. See ibid., H. no. 26, 65ff.; Gaudé, no. 26, 59ff.

289. See ibid., H. no. 65.

Therefore, when someone is in doubt concerning whether or not there is a command prohibiting or commanding something (as happens when two opinions of the same equally probable weight come together into consideration), then one does not have certain knowledge [*scientia*] of the command, and therefore one is not bound to keep the precept."

A *confirmation* of this can be found in St. Thomas,[290] and in other authors found in St. Alphonsus's work,[291] especially in no. 66[292]:

> The most learned Melchior Cano, O.P., writing against Scotus who obligated sinners to elicit contrition on whatsoever feast day, teaches, "There is nothing in human law nor in the Gospel on which this precept could be asserted. Let them bring it forth, and we will be silent." The same is expressed by Suarez, S.J., Ildephonse, O.P., the Salamanca Carmelites, and others.

Now, we will move on to the proof of the minor premise of the syllogism offered above, namely: "Now, in a contest between two opinions that are equally (or nearly equally) probable, the law is doubtful and uncertain." Again, we will break this apart in our proof.

First, "The law is doubtful." When one is faced with equally strong reasoning and arguments, there can only be doubt. Indeed, our intellect is related in various ways to the sides of a contradiction. Sometimes, it is not inclined more to one side than to the other. This can occur for two reasons. On the one hand, this can be on account of a defect of the motivating factor (as happens in problems when reasons are not at hand). On the other hand, such a lack of inclination can occur because of the apparent equality of those things that would move one to assent to either side. And this latter is the disposition found in the doubting person who fluctuates between two sides of a contradiction.[293]

Now, in the contest between two equally probable opinions, the arguments and reasons for and against freedom are equal. This is so because, as St. Alphonsus says in no. 71:

290. *ST* I-II, q. 19, a. 10; q. 90, a. 1; II-II, q. 104, a. 4.

291. See St. Alphonsus, op. cit., H. no. 66; G. no. 65.

292. Edit. Helig, p. 31-34; ed. Gaudé, no. 66, pp. 36-38 relates something almost the same, although rendered in a different manner. (Editor's Note, Ambroise Gardeil)

293. See St. Thomas, *De veritate*, q. 14, a. 1, presented in St. Alphonsus, op. cit., no. 71.

> When there is only probable knowledge for the law present to us, then...a kind of moral certitude would defend the law. When on the other hand, however, there is an equally probable opinion for freedom, then probability cannot survive on either side of the issue. (By "probability," I mean the kind of probable reasoning that would be apt for drawing to itself the assent of a prudent man.) This is so because from these equal probabilities only a mere doubt results and one wonders whether or not the law exists.[294]

Therefore, in a contest between two equally (or nearly equally) probable opinions, the law remains in doubt.

Second, "The law is uncertain." A human or divine law that has not been sufficiently *promulgated to conscience* is uncertain. This is so because, as St. Alphonsus says, with respect to [such] conscience it is certainly the case that someone who does not keep a law that is unknown to him does not sin in any way, so long as his lack of knowledge was not on account of his own negligence.[295] This is what is taught by St. Thomas in *ST* I-II q. 101, a. 4, ad 2, Cajetan (in his comments on this article), Suarez, the Salamanca Carmelites, and others.[296]

Now, in a contest between two equally probable opinions:

> It cannot be said that probable knowledge of the law suffices for it to be promulgated. Indeed, in that case, one by no means has sufficient knowledge in order to say that the law has been promulgated. All that one has is sufficient knowledge for the promulgation of a doubt or a mere hesitation *concerning whether there is a law present in this matter.* This is so because when two opinions of equal weight coincide, it happens (as we have said) that neither of them has weight.[297]

Therefore, in a contest between two opinions that are equally (or nearly equally) probable, the law is uncertain.[298]

Now, this is confirmed in two ways.

294. See St. Alphonsus, op. cit., no. 72 (H. p. 47); G. no. 68 (p. 40).
295. See ibid., no. 72 (H. p. 47); G. no. 69 (p. 41).
296. See ibid.
297. See ibid., no. 71 (H. pp. 46-47); G. no. 69 (p. 40).
298. ibid., H. no. 75 and 84; G. no. 73 and 80.

Confirmation 1

For two equally probable coinciding opinions, although the *less safe* one cannot be held because, as we said, *probability alone* by no means presents a firm foundation for acting in a permissible manner, nonetheless, the opinion that stands on the side of freedom (since it has a probability that is equal to the opposed opinion that stands on the side of the law) indeed brings about a grave doubt whether a law exists that would prohibit the action. Thus, it cannot itself be said *to be sufficiently promulgated*. Therefore, in that case, it is not promulgated and cannot obligate. For all the more reason is it the case that an uncertain law cannot bring about a certain obligation.[299]

Confirmation 2

From what we have already said, it has been sufficiently shown that in a contest between two equally probable opinions the law is doubtful, uncertain, and obscure. Now, St. Alphonsus says, "Time-honored authors commonly taught that where a law is obscure and where a determination or evident reasoning concerning the matter is not found in the texts of Scripture or of the Church, one need not fear being condemned of a grave sin, for they hold with certitude that a law that is in doubt does not obligate."[300]

He cites the Holy Doctor St. Raymond, O.P., St. Antoninus, O.P., and St. Thomas who writes, "Unless truth is had in an express manner, every question where the problem of mortal sin is raised is determined in the midst of great perils."[301] "Therefore," St. Alphonsus says, "the principle held by those opposed to this is false, namely that in a doubt the law has force and hence that in a doubt the safer path must be chosen." And he confirms this dictum by basing himself on St. Antoninus's exposition of St. Thomas's opinion in the following manner[302]: "For if one determines that it was mortal and it is not, he will mortally sin in acting against [that law] because everything that is against conscience leads one to hell...;

299. Ibid., H. no. 59 (pp. 27-28); G. no. 56 (p. 25).
300. Ibid., H. no. 77, §*Hinc est* (p. 60); G, no. 75 (p. 51).
301. St. Thomas, *Quodlibet* IX, q. 7, a. 2.
302. Loc. cit.

however, if one determines that it is not mortal and it is, his error will not excuse him from mortal sin."[303]

Objections

ANTECEDENT. *In the contest of two opinions that are equally (or nearly equally) probable, one is not permitted to follow the less safe one, thus forsaking the safer path.*

Therefore, the thesis is false.

The antecedent is proven as follows. "He who loves danger will die in it" (Sir. 3:27). Now, the equiprobabilist places himself in danger of transgressing the law.... Therefore, he will die in it (i.e., will sin).

Response to the major premise. I accept the authority cited, but *I make a distinction regarding its meaning.* I concede the point for him who prolongs his conversion all the way to death or for him who refuses to remove a proximate occasion for sinning voluntarily. And, as St. Alphonsus observes, this position implies this point. Indeed, in context the text says: "The hard heart will face evil in the end, and he who loves danger will die in it."[304]

I deny, however, that such a person follows an equally probable opinion, for the authority brought forth does not say this.

I have two responses to the minor premise. First, I respond by turning the argument around. Indeed, to the eyes of a probabiliorist, following a less safe but certainly more probable opinion, they similarly place themselves in danger, for that which is more probable is not certain, since some probability militates on behalf of the opposed opinion that favors the law. In order to always avoid this danger, one would be strictly bound to embrace tutiorism which alone is immune and free from every peril of transgressing the law.[305]

Second I also respond by making a distinction regarding the minor premise. I concede that such a person places himself in danger of transgressing the law *materially.* I deny, however, that he puts himself in danger of transgressing it *formally.*

And in this distinction, we make use of the same right as that which the probabiliorists assert against the tutiorists.

303. St. Antoninus, *Summa theol.*, pt. 2, tit. 1, ch. 11, §28 (edit. cit.), vol. 2, col. 188.

304. See St. Alphonsus, op. cit., H. no. 68 (p. 38); G. no. 63 (p. 34).

305. See ibid., H. nos. 81-82; G. no. 80-81.

Counter-Assertion 1: The equiprobabilist, however, places himself in danger of transgressing the law formally. Therefore, the difficulty stands.

The proof for this subsumed minor premise runs as follows. In doubts, the safer path must be chosen. Now, in a contest of two opinions, we find ourselves to be in a doubt, strictly speaking. Therefore, the safer path must be chosen, and one is not permitted to follow the less safe path without thereby sinning.

I respond first by *making a distinction with regard to the major premise.* I concede that the safer path must be chosen in *practical* doubts. I deny, however, that this is the case in *speculative* doubts.

I make the same sort of *distinction for the minor premise.* I concede that in a contest of two opinions we are faced with a *speculative* doubt. I deny, however, that we are faced with a *practical* doubt.

Thus, I also *make a distinction regarding the consequence drawn.* I concede that when it is a question of *practical doubt* one must choose the safer path, etc. I deny, however, that this is so for *speculative* doubt. And I deny the inference.

Indeed, we must declare on this point that the law brought forth (i.e., "In doubt the safer path must be chosen") does indeed prevail in a practical doubt that someone does not wish to set aside or cannot set aside.[306]

When, however, someone reflects on a speculative doubt, before he may act, he can and must set aside this directly and speculatively doubting conscience and form a practically certain *dictamen* for himself on the basis of reflex principles, by means of which he permissibly proceeds to act.

Counter-assertion 2: In speculative doubt, however, between two equally probable opinions someone cannot form for himself, on the basis of the reflex principles offered by St. Alphonsus, a practically certain conscience. Therefore, the difficulty stands.

The subsumed minor premise offered in this counter-assertion will be proven in parts. Probable knowledge suffices for adequate promulgation of the law. Now, a safer opinion favoring law possesses the character of being probable. Therefore, the law is sufficiently promulgated, and consequently one is not permitted to make use of the reflex principle, "A law that is not sufficiently promulgated does not obligate."

306. See ibid., H. no. 79; G. no. 77.

I respond as follows.

First, I *make a distinction regarding the minor premise*. I concede that it suffices for promulgating the law *in a doubtful manner*. I deny, however, that it suffices for promulgating it *in a certain manner*.

Likewise, *I make a distinction regarding the minor premise*. I concede that it suffices for promulgating the law *in a doubtful manner*. I deny, however, that it suffices for it to be promulgated as being *certain*.

I make a distinction regarding the *consequent* along the same lines. I concede that the law is sufficiently promulgated as *doubtful*. I deny, however, that it is promulgated as being *certain*. And simultaneously I deny the inference and ultimate conclusion, namely that one would not be permitted to make use of the principle, "A law that is not sufficiently promulgated does not obligate."

Indeed, awareness [*cognitio*] or certain knowledge [*scientia*] of the law entirely differs from opinion or probable knowledge. Thus, it is not correct to say that probable knowledge of the law suffices for it to be promulgated. Instead, it suffices only that a doubt or mere hesitation be promulgated, namely, "Is this a law or not?" Indeed, when a probable opinion exists on behalf of the law and, on the other hand, another equally probable opinion exists on behalf of freedom, then probability cannot survive on either side (i.e., a probable reason apt to drawing to itself the prudent assent of man). This is so because these equal probabilities only give rise to mere doubt concerning whether or not this law exists. St. Thomas clearly teaches this in *De veritate*, q. 14, a. 1 and elsewhere more briefly: "In the midst of equality of reasonings and arguments, only doubt remains."[307]

Counter-assertion 3: The law, however, is sufficiently promulgated as certain. Therefore, the difficulty stands.

The *subsumed minor* is proven as follows. The promulgation of the law is performed for the community. Now, every promulgation of the law had been performed well enough for the community. Therefore, the law is sufficiently promulgated and certain.

I respond as follows.

I concede the major premise.

I deny the minor premise, or, *rather, I make a distinction regarding what*

307. See ibid., H. no. 71; G. no. 68.

it says. I concede that this is sufficient for human law. I deny it, however, for the divine law.

I make a distinction in the consequent along the same lines and deny the inference. As St. Alphonsus says:

> We concede that for human law to have the power to obligate, it suffices that it be promulgated to the community, and it is not necessary that knowledge concerning the law immediately arrive at every single person. One must heed, however, that this holds only as regards the material object of the law, that it had been commanded or forbidden by the law, not however as regards the obligation in conscience for one to keep the law.
>
> Let me explain what I mean. If, for example, a given contract entered into without particular civil formalities is declared to be invalid, when the person who entered into that contract receives knowledge concerning it, then he is immediately bound to stand by the law's prescript, even though he might be unaware of the law... With respect to his conscience, however, he who does not keep that law which he does not know certainly does not sin in any way so long as he was not aware of his negligence.[308]

And the same thing must be said about a divine law that is not sufficiently promulgated in relation to human conscience.

COUNTER-ASSERTION 4: The divine law, however, has been sufficiently promulgated as something certain. Therefore, the difficulty stands.

The subsumed minor premise is proven as follows. The Divine and Eternal Law is the natural law. Now, the natural law is certainly promulgated precisely because God creates the soul and infuses it into the body. Therefore, the Divine and Eternal Law is sufficiently promulgated as something certain.

I respond by making distinctions regarding the major premise, the minor premise, and the consequent. In all of these propositions, I concede the point if one means that this is so *in first act*. I deny it, however, if one asserts them with regard to *second act*.

308. ibid., H. no. 72; G. no. 69.

As St. Alphonsus says:

> The Eternal Law is not the law that is proper [and immediately the law that belongs] to man, whose proper law is the Natural Law. Now, although the natural law is a participation in the Eternal Law, nonetheless the natural law is what, properly speaking, binds men since the natural law alone was promulgated to men and is applied by the light of reason. In any case, I say (as do other theologians) that although the Eternal Law in itself has the power to obligate in first act, nonetheless it is not the law obligating actually and in second act, until it has been proposed and applied to creatures through knowledge of it. Thus, I emphatically assert that this is taught by St. Thomas and by all theologians.[309]

COUNTER-ASSERTION 5: The natural law, however, is sufficiently promulgated as certain in second act. Therefore, the difficulty stands.

The subsumed minor is proven as follows. The position held by the possessor is better. Now, the natural law holds sway before freedom. Therefore, the natural law is sufficiently promulgated as certain in second act.

I respond as follows.

I concede the major premise. I have distinctions, however, to make regarding the minor premise and the consequent. I concede that the natural law holds sway over freedom *in potency or habitually*.I deny this, however, if it is considered as being *as known in act*.

Indeed, although the natural law of itself has obligatory force in potency, it nonetheless does not bind conscience unless it is promulgated in act to someone by the light of reason. Thus, the law holds in first act and thus is sufficiently promulgated as something certain, namely in potency, but because it is not actually applied, it does not bind the freedom that one possesses. Let us hear what St. Alphonsus has to say:

> "From the beginning, God established man and left him in the hand of his own counsel." He adds his commands and precepts: "If thou wilt keep the commandments and perform acceptable fidelity forever, they

309. Ibid., H. no. 72 (p. 48); G. no. 70 (p. 41). Cf. *ST* I-II, q. 71, a. 6; q. 90, a. 2; q. 91, a. 1 and 2. Also, St. Alphonsus, op. cit., H. no. 73; G. no. 71.

shall preserve thee" (Sir. 15:16; DR). And first the Lord created man as a free being, giving him, from His good pleasure, freedom, according to that which the Apostle writes in 1 Cor. 7:27 (DR): "Having power of his own will." And then, he laid down and imposed the commands that man is bound to keep; and therefore, since man's freedom is certain and holds before the obligation of the law, it is bound only by a law which is certain.[310]

COUNTER-ASSERTION 6: Those who embrace safer opinions, however, at least move toward what is safer. Therefore, in a contest between equally probable opinions, the opinion of the Probabiliorists must be followed in practice.

I respond with St. Alphonsus:

> It is indeed an impiety to relax the observance of divine laws more than one is permitted. It is no less an evil, however, to make the divine yoke heavier for others than is necessary. Indeed, the severity is too great... when it compels men to things that are too difficult and closes off the way of eternal salvation. As St. Bonaventure says, one damns those who are to be saved, and consigns those aware of their own infirmity to desperation... Therefore, St. Bonaventure rightly says that one's conscience must take care to be neither too lax nor too strict, for a lax conscience generates presumption, whereas strictness generates desperation. Likewise, a lax conscience often calls that which is evil good and a strict conscience, on the contrary, calls that which is good evil. Likewise, a lax conscience often saves those who are to be damned, whereas a strict one damns those who are to be saved.[311]

Moreover, as St. Alphonsus says, there two sorts of confessors that who are problematic. On the one hand, there are those who, clinging to their overly austere outlook, flippantly condemn the use of many opinions that are based on weighty foundations. On the other hand, there are those confessors who easily heap acclaim on opinions that lack a certain foundation, claiming that they are probable. Before a confessor may embrace a

310. St. Alphonsus, op. cit., H. no. 77; G. no. 75.
311. See St. Alphonsus, op. cit., no. 77, G. no. 75.

given opinion, he is utterly bound to carefully assess the intrinsic reasons at play. Indeed, when he is aware of a given reason that persuades on behalf of the safer opinion and does not at that time perceive an adequate response to it, he cannot embrace the less safe opposed position, even if the authority of many teachers were to favor it. This holds so long as the authority is not of such weight that that it would seem to call for deference more than does the reason in question. As St. Thomas says: "Someone of little knowledge [*scientiae*] is more assured concerning those things that he hears from some learned man than about those things that that he knows through his own reasoning."[312] St. Alphonsus states that this case is quite rare.[313]

Finally, through moderate use of equiprobabilism (doing so in accord with St. Alphonsus's thought) someone can proceed along the safe path and avoid danger of laxity or damnation, as we will immediately explain in the second conclusion.

Conclusion 2

One is not always permitted to follow a less safe opinion that is equally or nearly equally probable in contrast with a safer probable one.

This conclusion is expressed against the probablists in general and against certain equiprobabilists who lay hidden under an equivocation of terms and, falsely glorying in St. Alphonsus's own authority, teach that one is always permitted to follow a less safe option that is equally probable.

I will prove the conclusion in four manners.

First, as all authors profess, one is never permitted to act in doubt or with doubting conscience. "For everything that is not from faith [i.e., certitude] is sin." In a contest between two equally probable opinions, however, the only thing that results is a doubt, strictly speaking. Now, if an opinion standing on the side of freedom is only probable or equally probable as the other opinion standing on the side of the law, they cancel each other out, with neither being able to draw to itself the assent of a prudent man. Thus, on neither side does one have the moral certitude necessarily required for one to act. In such a case, the intellect cannot turn toward either side, and consequently, one is not permitted to act. Hence,

312. *ST* II-II, q. 4, a. 8, ad. 2.
313. Ibid.

as St. Alphonsus says, I hold that the probablists's claim, namely that "he who acts in a probable manner acts prudently," is false.[314]

Second, however, the other—which St. Alphonsus in no. 57[315] supposes as certain and which the Probabilists admit—is: When moral certitude is not discovered by means of direct principles, it can be had indirectly by means of reflex principles.

Now, on the use of reflex principles, it is sometimes clear that favor lies on the side of the law. At other times, however, it is on the side of freedom.

Therefore, one is not always permitted to follow a less safe but equally probable option.

The minor premise is proven both on the basis of authority and by reasoning the matter out.

By authority, it is proven through the universal principle, "The position held by the possessor is better." This is taken from the 65th rule of Canon Law in the sixth book [of the *Decretals*]: "In an equal fault or [otherwise equal] cases, the condition of the possessor makes a stronger claim."[316] And, in civil law, one reads, "In cases that are [otherwise] equal, the possessor ought to hold a stronger claim."[317] According to St. Alphonsus, this principle determines the other principles given above: "A dubious law does not obligate. An uncertain law does not lead to a certain obligation." "The anti-probabilists say that the law always holds sway. We say, however, that the law sometimes holds and, on other occasions, freedom does, namely when the law has not yet been promulgated. Therefore, in the case in which the law holds, one must stand on its side. If freedom holds sway, however, one must stand on the side of freedom."[318] Thus, according to St. Alphonsus, when the law is in doubt, it is not always permitted that one follow an opinion in favor of freedom. The doubt must be resolved, however, and, in order to form a practically certain conscience, one must see on what side possession holds sway.[319]

314. See St. Alphonsus, op. cit., H. nos. 57-58; G. no. 55.

315. See ibid., H. p. 27. This is omitted in Fr. Gaudé's edition on p. 25.

316. *Liber sextus decretalium* (ed. Taurini, 1588), col. 918-19.

317. *Digestorum*, bk. 50, tit. 16, *De diversis regulis iuris antiqui*, 128, cf. *Vindicias alph. Diss. apol.*, nos. 118-19.

318. St. Alphonsus, op. cit., no. 26, H. (p. 12); G. (p. 13).

319. Fr. Janvier, of the metropolitan church of Paris, and now of the cathedral, proposes and embraces this opinion of his former instructor in St. Thomas's Moral Theology. See his

Proof of the minor premise by reason. When each of them presents an equal case, the rights of freedom and of the law must be held as being equals. Now, in a contest between two equally probable opinions, the law and freedom are equally in doubt. Hence, for the same reason, one concludes against the probabiliorists that we are not always bound to follow that which is safer, and one likewise concludes against the probabilists that one is not always permitted to follow the less safe option. Indeed, we are here concerned with a strict doubt, and in such matters, one must discern between law and freedom by making use of a reflex principle. We confidently say with St. Alphonsus, however, that his reflex principle is universal and holds a special place among the others: "The position held by the possessor is better."

Third, likewise, *a proof is offered on the basis of the unsuitable consequences that would follow if this conclusion were not correct.*

In general, since equiprobabilists do not admit the principle, "The position held by the possessor is better," they must offer another by which one may have indirect practical certitude concerning the moral fittingness of the act. In general, they make use of the universal principle, "A law that is in doubt does not obligate. There is no obligation unless one can be certain concerning it," or, "It is not clear that one has an obligation to keep a law that probably does not exist." As Marc observes, however, when this principle is understood universally and for every case, it is quite doubtful and cannot be held to be morally certain. Indeed, when the existence of the law is certain and there is only a doubt concerning its cessation, can it be said that the law is doubtful, that it is probable that no doubt exists, and that it leads to no obligation? Hence, the principle gives way, as is noted by Fr. Gury, the editor of the Regensburg Compendium, no. 80, and since it does not have direct certitude, it cannot generate indirect certitude in practice.

Fourth, a proof is offered based upon an authentic exposition of each system, namely that of St. Alphonsus and common probabilism or the

---

Exposition de la Morale catholique, bk. 2, *La liberté*, Lent 1904, Paschal Retreat, 4th teaching (Paris: Lethielleux, 1904), p. 297. He cleverly notes, however, by the help of the *principle of possession*, that these decisions of St. Alphonsus scarcely differ from those that are pleasing to Probabiliorism. See Le Vedff, "Saint Alphonse est-il probabilioriste?" *Revue thomiste*, Vol. 12 (1904): pp. 129-50. Ambroise Gardeil, "Election, acte humain," in *Dictionnaire de théologie catholique*, III *Applications théologiques*, §2: Question of Probabilism. (Editor's Note, Ambroise Gardeil)

equiprobablism fabricated by probablists. Indeed, since they proceed according to different pathways, they are sometimes led to practically contrary opinions. It will be useful to explain each so that the even-handed reader may judge matters concerning these systems.

1. *The System of Equiprobabilism, According to the Reckoning of St. Alphonsus of Liguouri*

From the universal principle, "A law that is in doubt does not obligate," the Holy Doctor concludes that an equally probable opinion that is safer or favoring the law does not certainly bind. Since (on the other side), however, freedom is doubtful, it follows that a less safe, equally probable opinion does not loosen the bonds of the law. Hence, when we experience a strict doubt, a dispute between the law and freedom must be settled indirectly on the basis of the universal principle, "The position held by the possessor is better," and the entire question is reduced to this point. For one to discover, however, on what side *possession* may stand in doubtful matters, one must know on what side *presumption* stands. Now, presumption stands on the side that is not bound to prove the fact itself, but it transfers the burden of proof to the other option. [*Praesumptio verò stat pro eâ parte quae non tenetur ipsum factum probare, sed onus probandi illud transfert in alterum.*][320] And since the doubt sometimes is concerned with the law [*circa legem*], and sometimes with the fact [*circa factum*], one must consider how one is to form an indirectly certain conscience in either case by means of reflex principles.[321]

(a) *When the doubt is concerned with the law, one finds oneself in doubt either*, first, *concerning the law's existence, promulgation, or its extension*, or, second, *on the law's cessation, abrogation, revocation, dispensation, or reception.*

First: "*Indeed, that which is prohibited by no law is called 'permitted.'"*[322] The law binds in a prohibiting or commanding manner only if it is certain. Now, when one is in doubt about whether it is promulgated, or about its extent, that law is not certain (as has been shown). Therefore, it does not obligate, and in that case, man remains unbound and free, thus

320. Translator's Note: There is a closing quote here without an opening quote. Part of it seems to come from tr. 3, ch. 3 of Neyraguet's *Compendium theologiae moralis S. Alphonsi Mariae de Ligorio*.

321. See Marc, op. cit., no. 44 and 47.

322. St. Thomas, *In IV Sent.*, bk. 4, dist. 15, q. 2, a. 4, qa. 2.

being able to make use of his freedom, which he possesses. St. Alphonsus expressly says:

> If the law is doubtfully founded or is doubtful in its promulgation, it does not obligate, for possession does not stand on its side but, instead, stands on the side of freedom. Likewise, it must be said that if one is in doubt (regarding how far the law extends) concerning whether or not a given work is included in a promulgated law, then we are not bound to fulfill it because it does not hold for that side on which the law is doubtful.[323]

Second: *In a doubt concerning the cessation, abrogation, revocation, dispensation, or reception of the law, possession stands on the side of the law.*

St. Alphonsus's opinion is clear on this matter. "On the other hand, however," he says, "if the law is certainly founded and certainly promulgated and in this situation one wonders whether the law is abrogated, revoked, or dispensed, one must observe that the law then possesses [binding force]."[324] And, in another text, he says, "When one doubts whether a law is abrogated or dispensed, or whether one is faced with a reason that would excuse one from the law, we are in general bound by that law."[325] And again: "Thus, even when one is in doubt about whether a law that is just in itself had been received, it still must be observed. This is so because one must presume that it has been guaranteed by another principle, namely: 'When in doubt, one is to presume that what by rights ought to have been done was done [*In dubio praesumitur factum quod de iure faciendum erat.*]'"[326]

From what has been said, *you will infer* two things.

First, one is in doubt whether the law and freedom possesses standing in cases like the following: when one doubts whether a vow has been discharged, whether a promise has been made, whether a debt has been contracted, whether toward the middle of a Thursday night a day of abstinence has already begun, whether one has completed the period of time for observing one of the Church's laws, and so forth.

323. St. Alphonsus, op. cit., nos. 26 and 27 (H. pp. 12-13); G. no. 25 (p. 13). See Marc, no. 55, I.

324. Ibid., no. 27 (H. p. 12; G. p. 13).

325. Ibid., no. 99 (H. p. 95; G. p. 79).

326. Ibid., no. 27. Cf. Marc, no. 55, II.

Second, by contrast, the law stands in possession and freedom is bound in cases like the following: if one is in doubt as to whether the obligation of a law has ceased (e.g., whether [it does for a] sixty-year-old person), whether a day of abstinence has totally come to a completion (e.g., on a Saturday [*sabbato*] in the middle of the night), whether the Divine Office has been recited, or whether satisfaction has been reached for the precept of confession, for sacramental penance, for a vow, for a promise, for the repayment of something that is certainly owed, and so forth.

(b) *When the doubt is concerned with a fact, one can doubt either*, first, *whether a given fact exists*, or second, *whether it was rightly done.*

Nota bene: We are not here concerned with the same meaning of "doubt of fact" as was the case in Article 3 where we contrasted such doubt of fact with doubt of right. Instead, here, we are taking the term "fact" as meaning the effect of a virtue or as an activity that has been done for or against the law.

First: *When there is a doubt as to whether something has been done*, St. Alphonsus reflects on the pros and cons of freedom by making use of the principle, "A fact is not presumed unless it is proven," which is another principle taken from the 2nd Law Concerning Inspections into a Case [*Lege 2a de Probationibus*].[327] Therefore, in a doubt, the fact is not presumed but, rather, must be proven.[328] Thus, if there is a doubt as to whether someone had stolen something, the fact is not presumed but must be proven, for *nobody is presumed to be evil unless this is proven*, and *in a doubt the burden of proof falls upon the plaintiff.*[329]

Second: When something certainly has been done and *there is a doubt as to whether it has been done rightly*, St. Alphonsus makes use of other principles by means of which freedom may be assisted: "In a doubt one must judge based upon what ordinarily happens." This is taken from the 45th Rule of the Law in the sixth book of the Decretals, "What is ordinarily and regularly done is to be assessed as being the fact."[330] Hence, speaking about the Divine Office, St. Alphonsus teaches that one is ex-

327. *Digestorum*, bk. 22, tit. 3, *De probationibus*m 2: "And proof falls to him who says that something is so, not to him who denies that it is."

328. St. Alphonsus, op. cit., a. 26.

329. Cf. Marc, nos. 48 and 49.

330. *Sextus liber decretalium*, ed. cit., col. 898-99: "In unclear matters, we observe what is more likely or what generally is done."

cused from repeating it [in given cases]: "If you recall that you have begun a psalm, reading, or hours, and afterwards, not having stopped your recitation, you find yourself interrupted at the end of the hour in question, whether distracted or not, reading or reciting from memory those things you would not *ordinarily* be in the habit of erring about, etc..."[331]

Another principle that is used is: "In a doubt one must stand for the value of the act." That is, when the substance of a fact is already certain and one is in doubt concerning the value or quality of the act posited, then "that which by rights ought to have been done is presumed to have been done; that which has been done is presumed to have been done rightly." Hence, St. Alphonsus says, "Penitents are not to be told to repeat their confessions unless it is morally certain that they were invalid...because possession stands on the side of previously performed confessions so long as their nullity is not clear."[332]

Certain other supporting principles can be brought forward as well. They include, for example: "In a doubt, presumption stands on the side of the superior"; "In a doubt, positive biases are to be enlarged, hostilities restricted"; "A command does not obligate when it causes great difficulty [*cum tanto incommodo*]"; "In a conflict of laws, the superior law is to be preferred to an inferior one"; etc.[333] These have their proper consideration in the Treatise on Laws, however, and we refer the reader to that particular theological treatise. Indeed, sometimes these rules are handed on in a dangerous form, not being determined in accord with their proper principles.[334]

2. *The System of Equiprobabilism, According to the Reckoning of the Probabilists*

With St. Alphonsus, the probabilists make use of the universal principle, "A law that is in doubt does not obligate." They make particular use, however, of another principle, namely: "In a doubt, the position held by the

331. St. Alphonsus, in *Vindicias alph.*, pt. 1, ch. 1, p. 22, col. 2.

332. *Vindicia Alph.*, pt. 1, ch. 1, p. 23, col. 2. Cf. Marc, no. 51.

333. See Marc, nos. 51-54; *Vindicias alph.*, loc cit.

334. Translator's Note: This point, combined with his references to the treatises on the virtues, helps to expand the doctrine being handed on here, helping to avoid the truly dangerous and dessicating situation wherein these utterly general maxims end up being bandied about in the various probabilist debates.

possessor is better," although they accept and explain them in a different manner.

Some judge, with the probabiliorists, that this axiom is of use only in matters of justice but not in matters concerning the other virtues. But the two parties hold their respective positions through different reasons. The probabiliorists do indeed accept the principle, "A law that is in doubt does not obligate." The [robabilists do not, however, strive to limit the extension of the same principle. Indeed, if the title of possession is conceded, since presumption sometimes would be on the side of the law, freedom is not always free to itself, which they hold to be unsuitable and contrary to the liberality that they profess.

Others distinguish between the natural or divine positive law and ecclesiastical or civil law. If it is a question of the natural or divine positive law, they seem to admit a right of possession. If it is a question of ecclesiastical and civil law, however, they always resolve matters on behalf of freedom because, they say, the human legislator seems to urge obligation only when it is morally clear. But it could be said, with the probabiliorists, that the legislator is prudently presumed to will his laws to obligate in doubts and that observation of them does not depend on various interpretations offered by casuists. Thus, since from St. Alphonsus, following Suarez and others more generally, those distinctions and restrictions are unfounded, probabilists in general withdraw from this position and admit *that the right of possession is to be preferred in any case whatsoever*. They weaken the power and efficacy of this principle in another way, however.

They teach that this rule had been understood and received in the various schools only as regards a state of doubt strictly speaking [*presse sumpti*] (i.e., a state of negative doubt) and never concerning a state of opinion. In other words, contrary to the express opinion of St. Alphonsus, they pronounce that a principle of this kind is never to be used in a *strict doubt* (i.e., in a contest between two equally probable opinions) but, instead is to be used first in a doubt that is only negative (i.e., when there are not reasons present on either side, or when they are present but only express trivial reasons on their behalf) and second in a doubt formally taken (i.e., when the mind suspends its assent between two contradictory options). Thus, without qualification, they reject the principle of possession and for the formation of practically certain conscience, they in general solely make use of the principle, "A law that is in doubt does not obligate"; "An obligation is not to be imposed unless it quite clearly holds." They bring forth other secondary and subsidiary principles only inasmuch as they favor freedom. The reason for this, however, is that if they were to admit the right of possession in a strict doubt, the probabilists' first principle, "He who acts in a probable manner acts prudently," would come into question [*actum esset de primario Probabilistarum principio: Qui probabiliter agit, prudenter agit*].[335]

Hence, when there is a doubt concerning law [*legem*] or concerning the fact, the probabilists do not make use of the same method as St. Alphonsus.

(a) *Concerning the law.* First, when there is a doubt concerning the *existence*, *promulgation*, and *extension of the law*, the probablists argue as follows: "A law that is in doubt does not obligate. Now, in the aforementioned cases the law is doubtful. Therefore, it does not obligate, and one is permitted to follow the less safe option in favor of freedom." St. Alphonsus advances the same conclusion. While the opinion is the same, however, their methods differ.

Second, when there is a doubt concerning the *abrogation*, *cessation*, *dispensation*, or *reception* of the law, not only do they differ with regard to method but they also are led to an opinion contrary to that of St. Alphonsus. Indeed, equiprobabilists following St. Alphonsus's thought (and making use of the principle of possession) conclude that in these cases possession stands on the side of the law and that we are bound to follow the safer opinion. This is not, however, what the Probabilists hold. Since a doubtful law would not obligate, they infer that a law is doubtful when there is a doubt concerning the law's cessation, abrogation, dispensation, or acceptation, and hence that we are not bound to follow the safer option.

(b) *Concerning the fact.* First, when there is a doubt as to whether that which has been done *had been done rightly*, by the same method or a different one, they offer solutions that are nearly the same as those of St. Alphonsus.

Second, when there is a doubt as to whether something *had been done so as to satisfy the law*, they admit principles in support of freedom. They do not, however, always admit those that favor the law. Consequently, they do not embrace all of the Holy Doctor's opinions.

---

335. See Marc, no. 97 note.

Objections
They fall into the arguments that are proposed against the following thesis and that are setforth below.

Article 6: *Concerning Conscience Formed from an Opinion That Is Less Safe and Less Probable, in a Contest with a Safer and Certainly More Probable One; and Concerning Its Obligation*

§1. CONCERNING CONSCIENCE FORMED FROM AN OPINION THAT IS LESS SAFE AND LESS PROBABLE, IN A CONTEST WITH A SAFER AND CERTAINLY MORE PROBABLE ONE

The terms of this question were explained above and, in order to understand what must be said, they only need to be reflected on, especially the words "certainly probable."

Up to this point of the discussion, we have seen (in Articles 4 and 5) that, in a contest between what is safer and what is less safe, one is permitted to form for oneself a practically certain conscience from an opinion that is less safe but certainly more probable (and sometimes from a less safe and equally probable opinion). And on this point, teachers today seem to be in agreement. We reject, however, the opinion of the probabilists who hold that in a contest between equally probable opinions one is always permitted to follow the opinion that is in favor of freedom. Now, what must still be determined is whether in a contest between a safer opinion that is also certainly or more notably probable one is permitted to form for oneself a practically certain conscience from an opinion that is less safe and less probable.

Absolute probablists affirm that it is permitted. The probabiliorists and equiprobabilists, with St. Alphonsus, deny that it is. We embrace and defend this negative opinion, and against absolute probabilists, we declare the conclusion stated at the beginning of the next section.

§2. ON THE OBLIGATION OF THIS KIND OF CONSCIENCE

Conclusion
In a contest between two opinions concerning the objective moral fittingness

of an act, one is not permitted to follow an opinion that is less safe and less probable, leaving aside one that is certainly safer and notably more probable.

Stated another way: We are bound to follow a safer opinion that is certainly and more notably probable when it is in a contest with an opinion that is less safe and less probable.

This conclusion will be proven first from authority and then from reason.

First: Proof from Authority.

Negatively. The opinion held by absolute probabilism has no authority on its side when it is considered in itself, separately from St. Alphonsus's equiprobabilism. It enjoys only the tolerance of the Church. When it argues from authority, however, it creeps about beneath verbal equivocation, hiding under the patronage of doctors whose testimony is of no weight or who thought quite differently than is claimed. This is quite clear when you consider the way that probablists glory in St. Alphonsus's authority, for the Holy Doctor clearly teaches the contrary, as is clear even upon a cursory reading of the works that are praised by the Sacred Pontiffs.[336]

Positively. Clement III (ch. Capellanus, *de feriis*) declares that one must follow the opinion "that is better and more subtly founded upon reason."[337] Moreover, where there is a greater probability, there is a better and subtler reasoning.[338] Now, time-honored authors like Sts. Thomas and Bonaventure followed this rule, and did the probabiliorists did not recognize something different from this. The probabilists of greater note subscribe to it as well, including Suarez, who says: "A greater probability is a kind of moral certitude, if the excess of probability is certain."[339]

It is also proven on the basis of St. Alphonsus's authority, which the probabilists proclaim to be great (and rightly so). Let us listen to the Holy Doctor: "Therefore, I say that if the opinion standing on the side of the law seems *certainly* more probable, we are utterly bound to follow that, and we cannot embrace the opposite position that stands on the side of freedom."[340] And elsewhere, "For a century [*elapsi saeculi*] authors have

336. See Gury, nos. 64 and 65.

337. *Decretalium Gregorii* IX, bk. 2, tit. 9, ch. 4 (Turin, 1588), col. 672.

338. See Scavini, op. cit., no. 97. Marc, no. 100.

339. Suarez, *De legibus*, bk. 8, ch. 3, no. 19, p. 237. See Scavini, op. cit., no. 94.

340. St. Alphonsus, op. cit., H. no. 56 (p. 26); G. no. 54 (p. 25).

quasi-commonly held this position (namely, that of the probabalists). We say, however, that it is lax and cannot permissibly be embraced."[341] We bring forward this position (with the *Vindiciae alphonsianae*, pt. 1, ch. 1, §2, a. 2), not in order to brand or condemn the opinion of probabilism but rather, in order to refer to St. Alphonsus's thought on the matter, which is faithfully followed by Scavini, Bouvier, Gousset, and indeed by the Holy Doctor's [spiritual] sons in the work *Vindiciae alphonsianae*.

Second: *Proof by reason*. In order to act in a permissible manner, one must form for oneself (either directly or indirectly) a practically certain judgment concerning the objective moral fittingness of the act. Now, a person who relies on an opinion that is less safe and less probable in contest with one that is safer and certainly more probable cannot form for himself (either directly or indirectly) a practically certain judgment concerning the objective moral fittingness of the act. Therefore, he cannot permissibly follow the less safe and less probable opinion.

The major premise is certain and admitted by all.

The minor premise is proven as follows.

(a) *One cannot directly form a practically certain judgment* [based on an opinion that is less safe and less probable]. We will address this on three heads.

One, a scarcely probable opinion does not present a sufficient and certain foundation for one to act in a permissible manner. Now, in a contest with another opinion that is certainly more probable and safer, the less safe and less probable opinion is scarcely or doubtfully probable in relation to the opposed opinion. This is so because the power and efficacy of the motives militating on behalf of the less probable opinion are overcome and canceled out by the stronger motives of the more probable and safer opinion. Indeed, the more that the probability of one increases, the more the probability of the opposed one decreases. "Thus, it then happens," as St. Alphonsus says, "that a less safe opinion that lacks a certain foundation remains either scarcely probable or at least doubtfully probable in comparison to the safer one. Therefore, he who embraces it does so through imprudence, not prudence."[342]

341. *Homo apostol.*, no. 31.

342. St. Alphonsus, op. cit., H. no. 56 (p. 26); G. p. 55, note 54. See Billuart, *Summa sancti thomae*, *De conscientia*, diss. 6, a. 3.

Two, in order that the prudent man may act in a permissible way in doubtful matters, he is bound to look into the truth and to follow it. Where the truth cannot be clearly found, however, he is at least bound to embrace that which more closely approaches the truth. Now, this is the case for a certainly more probable opinion, so that, in such a case, "The safer option is not still doubtful (understood in the sense of 'doubt strictly taken' as we discussed in an earlier question). Instead, it is morally or quasi-morally certain. At least it cannot be called more doubtful, strictly speaking, since the possibility of its truth rests on a certain foundation."[343] Therefore, the prudent man is bound to follow the safer and more certainly probable opinion, and he is not permitted to embrace the less safe and less probable one.

Confirmation: "In all thy works let the true word go before thee, and steady counsel before every action."[344] Now, a less probable opinion in contest with one that is notably more probable cannot be called a "true word," since it more greatly approaches toward falsity than it does toward truth; and it cannot be called "a steady counsel" since it is based upon weaker motives than the opposed opinion. Therefore, [it cannot be the rule of action].[345]

Third, the will moves to assent only by first being moved by reason, as was said above, and every judgment about things to be done must be from faith (i.e., from certitude). Now, as St. Alphonsus says:

> In such a case, a man does not act based upon his own judgment or his own credulity [*sic*] (i.e., faith [in the sense used above]). Instead, he acts on the basis of a kind of impulse which would be inspired into his intellect by his will, so that he would draw back from the opinion that appears to be more likely and would be bent toward the opinion that does not appear true to him (nay, which seems not to have a certain foundation that could be true). And this is in line with what is said by the Apostle in Rom. 14:23 (DR): "For all that is not of faith [i.e., certain] is sin."[346]

343. St. Alphonsus, loc cit.

344. Sirach 37:20 (DR).

345. See Billuart, loc. cit.—Scavini, op. cit., no. 97.

346. See St. Alphonsus, op. cit., H. no. 56; G. note 54, p. 25.

Therefore, one is not permitted to follow an opinion that is less safe and less probable in contest with a safer and more certainly probable opinion.

(b) *One cannot indirectly* form for oneself a practically certain conscience [based upon an opinion that is less safe and less probable].

This can be proven in four ways.

One, indirect certitude is established on the basis of reflex principles. Now, in a contest between an opinion that is safer and certainly more probable, no reflex principles can supply for the deficiencies flowing from certitude that is less safe and less probable. Indeed, insofar as opinions considered in relation to one another are equal to each other, they cancel each other out or, if one may so speak, *neutralize* each other in the view of the prudent man's assent. Hence, after a comparison of this sort, a certainly more probable opinion would remain solely probable and consequently morally certain (since it at least exceeds a less probable opinion by at least one moral degree). Since the contrary, less probable opinion, however, would have no greater motive for itself, it ends up being utterly improbable and cannot be rendered certain by any subterfuge of reflex principles.[347] Therefore, [one cannot indirectly form a probably certain conscience in such cases.]

Two, nor will support be found in the principle of which they make use, namely, "A law that is in doubt..." Indeed, a law that is certainly more probable is already morally certain, and freedom cannot hold sway over it. In fact, one cannot claim that it is not sufficiently promulgated. Therefore, in such a case, it is contrary to reason to say that the law would be doubtful.[348]

Three, even less proven is the pronunciation, "He who acts in a probable manner acts prudently." Indeed, this principle is too universal and labors under an equivocation. One must confess that someone could prudently follow an opinion that is only probable. If both propositions are equally probable, however, the safer path must be followed when it is a question of the truth of fact. When it is a question concerning *probability of right*, however, it is not certain, as we saw with St. Alphonsus, and the intellect remains in a strict doubt. *A fortiori*, therefore, in a contest be-

347. See Marc, no. 101, II, 2.

348. See Marc, no. 101, 1.

tween what is certainly more probable and what is less probable, it would be the greatest imprudence for one to will to follow the opinion that is less safe and less probable since, as St. Alphonsus testifies, such a teaching would lead one to laxism. Indeed, they say that in order for someone to be able to follow an opinion, it must be truly and solidly probable. In this way, they seem to evade the 3rd proposition condemned by Innocent XI: "In general, when we do something confidently according to probability, whether intrinsic or extrinsic, however slight, provided there is no departure from the bounds of probability, we always act prudently."[349] Their supposition must be denied, however—namely that the less probable opinion would remain truly and solidly probable in a contest with one that is certainly more probable. And who will judge among so many opinions which are asserted as being truly probable? As St. Alphonsus writes: "And indeed, in this matter, many abuses were committed in the last century concerning the selection of opinions, so that many intrinsically lax opinions were admitted as though they were probable. Now, this was the reason why the Church condemned many of them, for they baselessly held various positions to be probable."[350]

Four, the probabilists, moreover, do not wish to establish a comparison between contrary opinions, suspend their judgment concerning the safer or more probable opinion, and only bother to weigh out the probable foundations favoring freedom. As St. Alphonsus writes, however, "Such a voluntary suspension of judgment is in fact joined to a kind of vincible, nay, affected, ignorance."[351] On this matter, Martinet writes, "Once one grants everyone the right to hold that obligations can be considered uncertain and of no weight, thereby allowing anyone to privately judge that the opposed position has some probability of being true and solid, we do not truly know: First, whether any of the most certain received obligations of the Christian life would remain safe and second, whether there would be any condemned laxist proposition which would fail to come back to life."[352]

Objections

349. Denzinger, no. 2103 (43rd edition).

350. St. Alphonsus, *Homo apost.*, no. 73. Also, see the end of Marc, no. 102.

351. Marc, no. 102, 1.

352. *Theol. Moral.*, bk. 1, a. 13, §3, *in fine*. See Marc, no. 102.

Antecedent. *One is permitted to follow the less safe and less probable opinion in contest with a safer and certainly more probable one.*

Therefore, the thesis is false.

Proof of the Antecedent. Obligation only exists concerning those things that are certainly clear, for a law that is in doubt does not obligate, as St. Alphonsus shows.

Now, in a contest with something that is safer and more probable, it is not clear that there is an obligation to keep the law against which a true and solid probability militates. Indeed, on this hypothesis, the law is uncertain, given that there is a true and solid probability presupposed as being contrary to it.

Therefore, there is no obligation for one to follow the *safer* ([and] more probable) path, setting aside a *truly probable* opinion. Thus, one is permitted to follow a truly probable opinion, setting aside the safer one, even when it is more probable.[353]

I respond by conceding the major premise.

I do, however, *make a distinction regarding the minor premise.* I concede it if one understands it as saying, "Now, in a contest with an opinion that is safer and *more probable*...it is not clear, etc.... [if it is] *insufficiently more probable.*" I deny the minor premise, however, if it is *certainly and notably more probable.*

Likewise, I make the same sort of *distinction regarding the consequent.* I concede it if one thus sets aside an opinion that is a safer and even more probable one, *when it is insufficiently more probable.* I deny the consequent, however, if it is a case of an opinion that is certainly more probable.

Allow me to explain this as follows.

The objection is taken from an argument from reason.[354] As it stands, the proposition labors under an equivocation, for in the thesis it is explicitly said that one is permitted to follow a truly and solidly more probable opinion, setting aside a safer and equally probable (or even *truly more probable*) one. What is meant by the words "truly more probable"? According to St. Alphonsus, a *truly* more probable opinion is the same thing as an opinion that is certainly and notably more probable, as we have said. This is not, however, how Fr. Gury understood the matter in later editions

353. See Gury-Ballerini, no. 60.

354. See ibid.

[of his work][355] and, in reality, it stands for what is certainly and notably more probable. Therefore, the author should prove what is intended, but in the argument he only makes use of the expression "more probable," not including the words "truly or notably more probable." And thus, he offers no proof against equiprobabilism, which speaks about a safer opinion that is certainly more probable and concedes that we are sometimes permitted to follow a less safe but truly and solidly probable opinion in a contest with a safer but insufficiently more probable opinion.

Beyond this equivocation involved in the minor premise and the consequent, there is also a begging of the question. They say that this holds in the case when a law is uncertain, since it is supposed that there is a true and solid probability against it. This is affirmed but is not proven. And, indeed, behold the argument that the probablists introduce like an Achilles heel [*ut Achilleum*]. Formally, it is reduced to the following: If a less safe opinion is truly and solidly probable in a contest with a more probable one, the law is not certain but, instead, is doubtful and, consequently, does not obligate; now, this is the case, namely, that the less safe opinion is truly and solidly probable in contest with a more probable opinion; thus, the law is doubtful, not certain, and therefore does not obligate."

I respond by allowing the major premise to pass. It is a hypothetical or conditional proposition whose truth depends on the logical connection between the antecedent and the consequent, as if it were said, "If something is a man, then it is an animal."

With regard to the *minor premise*, I apply the same distinction as I used above, namely between insufficiently more probable opinion and that which is certainly more probable. Thus, I deny that in a contest with a certainly more probable opinion the less safe and probable opinion would remain truly and solidly probable. Consequently, I also deny that one would be permitted to follow the less probable opinion, setting aside that which is certainly more probable.

Counter-assertion 1. Now, a less safe opinion remains (and is) probable in a true and solid manner in a contest with a safer and notably more probable one. Therefore, the difficulty stands.

355. See pp. 310–11, n. 373, below.

The subsumed minor premise is proven as follows. A probable opinion is one that is based on a weighty and solid motive. Now, the motive on which the less safe opinion is based remains weighty and solid in a contest with the notably weightier motive on which the more probable opinion is based. Therefore, a less safe opinion remains (and is) probable in a true and solid manner in a contest with one that is safer and notably more probable.

I respond to this first by *conceding the major premise* (although I could make a distinction in it, as I will for the minor premise).

I make a distinction regarding the minor premise. I concede it if it is the case that a weighty and solid motive remains, *absolutely speaking*. I deny the minor premise, however, if it claims that it remains such *in relation* to the notably weightier motive of the opposed, more probable opinion.

Therefore... I make a distinction in the conclusion along the same lines.

Indeed, although an opinion that is less safe absolutely speaking and considered in itself may have a weighty and solid foundation for itself, nonetheless, in relation to one that is notably more probable, it cannot be truly and solidly probable. Indeed, given that a more probable motive would be notably and certainly preponderating, it either entirely cancels out the foundation of the other, less probable one or so weakens it that it could not be called[356] truly and solidly probable in relation to the certainly more probable opinion.[357]

Counter-assertion 2. Now, a less safe opinion remains (and is) truly and solidly probable *in relation to a notably more probable one*. Therefore, the difficulty stands.

I prove the subsumed minor premise as follows. Those things that are wholly directed to another thing (i.e, relations) seem to be simultaneous by nature, as Aristotle says.[358] Now, an opinion favoring freedom is called less probable in relation to what is notably more probable favoring the law. Therefore, the less probable opinion is simultaneous by nature with a certainly more probable one and remains truly and solidly probable in relation to it.

356. **Translator's Note:** Reading "dici nequeat" for "dicit nequeat."

357. See *Vindicias Alph.*, p. 123.

358. Aristotle, *Categories*, ch. 7, txt. 5.

I respond first by *making a distinction regarding the major premise.* I concede this if one means a relation *secundum esse.* I deny it, however, if one means a transcendental relation [*secundum dici*].[359]

359. **Translator's Note:** For a brief overview, see the following passage (ed. Matthew K. Minerd) from Austin M. Woodbury, *Ostensive Metaphysics*, The John N. Deely and Anthony F. Russell Collection, St. Vincent College Library, Latrobe, PA, n. 1201 (pp. 930-932):

"But *real* relation itself is *twofold*, according as it is either a pure relation, i.e. nought except a relation, such as sonship, or is together some absolute being, [e.g.] a quality, such as sight, which besides being a relation to vision and to colour, is also a quality. A *pure* real relation is called a *predicamental relation*, which is *a pure order towards other*, so that it is not together some absolute being; wherefore it is named '*predicamental*,' since it constitutes a *special mode* of being really distinct from every absolute mode of being. This predicamental relation is a real purely relative accident superadded to its subject, this subject being constituted related to another: not formally through itself, but formally through this accident really distinct from itself. *Examples* are fatherhood, sonship, equality, similarity.

"But a *real relation which is together some absolute being* is called a *transcendental relation*: because it extends itself beyond the special predicament of relation and is found in all the predicaments or modes of being ([e.g.] in substance, quality, etc.). A transcendental relation accordingly is the *very entity of some absolute being from its very essence ordered towards another*, or proportioned or adapted or adjusted to another, as matter from its very essence is ordered towards form, or essence towards be [i.e. existence], or act towards object. Therefore, a transcendental relation is nothing else than the very *essence* of a being, which is not only a relation, *as it is adapted or ordered towards another*—as the essence of sight (which is not merely a relation, but is a quality) is adapted or ordered towards vision and color; wherefore, it is nothing else than an *essential adaptation* of a thing that is not a mere or pure relation. Accordingly, that which is related through a transcendental relation is constituted related: *formally through its own entity*, so that it *is* its own relation, not formally through a relation really distinct from its entity—in this case, its order or adaptation to another would be only accidental, not essential.

"It is manifest from what has just been said that: whereas, as will be explained later (cf. n. 1206), in predicamental relation there is *real* distinction between these *four*: the *relation* itself, its *subject*, its *foundation*, and its *term*; when it is a question of transcendental relation, there is real identity between the relation itself and its subject, and its foundation, the *only* real distinction lying between tht one reality which is together these three and the term.

"From what has just been said follow *two further distinctions* between predicamental and transcendental relation. *First* indeed, whereas *predicamental* relation respects its term as a *pure* term; *transcendental* relation, on the contrary, respects its term, not as a pure term, but as that whereunto the subject is essentially adapted, to wit, as specificative, or perfective, or complement, or proper subject. But *second*, whereas *predicamental* relation perishes if its term does not *really actually exist*, since its sole office is to refer the subject to that term *as to a term*—which it cannot do if that which is the term does not exist; *transcendental* relation, on the contrary, does not require that its term really exist actually, since something can be essentially adapted to another without the real actual existence of that other; thus, for example, [the] human soul is transcendentally related to the human body, but can exist after the body has ceased to exist; also, there can be science of an object which does not exist really ([e.g.] logic, whose object is mental being [*entia rationis*, namely *relationes rationis* that are second intentions]. [continued next page]

I make a distinction regarding the minor premise as well. I deny that the less probable is so called if one means a relation *secundum esse*. I concede it, however, if one means it is a transcendental relation.

I make a distinction in the conclusion. I do so with regard to the claim, "Therefore…it is simultaneous in nature." I concede it as transcendentally relative to a probable motive. I deny it *of itself*, however, as ordered to the prudent man's assent.

This somewhat obscure objection first of all labors under an equivocation concerning the nature of relatives, which are of two kinds, namely *secundum esse* and transcendental [*secundum dici*]. That which is relative *secundum esse* is that whose essence [*quidditas*] is nothing other than *to be toward the other*, and the name of such relatives signifies nothing other than the relationship [*habitudinem*] between two things (e.g., *the double* and *the half*). Therefore, we concede that such relatively said things are simultaneous by nature. Indeed, they mutually infer each other and mutually fall away, for if the double exists, the half will exist, and vice-versa. this is not, however, how an opinion is called less probable in relation to one that is more probable. Instead, it is so designated according to a transcendental relation.

Now, a transcendental relation is one whose essence does not consist *in being toward another thing* but nonetheless can only be explained *through an order to another thing*. Hence, things of this sort are not truly relative but are *things* which designate a consideration, that is, which signify one thing and are turned toward something and therefore are relative *secundum quid*. For example, scientific knowledge signifies a quality upon

"*It is to be noted* that the distinction of *real* relation into predicamental relation and transcendental relation does not fully coincide with the distinction, commonly made by *St. Thomas* and the ancient scholastics, of relation into 'relation according to [existence] (*secundum esse*)' and 'relation according to be-spoken (*secundum dici*).' See ST I q.13 a.7 ad 1. For, they called by the name of '*relation according to [existence]*' every pure relation or relation whose whole [existence] is *[to]-[exist]-towards-other*, wheter such relation be real (and then it is predicamental) or mental; for also of mental relation is it true that its whole [existence] is towards other. See *De potentia*, q.7 a.10 ad 11. While, they called by the name '*relation according to be-spoken*,' the relation that is together some absolute being (and this is transcendental relation): inasmuch as such absolute beings are understood and are defined and therefore are-spoken through reference to another; as potency is understood and is defined and is-spoken through reference towards act, and similarly matter through reference to form, and similarly sight through reference to vision and colour, and similarly habit through reference to its operation and object.]

which there follows a relation to a knowable object (for it is a scientific knowledge of the knowable).[360] the term "science [*scientia*]," however, is not used so as to signify that relationship [*habitudinem*]. Instead, it is used so as to signify the quality itself inasmuch as it is a *habitus* perfecting the intellect. Now, according to Aristotle, it is not true to say that things of this sort are simultaneously relative by nature. Indeed, the knowable seems to be prior to science, and if every scientifically knowable thing were destroyed, so too would science be destroyed, but not vice-versa. Indeed, even if there were no science, nothing would prevent the knowable from existing.

Moreover, *by applying the distinction to the minor premise*, what we have said about scientific knowledge is proportionally suitable for the case of opinion. Indeed, opinion is an assent with fear that the opposed side might be true, and it signifies the disposition of the intellect upon which follows a relation to a likely or probable object. Thus, if the probable thing is destroyed, the opinion will be destroyed. If the opinion is destroyed, however, the probable thing will not be destroyed. Therefore, more and less probable opinions are not said to be relative *secundum esse* but instead are transcendentally relative [*secundum dici*], and it does not follow that they would be simultaneous by nature. Indeed, it can happen that some probable object could remain on account of a motive that is weighty and solid of itself and that nonetheless the opinion concerning it would be destroyed. And this happens in a contest between a less probable opinion and one that is certainly more probable, as is clear in the application of the same distinction *to the consequent.*

Indeed, we have said that an opinion remains transcendentally [*secundum dici*] probable as regards the relationship [*habitudinem*] that it has to the probable object. It does not, however, remain so of itself inasmuch as it is a disposition of the intellect as ordered to the assent of a prudent man.

The reason for this is that "more" and "less" is said about an opinion inasmuch as it signifies a disposition of the subject (i.e., of an intellect that is more or less inclined to one or the other side of a contradiction).

360. Translator's Note: Throughout this paragraph, Fr. Beaudouin uses "scibile," not "cognoscibile." It is not clear whether he is using the expression in the strict Thomist sense, for *scibilitas* indicates the *scientific knowability* of something, in distinction from the mere knowability that the thing has. Given the distinction of the sciences based upon abstraction, one knowable thing can have many kinds of scientific knowability.

Indeed, properly speaking, *the more* and *the less* are not found in relatives but in qualities because, through a lesser admixture of contrary factors, that quality is *intensified*, and through a great admixture of such contrary factors that quality is *remitted*. For example, that which is warmer is something that has less coldness. Now, opinion stands between scientific knowledge and ignorance. Thus, the more that someone opines on account of stronger motives, the more does that person approach the perfection of science and of truth. Likewise, to this same degree does he recede from the imperfection of ignorance and of error. Now, truth is the first law of the intellect, and in doubtful matters, where perfect scientific knowledge is not found, we follow that which is more likely. Therefore, the intellect that is more attracted and enticed by that which is notably probable will not turn away from assenting to that which is truly and solidly probable. This would be against the nature and perfection of counsel and judgment. Thus, although that which is absolutely less probable is probable in relation to its probable object, nonetheless in a contest with that which is certainly more probable, it does not remain probable as ordered to disposing the intellect and does not suffice for motivating the prudent man's assent.

Counter-Assertion 3. Now, a less probable opinion suffices for motivating the assent of a prudent man. Therefore, the difficulty stands.

I prove the subsumed minor premise as follows. As is taught by St. Augustine and St. Thomas, choice is an act of prudence.[361] Now, when the will finds itself faced with a choice that is more eminent than others presented to it, it can choose that which is less worthy. Therefore, the prudent man can choose that which is less probable.

I respond first by *making a distinction with regard to the major premise*. I deny the major premise if one means that it is *essentially* an act of prudence. I concede it, however, if one means that it is *consequently* an act of prudence.

I make a distinction regarding the minor premise as well. I concede that the will can choose that which is less worthy *physically*, by way of a freedom of exercise and specification. I deny this, however, if one means that it is less worthy *morally*, according to the order of reason and of prudence.

361. See *ST* II-II, q. 47, a. 1.

I make a distinction regarding the consequent along the same lines and deny the inference.

Regarding the major premise. Indeed, as St. Thomas observes, choice implies a kind of prior comparison.[362] The conclusion of the syllogism, however, that is brought about in things to be done [*operabilibus*] pertains to reason and is called the decree [*sententia*] or judgment upon which choice follows. Thus, the choice that is in the appetite [i.e., the will] always follows the counsel or judgment that is in reason. Of these two, however, counsel pertains more to prudence. Indeed, in his comments on book six of the *Nicomachean Ethics*, St. Thomas says that the prudent man is he who takes counsel well, and since choice is [an act] of a previously counseled appetite, it is attributed to prudence consequently, namely inasmuch as it directs choice through counsel.[363]

Regarding the minor premise. Therefore, we concede that the will can choose that which is less probable. Indeed, nothing prevents it from doing so if it has proposed to it things that are equal or more eminent from one perspective, although without considering some condition on the other side that renders that other side more eminent, thus leading the will to bend itself toward that which is less probable in itself rather than toward the other option. This demonstrates [*evincit*], however, nothing other than the freedom of exercise and of specification that man can make use of either for good or for evil. In order for the choice to be that of a prudent man, it must be in accord with right reason and the right judgment of prudence, which is denied in this case.

Regarding the consequent, the following may be said.

Indeed, as Thyrsus González de Santalla, a former Superior General of the Jesuits, observes: "Although the opinion of the Probabilists is not touched (by Innocent XI's condemnation), nonetheless, its foundation seems *a priori* to be weak. Indeed, this foundation was that a less probable opinion would be, absolutely speaking, probable and hence would be based upon a weighty and prudent foundation. Thus, anyone would be

362. See *ST* I-II, q. 13, a. 1, ad 1.

363. See *ST* II-II, q. 47, a. 1c and ad 2.

Translator's Note: It is important to note, however, that this dependence is in the order of formal causality, while the intellect here depends on the will in the order of efficient causality. This mutual causality, admitted in certain passages by Fr. Beaudouin, is not always presented in full clarity by him.

able act in accord with it, for in that case one would act according to a weighty and prudent reason. Hence, such a person would not sin, given that he thus acts prudently. This foundation, however, has already been overturned by the Pope's definition. This is so because he who makes use of a barely probable opinion that is contained within the limits of probable opinion [precisely] as such makes use of an opinion that, absolutely speaking, is based on a weighty and prudent foundation and nonetheless does not act according to right and prudent reason."[364]

Hence, St. Alphonsus most rightly pronounces that a less probable opinion in contest with one that is certainly safer and more probable would not remain truly and solidly probable but, instead, would be only scarcely probable. Consequently, it cannot be chosen by a prudent man.

Counter-Assertion 4. Now, an opinion that is certainly more probable is not more sufficient than a less probable one in drawing to itself the assent of a prudent man. Therefore [the difficulty stands].

The subsumed minor premise is proven as follows. Everything that is not from faith (i.e., from certitude) is a sin. Now, a certainly more probable opinion is not certain and remains within the limits of probability, just like a less probable one. Therefore, as ordered to the assent of a prudent man, it is not more sufficient than is a less probable one.

I respond first by *conceding the major premise.* (Or, I could make a distinction. I deny the major premise if it refers to certitude that is only direct. I concede it, however, if it means direct or [*et*] indirect certitude.)

I also make a distinction regarding the minor premise. I concede that it is not directly and speculatively certain. I deny, however, that it is not indirectly and practically certain.

Finally, I make a distinction regarding the consequent along the same lines and *deny the inference.* There is no difficulty concerning the distinction offered. All must admit it, and it was sufficiently explained above. Hence, although an opinion which is certainly more probable may be called "quasi-morally certain" in St. Alphonsus's writings, nonetheless it does not approach the dignity of a moral declaration [*sententia*]. It can and must, however, be rendered certain by means of reflex principles.

364. See Thyrsus Gonzalès, *Fundamentum theologiae moralis*, dissert. 7, §3, Colon. (Agrip., 1664), p. 131.

Now, this concession does not help the probabilists, nor does it establish that equality exists between a more probable opinion and one that is less probable when forming an indirectly and practically certain conscience. Accordingly, with time-honored authors and St. Alphonsus, we say that where certitude is lacking, we follow that which is more likely, and no reflex principles of the probabilists can break this natural law of the intellect. Indeed, as has been said, the laws that they bring forth (e.g., "A law that is in doubt does not obligate," and so forth) are not useful for forming a practically certain conscience in a contest between equally probable opinions. Thus, *a fortiori*, they are not useful in a contest between a certainly more probable opinion and one that is less probable.[365]

Counter-assertion 5. Only the probablist position is practical. Therefore, the difficulty stands.

The subsumed minor is proven as follows. The probabiliorists' system creates too grave a difficulty for both confessors and penitents in weighing out the various degrees of probability. It also leads to a perpetual fluctuation of teaching and confusion in decisions, for what appears to be more probable to one person is less probable to another.

Now, probabilism, when it is correctly understood, generally takes care to avoid disadvantages of this kind. Indeed, there are only two things to be weighed out for Probablists, namely, certain obligations and merely probable obligations. Although one is not always clear about the true probability, nonetheless, ordinarily speaking, it is clear to everyone that it is much easier to discern whether a solid reason or authority holds against the law than it is to bring forth a judgment concerning a given excess of probability.

Therefore, only the probabilist position is practical.

I respond first by *making a distinction regarding the major premise.* I concede that a difficulty follows if one is concerned with an opinion that is *insufficiently more probable.* I deny it, however, if one is concerned with an opinion that is *certainly and notably more probable.*

I deny the minor premise and the consequent.

This objection touches on the fundamental distinction between probabiliorism, equiprobabilism, and probabilism. Indeed, probabiliorists and

365. Cf. *Vindicias, Diss. apol.,* no. 112.

equiprobabilists (with St. Alphonsus) hold that to form a practical judgment in a contest of opinions, a given person must establish a comparison, weighing out the reasons for either side of the matter. If it appears to such a person's intellect that the truth stands more greatly on the side of the law than on that of freedom, then the will cannot prudently and sinlessly adhere to the less safe side. Some probabilists seem to reject this comparison and weighing-out of matters because it would be too troublesome for confessors and penitents. We do not deny this troublesome effect in cases when the opinion is insufficiently more probable, for such a small amount is [rightly] held to be nothing (and in moral matters, mathematical equality is not what is required). When concerned, however, with an opinion that is certainly and notably more probable (i.e., that it exceeds the other by a single moral degree), this troublesome situation vanishes. Indeed, one degree of probability makes it probable, and both the probabilists and probabiliorists weigh out and judge a weighty motive with the same easiness or difficulty. When one objects, however, that the necessary comparison is also too troublesome, we respond with St. Thomas that comparison is a[366] proper activity of the intellect. "Indeed, knowledge pertains to reason, which has as its office the activity of distinguishing between those things that are of themselves conjoined, as well as the activity of in some manner bringing together those things that are different by comparing one to the other."[367]

To the minor premise, we say the following. We do not wish to concede the claim that probabilism would free itself from troubles of this sort (if however, in reality, such troubles properly would belong to some particular domain and not, rather, be common to every discipline). For if probabilist confessors and penitents have had no such troubles, the usefulness of their mode of evaluation has not led to the recommendation of these kinds of Probabilist systems in the writings of eminent Catholic teachers who, being learned in moral science, unanimously proclaim its obscurity and difficulty. Thus, the minor premise is denied without qualification. Indeed, for a Probablist to act on the basis of his own principles, he must discern true, weighty and solid reasons that are contrary to the

366. **Translator's Note:** Such comparison is technically proper to the intellect *as rational*, not *precisely as an intellect*, that is, according to the characteristics that man's intellectual capacities analogically share with the angels and God.

367. *ST* I-II, q. 27, a. 2, ad 2.

law. A weighty motive, however, is opposed to a tenuous one, and a solidly probable one to one that is scarcely probable. Therefore, one must distinguish between an opinion that is gravely probable and one that is scarcely probable. Making such a distinction is at least as difficult (if not more so) than is the making of a distinction between what is certainly more probable and certainly less probable. This is so because we cannot make this kind of judgment without comparing the reasons that militate for an opinion that is scarcely or gravely probable on either side. And this gives rise to no small difficulty in weighing out the various degrees of probability, along with doctrinal confusion and a fluctuation in the making of decisions. Indeed, what seems only scarcely probable to one person can seem gravely and solidly probable to another. Those who refuse to take up this kind of comparison fall into a doubly problematic situation. First, in a contest with a certainly more probable and safer opinion, they leave freedom open, although such freedom is doubtful and, relatively speaking, does not have a solid and true foundation for itself. Second, however, in a contest between a probable and a scarcely-probable opinion, they expose themselves to the peril of following that which is scarcely probable, which all admit cannot offer a foundation for forming a practically certain judgment of conscience.

Finally, this method of probabilism (which consists in a weighing out of the probability that stands for freedom, neglecting a comparison of the motives that favor the law) is not only contrary to the nature of the intellect and of reason, but is also contrary to the way that this method has been used by the eminent and weighty teachers of moral theology both classically and in more recent days. Nay, as the authors of the *Vindication* [of Alphonsus] note, "Any confessor and any prudent man make use of the virtually the same rule, when after reading proven authors or consulting a given learned man, he finally proceeds to act."[368] And in at least one case, Fr. Ballerini is compelled to admit this. He says that, at times, someone must abandon the use of a probable opinion and, indeed, is bound to make use of a more probable opinion whose opposite is defended by others as being very probable (and in fact as being morally certain).[369] "Then the very matter at hand, however, warns the prudent reader that

368. *Dissert. Apol.*, no. 76.

369. See St. Alphonsus, *Theol. Mor.*, bk. 4, no. 443, 1st opinion.

he must look into the matter more diligently. Hence, it will quite easily become clear either that the other opinion is called very probable without cause or that one can be sure that the other has been vainly judged to be probable."[370] This sensible, more diligent inquiry, terminating in a judgment cannot be engaged in without the activity of comparing.

COUNTER-ASSERTION 6. Now, the opinion of probabilism has so firm a basis on authority that, in practice, someone can follow it with a safe conscience. Therefore, the difficulty stands.

The subsumed minor is proven as follows. First of all, there is the quite-common assent of authors through many centuries, including the eminent names of Suarez, De Lugo, Lessius, Eusebius Amort, Bonancia, and others.

Second, also, this is based upon the authority of St. Alphonsus whose works enjoy the Church's approval, at least implicitly.

Third, also, there is the fact that the doctrine of Probabilism has never been condemned. Therefore, [one can follow it with a clear conscience.]

I will respond to each of these claims in part.

To the first proof: Suarez, De Lugo, Lessius, Bonacina, and many others, generally admit that one can make use of a probable opinion in favor of freedom when there is a contest between that opinion and one that is more probable. They do not explain more distinctly, however, what kind of probability is required or suffices, and they do not distinguish between that which is more probable and that which is notably more probable. Eusebius Amort teaches the contrary, as the authors of the *Vindiciae alphonsianae* show.[371] Moreover, not all of those who are cited for Probabilism in reality hold it as a position, for the terms "more probable" and "less probable" are not used in the same sense by various authors, as Thyrsus Gonzalès observes and as is clear from what was said above concerning the definition and breadth of probability. So many and sundry things are said in theology concerning this matter that [Julius] Mercorus, O.P. ([*Basis totius moralis Theologiae*], pt. 2, a. 28) refers to fourteen manners of speaking that are used in these matters. Therefore, one must receive with a grain of

370. Gury-Ballerini, no. 78, note C.

371. See *Vindiciae alphonsianae*, ch. 3, a. 1 *in fine*, p. 91. Also, see St. Alphonsus, op. cit., H. no. 70; G. no. 66.

salt the listing that is everywhere found in the writings of the summulists and in which one finds it asserted that various authors of note embrace tutiorism or probabiliorism or equiprobabilism or probabilism (whether lax, common, or absolute).

Hence, this question had been quite obscurely and confusedly treated before St. Alphonsus. Today, however, after it has been explained in clear terms and adequately judged, we believe that a prudent man must adhere to the opinion of the Holy Doctor whom the Church at least implicitly has approved and whom the Holy Pontiffs have so greatly commended.

To the second proof, namely, the one bringing forward St. Alphonsus: it absolutely is not the case that St. Alphonsus teaches that one is permitted to follow an opinion that is less safe and less probable when it is in a contest with one that is safer and notably more probable. He expressly holds the opposite, as was clearly shown above. The testimonies drawn from the *Dissertatione*, according to the Naples edition of 1755, do not favor probabilism, since they are brought forth in accord with the rules of sound criticism. Indeed, one must judge the nature of his genuine system on the basis of his later works and not his earlier ones, which the Holy Doctor never received, argued for, nor commended as being part of his body of works of moral theology. Now, at least from 1762 until his death in 1787, St. Alphonsus very consistently taught the opinion that we have expressed, as one can see in the *Vindiciae*. Thus, one is not permitted to forcibly claim that St. Alphonsus bestowed approval upon absolute probabilism.

If one expresses the assertion in certain equivocal terms, however, (e.g., when the Holy Doctor, speaking without qualification and not making use of the term "notably," teaches that one is permitted to follow a less probable opinion in a contest with one that is more probable), an interpretation must be taken from other places in which he expressly manifests his opinion, and we say with Cajetan, who, responding to sophistries that have been expressed concerning St. Thomas's doctrine, said: "When one is clear about a certain conclusion [in St. Thomas], the words that sometimes appear to be out of harmony with this must be reverentially [*pie*] interpreted."[372]

Certain more recent authors seem to be deceived by the fact that they did not distinguish between the scarcely more probable and the notably

372. *In ST* I-II, q. 4, a. 1.

more probable in accord with St. Alphonsus's way of thinking. And for this reason, they proposed in the schools a system of absolute probabilism under the banner of the authority of such a name, although it was utterly alien to his thought.

A great number of people, however, clearly perceived and followed his opinion, among whom we may number Bouvier, Gosset, and Ernest Müller, the rector and emeritus professor of moral theology at the University of Vienna. It suffices that we refer to Scavini, who asks in no. 97, "Is one permitted to follow an opinion that is less safe and less probable in a contest with one that is safer and simultaneously also more probable?" He responds negatively. Now, this illustrious author was praised by Pope Pius IX on April 7, 1847: "We offer you the greatest of thanks, that in having brought together these theological instructions you considered nothing more venerable than to more broadly propagate the salutary doctrines of the most holy and learned man Alphonsus Mary di Liguouri and to give instruction to the souls of the Church, especially those of the young."

To the third point and to the consequent (i.e., that the opinion of probabilism never has been condemned and therefore one is permitted to follow it in practice), I respond as follows. I concede that this opinion has not been condemned. Probabilists must admit, however, that it has never been approved. We have never seen the authority or reasoning on which it can be supported,[373] and consequently we cannot recommend its use.

373. To take one example among many, there may be a way in which Gury clads himself with the authority of St. Alphonsus. In earlier editions (Lyons, 1850; Parma, 1852), no. 60, the author establishes this thesis: "One is permitted to follow an opinion that is truly and solidly probable, setting aside one that is safer and equally probable or even more probable, where it is a question only about what is permitted or not permitted, though only if the excess of probability of the safer opinion is not significantly more probable." He proves this as follows: "Thus, as St. Alphonsus did before us, we follow the middle way between the opposed opinions of theologians, indeed tempering the rigor of the probabiliorists, and simultaneously restricting within stricter limits the sometimes-excessive liberality of not-too-few probabilists. Indeed, the Holy Author is in agreement with us. Accordingly, he teaches that one is permitted to follow an opinion that is not only equally probable but one that is nearly equally probable, so long as the opposed opinion is not certainly, evidently, and much (or, notably) more probable. (*Homo apost.*, no. 77). Opining, however, that it is permitted even to follow a less probable opinion favoring freedom, we apply this restriction, namely: *so long as the excess of the safer opinion's probability is not significantly notable*, which comes back to St. Alphonsus's opinion. We thus believe that the use of probabilism is to be tempered in this manner. And indeed, if there is such an excess of probability favoring the law before the other opinion, the former seems to revert to being very probable, and hence, the latter becomes dubiously or scarcely probable." (Gury, in the *Vindiciae*, pt. 1, ch. 1, §2, p. 34.)

Let them who follow it judge upon what principles they can form their conscience for themselves and upon what knowledge they will be able to distinguish between what is scarcely and solidly probable. Indeed, above all, let them take care lest they lead the faithful into laxism or, under the pretense of fighting Jansenism or rigorism, loosen the reigns of morals far too much.

CONCLUSION

Therefore, let us conclude this disputation by briefly gathering together the ways that Catholic teachers today seem to agree and disagree.

They agree in what they say about conscience considered from the perspective of the object, namely inasmuch as it is right or erroneous. Now, when in comes to the question of conscience considered from the perspective of the subject (i.e., the perspective of the intellect's assent) they unanimously teach, with the Apostle, that activity that is not from faith [i.e., certitude] is a sin, commonly admitting that imperfect certitude in moral matters suffices for forming practically certain conscience. Some teachers seem to have less approval for the certitude that is had indirectly,

---

In later editions, however, the restriction that was applied was expunged, and the thesis was proposed thus: "One is permitted to follow a truly and solidly probable opinion, setting aside one that is safer and equally probable, or even more probable, when it is only a question of what is permitted or not permitted."

And finally, the last thesis is converted into pure and absolute probabilism: "One is permitted to follow a truly and solidly probable opinion, setting aside one that is safer and equally probable, or even truly more probable, when it is only a question of what is permitted or not permitted." (See Gury, Lyon / Paris, 1869, p. 54). In St. Alphonsus's writings, that which is truly more probable is the same as that which is notably more probable. Thus, the final thesis proposed is opposed to the prior one. So be it! [*Libuit*!] The author has changed his opinion. Let the evenhanded reader, however, judge by what right he brings this opinion under the patronage of St. Alphonsus and proves it on his authority. (Cf. Gury, nos. 60 and 65, 3: From the Church's authority, at least in her implicit approval of St. Alphonsus's works. Roman edition from 1882 with notes by Fr. Ballerini, p. 59.) Lehmkuhl, S.J., in no. 77, thinks up another means of escape. He believes that, in his last writings, St. Alphonsus professed equiprobabilism. "However," he says, "he hardly ever expunged [*expunxit*] any opinion of the probabilists', so long as it was probable, nor did he ever deny that it is practically permitted." [*Theol. Mor.*, Fribourg im Brisgau, 1893, p. 60.] No wonder! Indeed, according to St. Alphonsus, an opinion cannot be called more probable in a contest with one that is truly and solidly probable. Therefore, let the probabalists profess with St. Alphonsus that, on the contrary, opinions that are upheld as being probable are not all truly probable, neither speculatively nor practically, in a contest with one that is certainly more probable; and thus, the controversy between the probabilists and equiprobabilists is brought to a close.

but they disagree more as regards their terminology than as regards the actual matter itself.

They all deny that one can form a practically certain *dictamen* on the basis of doubting conscience (whether it be lax or scrupulous).

Finally, concerning probable conscience absolutely considered, both time-honored authors and more recent ones believe that, on the basis of a very probable opinion and one that is only probable, one can form practically certain conscience for himself. Similarly, when one is discussing a probable opinion that having *probability of fact*, comparatively understood, all agree among themselves and teach that the safer option must be chosen.

A difficulty arises, however, when it comes to the question of a probable opinion having *probability of right*.

Probabiliorists, against the Jansenists and absolute tutiorists, invincibly prove that in a contest with an opinion that is safer but less probable one is permitted to follow the more probable but less safe opinion. And today, among Catholic doctors, there are none who refuse to admit this conclusion.

Therefore, disagreement or freedom of opinions short of ecclesial condemnation organizes itself around three systems:

Probabiliorists, after defending against the tutiorists the use of a more probable opinion in a contest with one that is less probable, stop here and deny that one is permitted to follow a less safe but probable opinion in a contest with one that is equally probable but safer.

Equiprobabilists, by contrast, with St. Alphonsus and with the approval of the whole Church, teach that one is sometimes permitted to follow an opinion that is less safe yet equally probable in a contest with one that is probable and safer. And, on the basis of the declaration of the Sacred Penitentiary, all theologians can safely follow this opinion of the equiprobabilists.

Probabilists, however, proceed even further, and professing liberality or mercy, favor freedom even more, and wish that it be always permissible for one to follow an opinion that is less safe and probable in a contest with one that is equally probable, nay even in a contest with an opinion that is safer and also certainly more probable.

Thus, the entire question remains disputed among the probabiliorists, equiprobabilists, and the probabilists.

We have embraced St. Alphonsus's opinion saying, in line with the Holy Doctor's thought: Just as one must not approve of confessors who, retaining far too much austerity, easily condemn the use of many opinions that are based on a weighty foundation, so too, on the contrary, one must not approve of those who vociferously and easily approve of opinions without a certain foundation as though they were probable.

Moreover, given that, in our days, the error of the Jansenists has been overthrown, incautious laxity is the danger that threatens men, not too much austerity. Indeed, the sons of men find that truths are diminished among them, and on the pretext of liberality, it is too frequently the case that the judgments of God are emptied of their power.

* * *

Because the probabiliorists and probabilists, just as the equiprobabilists, however, can each follow his own opinion with the Church's tolerance, practical doubts arise and must be resolved in order that each person may consult his conscience.

Thus, we have several sub-questions that may be asked.

Sub-question 1: *Are probabiliorists permitted to indifferently follow one or the other opinion or system and to conduct themselves at one time like equiprobabilists and at another time like probabilists? (And the same thing can be asked concerning equiprobabilists and probablists.)*

I have two responses. First, *per se*, no. Indeed, since the Probabiliorists believe that one is not permitted to follow a less safe but equally probable opinion in a contest with one that is safer and more probable, were one to act in this manner, he would not act out of the certitude of science [in the prudential sense explained earlier] and thus would sin, for everything that is not from faith [i.e., certitude] is a sin.

Second, *per accidens*, however, yes: namely, if one sets aside such conscience and on the basis of intrinsic or extrinsic reasons changes his opinion universally or particularly, thus forming for himself a practically certain *dictamen* so as to act prudently.

The same thing must be said concerning those equiprobabilists who would like to follow probabilism. One can, however, follow an opinion that is equally probable or more probable in favor of the law.

Probabilists, however, always permissibly (at least in virtue of a counsel) can follow an opinion that is certainly more probable or equally probable, since such an opinion approaches more closely to the truth and sometimes is safer.

Sub-question 2: *Are probabiliorists, equiprobabilists, and probabilists permitted to follow the opinion that is held by others as being more probable, equally probable, and probable, although it does not appear to him as such?*
I have two responses.

First, *per se,* no, for the same reason given in the preceding response, namely that by acting in this way, one would not act from faith [i.e., certitude]. Indeed, in order to act prudently, probabiliorists must judge that a given opinion is truly more probable. If, however, someone weighs out the intrinsic or extrinsic reasons and recognizes that an opinion which others hold as being more probable in reality is not more probable but, instead, is less probable or false, such a person cannot form a practically certain conscience for himself from such an opinion. And the same must be said from the perspective of an equiprobabilist and a probabilist. Indeed, as Gury says (cf. no. 77, 2): "You are not permitted to follow an opinion that is probable for others but is entirely false to you, for if you actually judge that something is not permitted and then do it, you are aware of the sin involved in that action and therefore act against your conscience."

Second, *per accidens,* I answer affirmatively. This is so because, without a doubt, someone can set aside such conscience and, after looking further into the matter and taking both sides back into account, judge that such an opinion that is defended by others is truly more probable, equally probable, or probable.

Sub-question 3: *Must a probabiliorist or equiprobabilist who is consulted about the permissibility or impermissibility of a given action respond to someone taking counsel about the position that he holds?*
I respond affirmatively but not, however, *without qualification* and *absolutely.* The first reason is that counsel, like other moral acts, must proceed from certitude of conscience. The second reason is that, as St. Alphonsus says, he himself is not the judge of the opinions that are held by others as being truly probable and sometimes being certainly probable.

Sub-question 4: *Can (and ought) a confessor absolve a penitent who wishes to follow an opinion opposed to the position that he holds?*
I have two responses. First, I respond *affirmatively*, if the penitent adheres to a truly and solidly probable opinion[374] and has a different disposition on the mater than does he [*et aliundè sit dispositus*]. The reason for this conclusion is that because the penitent who is correctly disposed and has made his confession has a strict right to absolution, and the confessor is not the judge of opinions but only of the disposition of the penitent.[375]

Second, I respond that if the penitent holds an opinion that may have some probability, so that the confessor, although he may not hold that it is solidly probable, nonetheless cannot think that it is entirely false, then one should follow St. Alphonsus in making a distinction. (1) On the one hand, if the penitent is so unlearned [*indoctus*] point that he could not form a right conscience for himself on the basis of that opinion's probability, it is certain in that case that he cannot be absolved. (2) On the other hand, however, when the penitent is capable of forming a right conscience for himself, the common opinion teaches that in that case the confessor can provide absolution and must do so under pain of mortal sin [*sub gravi*], at least if the confession was made concerning a weighty matter.[376]

Third, I respond that if the penitent holds an opinion that appears to be clearly false, he must not be absolved, as St. Alphonsus says[377] along with St. Antoninus.[378]

Sub-question 5: *Is a probablist, faced with a number of probable opinions, permitted to follow sometimes this one, and sometimes that one?*

374. Namely that which, taken by itself, one judges to be such. (Editor's Note, Ambroise Gardeil)

375. St. Alphonsus, *Theol. Mor.*, bk. 7, H. no. 604.

376. See St. Alphonsus, *Homo apost.*, tract. 16, no. 118.

377. See St. Alphonsus, *Theol. Mor.*, bk. 6, no. 604.

378. Lehmkuhl responds, in no. 118 of the 6th edition (1874) of his *Theologia moralis*: "Even if a given opinion seems certainly false, one can and must absolve the penitent who, instructed either by himself or by another learned person (a confessor), wishes to follow the contrary opinion which externally is sufficiently probable. Yet, it is likewise the case that the confessor who holds that a given opinion is certainly false can (nay sometimes out of charity must) indicate that he is someone who holds a contrary opinion." I only refer to this position. Let the prudent reader judge this matter.

In the 9th edition in 1910, Fr. Lehmkuhl has indeed changed the place of this opinion but has not changed the opinion itself. See no. 209, vol. 1, p. 130. (Editor's Note, Ambroise Gardeil)

I respond negatively as regards the opinion of equiprobabilism, for [they hold that] in a contest between equally probable opinions, we are bound to follow the safer opinion which the title of possession favors.

I respond positively as regards the opinion of certain probabilists. "Because," writes Gury,[379] "among probable opinions nothing is given as being safer or more secure to the other one. Indeed, all are equally secure."[380]

Sub-question 6: *Is a Probabilist permitted to make use of two opinions in one and the same act?*

If one law would thus be violated, I respond negatively. (Cf. Marc, no. 90.) On this matter, see Ballerini in no. 80, q. 7, note b, summarizing Fr. Gury's response. He writes:

> Take care, however, lest you draw the matter into such an absurd contradiction that, while doing something as being morally befitting (on the basis of one opinion), you [simultaneously] would reject something as morally unbefitting (precisely because of the opposite opinion). Thus, you would act absurdly if, through the use of one probable opinion you were to take possession of an inheritance coming from a will that would be lacking in legal form and, then, on the pretext of another opinion, which refuses to allow this will to be valid, you would refuse to pay out a bequest. Indeed, he who accepts the inheritance also assumes the burdens necessarily joined to it.[381]

---

379. Gury, op cit., no. 80, q. 7.

380. See Lehmkuhl, no. 114: "*Per se* nothing prevents me from practically following one or the other opinion either of which is probable in itself and to me. On account of something else, however, it can happen that one sometimes is not permitted [to act in this or that way] or that it *would not be expedient*. For example, consider a judge who, if he were to follow either of the opinions, would not escape just censure for being fickle or, in certain circumstances, even the stain [*labem*] of injustice.)" Here, our author puts in his own manuscript the emphasis upon this astonishing expression, "would not be expedient [*non expediat*]." Moreover, it is entirely the same as what Fr. Lehmkuhl advances in the most recent, 9th edition of the text, 1910, no. 204, vol. 1, p. 128. (Editor's Note, Ambroise Gardeil)

381. See Lehmkuhl, op. cit., no. 115 (ed. 1910, no. 205).

BIBLIOGRAPHY

An index of works used in the course of this book, with the editions that the author most frequently utilized.

St. Albert the Great, O.P. *Opera omnia*. 21 vols. in folio. Lyon, 1551; 38 vols. in quarto. Paris: Vivès, 1890.

St. Antoninus (O.P.). *Summa theologica*. 4 vols. in folio. Verona, 1740.

Aristotle. *Opera omnia*. Edited by Ambroise Firmin-Didot. Paris: Didot, 1850.

St. Augustine. *Opera omnia*. Migne, *Patrologia latina*, vols. 32–47.

Billuart, Charles René (O.P.). *Summa Sancti Thomae Aquinatis hodiernis academiarum moribus accommodata*. 8 vols. in quarto. Arras, 1876; 9 vols. in octavo. Lyon / Paris: Guyot / Mellier, 1847, and Paris: Lecoffre, 1874.

St. Bonaventure (O.F.M.). *Opera omnia*. 10 vols in folio. Quaracchi, 1882–1901.

Boniface VIII. *Decretalium sextus liber*. 1 vol. in folio. Turin, 1588.

Digestorum. See *Corpus iuris civilis*. 1 vol. in folio. Turin, 1588.

Thomas de Vio Cajetan, O.P. *Commentaria in Summam theologicam D. Thomae Aq*. 5 vols. in folio. Padua, 1698. Leonine edition, 9 vols. in fol. Rome, 1888ff.

____. *Summa de peccatis et Novi Testamenti ientacula*. 1 vol. in octavo. Rome, 1523.

Mechior Cano, O.P. *De locis*. 2 vols in octavo. Madrid, 1776.

Daniello Concina, O.P. *Ad theologiam christianam dogmatico-moralem Apparatus*. 2 vols. in quarto; 2nd vol. (*De conscientia et Probabilismo*). Rome and Venice, 1751.

Denzinger, Heinrich. *Enchiridion Symbolorum et definitionum etc.* Würtzburg, 1865. Fribourg im Breisgau: Herder, 1908.[382]

Gonet, Jean-Baptiste (O.P.). *Clypeus thomisticus.* 6th ed. 6 vols. in folio. Lyon, 1681.

González, Thyrsus (S.J.). *Fundamentum theologiae moralis.* 1 vol. in octavo. Coloniae Agripp., 1694.

Gosset. *Théologie morale.* 2 vols. in octavo. Paris, 1848.

Gratian. *Decretum.* 1 vol. in folio. Turin, 1588.

Gregory the Great, O.S.B. *Pastoralis liber.* Migne, *PL* 77.

Gregory IX. *Decretales.* 1 vol. in folio. Turin, 1588.

Gury, Jean-Pierre (S.J.). *Compendium theologiae moralis.* Lyon: Perisse, 1850; Parma: 1852; Lyon / Paris: H. Pelagaud, 1869.

______., and Antonio Ballerini, S.J. *Compendium theologiae moralis.* 2 vols. in octavo. Rome-Turin: Ex Typographia Polyglotta, 1872 and 1882.

John of St. Thomas, O.P. *Cursus theologicus,* 9 vols. in quarto. Paris: Vivès, 1883ff.

Lehmkuhl, Augustin (S.J.). *Theologia moralis.* 2 vols. in octavo. Fribourg im Bresgau, 1893.

De Liguouri, St. Alphonsus Marie (C.SS. R.). *Theologia moralis.* 6 vols. in duodecimo. Edited by Michael Heilig. Paris, n.d.[383]

382. Compare this 4th Würzburg edition, which the author used, with the 10th edition of Friburg im Breisgau.

383. Compare the texts taken from this edition with the most recent primary edition: S. Alphonsi Mariae de Ligorio, C.SS.R.F., *Theologia moralis,* ed. Leonardo Gaudé, 4 vols. in quarto (Rome: Typis Polyglottis Vaticanis, 1905ff.). In the footnotes, the *Heilig* edition is indicated by "H" and the *Gaudé* edition by G.

Mandonnet, Pierre (O.P.). "Le décret d'Innocent XI et le Probabilisme." *Revue thomiste* (1901): 460–481, 520–539, 652–673; (1902): 676–698.

____. "La position du Probabilisme dans l'Eglise catholique." *Revue thomiste* (1902): 5–20.

____. "De la valeur des theories sur la probabilité morale." *Revue thomiste* (1902): 314–335.

Marc, Clément (C.SS.R.). *Institutiones morales Alphonsianae.* 2 vols. Rome: Cuggiani, 1887

Neyraguet, Deotat. *Compendium theologiae moralis S. Alphonsi de Ligorio.* Toulouse, 1839.

St. Raymond of Peñafort, O.P. *Summa.* Edited by Laget. Lyon, 1718. Appendix *De regulis iuris canonici*, after the *Index Rerum*, extracted from the Sixth Book.

Redemptoris (cura et studio quorumdam theologorum e Congretatione SS). *Vindiciae Alphonsianae, seu Doctoris Ecclesiae S. Alphonsi de Ligorio, doctrina moralis vindicata.* Amended and augmented edition. 2 vols. in octavo. Paris and Turin: Casterman, 1874.

____. *Prefatio apologetica* of the other edition the *Vindiciae Alphonsianae.* This brings together a prefatory discussion of the authority of St. Alphonsus's moral doctrine as well as an apologetic discussion of St. Alphonsus's moral system, 213pp. (These are excerpted from the former work.)

Salmanticenses (O.C.). *Cursus theologicus.* 20 vols. in octavo. Paris: Palmé, 1876.

Salmanticenses (O.C.). *Cursus theologiae moralis.* 3 vols. in folio. Venice, 1734.

Scavini, Pietro. *Theologia moralis universa, ad mentem S. Alphonsi.* 4 vols. in octavo. Paris: Lecoffre, 1863.

De Soto, Domingo (O.P.). *In Dialecticam Aristotelis.* 1 vol. in quarto. Salamanca, 1554.

Suarez, Francisco (S.J.). *Opera omnia.* 28 vols. in quarto. Paris: Vivès, 1856ff.

St. Thomas Aquinas, O.P. *Opera omnia.* 25 vols. in folio. Parma, 1852–1873.

Zigliara, Tommaso Maria (O.P.). *Summa philosophica.* 3 vols. in duodecimo. 5th edition. Lyon and Paris: Delhomme et Briguet, 1884.

BENOÎT-HENRI MERKELBACH, O.P.

* * *

Treatise on Conscience in General

ORIGINAL TEXT

Merkelbach, Benoît-Henri. "Tractatus de conscientia in generali." In *Summa theologiae moralis*, 5th ed., vol. 1, 186-206. Paris: Desclée de Brouwer, 1946.

* * *

TRANSLATOR'S INTRODUCTION

As I noted earlier in my introductions, I have chosen, in the interest of space, not to include Fr. Merkelbach's lengthy, yet certainly deserving, extension of the treatise on prudence, wherein he lays out a presentation of how he believes the various virtues connected to prudence (above all *synesis* and *gnome*) are involved in forming a right and certain judgment of conscience. Nonetheless, just as Fr. Beaudouin's *Tractatus de conscientia* is placed in the context of the treatise on human acts in the *Prima secundae* (precisely after the so-called subtreatise on morality), Fr. Merkelbach also includes a sub-treatise on conscience *in generali* in the same treatise. His presentation is quite clear and testifies to the great strength of the developed scholastic tradition in his time. Indeed, in the full "manual" on moral theology, this text is no mere "handbook" summary but, instead, a systematic and quite-detailed exposition of the state of Thomist moral theology (arguably the best of all the Thomist manuals of the day, better even than that of Prümmer—although more technical and, hence, more difficult). This selection is relatively brief, but the clarity summarizes much of what had been inherited by the Thomist school up to the 1930s. Textbooks of this level of detail, concern for the preceding tradition, and synthetic outlook are a great *desideratum* in our contemporary theological environment. We can only draw a small sampling from so excellent a text, today almost forgotten after the recent spate of anti-scholasticism.

* * *

TREATISE ON CONSCIENCE IN GENERAL

Benoît-Henri Merkelbach, O.P.

INTRODUCTION

198. *Object of this treatise.* After considering the *end* [in the treatise on beatitude] and *human acts* in themselves (i.e., from the perspective of their *material* and *formal* elements), we must now treat of: first, *the rules* which must measure these acts (i.e., their exemplar cause) and second, their *principles* (i.e., their efficient cause). The principles of human acts are man's *powers*, a topic that is treated in philosophy, as well as *habitus*[1] (whether good or evil), which are treated in the treatise on *habitus* and virtues. There are, however, two rules of human acts: *law* (their remote, objective, and extrinsic rule), and *conscience* (their proximate, subjective, and intrinsic rule). Thus, after having treated human acts, the next treatise that logically follows is that which is concerned with their proximate rule (i.e., conscience). Indeed, just as the archer must know the rules for aiming correctly at his target, so too man must know the rules by which his acts may are rendered orderable to the ultimate end.

Moreover, general moral theology is only concerned with conscience *in general.* In other words, it is concerned with what it must be in order that it may be the rule of our acts, as well as the qualities required for this to be the case. In no way, however, does general moral theology considers each particular state of conscience or all the various species of conscience; nor does it consider the ways that one may prudently form one's conscience, nor the ways that one can sin against it. All of this belongs to special moral theology,[2] indeed to the treatise concerned with the cardinal virtue of prudence, which has right and well-formed conscience as its act. Accordingly, we are here concerned with discussing the following three issues:[3]

1. On moral conscience considered in itself (i.e., in its *physical* or *psychological existence*).
2. On conscience as the rule of moral acts (i.e., in its *moral existence*) and the qualities required for moral conscience, namely: (a) its truth and rectitude, considered from the perspective of the object; and (b) its certitude, considered from the perspective of the subject.
3. On conscience as the rule of supernatural acts (i.e., according to its *supernatural existence*).

QUESTION I: ON MORAL CONSCIENCE, CONSIDERED IN ITSELF IN ITS PSYCHOLOGICAL BEING

ST I, q. 79, a. 13; *De Veritate*, q. 17, a. 1-3; *In II Sent.*, d. 24, q. 2, a. 4

199. *Notions.* "Conscience" (συνείδησις), is taken from the term "*conscire*" (i.e., to know together). Etymologically speaking, it means, in a way, "with another knowledge." Therefore, it sometimes signifies knowledge had *with others*, or, the common knowledge had by multiple people (Cicero, *First Oration Against Catiline*, 1; Tacitus, *Agricola*, 2). More commonly, however, it means knowledge of one thing with its own intrinsic meaning [*scientiam unius apud se servatam*], although considered and applied *to something else*. Thus, *properly speaking*, it implies the ordering of knowledge

1. **Translator's Note:** As a rule, I do not translate "habitus" as "habit", given that the latter can seem too passive an expression. For a discussion related to this issue, one might consult the excellent work, Yves R. Simon, *The Definition of Moral Virtue*, ed. Vukan Kuic (New York: Fordham University Press, 1999).
2. **Translator's Note:** That is, to the treatises on the particular virtues, included by St. Thomas in his *ST* II-II.
3. For the *general* part of the doctrine on conscience, see *ST* I-II, q. 19, a. 3, 5, and 6; *De veritate*, q. 17; *In II Sent.*, d. 24, q. 2, a. 4 and d. 29, q. 3, a. 1-3; *Quod.* III, q. 12; VIII, q. 6, a. 3 and 5. Also, see the relevant treatment in St. Antoninus's *Summa theologica moralis*, St. Alphonsus's *Theologia moralis*, as well as in Billuart, Bouquillon, Raphaël a S. Joseph, Theologia Mechliniensis, and Haine. Likewise, consult Fr. Beaudouin's *Tractatus de conscientia*; Noble, *La conscience morale*; Dumas, *Theologia moralis thomistica*, vol. 1.

to something and is *the act* by which we apply knowledge to a particular thing that is done. Now, this can take place in two ways:

1. By applying knowledge to considering that something may exist or will come into existence. In this case, we are speaking of the merely *psychological* conscience by which we know that we are doing something or recognize that we did or did not do something. This kind of conscience is said to testify and is enclosed within our interior senses and memory. (Cf. Gen. 43:22; Rom. 9:1; Eccl. 7:23; 2 Cor. 4:2 and 5:11.)
2. It can also come about by applying knowledge to considering whether something is or was rightly done or not, and this is *moral* conscience, which is a judgment about good and evil acts and an application of moral knowledge to our human works. In its own turn, this kind of conscience is itself twofold, for moral knowledge [*scientia*] can be applied:
   a. To examining something that was done and to judging whether or not it was done rightly. This is *consequent* conscience, which is said to excuse or accuse (or, gnaw) (cf. Heb. 9:14; Rom. 2:15; Tit. 1:15; 2 Tim. 1:3; 2 Cor. 1:12; Is. 66:24; Mk. 9:40; DR): "Where their worm (i.e., conscience) dieth not."
   b. To directing something that still can be done and to judging that this is good and to be done or evil and not done. This is *antecedent* conscience, which is said to incite, induce, bind, urge, or hinder (cf. Rom. 13:5). This is a judgment about the morality of an act to be individually posited here and now and is an application of moral knowledge [*scientiae*] to a determinate act. And this is moral conscience in the strict sense, for it alone is the rule of human acts. This is what we are discussing here in the current treatise.

The term "conscience," is sometimes, however *improperly* understood as referring to either: (1) its object (or, the thing decided upon [*re conscita*]), i.e., that which is in our conscience (cf. 1 Tim. 1:5) as when someone says, "I will tell you my conscience," "to examine one's conscience or stain or purify it"; or, (2) its causes and, then, it is understood as being the *habitus* by means of which we are rendered able to judge good and evil[4] as well as the habitual disposition by which we are inclined toward judging in this or that way about an actions moral goodness [*honestate*]. And it is also understood as being knowledge of the law, that is to say, a universal judgment concerning the morality of acts in general without us applying that to a determinate act. Thus, we say that a human person having reached the age of reason [*hominem septennium*] has awareness [*conscientiam*] of good and evil.

200. *Antecedent conscience is a judgment,* but not every antecedent judgment is conscience. Indeed, a variety of judgments exist:

1. First, there is a *merely speculative* judgment, *solely* concerned with the *truth* of the thing under consideration, without any relation to activity. For example, one may ask whether Peter possesses any money.
2. Second, there is a *speculatively-practical* judgment (i.e., a speculative judgment concerning doable things [*praxim*]) concerning *the morality* of our acts *in general* and in the abstract, to the extent that they are considered in themselves and without being ordered to a subject who is active here and now. That is, it is a judgment concerning *objective and material moral fittingness,* which itself can be considered from two perspectives.
   a. On the one hand, man can make entirely universal moral judgments by which he assents to the first practical principles (e.g., "Good is to be done and evil avoided"; "No injury is to be inflicted upon someone"; "Do not do to another what you would not wish to be done to yourself"; "The Highest Good is to be loved"; and so forth). The intellect does not fall into error about these sorts of things, for it naturally possesses a *habitus* (or, facility [*facilitatem*]) for perceiving and enunciating them, namely, *synderesis.*
   b. On the other hand, man can make less universal judgments, by which he assents to general conclusions de-

4. This is called "synderesis" (συντήρησις = maintenance, namely, of the first principles of moral matters) which, therefore, is called the "spark of conscience" and a small flame that is derived from the divine light.

duced immediately or mediately from first principles (e.g. "Theft must be avoided"; "Fornication is not permitted"; and so forth). The intellect can sometimes fall into error about these sorts of things. Nonetheless, it can acquire a *habitus* for drawing such conclusions, namely the *habitus* of *moral science*.

3. Third, there is a *practically-practical* judgment concerning *the morality* of an act *in particular*, to be concretely posited here and now by an acting subject. By means of this kind of judgment, we apply the first, universal principles, as well as moral science, to a particular case in particular conclusions. For example: "To [here and] now take this sum of money from Peter, without any reason and without him knowing that I am doing so, would be to commit theft, which is something to be avoided." This is a particular judgment of conscience, which is immediately ordered to activity and concerned with *subjective and formal moral befittingness*. Moreover, it is proximately practical in relation to the universal judgments made by *synderesis* and moral science, which are remotely practical. Hence, some people call it the *ultimate practical judgment*, not *simpliciter* but, rather, among the three judgments that are *concerned with moral befittingness*.
4. Finally, there is the *ultimate-practical* judgment (or, the one that discerns the choice to be made). Here, we are not speaking about a judgment concerned with the morality of the act but, rather, with the *suitability* [*convenientia*] of the act (i.e., concerning what is suitable to choose and do here and now, whether it is good or evil). This follows upon the [judgment of] conscience by which one ought to be directed and yet can be contrary to it, for example, if I were to take Peter's money although [my judgment of] conscience were to declare that this action is prohibited.

201. *Conscience is defined*: "A *dictamen* or judgment of the practical intellect affirming that a particular act is permitted or not permitted and therefore must be done (or, can be done) or must be set aside by us. The definition indicates the following:

1. The *genus* to which conscience pertains, namely "a judgment or *dictamen*." In this way, it is distinguished from: *reason*, which is a power; from *synderesis*, which is the *habitus* of first practical principles by which we are rendered capable of having conscience; from *moral science*, which is habitual acquired knowledge concerning the morality of acts in general; and from *prudence*, which is a virtue inclining one to make a right assessment concerning all the circumstances of a concrete act and to make a right judgment concerning its morality (in other words, inclining one to have right conscience and to command what it declares). Indeed, conscience is not a *habitus* but, instead, is an act. Therefore, it is easily reformed and set aside; and if it is said to "abide," this must not be understood as though it would abide in itself but, rather, in its causes, which are reason and *synderesis*, or even in the others [i.e., moral science and prudence].
2. The *subject* in which it resides:
   a. *The intellect*: For a judgment does not exist in the will but, rather, precedes it so that it may will the good and flee evil. And if conscience is said to be good or evil, it is not such formally in itself (as if it were the subject of goodness) but, instead, is called good or evil in its role as a rule [*regulative*] and based on its effect inasmuch as it directs good or evil deeds.
   b. Indeed, it is said to be in the *practical* intellect, for it does not stop in the contemplation of the truth but, rather, directs the deed to be pursued. Thus, it is distinguished from merely speculative judgments and from psychological conscience.
3. *It specific object*:
   a. *Affirming that a particular act* (i.e., how it can be posited, concretely, with an eye to the end and the circumstances involved here and now). Thus, it is distinguished from the speculatively practical judgments of moral science.
   b. *Is permitted or not permitted*. Thus, it differs from other practical judgments which are concerned with usefulness, appropriateness [*convenientia*], easiness, and so forth,

among the various other things [involved in / presupposed by] the ultimate practical judgment [*inter alia a iudicio ultimo practico*].

c. *And therefore here and now must be done or set aside*: for it judges concerning the act to be done, not concerning an act that was done in the past. In this way, it is distinguished from consequent conscience.

d. *By us*: for conscience is only concerned with one's own acts and not with someone else's (cf. Rom. 14:4; 1 Cor. 4:4–5).

202. *Conscience is a conclusion of practical reasoning.* Its major premise is drawn from *synderesis* (e.g., "Evil is to be avoided")[5] and its minor from reason (e.g., "Now, to have sex with a given married woman is evil"). Conscience infers the conclusion, "Therefore, here and now it is not permitted for me to have sex with this woman."

Just as there can be a false conclusion in speculative reasoning, however, so too can there be a false conclusion in conscience. This can happen either:

1. *From the perspective of the form of one's reasoning*, because the conclusion is wrongly deduced from true principles which are not validly applied [in these circumstances]. Thus, for example: "God is to be obeyed. Now, God commands that we come to the aid of the poor. Therefore, here and now, I must come to the aid of this neighbor of mine."
2. Or, *from the perspective of the matter reasoned about*, because it is deduced from a false principle. For example: "That which is not prohibited is not evil. Now, sexual intercourse with a given

5. More recent authors are in the habit of saying that the major premise of the syllogism giving rise to conscience is a principle of law, also thinking of a principle deduced from the first and most universal principles of morals. Nay, certain people even say that the major premise must always be a principle, not indeed of *synderesis*, but of moral science, and that the minor alone asserts the fact to which the principle would be applied. In contrast, however, to this, St. Thomas clearly and constantly teaches that the major premise is an utterly universal principle *of synderesis, which cannot err.* If conscience is said to be an application of *science* to a particular case, this must be understood as pertaining to the syllogism's minor premise, which is affirmed by reason. Finally, moral science, together with a right estimation of the particular circumstances, together concur in the enunciation of this premise. See *De veritate*, q. 17, a. 2 and *In II Sent.*, d. 24, q. 2, a. 4.

> unmarried woman [*mulieri solute*] is not prohibited. Therefore, it is not evil." For, although there cannot be falsity in the major premise (since synderesis cannot err concerning first principles), reason nonetheless can err in the minor concerning particular principles.[6]

203. *Principle: Conscience is the proximate and subjective rule of human acts.* It does not obligate by itself [*per se*] and in virtue of itself alone. Instead, it obligates in virtue of the divine precept because it applies the objective and remote rule (or, the law) to a particular case as ordered to a [given] subject's activity. This is akin to the decreeing of a command by the emperor through a legate. If the emperor's command could only reach the citizens by means of a legate, the legate's command only obligates because it promulgates the emperor's command (cf. *ST* I-II, q. 19, a. 4, ad 2; *In II Sent.*, d. 39, q. 3, a. 3, ad 3). Thus, conscience is an intimation and kind of promulgation of the law concerning an act to be posited here and now:

> As St. Bonaventure says, in *In II Sent.*, d. 39, a. 1, q. 3, conscience is, as it were, *God's herald* and envoy, and it does not command what it says on its own authority but, instead, commands as if it were coming from God, as does a *herald* when he makes the king's edict known. Hence, conscience has the power of binding.

---

6. Not every [act of] conscience can be false, however, for falsity is not always possible for every minor premise. This happens when it is a question of immediate conclusions which are directly taken from first principles and are in the minor premise only as a particular enunciation of that which is universally contained in the major premise. Thus, "No injury is to be inflicted upon a man. Now, Peter is a man. Therefore, no injury is to be inflicted upon Peter." Or, "The highest Good must be loved. Therefore, God must be loved by me." Let St. Thomas himself be heard on this matter, in his words drawn from *De veritate*, q. 17, a. 2: "Nonetheless, note that conscience cannot err about certain things, namely, when that particular act to which conscience is applied has a universal judgment concerning it in *synderesis*. For, just as in speculative cognition there cannot be errors concerning particular conclusions that directly fall under universal principles in the same terms (e.g., as nobody is deceived in the judgment, 'This whole is greater than its part,' just as nobody is deceived in the judgment, 'Every whole is greater than its part'), so too nobody can err in judgments such as, 'God must not be loved by me,' or 'A given evil must be done.' This is so because in either sort of judgment (i.e., whether concerning things to be known or things to be done) the major premise (inasmuch as it exists in a universal principle) as well as the minor premise (by means of which the same thing is predicated in a particular fashion) are *per se nota*, as when one says, 'Every whole is greater than its part. This is a whole. Therefore, it is greater than its part.'"

St. Thomas makes use of another comparison in *De veritate*, q. 17, a. 3, namely, to a physical chain by which we are bound only if it is in contact with the body and applied to it. Thus, the moral chain (or, the law) binds only through the application of the law which takes place through knowledge of the precept and conscience:

> Thus, in matters pertaining to the will, the command of a ruler is related to the kind of binding that the will can undergo, just as a bodily action is related to the binding of bodily things with a coercive necessity. The action of a bodily agent, however, never imposes necessity upon another thing unless its action comes into contact with the thing upon which it acts. Thus, someone is not bound by the command of a given king or lord unless his command reaches the person who is commanded. Now, it reaches such a person through knowledge. Thus, someone is bound by a precept only through knowledge of that command.... In bodily beings a bodily agent only acts through contact; so too, in spiritual beings, a command binds only through knowledge. And therefore, just as touch acts through the same power as that through which the power of the agent acts (since touch acts only through the agent's power, and the agent's power acts only through touch), so too *the precept and conscience both bind through the same power, since the command binds only through the power of knowledge and knowledge through the power of the precept. Thus, since conscience is nothing other than the application of knowledge to an act, it is clear that conscience is said to bind in virtue of the divine command.*

Therefore, it follows that conscience obligates more than the command of a human superior: "Conscience binds only on the strength of the divine command... Thus, since the divine command obligates against the command of a superior and obligates more than a superior's command, the bond of conscience will be greater than the bond of a superior's command and conscience will bind even when a superior's command exists but is opposed to what conscience commands" (*De veritate*, q. 17, a. 5).

As is the case for law, however, conscience also, on account of the way it binds (that is, on account of its obligation) is: *binding* (or prescriptive) whether negatively *prohibiting* or positively *commanding*; or *non-binding* (or non-prescriptive), which is either *permitting* or *counseling*.

204. *An observation.* Only antecedent conscience is the rule of acts, for it alone flows over into an act. Consequent conscience, however, which presupposes that an act has occurred is not such a rule. Unsophisticated thinkers [*rudibus*] think that the opposite is the case. Such people must be told, however, that the goodness or wickedness of a past act must be judged in accord with the knowledge which the agent had before performing the act, not in accord with the knowledge had after the fact.

QUESTION 2: ON CONSCIENCE INASMUCH AS IT IS THE RULE OF MORAL ACTS

205. *Principle.* Thus, we may never permissibly act against the rule of human actions when it commands or prohibits something. We may always, however, permissibly act in accord with it if it has the appropriate qualities.

Proof. To act against conscience includes an evil will, for that is nothing other than to do what one judges to be prohibited by God or to not do what is commanded (cf. Rom. 14:23). Thus, we have this axiom: "Whatever is done against conscience advances us on the road to Gehenna." This must be understood as holding for commanding and prohibiting conscience, not, however, for counseling and permitting conscience, given that those forms of conscience do not bind in an obligatory manner. In contrast, to act in accord with conscience is to do what we judge to be commanded (or at least permitted) by God. Now, to do what we judge to be commanded or permitted by God *of itself* includes the intention to conform oneself to the law and to God's will. Therefore, it is *per se* permitted, that is, when that judgment of conscience has the appropriate qualities, which we will now discuss.

There are two kinds of such qualities. On the part of the object, truth and rectitude must be present. On the part of the subject (or, of the assent) there must be certitude. Indeed, conscience is the rule and measure of human acts. Now, every measure must be adequate (i.e., true and right, not false) and certain (i.e., not ambiguous). Therefore, conscience must be true and right (from the perspective of the object) and certain (from that of the subject).

Article 1: *On Rectitude of Conscience*

ST I-II, q. 19, a. 3, 5, 6; *De veritate*, q. 17, a. 2-4; *In* II *Sent*, d. 39, q. 3, a. 3; Quodl. III, q. 12, a. 1 and 2.

206. *Notions*. Conscience must be *right*. Two kinds of conscience are distinguished, however, *from the perspective of the object* (or, conformity with the law), namely, true and erroneous conscience, inasmuch as it declares truth or falsity. *True* conscience is that which, on the basis of true principles, declares that some particular action is permitted or not permitted when it truly is such (namely, when it is truly good or evil). *Erroneous* conscience is that which, on the basis of false principles that nonetheless are thought to be true, declares that some particular action is permitted or not permitted when it in reality is not such (e.g., declaring to be evil that which is either good or intrinsically indifferent or declaring to be good that which is intrinsically evil). It is said to be *vinicibly* erroneous if it can be overcome with moral diligence. It is said to be *invincibly* erroneous if it cannot be overcome with moral diligence either because someone has not had a thought concerning the truth being looked into (being completely ignorant thereof and also not having some sort of vague idea about it), or because even upon sincere inquiry into the truth he does not arrive at it. Now, if conscience were to err from an error that formerly was vincible but now is invincible, even if the antecedent error was a sin (and all the graver so, to the degree that the foreseen course of action was, of itself, more evil) nonetheless, this *current* judgment of conscience is in fact invincibly ignorant.

Some wonder,however, whether both forms of conscience (i.e., true and erroneous) are rules of action and, in some manner, sufficiently right. To resolve this question, many have distinguished negative conformity from positive conformity with conscience, saying that every form of conscience always obligates so that we cannot act against it. They add, however, that some forms (namely, erroneous conscience) do not obligate so that we may act in accord with it. In other words, it negatively is the rule of action, meaning that it is never permitted that one act against any form of conscience, but we are not always required to positively act in accord with it. In general, however, this distinction is useless. For he who does not act in accord with commanding and prohibiting conscience, not doing what it commands nor avoiding what it prohibits, by that very fact also acts against conscience, for he does what is prohibited or fails to do what is commanded. Hence, we will simultaneously respond to both cases with the same answer.

207. *Principle 1.* True conscience is essentially [*per se*] the rule of acting so that if it is commanding or prohibiting, we are bound to be in conformity with it both negatively (i.e., by not acting against it) and positively (i.e., by acting in accord with it).

Let us consider the parts of this principle.

1. "*Per se.*" In other words, this holds of its very nature, for it faithfully presents the law as it is in itself. Hence, it binds absolutely and in every occurrence. Therefore, the act that is conformed to it is *essentially* [*per se*] good.
2. "If it is commanding or prohibiting." If it counsels or permits, one is not unpermitted to act against it, for we are not bound to do or not do something which is neither commanded nor prohibited by any law. Indeed, counseling conscience binds insofar as we may not hold in scorn what it counsels, but its binding force does not go so far as to require us to fulfill what it counsels. We always, however, can act according to true conscience, nay, we even have the *right* to act thus.

Proofs. First, *from Scripture* (Rom. 14:23): "Everything that is not from faith (i.e., good faith) is a sin." That is, he who does not act out of belief [*credulitate*], persuasion, [or] the judgment of conscience sins. This is how the Fathers generally understood the meaning of this passage.

Second, *from reason*: Since conscience intimates and applies the law, it is the proximate rule of human acts according to which their moral being [*esse morale*] is measured. True conscience, however, rightly applies the law, for it is a faithful herald. Therefore, the act which falls short of this measure is not conformed to the law but, instead, is morally evil. The point is confirmed as follows: true conscience is the law itself, certainly known by us and applied to an act; now we are bound to follow the law when it is known; therefore, [we are bound to follow our conscience.]

208. *Principle 2.* Invincibly erroneous conscience is accidentally [*per accidens*] the rule of action, so that if it is a commanding or prohibiting form of conscience, we are bound to be conformed to it both negatively (i.e., by not acting against it) and positively (i.e., by acting in accord with it).

Let us consider the parts of this principle:

1. "*Per accidens.*" In other words, not of its very nature (for it is not conformed to the law) but, rather, on account of ignorance (for it is believed to be in conformity with it). Therefore, it does not bind in every occurrence but, rather does so conditionally [*sub conditione*], as long as it lasts and for as long as it is not set aside. Therefore, the act conformed to it is good *per accidens*.
2. "If it is a commanding or prohibiting form of conscience." For if it were counseling or permitting conscience, it is not impermissible to act against it, for invincible error excuses from sin. We do not, however, have a *right* to act in accord with it, for there is no such thing as a right to follow error.

Proofs. First, *from Scripture*. He who acts against invincibly erroneous conscience does not act from faith (or from persuasion) and, hence, according to the Apostle (in Rom. 14:23), he sins. This is even more obvious from the context here. In this passage, the Apostle is speaking about the eating of foods which are not *per se* evil but, instead, were erroneously held by many to be unclean inasmuch as they were prohibited by the Law of Moses. Thus, St. Paul taught that anyone who truly believed that such food was unclean but nonetheless ate it sinned, for, as he writes in v. 14 (DR): "I know, and am confident in the Lord Jesus, that nothing is unclean of itself: but to him that esteemeth any thing to be unclean, to him it is unclean"; that is: *I am certain that no food is unclean by its very nature, except in the case of the person who believes that it is unclean*. And, in v. 23 (DR) he writes: "But he that discerneth, if he eat, is condemned; because not of faith. For all that is not of faith is sin"; that is: if someone doubts the permissibility of eating a given food but nonetheless eats it, doubting whether it is "clean," that person is condemned, for he does not eat out of persuasion of conscience (i.e., in good faith). *A fortiori*, this holds true for the person who eats what he certainly judges to be unclean.

Similarly, St. Paul writes in 1 Cor. 8:7 (DR): "For some until this present, with conscience of the idol, eat as a thing sacrificed to an idol: and their conscience, being weak, is defiled." And he writes in Gal. 5:3 (DR): "And I testify again to every man circumcising himself that he is a debtor to do the whole law." In other words, for as long as someone falsely thinks that circumcision is necessary for his salvation, he is bound to observe the whole Law. Thus, Christ the Lord teaches that invincible error excuses, not vincible error. (See John. 9:41 and 15:24.)

Second, *from reason*.

1. If invincibly erroneous conscience proposes something as being the law of God, that thing is accepted by the erring person as being the law itself. Therefore, if he draws back from it, he intends to draw back from God's law and thus holds it in scorn, thereby acting in an evil way. This is akin to the person who scorns the command of the man whom he falsely believes to be the emperor's legate, thus holding the emperor's command in scorn (cf. a. 5, ad 1 and 2).
2. The human act tends toward its object as it is proposed by reason. Therefore, if erring reason proposes something as being evil and a man wills it, he does something that he judges to be evil and thus performs that act out of an evil formal notion and wills evil. (And vice-versa for the good.) This is confirmed as follows: the will is a blind power; thus, its goodness and wickedness does not depend upon the object as it is in itself but, rather, as it is proposed by reason and in the way that it is proposed (a. 5; *Quodl.* III, q. 12, a. 2).

209. *Principle 3.* Vincibly erroneous conscience is not a legitimate rule of action. Indeed, even if it obligates, such that we may be conformed to it when it commands on the condition that it is not set aside, nonetheless, there is an obligation to set it aside if perhaps it is the cause of doing evil or of not doing a good that should be done. Thus, we can neither act against it nor in accord with it.[7]

---

7. Do not, however, let it be said that a man would necessarily sin in this case and that he is entangled, not knowing what to do in order that he may avoid evil. For, as St. Thomas says in q. 19, a. 6, ad 3: "Just as syllogistic argumentation, when a given unfitting thing is granted, others necessarily follow; so, in moral matters, when a given unfitting thing is posited, others necessarily follow. For example, suppose that there is a person who seeks vainglory. This person will always sin, whether he does what he is bound to do but does so out of vainglory or does not do that thing. He is not entangled, however, for he can always set aside this evil intention. And similarly, if we suppose an error of reason or of conscience proceeding from non-excusing ignorance, evil necessarily follows in the will. And nonetheless, this man is not entangled, for he can draw back from his error since his ignorance is vincible and voluntary." Similarly, in *De veritate*, q. 17, a. 4, ad 8: "It must be said

Proof. First, he who acts against this form of conscience does what he judges to be evil and thus sins. He who acts in accord with it, however, does what he cannot rightly judge to be good and, by that very fact, negligently judges concerning its morality, thus exposing himself to the proximate danger of acting in an evil way, likewise acting rashly and [hence] in an evil way. This is confirmed as follows: for although he becomes aware that he must make further inquiry into the truth, he voluntarily neglects to do so; thus, he should have feared that his action would be evil and cannot be securely certain concerning its goodness (cf. John. 9:41 and 15:24).

Second, he who does not set aside vincibly erroneous conscience by this very fact acts in an evil way, for the evil that is done is at least indirectly willed, given that he willed this very ignorance (that is, this [act of] erroneous conscience), laying at the foundation of his action. And, quite understandably, vincible ignorance does not excuse one from guilt; therefore, it does not excuse from actual guilt if it is actually vincible.

210. *What kind of conscience is right?* Many people only call true conscience "right" conscience. Others call invincibly erroneous conscience right if it is conformed to the law, as happens if it arises from a speculative error (e.g., the conscience that Jacob had when he approached Leah, thinking her to be Rachel) and not right if it is not conformed to the law, as happens if it arises from a practical error (e.g., the conscience of the person who thinks that theft is permitted). Others call invincibly erroneous conscience right if it is logically deduced from a false principle and not right if it is illogically deduced. Finally, inasmuch as it is prudently formed, others call all invincibly erroneous conscience "right," not *simpliciter* but, rather, *secundum quid* (and with respect to the agent, that is, *quoad nos*) in the order of acting, given that it is a right and legitimate rule of acting. Although it may be speculatively false, it is nonetheless practically true and declares a practical truth, namely, that which *truly* is permitted here and now, as being in conformity with right appetite, that

that he who has (vincibly erroneous) conscience informing him that he should commit fornication is not *simpliciter* entangled, for he can do something by means of which he would not fall into sin. Namely, he can rid himself of his erroneous conscience. However, he is entangled *secundum quid*, that is, for as long as the erroneous conscience remains. And there is nothing unsuitable in holding that, if some given thing is presupposed a man cannot avoid sin, just as supposing the intention of vainglory, he who is bound to give alms cannot avoid sin—for if he gives them out of such an intention, he sins, but if he does not give them, he is a transgressor."

is, with a morally befitting will (namely, it is true in these circumstances that this is permitted or not permitted for me). That is, such a *dictamen* of conscience comes from a right intention to do good and avoid evil, which is conformed to the true, loftier principle of morality: "The good is to be done and evil avoided." In this way, it is conformed to the eternal law of God. The truth of this point will be much clearer based on what we will say in the relevant place in the treatise on prudence.

211. *Corollaries.* From what has been said thus far, the following conclusions can be drawn with ease:

1. Conscience *binds*. True conscience binds *per se*, and erroneous conscience does so until it is set aside. Moreover, invincibly erroneous conscience *excuses*, whereas vincibly erroneous conscience does not.
2. Man has an absolute right to follow a conscience that is entirely true, and this is the freedom that, in a strict sense, is *freedom of conscience*. As regards invincibly erroneous conscience, although man can and must follow it in the internal forum, he does not have a true and proper right to do this, for he has a right that exists only upon a supposition and not upon a foundation in the objective relations of things. And he especially does not have an absolute right to follow it in an external act, for a legitimate authority can indeed choose not to punish him who *proves* that he follows the dictate of his conscience but can impede him so that he may not follow it externally. For example, a Catholic state [can] impede the practice of worship by heretics or those who do not believe in Christ, although it is not uncommon that those adhering to them follow the *dictamen* of their consciences.
3. An act (or, sin) against the law can exist while itself not being against conscience for as long as such a person committing it is not aware of the law. In that case, however, the act is only materially, not formally, evil. On the other hand, there can be an act (or, sin) that is formally contrary to erroneous conscience while, however, not being contrary a law that in fact exists; nonetheless, it is contrary to the supposed law; hence, although it is not materially contrary to the law it is nonetheless formally contrary to it and, thus, is contrary to the eternal

law, which declares that one must not act contrary to what he believes to be commanded or prohibited. Finally, every formal sin against the law is also contrary to conscience.

Hence, this means that conscience in some sense obligates, *per accidens*, *more* than the law of God.

Conscience obligates not in virtue of itself but, rather, in virtue of the divine precept, for conscience does not declare that something is to be done merely because it seems to be so but, rather, because it is commanded by God. Hence, *per accidens*, it obligates in virtue of the divine precept inasmuch as its makes its declarations as things being commanded by God. And therefore, conscience obligates *more greatly* than does the divine precept in virtue of which it binds. To give a parallel example: it is clear that if the king's command were not to arrive at the people except through the mediation of some prince, if the prince were to say, "This is commanded by the king"' even though it is not truly his declaration, it would obligate as though it were the king's command (*In II Sent.*, d. 39, q. 3, a. 3, ad 3).

4. Nonetheless, purely erroneous conscience (or erroneous precisely as such [*qua talis*]) cannot *per se* be binding, for obligation presupposes a law that really exists and is applied to the subject, not one that is imaginary. Hence, in the case of invincibly erroneous conscience, we are obligated not by the law which does not exist and which conscience erroneously affirms, but rather, by the certain, superior principle of the law (or, by the universal natural law, "The good is to be done and evil avoided," which prohibits acting contrary to that which, after careful examination, we judge to be good and commanded by God or an evil forbidden by Him. Hence, such a form of conscience is in some way true, namely practically true, because it is true that so long as such conscience remains one is permitted to act in accord with it, and it is right inasmuch as it is conformed to a right intention [of the end of some moral virtue] which itself is right because it is conformed to a superior principle and, thus, to the eternal law.

This applies to every form of conscience that here and now is invincibly erroneous, even if this comes from prior vincible and culpable ignorance, provided that it now is actually invincible because one is not aware of it. Such conscience was culpable *in its cause*, but it is the legitimate rule of acting here and now, and an action following from it is not culpable *in itself*, even though it may well be culpable in its cause.[8]

5. By contrast, vincibly erroneous conscience in no way can be called right or true, for, because he does not sufficiently look into things, the agent cannot sincerely and in truth judge that a given act is good or evil; nor can he sincerely will to do the good and avoid evil. Therefore, this conscience is erroneous in an unqualified manner [*simpliciter*].

212. *An observation.* In the treatise on prudence, we will discuss the way that erroneous conscience is discerned and set aside, as well as the obligation to reeducate those who err in conscience, along with the nature of the sin of acting against conscience.

Article 2: *On the Certitude of Conscience*

In IV Sent., d. 21, q. 2, a. 3; Quodl. VIII, q. 6, a. 3

213. *Notions.* Conscience must also be *certain. On account of its subject* (i.e., on the part of the act, assent or [*seu*] adherence to the object), however, conscience is either *certain* (if its judgment firmly clings to something) or *uncertain* (if it does not cling firmly). The latter is *doubtful* if it does not cling to what it judges to be so but, instead, suspends its judgment. It is said to be *opining* if it clings to it, although with fear that the opposed judgment might be true. Accordingly, certain conscience is that which, in itself and in all of the principles from which it is formed, excludes fear that an opposed judgment might be true. Therefore, it firmly and without fear of error judges that some particular course of action is permitted or not permitted. We will now, however, ask whether in order to be the rule of action, conscience must be certain.

214. *Principle.* The only legitimate rule of action is certain conscience, namely, that by means of which man prudently forms for himself a certain

8. In this sense, St. Thomas absolutely affirms the culpability in a. 6.

judgment that the action to be performed here and now may be permissibly and morally [*honeste*] performed. Hence, this kind of conscience is required so that one may act in a permissible manner.

Proof. First, *from Scriptural texts.* To begin, there is Rom. 14:23: "Everything that is not from faith is a sin"; however, he who is not certain does not act from conviction, and, therefore, what he does from uncertain conscience is not from faith (or, persuasion); therefore, it is a sin. The Apostle himself explicitly draws this conclusion, inferring it from the aforementioned principle (DR): "he that discerneth," that is, he who hesitates or doubts whether a given food to be eaten is permitted, "if he eat, is condemned; because this is not of faith." Thus, it is said in Sirach 37:20 (DR): "In all thy works let the true word go before thee, and steady counsel before every action."

Second, *from reason.*

1. He who acts with an uncertain conscience has a reasonable and founded fear concerning the wickedness of the act in question and uncertainty about its goodness. He who is uncertain concerning the goodness of his act, however, but acts nonetheless, wishes to perform it whether or not it is against the law and, thus, hypothetically consents to the evil in question, has an evil will, scorns God's law, and does evil. This is confirmed by the example of the servant who, doubting whether something is against his lord's will, would neglect to discover what his lord's will is, while nonetheless choosing to act. All would judge that such a man was guilty in taking this course of action. Likewise, when someone does something that he suspects would offend his friend, we judge, by that very fact, that he offends his friend and also holds his friendship in scorn.
2. He who voluntarily exposes himself to the proximate danger of formally sinning and of offending God does evil. He who says, however, "It is uncertain whether this is actually evil," and nonetheless acts, thereby acts rashly, for he does that which he fears would offend God and thus exposes himself to a proximate danger of formally sinning and of offending God. Therefore, he performs an evil act. Hence, Augustine wrote against the Donatists: "If, therefore, it is doubtful whether it be not a sin to receive baptism from the party of Donatus, who

can doubt but that it is a certain sin not to prefer receiving it where it is certain that it is not sin?"[9]

3. Conscience is the rule and measure of our acts. Now, the measure cannot be ambiguous but, instead, must be certain. Therefore, conscience must be certain.

215. *Applications.* From what has been said, the following points follow.

1. He who does not have a certain practical judgment concerning the permissibility of his action (i.e., certain conscience) cannot act; and if it is completely necessary that he act, he is bound to choose to do the safest action, namely, that which most favors the law (or, obligation) and most greatly withdraws from the danger of doing evil. Hence, we have the axiom: "In doubtful matters of practice, the safer path must be chosen."
2. He who does not have a certain, direct, speculatively-practical judgment concerning the objective and material moral befittingness of the action is not thereby always lacking in a certain practical judgment concerning the subjective and formal moral befittingness of the act. No, he sometimes can have certain conscience, forming it by means of a given superior principle and through a reflex judgment made by his intellect which thereby reflects upon its act and applies that principle to

9. Augustine, *On Baptism, Against the Donatists*, trans. J. R. King and Chester D. Hartranft, *Nicene and Post-Nicene Fathers*, First Series, Vol. 4. ed. Philip Schaff (Buffalo, NY: Christian Literature Publishing Co., 1887), rev. and ed. Kevin Knight (http://www.newadvent.org/fathers/14081.htm), bk. 1, ch. 5, no. 6. [**Translator's Note:** The full text is needed for the quote given by Fr. Merkelbach, who is citing it in a shortened form that one can find in St. Alphonsus (and likely others): "Accipere (Baptismum) in parte Donati...si incertum est esse pecatum, quis dubitet certum esse peccatum."]

A number of theologians call the value of this argument into doubt. If one considers it fully, however, he will clearly see that it does not substantially differ from the preceding argument; moreover, that particular manner of proposing it is already found in St. Thomas (*Quodl.* VIII, q. 6, a.3), having proposed the case in which someone "finds himself in doubt because he is faced with contrary opinions...*if while such a doubt remains*, he holds that there are many things that are permitted, *he commits himself to the danger* [*of sinning*], and thus without a doubt sins, inasmuch as he loves [some] temporal benefit more than his own salvation." And along the same lines, he writes in *In IV Sent.*, d. 21, q. 2, a. 3: "He who commits or omits an action that he thinks perhaps might be a mortal sin, commits himself to this danger [*discrimini se committit*]." Likewise, in Scotus's writings, see q. 2, prol., and *In IV Sent.* [*sic*], d. 30, q. 1; in St. Alphonsus, see, *Theologia moralis*, bk. 1, no. 22.

the situation in question. For example, however much I may be in doubt concerning the morality of a given action, I can be quite certain that I must perform it if my superior commands me to do so, both because presumption stands on the side of the superior who, hence, must not be deprived of his right to command (which he certainly has) on account of his subordinates' doubts, and because the right order of the common good forbids the subordinate to refuse his obedience unless it is completely certain that the superior is abusing his power. Although I might doubt whether a given work is servile, it is certain that I can do it if my pastor says I can. Although it may be uncertain whether a sacrament is valid when a given matter is used and whether it may be licitly administered thus, it is certain for me that, out of reverence for the sacrament, I must abstain from such an administration as a rule and, also, that in the case of necessity I must perform it. Although a given man is probably guilty, it is certain that a judge cannot condemn him unless he is proven guilty with certitude. And so forth... For many similar cases exist, as is determined in the specific treatises of moral theology [(i.e., in the particular treatises on the virtues, wherein such casuistic studies should properly be undertaken)].

3. In particular, a practical judgment is held to be certain, even while a speculative doubt remains, and a certain judgment of conscience concerning a specific obligation arises as often as there is a *certain and absolute obligation to attain a determinate end which otherwise may perhaps not be attained*—that is, as often as a good effect (e.g., salvation, a sacrament, or health) absolutely must be obtained or an evil (damnation, death, or injury) absolutely must be avoided—while there also is doubt not only concerning the moral befittingness of the act but also *concerning the necessity* or efficacy *of the means*[10] required for this as well as concerning the *validity* of the act or fact. In

10. Note that it is one thing to be necessary with a necessity of means and another to be necessary with only a necessity of precept. The latter is only necessary for the end because it is commanded (e.g., to hear Mass); the first is necessary because it is a means without which the end cannot be obtained (e.g., Baptism or contrition for sins).

short, then, in this case, there intervenes the superior and certain law which declares, "In doubtful cases concerning the validity of the act to be performed, the safer thing is to be done." By means of this kind of reflex judgment, objectively uncertain obligation becomes subjectively certain. This is so because, if the moral befittingness of the action depends upon our reason and upon conscience, this is not so for the value of the action or for aversion from harm, for our doubt or judgment does not change the nature of things. Therefore, it cannot render any act valid, nor can it make an appropriate [*debitum*] effect arise from the action, nor prevent harm from following upon it. For example, however probable a doubt or opinion may be, it cannot make that which is not a sacrament to be a sacrament or that which is poison to be medicine. Hence, in such a case, a sure dictate of the natural law [*lex naturalis certa*] forbids one to expose oneself to the danger of not obtaining the end or to the danger of inflicting harm, namely by making use of a means that perhaps is inefficacious or harmful. To expose oneself to danger in this way, in particular [*in specie*], is most unpermitted, [for] "When faced with doubts concerning things that are necessary with a necessity of means in relation to eternal salvation," namely, in these sorts of matters, "One must do that which is safest and most certain."

4. He who is uncertain, not indeed about the value of the act (or, about [something necessary] with a necessity of means), but only about its moral befittingness (or, about [something necessary] with a necessity of precept), must, before he can act, set aside the doubt either by undertaking a more diligent inquiry into the truth of the matter or by seeking counsel from those who are wiser than he, forming for himself certain conscience concerning the moral befittingness of the act, at least indirectly by means of a reflex judgment applying a given general and certain principle. Prudence, taking all of the circumstances into consideration, points out how one is to proceed in various cases and doubtful situations. Therefore, such matters will be discussed in the treatise on prudence. If such means are lacking here and now, however, one must refrain from acting. But, if

one cannot altogether avoid acting, one must choose the safer course of action, as was already said above in (1).

QUESTION 3: ON CHRISTIAN CONSCIENCE INASMUCH AS IT IS THE RULE OF SUPERNATURAL ACTS

216. *What is supernatural conscience?*[11] In the supernatural order, there also must be supernatural conscience, which judges concerning the supernatural quality and worth of our acts (that is, concerning supernatural morality). It can be defined thus: "A judgment (or, *dictamen*) of the practical intellect affirming that a given particular act to be performed here or now is or is not supernaturally good and even meritorious in relation to eternal life."

It differs from natural conscience in the following ways.

1. *In its object*: Natural conscience considers only the natural goodness of an act, whereas supernatural conscience also considers its supernatural goodness. That is, beyond the natural goodness of the act, it asks whether an act tends toward the supernatural end or whether it does not tend toward it—or even turns one away from it.
2. *In its end (or, motive)*: Natural conscience proceeds from love of natural moral befittingness and strives to conform our acts to reason. Supernatural conscience goes beyond this, proceeding from a kind of love for God Himself, at least an initial and imperfect love, striving to conform our acts to the divine life, [whether] in its inchoate form or as consummated, and also to avoid the eternal loss of this life and of God Himself.
3. *In the law* that it applies to action: Natural conscience applies the natural law, as well as human law which perfects and determines the natural law. Beyond this, supernatural conscience applies the divine positive law,[12] as well as ecclesiastical law which determines and completes the former.

11. Cf. Noble, *La conscience morale.*
12. TRANSLATOR'S NOTE: This is an example of one of the grave weaknesses of the language used here. Beyond the divine positive law, supernatural conscience is involved in the "application" (or, as I like to say, the "existentialization in human acts") of the supernatural virtues. Of course, this occurs in different ways depending on whether we are talking about the

217. *The relationship between natural and supernatural conscience.* Supernatural conscience does not exist separately and independently from natural conscience so that the believer would have two separate and collateral forms of conscience within himself, alternating between one another (e.g., the philosophical conscience of the stoic and the Christian conscience of the faithful man). Rather, supernatural conscience includes natural conscience and subordinates it to itself, so that harmony and unity exist in the complete life and activity of man, and this whole, with all its acts, is ruled by supernatural conscience. Hence, in the believer, natural conscience is transformed and becomes supernatural; however, by becoming supernatural, it *includes* (albeit *surpasses*) natural conscience, so that the believer is bound...

1. Indeed to act *as a man* but, above all, to act *as a son of God.*
2. Indeed, to live *his natural life with moral befittingness* but, in an even greater way, namely, to live *the divine life in a supernatural way.*
3. To keep *the natural law* but also *the new and positive commands of God and of the Church* relative to the sacraments, penance, religious piety for God, and divine friendship.[13]
4. To do good and *cultivate virtue according to the measure of reason* but also to do so *in accord with the more excellent measure of the divine law*, as ordered to the more excellent divine life in accord with the exemplar of Christ Jesus who humbled Himself, suffering and being obedient to the point of death.

In short, supernatural conscience does not destroy natural conscience but, rather, perfects it, just as grace does not destroy nature but, rather, perfects it.

---

theological virtues or merely about the infused moral virtues. Nonetheless, it is not a question of merely applying the divine positive law, as though that were the whole content of the new law of the Spirit. Other things said by Merkelbach correct this, however. To this end, much is contained in the powerful expression of Fr. Lemonnyer: "the natural law of our supernatural life." See Antoine Lemonnyer, *Notre vie divine* (Paris: Éditions du Cerf, 1936), p. 14. This new law, pertaining to the "nature" of our "supernaturalized" existence, is what Christian conscience applies, through the theological virtues and the infused moral virtues.

13 **Translator's Note:** Again, this needs greater clarity regarding the way that the *new law* is the internalized life of the spirit in grace. The language here tends toward a kind of extrinsicism that risks not drawing attention to the true grandeur of the true Christian life in grace. The fourth point helps to overcome this deficiency, but it should be at the center of the presentation.

218. *The formation of supernatural conscience.* Supernatural conscience does not follow a different process than that which is followed by natural conscience, for grace perfects nature without destroying it. Nonetheless, it is ordered to human acts of greater excellence. Thus, it too is a conclusion of [supernaturalized] reason. Indeed, just as natural conscience is founded on the first principle of *synderesis*, "The good is to be done and evil avoided," and in the natural inclination of the will to the morally befitting good (or, the good of reason), so too supernatural conscience is founded: (1) in the first practical principles of faith (e.g., "One is to tend toward God as to one's supernatural end"; or, "The Highest Good, to be possessed in Himself in the beatific vision, must be loved above all things"; or, "The felicity which consists in the vision of God must be secured"; or, "One must be obedient to God who destines us to friendship with Him and to a sharing in His life"); and (2) if it is to be perfect, it must be founded on faith that is informed by charity, which inclines one to the divine good, as well on sanctifying grace.

Its major premise is not from *synderesis* alone,[14] but especially comes from faith, informing reason and *synderesis*, while also elevating and subordinating them. In the just man, however, faith holds fast by means of the gifts of understanding, knowledge, and wisdom under the influence of the gifts of the Holy Spirit dwelling in the soul and moving it.[15]

Its minor premise is from reason, under the influence of grace inspiring supernatural prudence with its connected virtues. In the just man,

14. Faith informs and elevates reason and *synderesis*, subordinating them to itself. Consequently, under the light of faith, *synderesis* is able to enunciate the first supernatural practical principles. And reasonably so, for supposing that faith teaches that God has elevated us to a supernatural end and that our ultimate good is only found in the beatific vision of God Himself, *reason* sees already that we must tend toward that end and that the ultimate good to be possessed in this manner must be loved in all of our acts. And do not say that *synderesis* does not have an idea of the supernatural end, for *synderesis* does not exist for conceiving ideas but, supposing these ideas, it sees and with ease enunciates their befittingness or unbefittingness.—St. Thomas does not expressly speak about supernatural conscience but everywhere says that the major premise is placed in conscience by *synderesis*; however, he is not speaking only about the conscience of philosophers but also is speaking of the conscience of believers; [therefore, supernatural conscience enunciates its major premise by means of synderesis, elevated by, and subordinated to, faith.]

15. **Translator's Note:** Here, however, we see the lofty heights to which the Thomist position can push our understanding of conscience. Even before discussing the gift of counsel (in the treatise on prudence), we see here the loftiness of the supernatural knowledge standing at the very foundation of our basic insights orienting and driving our supernatural moral reasoning.

however, it is from reason under the influence of the *habitus* of infused prudence (with its connected virtues) and even sometimes under the influence of the gift of counsel given by the Holy Spirit. Indeed, just as to live a natural morally befitting life we seek out wise and prudent men, so too in place of human counsel the Holy Spirit Himself, dwelling in our souls, deigns to become our Counselor by ordering us to eternal life.[16]

The conclusion is enunciated under the influence of supernatural prudence with its connected virtues.

Therefore, the immediate principle of supernatural conscience is infused prudence, along with its connected virtues. Its mediate principles are the theological virtues and the gifts of the Holy Spirit dwelling in our soul and moving it, so that God Himself may immediately bestow all the powers of this conscience. In other words, Christian conscience is a work of divine grace in its birth, progress, and perfection.

219. *Corollaries.*

1. Thus, supernatural conscience is *more perfect* than natural conscience and perfects it, for it: (a) *surpasses* natural conscience, as was said above in no. 217; (b) is *clearer* than natural conscience, because it rests on principles of faith, is illuminated by faith, and is formed with the aid of grace; (c) is *more certain* than natural conscience, because the divine revelation on which it is founded is more certain than human reason inasmuch as it is given to us on the infallible authority of God and is proposed by the infallible authority of the Church and also because it has surety from the light of the Holy Spirit.
2. Since Christian conscience includes natural conscience, in order for it to be the rule of acting in a morally befitting way [*honeste*] it must have the same qualities needed by natural conscience, namely rectitude and certitude.
3. Nonetheless, in order for conscience to be the rule of supernatural acts, it does not suffice that it be invincibly erroneous, namely, that by which someone would in good faith judge that an act is supernatural or meritorious for eternal life. Good faith can suffice for [natural] moral goodness [*ad honestatem*] because such moral goodness [*honestas*] depends

16. See *ST* II-II, q. 52, a. 2 and ad 3.

upon conscience (that is, upon our judgment) and not upon the supernatural worth [*valor*] of the act. Indeed, the judgment of reason or conscience cannot make an act supernatural, proceeding from grace, nor can it make it be efficacious for obtaining eternal life. Here, in short, what is involved is not only the moral befittingness of the act but also the validity [*validitate*] of the act and the efficacy of the means for reaching the end (see no. 215, 3, above).

* * *

INDEX

CLUNY MEDIA

Designed by Fiona Cecile Clarke, the CLUNY MEDIA *logo*
depicts a monk at work in the scriptorium,
with a cat sitting at his feet.

The monk represents our mission to emulate
the invaluable contributions of the monks
of Cluny in preserving the libraries of the West,
our strivings to know and love the truth.

The cat at the monk's feet is Pangur Bán, from the
eponymous Irish poem of the 9th century.
The anonymous poet compares his scholarly
pursuit of truth with the cat's happy hunting of mice.
The depiction of Pangur Bán is an homage to the work
of the monks of Irish monasteries and a sign
of the joy we at Cluny take in our trade.

"Messe ocus Pangur Bán,
cechtar nathar fria saindan:
bíth a menmasam fri seilgg,
mu memna céin im saincheirdd."

Made in the USA
Middletown, DE
15 April 2025